ENGLISH PRACTICE GRAMMAR

With answers

Michael Macfarlane

Arabic consultant:
Dr Abdel Halim A. Abo Jalalah

Garnet
EDUCATION

Published by Garnet Publishing Ltd
8 Southern Court, South Street, Reading,
Berkshire RG1 4QS, UK

© 1995 Garnet Publishing Ltd

First edition 1995
reprinted 1998, 2003
British Library Cataloguing-in-Publication Data
A catalogue record for this book is available from the
British Library.
ISBN 1 85964 065 6

Editor: **Jane Hobbs**
Arabic consultant: **Dr Abdel Halim A. Abo Jalalah**
Design: **David Rose and Mark Slader**
Illustration: **Mark Stock**
Typesetting: **Samantha Abley and Vicky Henriksen**

Printed in Lebanon

Contents

Introduction   6

Acknowledgements and dedication   7

Basic verb forms

  1 Imperatives   8
  2 Present simple   10
  3 Present simple: *be*   12
  4 Present continuous   14
  5 Present simple or present continuous   16
  6 Past simple   18
  7 Past simple: *be*   20
  8 Past continuous   22
  9 Present perfect 1   24
10 Present perfect 2   28
11 Present perfect or past simple   30
12 Present perfect continuous   32
13 Past perfect and past simple   34
14 Future with *going to*   36
15 Future with *will*   38
16 Future continuous   40
17 Future perfect   42
18 Future review   44
19 *have* and *have got*   46
20 Review: main verb forms   48
21 Review: auxiliary verb forms   50
22 Short form or full form   54

Question forms and answers

23 Question forms 1   56
24 Question forms 2   58
25 Tag questions   60
26 Short answers   62
27 Indirect forms   64
28 *So* and *Neither/Nor*   *so* and *not*   66

Modal auxiliary verbs

29 Modal auxiliary verbs 1   68
30 Modal auxiliary verbs 2   70
31 Modal auxiliary verbs 3   72
32 Modal auxiliary verbs 4   74
33 Modal auxiliary verbs 5   76
34 Modal auxiliary verbs 6   78
35 Modal auxiliary verbs 7: past forms   80
36 Review: modal auxiliary verbs   82

Passive verb forms

37 Passive verb forms 1   86
38 Passive verb forms 2   88

Infinitives and *ing* forms

39 Verb + *to* + infinitive or verb + *ing* form 1   90
40 Verb + *to* + infinitive or verb + *ing* form 2   92
41 Verb + object + *to* + infinitive   96
42 Verb/adjective + preposition + *ing* form   98

Conditional forms

43 Conditional forms: type 0 and type 1   100
44 Conditional forms: type 2   102
45 Conditional forms: type 3   104

Reported speech

46 Reported speech 1: statements   106
47 Reported speech 2: questions   108
48 Reported speech 3: orders, promises, etc   110

Nouns and articles

49 Singular and plural   112
50 Irregular noun forms   114
51 Countable and uncountable nouns   116
52 Articles 1: *a*, *an*, *the* and *some*   118
53 Articles 2: general and specific   122

Other determiners and pronouns

54 Demonstratives   *one* and *ones*   126
55 *some* or *any*   128
56 *There, It* and *They*   130
57 Quantity   132
58 Partitives   134
59 Pronouns: subject and object   136
60 Pronouns: possessive   138
61 Pronouns: reflexive   140
62 Direct and indirect objects   142
63 *something, anybody, everyone*, etc   144

Relative clauses

64 Relative clauses 1   146
65 Relative clauses 2   148
66 Relative clauses 3   150
67 Relative clauses 4   152

Adjectives and adverbs

68 Adjectives 1	**154**
69 Adjectives 2	**156**
70 Adjectives and adverbs	**158**
71 Adverb positions	**162**
72 Adverb types	**164**
73 Comparison 1: adjective and adverb forms	**168**
74 Comparison 2: sentence patterns	**172**
75 *too* and *enough*	**174**
76 *a bit, very much, a lot so, such*	**176**

Prepositions

77 Prepositions 1: place and movement	**178**
78 Prepositions 2: place	**182**
79 Prepositions 3: time	**184**
80 Prepositions 4: time	**188**
81 Preposition + noun, noun + preposition	**190**
82 Adjective + preposition	**192**
83 Prepositional verbs	**194**
84 Phrasal verbs	**196**

The sentence and its parts

85 Word classes	**198**
86 Sentence: types and structure	**200**
87 Connecting clauses	**202**
88 Connecting sentences	**204**

Appendices

1 Irregular verbs	**206**
2 Some spelling rules	**209**
3 Punctuation	**212**
4 Numbers	**214**
5 Days, dates and times	**216**

Index	**217**

Answer key	**225**

Introduction to the student

Is *English Practice Grammar* the right level for me?

- Yes, if you are no longer a beginner.

- Yes, if you are not yet an advanced user of English.

- Yes, if you feel that you still need further explanation in your own language.

How can this book help me?

Study *English Practice Grammar* when you have a problem with a particular point. It will help you to understand it and practise it.

Do not try to read the book from the beginning to the end. It is not a course book!

What does the book contain and why?

The Contents on pages 3 to 5 and the Index on pages 217 to 224 help you to find the grammar point you want.

The 88 Units on pages 8 to 205 explain the essential grammar of English and provide practice exercises for each point. Most of the Units have two pages – a page of grammar on the left and a page of practice exercises on the right. Some important grammar points have two pages of explanation and two pages of exercises.

The Answer key on pages 225 to 245 allows you to check the answers to the exercises.

The Appendix sections on pages 206 to 216 give you information about irregular verbs, spelling rules, punctuation, numbers, days, dates and times.

What's in a Unit?

Grammatical forms

Illustrated grammar situation

Explanations and examples

Exercises

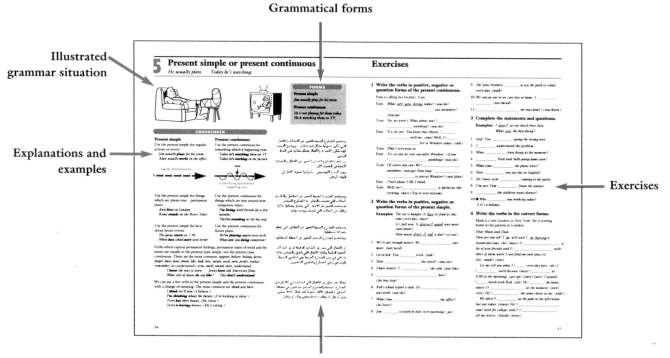

Explanations in Arabic

How do I use the book?

1 Find the grammar point you want to study in the Contents or the Index.

2 Turn to the correct Unit. Study the illustrated grammar situation, the grammatical forms, explanations and examples. Study the explanations in Arabic to make sure that you have understood everything.

3 Do the exercises.

4 Check your answers in the Answer key.

5 If you have made any mistakes, read the grammar explanation again to understand what you did wrong.

6 Study the Appendix sections if you want information about irregular verbs, spelling rules, punctuation, numbers, days, dates and times.

Introduction to the teacher

English Practice Grammar is designed mainly for self-study by students who may be learning at secondary school, college or adult levels. You may want to recommend that students study particular Units to supplement, reinforce or revise work that has been done in class. The exercise material can of course also be used in class, the reference materials then being used as a reminder and summary of your own language presentations.

Acknowledgements

To my many students who have helped me find ways of explaining that thing that is so difficult to explain – English grammar.

To my Editor, **Jane Hobbs**, and **Tony Hobbs** for all their help and encouragement over a very long period.

To **Dr Abdel Halim A. Abo Jalalah** for his advice and Arabic explanations.

To **David Rose** and **Mark Slader** for the design.

To **Mark Stock** for the illustrations.

To **Samantha Abley** and **Vicky Henriksen** for preparing the typescript.

Dedication

This book is dedicated to Ishitaro Niioka who, more than most, understood the need for language and the power of communication.

1 Imperatives

Light the firework.

Light the firework ... and stand back!

The basic imperative is the infinitive, or dictionary form of a verb. Use a main verb infinitive for an action.

> **Light** the firework ... and **stand back**!

Make a formal or written negative imperative with *Do not*.

> **Do not hold** the firework.

Make an informal spoken negative with *Don't*.

> **Don't hold** the firework.

Use *be* + adjective.

> **Be careful! Don't be stupid!**

Use imperatives to give orders.

> **Be** quiet! **Don't talk**!

Use imperatives to give instructions, eg for operating machines and in cookery books.

> **Turn** the handle to the left and **press** the red button.
> **Chop** an onion and **fry** it in oil until it is brown.

Use imperatives for polite instructions.

> Please **turn** to page 15.

Use imperatives for warnings.

> **Look out**! It's going to fall!   **Be** careful not to hurt yourself.
> **Don't play** with that knife or you'll hurt yourself.

Use imperatives for friendly advice.

> **Relax! Don't worry!** Everything will be all right.

Use imperatives for invitations.

> **Come** and **have** dinner on Saturday.
> Hello! **Come in** and **sit down**. **Make** yourself at home.

Use imperatives for directions.

> **Go** straight on, **take** the first turning on the left, **cross** the bridge, and the bank is on the right.

Use *Let's* + imperative to suggest doing something together.

> **Let's buy** some fireworks.

Form the negative with *Let's not*.

> **Let's not go out** today.

تتكون الصيغة الأساسية للأمر من مصدر الفعل الرئيسي المستخدم.

اما الصيغة الرسمية التي تستخدم عند الكتابة فتتكون من Do not.

وتأتي صيغة الأمر التي تستخدم في الحوار العادي مختصرة مع Don't.

ويستخدم مصدر فعل الكينونة be + صفة.

وتستخدم صيغة الأمر لتصدير الأمر.

وتستخدم صيغة الأمر لإعطاء التعليمات كما هو الحال عند تشغيل آلة ما وكذلك في كتب الطبخ.

وتستخدم صيغة الأمر لإعطاء أوامر بصيغة مهذبة.

كما أنها تستخدم عند التحذير.

وكذلك عند إسداء النصح.

وكذلك تستخدم صيغة الأمر لتوجيه الدعوات.

كما أنها تستخدم عند إرشاد شخص ما كي يصل إلى مكان بعينه.

وتستخدم صيغة الأمر مسبوقة بـ Let's عند اقتراح القيام بعمل ما معاً.

وتتشكل صيغة النفي لهذا النوع من الأمر باستخدام Let's not...

Exercises

1 Complete the imperative sentences.

ـ١ اكمل تركيب الجمل التالية بصيغة الامر :

Example: The bus leaves at exactly 4.00, so _don't be_ late.

1 _____ quiet, everyone. You're too noisy.

2 ● Is the plane going to crash?

   ○ Oh, _____ silly. Of course it isn't.

3 _____ careful with that knife. It's sharp.

4 _____ mean, Joe. Give Sam the toys.

5 _____ quick, Larry. There isn't much time.

6 Drive carefully. _____ such an idiot!

7 _____ helpful to your mother. She's very busy.

8 Why are you crying? _____ so sad.

2 Complete the imperative sentences with these verbs.

ـ٢ اكمل الجمل التالية بصيغة الأمر مع هذه الافعال :

drive, forget, go, play, press, take, talk, turn off, write

Example: _Go_ home now. It's late.

1 _____ with matches. They're dangerous.

2 _____ this money to the bank, please.

3 It's time to sleep now. _____ the lights.

4 _____ to your sister like that. It's rude.

5 _____ to collect the air tickets on your way to the airport.

6 To open the machine, _____ this button.

7 _____ so fast. You'll have an accident.

8 _____ your name, age and address here, please, madam.

3 Complete the instructions with these verbs.

ـ٣ اكمل التعليمات مع هذه الافعال :

choose, enjoy, place, press, pull down, push, put, put in, take

Ben: How do I work this drinks machine, Sam? I'd really like some coffee.

Sam: It's easy. Do you want milk and sugar?

Ben: Sugar, please, but no milk.

Sam: OK, first _pull down_ a plastic cup from this hole on the right. Then [1]_____ your money. Now [2]_____ the cup under here and

[3] _____ the sugar button. Now

[4] _____ your drink – black coffee.

[5] _____ your cup under here,

[6] _____ the button and the coffee comes out.

And now just [7]_____ your coffee and

[8] _____ it!

Ben: Thanks, Sam.

4 Study the map and complete the directions to May's Garage. Use these verbs.

cross, drive, follow, go, pass, take, turn

1 To get to May's Garage, _go_ to the end of this road.

2 _____ right into the High Street.

3 _____ right again at the first traffic lights.

4 _____ the second left opposite the Plaza Hotel.

5 _____ the bank on the right.

6 _____ the road to the end and _____ right at the post office.

7 _____ the bridge and _____ right.

8 _____ along the side of the river and _____ the third left. May's Garage is near the corner, on the left.

2 Present simple
Ann works at A.B.C.

Ann works from 8.00 to 4.30 every day.

In positive statements a verb usually has no ending.
> *I* **work**.   *You* **talk**.   *We* **write**.   *They* **go**.

The 3rd person singular is different. The verb usually ends in *s*.
> *He* **works**.   *It* **moves**.

If the verb ends in *y*, change the *y* to *ies*.
> *cry → cries, fly → flies, try → tries*

If the verb ends in *o, ch, sh, ss* or *x*, add *es*.
> *go → goes, watch → watches, wish → wishes, miss → misses,*
> *box → boxes*

Verbs in negative statements and most questions have no ending. They all need the auxiliary verb *do/does*. (See Unit 21 for information about *do/does* as a main verb and auxiliary verb.)
> *I* **don't like** *this music*.   *She* **doesn't talk**.
> **Do** *you* **know** *him?*   **Does** *it* **work?**
> *When* **do** *they* **start?**   *Where* **does** *he* **live?**

Use the present simple for permanent states and situations.
> *I* **live** *in London*.   *I* **have** *two sisters*.

Use the present simple for things which always happen.
> *The sun* **rises** *in the east*.   *Water* **boils** *at 100° C.*

Use the present simple for repeated actions and events.
> *I* **get up** *at 7.00 most days*.   *Ann often* **has** *coffee at 11.00.*

Use the present simple for facts about future events.
> *Flight 765* **leaves** *at 10.30.*
> *The President* **arrives** *at midday tomorrow.*

Some verbs usually take the present simple and not the present continuous. (See Unit 5 for a list of these.)
> *I* **know** *what to do next*.   *Susan* **doesn't like** *cold weather.*
> *Do they* **understand** *English?*

عند تكوين الجمل الخبرية المثبتة، لا يضاف للفعل عادة أيّ نهايات.

وينتهي الفعل بـ S عادة مع ضمائر الغائب المفردة.

وعند استخدام فعل ينتهي بالحرف y يجري استبداله بـies.

وعند استخدام افعال تنتهي بـ o , ch, sh, ss او x نضيف للفعل es.

وعند استخدام الجمل الخبرية في حالة النفي، وكذلك في معظم الجمل الاستفهامية، لا تضاف اي نهايات للفعل، بل يستخدم الفعل المساعد do أو does (انظر unit 21 للمزيد من المعلومات حول do/does كفعل رئيسي وكفعل مساعد).

يستخدم المضارع البسيط للتعبير عن الحالات والمواقف التي تتصف بالديمومة.

ويستخدم المضارع البسيط للتعبير عن الاحداث التي تحدث دائماً.

ويستخدم المضارع البسيط للتعبير عن احداث وافعال تتكرر.

ويستخدم المضارع البسيط للتعبير عن الحقائق التي تتعلق باحداث مستقبلية.

وهناك مجموعة من الافعال التي تأتي عادةً في المضارع البسيط وليس في المضارع المستمر. (انظر اللائحة بهذه الافعال في unit 5)

Exercises

1 Write the verbs in the correct forms.

Example: Rob often _watches_ TV. (watch)

1 We _____ in London. (live)

2 I really _____ this picture of you. (like)

3 That baby _____ every night! (cry)

4 Ann and Mary _____ work at 8.30. (start)

5 Ann _____ home at 4.30. (go)

6 Mary's husband _____ her from work at 5.00. (fetch)

7 Our cat _____ fish for lunch every day. (have)

2 Write the verbs in positive or negative forms.

Examples: We _need_ to explain again. (need) She _doesn't understand._ (not/understand)

1 I _____ to visit Rome again. (want) I really _____ the city. (love)

2 We sometimes _____ the stereo, but it _____ very well. (use) (not/work)

3 Charlie's fat! He _____ any exercise, and he _____ too much! (not/get) (eat)

4 They aren't interested in sport. They _____ football, and they _____ volleyball either. (not/like) (not/enjoy)

5 Roy _____ very often, but Andy _____ swimming every day. (not/swim) (go)

6 I _____ coffee before bed time because it _____ me awake. (not/drink) (keep)

7 Sally _____ , so she always _____ to work. (not/drive) (walk)

3 Write the questions for the answers.

Example: (come/from Britain)
● _Do you come from Britain?_
○ Yes, I do. I'm from London.

1 (Tom/drive)
● _____
○ Yes, he does. He's got a blue Nissan.

2 (you/know/Ann Smith)
● _____
○ Yes, I do. She's an old friend.

3 (the TV/work)
● _____
○ No, it doesn't. It's broken.

4 (you/go out/much)
● _____
○ No, we don't. We usually stay at home.

5 (Marie/speak/French)
● _____
○ Yes, she does. She's fluent.

6 (Fred and Mary/live/near here)
● _____
○ Yes, they do. They live in the next road.

4 Change the statements into questions.

Example: I go swimming. (How often)
How often do you go swimming?

1 Tom goes to work. (How)

_____

2 Sally visits her parents. (When)

_____

_____

3 They go on holiday every year. (Where)

_____

_____

4 I get home in the evening. (What time)

_____

_____

5 We always make mistakes. (Why)

_____

_____

6 The children watch TV after school. (How long)

_____

_____

7 The cat has lunch at 1.00. (What)

_____

_____

3 Present simple: *be*

Jim is a really good player.

Jim is a really good player.

Use the present simple of *be* for any state.

Age:	*I'm 22. Carol isn't 10. She's 11.*
Description:	*Jim is tall and dark. How tall is Ann?*
Height:	*She's 1 metre 70. Is he as tall as me?*
Weight:	*Jim is 78 kilos.* *How heavy is the parcel?*
Feelings:	*We're tired, hungry and angry!*
Distance:	*The town is about five kilometres away.*
Size:	*The room is five metres by six.*
Price:	*How much are these shoes, please?*
Time:	*What time is it?* *What's the time?*

Use the present simple of *be* in *there is/there are*.

● *Is there* a post office near here?
○ Yes, *there's* one in the next street.

Use *Yes/No* questions to check information. Form them like this.

She *is* clever. → *Is* she clever?
The students *are* in Room 1. → *Are* the students in Room 1?

You can answer *Yes/No* questions with short answers.

● *Is* she clever?   ○ Yes, she *is*.
● *Are* the students in Room 1?   ○ No, they *aren't*.

We always use full forms in *Yes* answers, when the verb is the last word.

Yes, I *am*.   Yes, he *is*.   Yes, they *are*.

We usually use short forms in *No* answers.

No, she *isn't*.   No, we *aren't*.   (But No, I'm *not*.)

Use *Wh* questions to get more information.

● Who *is* she?   ○ Her name *is* Pam Woods.
● Where *is* she now?   ○ She's in Room 1.

يستخدم فعل الكينونة be في زمن المضارع البسيط للتعبير عن اي من الحالات المبينة.

ويستخدم فعل be في زمن المضارع البسيط للتعبير عن معنى «يوجد» there is/ there are.

يستخدم نوع الاسئلة التي يجاب عنها بـ «نعم» او «لا» للاستفسار عن معلومة معينة.. وتتكون كما هو موضح...

ويمكن الاجابة عن هذا النوع من الاسئلة بشكل مختصر.

ولا يستخدم الاختصار عند الإجابة بِ «بنعم» عندما يكون الفعل آخر كلمة في الجملة.

تستخدم عادة الصيغ المختصرة عند الاجابة بـ «لا».

تستخدم الاسئلة التي تبدأ بأداة استفهام للحصول على المزيد من المعلومات.

Exercises

1 Complete the statements and questions.

Examples: *This* _is_ *my book.*
Are *these your books?*

1 *Those* _____ *your shoes.*

2 _____ *that your teacher?*

3 *The time* _____ *10.30.*

4 _____ *I late for the bus? Oh, no!*

5 _____ *they the new students?*

6 *Ann* _____ *Rosie's best friend.*

7 _____ *you from Japan?*

8 *Dear Sir,*
My brother and I are writing in reply to your
advertisement today in the Daily Times. I _____ *20*
years old, and he _____ *19. We* _____ *both experienced*
drivers.

2 Write the short forms.

Examples: *she is* _she's_
we are not _we aren't/we're not_

1 *I am* _____ 5 *I am not* _____

2 *he is* _____ 6 *he is not* _____

3 *they are* _____ 7 *they are not* _____

4 *you are* _____ 8 *you are not* _____

3 Correct the statements.

Example: *Sue is a nurse. (doctor)*
Sue isn't a nurse. She's a doctor.

1 *I'm 80 kilos. (85)*
I _____
_____

2 *Alan is in Berlin. (Paris)*
Alan _____
_____

3 *You're 1 metre 75. (1 metre 80)*
You _____
_____

4 *They're at home. (school)*
They _____

4 Answer the questions. Use short forms.

Examples: ● *Are you from Britain? (Yes)*
○ _Yes, I am._
● *Is Sam from LA? (No) (Miami)*
○ _No, he isn't. He's from Miami._

1 ● *Is Sally from London? (Yes)*
○ _____

2 ● *Are we on time? (No) (very late)*
○ _____

3 ● *Is it 1st May today? (No) (30th April)*
○ _____

4 ● *Are there any people on the beach? (Yes)*
○ _____

5 ● *Are you 30? (No) (only 28)*
○ _____

5 Read. Then write questions and answer them.

Example: *(What/name)*
● _What's his name?_
○ _Nick._

Nick is 25. He is a designer at A.B.C. His office is on the second floor. There are six other people in the same room. Nick's desk is the one by the window.

1 *(How old)*
● _____
○ _____

2 *(What/job)*
● _____
○ _____

3 *(Where/office)*
● _____
○ _____

4 *(How many people)*
● _____
○ _____

5 *(Which/desk)*
● _____
○ _____

Present continuous

I'm flying!

Look! I'm flying!

Form the present continuous with *am, is, are* + main verb + *ing*. (See Unit 21 for information about *be* as a main verb and auxiliary verb.)
> Peter **is flying** to New York now.
> **Are** the boys **stopping** for a rest?

If the main verb ends in *e*, leave it out.
> *move → moving, come → coming, drive → driving*

If the main verb ends in a single consonant after a short vowel, double the consonant.
> *stop → stopping, run → running, swim → swimming*

If the main verb ends in *ie*, change *ie* to *y*.
> *die → dying, lie → lying*

Use the present continuous for things which are happening now.
> Look! **I'm flying**!
> Listen! Something **is moving** over there.

Use the present continuous for temporary states and activities.
> **I'm staying** with friends for a month.
> Paul **is painting** his house this week.

Use the present continuous for future plans.
> Sam **is playing** football tomorrow.
> **Are** you **doing** anything on Saturday?

Some verbs usually take the present simple and not the present continuous. (See Unit 5 for a list of these.)
> I **know** what to do next.   Susan **doesn't like** cold weather.
> **Do** they **understand** English?

يتكون المضارع المستمر من am أو is أو are + الفعل مضافاً له ing. (انظر unit 21 للمزيد من المعلومات حول be كفعل رئيسي وكفعل مساعد.

يحذف حرف e عند استخدام فعل اساسي ينتهي به.

عند استخدام فعل اساسي ينتهي بحرف ثابت مسبوق بحرف متحرك قصير، يكتب الحرف الثابت مرتين.

اذا كان الفعل الاساسي ينتهي بـ ie يجري ابدالهما بالحرف y.

يستخدم المضارع المستمر للتعبير عن الاحداث التي تجري في الوقت الحاضر.

ويستخدم المضارع المستمر للتعبير عن الحالات والناشط العارضة.

ويستخدم المضارع المستمر للتعبير عن الخطط المستقبلية.

هناك افعال تستخدم عادة، في زمن المضارع البسيط عوضاً عن المضارع المستمر (انظر لائحة بهذه الافعال في unit 5)

Exercises

1 Write the short forms.

Examples: *She is going.* <u>*She's going.*</u>
We are not going.
<u>*we aren't/we're not going.*</u>

1 *I am going.* _____

2 *You are not going.* _____

3 *He is not going.* _____

4 *They are going.* _____

5 *It is not going.* _____

2 Write the verbs in positive or negative forms.

Examples: *You* <u>*'re talking*</u> *too much. (talk)*
Let's go out. It <u>*isn't raining*</u> *now. (not/rain)*

1 *Stop the car. I _____ well. (not/feel)*

2 *Be careful! You _____ too fast. (go)*

3 *It's dark! The lights _____ (not/work)*

4 *The phone _____ , but Cathy _____ it. (ring) (not/answer)*

5 ● *I _____ Tim. Is he here? (look for)*
   ○ *I'm sorry. He _____ here this week. (not/work) He _____ our Paris office. (visit)*

6 ● *Hello. Can I speak to Alice, please?*
   ○ *I'm afraid not. She _____ a bath at the moment. (have)*

7 *Paul and Pat _____ television. (not/watch). They _____ to some of their favourite music. (listen)*

3 Complete the questions and answers.

Examples: ● *What* <u>*are you doing?*</u> *(you/do)*
   ○ *I* <u>*'m mending*</u> *the door. (mend)*

1 ● *What _____ (the children/do)*
   ○ *_____ in the garden. (they/play)*

2 ● *_____ the film? (you/enjoy)*
   ○ *Yes, I _____ It's really good.*

3 ● *Why _____ so much? (Bill/train)*
   ○ *_____ to get into the team. (he/try)*

4 ● *_____ to the party? (Sally/go)*
   ○ *No, she _____ She's very tired.*

5 ● *How fast _____ (we/fly)*
   ○ *_____ 700 kph. (we/do)*

6 ● *_____ the car? (the boys/wash)*
   ○ *No, they _____ . _____ the grass. (they/cut)*

7 ● *What _____ (the cat/eat)*
   ○ *_____ fish. (it/eat)*

4 Write these verbs in the correct forms.

choose, cut, get, have, leave, make, plan, write

Example: *She* <u>*'s having*</u> *a cup of tea.*

1 *He _____ his tools from the garage.*

2 *The boys _____ a library book.*

3 *_____ a new book, Professor?*

4 *I _____ to visit Canada next year.*

5 *We _____ in a minute. Give me your case.*

6 *Why _____ the wood into pieces, Dad?*

7 *Sarah _____ a cake. (make)*

5 Write these verbs in the correct forms.

build, do, go, start, study, train, work
Two old college friends meet by chance.

Nina: Hello, Alan! What <u>*are*</u> *you* <u>*doing*</u> *here?*

Alan: Oh, hi! I [1]*_____ for my uncle's construction company. We* [2]*_____ some offices here in London. Tell me,* [3]*_____ you still* [4]*_____ at college?*

Nina: No, I [5]*_____ . I* [6]*_____ to be a banker.*

Alan: And [7]*_____ your brother still* [8]*_____ to school?*

Nina: No, he's left school now. He [9]*_____ at college next month.*

5 Present simple or present continuous
He usually plays.   Today he's watching.

FORMS

Present simple

Jim usually plays for his team.

Present continuous

He is not playing for them today.
He is watching them on TV.

CROSSCHECK

Present simple	**Present continuous**

Use the present simple for regular actions or events.

*Jim usually **plays** for his team.*
*Alan usually **works** in the office.*

regular actions/events

Use the present simple for things which are always true – permanent states.

*Ann **lives** in London.*
*Rome **stands** on the River Tiber.*

Use the present simple for facts about future events.

*The game **starts** at 2.30.*
*When **does** school **start** next term?*

Use the present continuous for something which is happening now.

*Today he's **watching** them on TV.*
*Today he's **working** in the factory.*

now

a continuing action/event
happening now

Use the present continuous for things which are true around now – temporary states.

*I'm **living** with friends for a few months.*
*They're **standing** at the bus stop.*

Use the present continuous for future plans.

*We're **playing** again next week.*
*What **are** you **doing** tomorrow?*

Verbs which express permanent feelings, permanent states of mind and the senses are usually in the present/past simple, not the present/past continuous. These are the most common: *appear, believe, belong, detest, forget, hate, hear, know, like, look, love, mean, need, own, prefer, realize, remember, see* (understand), *seem, smell, sound, taste, understand.*

> *I **know** the way to town.   Jenny **loves** old American films.*
> *What sort of music **do** you **like**?   They **don't understand**.*

We can use a few verbs in the present simple and the present continuous – with a change of meaning. The most common are *think* and *have.*

> *I **think** we'll win.* (I believe.)
> *I'm **thinking** about the future.* (I'm looking at ideas.)
> *Terry **has** three houses.* (He owns.)
> *Terry **is having** dinner.* (He's eating.)

يستخدم المضارع البسيط للتعبير عن الأحداث او الأفعال التي يتكرر حدوثها بشكل شبه منتظم؛ ويوضح الرسم كيف تتكرر الاحداث والافعال بشكل متتابع على الخط الزمني.

ويستخدم المضارع المستمر للتعبير عن الافعال والاحداث الآخذة في الحدوث الآن.

ويبين الرسم التوضيحي استمرارية حدوث الفعل في الوقت الراهن.

ويستخدم المضارع البسيط للتعبير عن الحقائق وكذلك عن الحالات التي تتصف بالدوام. اما المضارع المستمر، فيستخدم للتعبير عن الأشياء التي يَصْدُق وصفها حالياً وكذلك عن الحالات المؤقتة.

يستخدم المضارع البسيط للتعبير عن الحقائق التي تتعلق باحداث مستقبلية.

ويستخدم المضارع المستمر للتعبير عن الخطط المستقبلية.

ان الأفعال التي تعبر عن المشاعر الدائمة او الحالات الذهنية الدائمة، وكذلك الأفعال التي تتعلق بالحواس تأتي عادةً في زمن المضارع البسيط وفي زمن الماضي البسيط، وليس في زمني المضارع والماضي المستمرين. واكثر هذه الافعال شيوعاً هي التالية:

وهناك عدد قليل من الافعال التي تستخدم في كلا الزمنين، المضارع البسيط والمضارع المستمر مع تغيير في معناها الحرفي. والفعلان الاكثر شيوعاً هما فعل think بمعنى يرى او يظن او يعتقد وفعل have بمعنى يملك او يتناول.

Exercises

1 Write the verbs in positive, negative or question forms of the present continuous.

Pam is calling her brother, Tom.

Pam: *What <u>are you doing</u> today? (you/do)*
¹_____ *out anywhere?*
(you/go)

Tom: *No, we aren't. What about you?* ²_____
_____ *anything? (you/do)*

Pam: *Yes, we are. You know that Marie* ³_____
_____ *with me. (stay) Well, I* ⁴_____
_____ *her to Windsor today. (take)*

Tom: *That's very near us.*

Pam: *Yes, so can we visit you after Windsor – if you*
⁵_____ *anything? (not/do)*

Tom: *Of course you can. We* ⁶_____
anywhere. (not/go) How long ⁷_____
_____ *to stay at Windsor? (you/plan)*

Pam: *Until about 5.00, I think.*

Tom: *Well, we* ⁸_____ *a barbecue this*
evening. (have) You're very welcome.

2 Write the verbs in positive, negative or question forms of the present simple.

Examples: *The cat is hungry. It <u>has</u> its food at this*
time every day. (have)

It's full now. It <u>doesn't want</u> any more.
(not/want)

How much <u>does it eat</u> a day? (it/eat)

1 *We've got enough money. We _____ any*
more. (not/need)

2 *Go to bed. You _____ tired. (look)*

3 *How _____ this word? (you/say)*

4 *I hate winter. I _____ the cold. (not/like)*

5 *_____ here?*
(the bus/stop)

6 *Rob's school report is bad. He _____*
any work. (not/do)

7 *What time _____ the office?*
(he/leave)

8 *Jim _____ to work by bike every morning. (go)*

9 The Jones brothers _____ across the park to school
every day. (walk)

10 *We can go out or we can stay at home. I _____*
_____ *(not/mind)*

11 _____ *the way home? (you/know)*

3 Complete the statements and questions.

Examples: *I <u>don't</u> go out much these days.*
What <u>are</u> the boys doing?

1 *Stop! You _____ going the wrong way.*

2 *I _____ understand this problem.*

3 *What _____ Ann doing at the moment?*

4 _____ *Nick and Sally going home soon?*

5 *What time _____ the plane leave?*

6 *How _____ you say this in English?*

7 *He's busy, so he _____ coming to the party.*

8 *I'm sure Tom _____ know the answer.*

9 _____ *the children want dinner?*

10 ● *Why _____ you working today?*
○ *It's a holiday.*

4 Write the verbs in the correct forms.

Mark is a new student in New York. He is writing
home to his parents in London.

Dear Mum and Dad,
How are you all? I <u>'m</u> well and I <u>'m having</u> a
wonderful time. (be) (have) I ¹_____
a lot of new friends and I ²_____
with three of them until I can find my own place to
live. (make) (stay)

  Let me tell you what I ³_____ *every day here. (do) I*
⁴_____ *early because classes* ⁵_____. *at*
8.00 in the morning. (get up) (start) Later, I usually
⁶_____ *lunch with Rod. (eat) He* ⁷_____ *the house*
where I ⁸_____ *at the moment. (own)*
(live) He ⁹_____ *the same classes as me.*
(take)

  We often ¹⁰_____ *at the gym in the afternoon,*
but not today. (train) He ¹¹_____
some work for college, and I ¹²_____
all my letters. (finish) (write)

6 Past simple
I washed them yesterday.

I washed your jeans yesterday.

FORMS

Statements		Yes/No questions		
I	*washed it.*	*Did*	*I*	*wash it?*
You			*you*	
He	*did not wash it.*		*he*	
She			*she*	
It			*it*	
We			*we*	
They			*they*	

Wb questions   **Full answers**
When did she do it?   *She did it yesterday.*
What did she do?   *She washed his jeans.*

Short form: *did not = didn't*

Use the past simple for actions which started and finished in the past. Look for past time markers such as *yesterday*.

> Ann **phoned** us yesterday.   Leo **arrived** home last night.

In past simple statements the verb usually ends with *ed*.

> She **washed** his jeans.   He **played** with his friends all morning.

If the verb ends in *e*, add *d*.

> We **moved** to our new house a month ago.

If the verb ends in a *y*, we usually cut *y* and add *ied*. (But not in *say*, *pay* and *lay*. See Appendix 1 for the past forms of these verbs.)

> I **hurried** to catch the bus.   She **carried** her baby to bed.

If the verb ends in a single consonant after a short vowel, double the consonant.

> We **stopped** work for lunch.   They **fitted** the pieces together.

A lot of important verbs are irregular, and their past forms do not end in *ed*. You have to learn these one by one. (See Appendix 1 for a list of these.)

> *come → came, go → went, drink → drank, eat → ate*

Positive statements need only a main verb.

> I **went** to the cinema last night. I **enjoyed** the film.

Most questions and negatives need the auxiliary verb *did*. (See Unit 21 for information about *do* as a main verb and auxiliary verb.)

> ● *What **did** you **see**? **Did** you **enjoy** it?*
> ○ *I **saw** Robocop 4. I **didn't enjoy** it much.*

Some verbs usually take the past simple and not the past continuous. (See Unit 5 for a list of these.)

> I **knew** what to do next.   Susan **didn't like** cold weather.

We can use the form *used to* + verb for something that often happened in the past, but does not happen now.

> I **used to go** training every day.   I **didn't use to smoke**.
> How often **did** Alan **use to go** abroad?

يستخدم الماضي البسيط للتعبير عن الأفعال التي بدأت وانتهت في الماضي... وتحوي الجمل كلمات تدل على الماضي مثل yesterday.

عادةً ينتهي الفعل في الجمل الخبرية في الماضي البسيط بـed.

اذا كان الفعل ينتهي بـ e يضاف اليه حرف d فقط.

اذا كان الفعل ينتهي بـ y يحذف هذا الحرف ويضاف، عوضاً عنه، ied ولكن الحال يختلف مع الافعال lay و pay و say (انظر الملحق 1 الخاص بتصريف الافعال).

اذا كان الفعل ينتهي بحرف ثابت مفرد مسبوق بحرف متحرك قصير، يكتب الحرف الثابت مرتين.

العديد من الافعال المهمة غير قياسية، ولا تنتهي صيغ الماضي الخاصة بها بـed.. وهذه الافعال يجب تعلمها كل على حدة. (انظر لائحة بهذه الافعال في الملحق 1.)

تحتاج الجمل الخبرية المثبتة إلى فعل أساسي واحد فقط.

وتحتاج غالبية الجمل الاستفهامية وكذلك الجمل المنفية الى الفعل المساعد did (انظر unit 21 لمزيد من المعلومات حول do كفعل رئيسي و كفعل مساعد).

وهناك من الافعال ما يأتي عادة، في زمن الماضي البسيط وليس في زمن الماضي المستمر (انظر لائحة بها في unit 5).

وتستخدم صيغة used to + فعل للتعبير عن فعل معتاد الحدوث في الماضي ولا يحدث في الوقت الحاضر.

Exercises

1 Write the past forms.

Examples: clean _cleaned_   sell _sold_

1 ask _____   11 invite _____
2 be _____   12 jump _____
3 break _____   13 keep _____
4 call _____   14 leave _____
5 do _____   15 meet _____
6 drive _____   16 need _____
7 eat _____   17 open _____
8 find _____   18 run _____
9 go _____   19 see _____
10 have _____   20 wake up _____

Which verbs are irregular?
Which verbs can be main verbs and auxiliary verbs?

2 Complete the paragraph with verbs from Exercise 1.

This morning, I _woke up_ late. When I ¹_____ the time, I ²_____ out of bed, and I ³_____ downstairs. I ⁴_____ a piece of bread, and I ⁵_____ a glass of orange juice. I ⁶_____ the house at 8.00, and I ⁷_____ at 100 kph all the way to work!

3 Write statements with positive and negative forms.

Example: (see/his parents ✓) (see/his sister ✗)
Sam _saw his parents_ last night, but he _didn't see his sister._

1 (find/my old suit ✓) (find/my new one ✗)
   I _____ yesterday, but I _____

2 (clean/her red shoes ✓) (clean/her black ones ✗)
   Tina _____ this morning, but she _____

3 (call/their mother ✓) (call/their sister ✗)
   They _____ the other day, but they _____

4 Write questions and short answers.

Example: I went to the beach. (Ben) (Yes)
● _Did Ben go to the beach too?_
○ _Yes, he did._

1 Andy visited Paris last year. (Tim and Fred) (No)
   ● _____
   ○ _____

2 Sue ran well in the race. (Ann) (Yes)
   ● _____
   ○ _____

3 They had a Maths test. (French) (No)
   ● _____
   ○ _____

4 Peter practised the violin. (piano) (Yes)
   ● _____
   ○ _____

5 Read. Then write questions for the answers. Use these question words.

How, What time, When, Where, Who, Why

Example: ● _Where did Susan Hill go?_
○ She went to London.

Susan Hill went to London last Thursday because she wanted to buy a wedding present for her sister. She went by train and she got there at 10.30. She met an old school friend at the station and they went shopping together.

1 ● _____
   ○ She went there last Thursday.

2 ● _____
   ○ She went by train.

3 ● _____
   ○ Because she wanted to buy a wedding present.

4 ● _____
   ○ She got there at 10.30.

5 ● _____
   ○ She met an old school friend.

6 ● _____
   ○ They met at the station.

7 Past simple: be

They were by my bed.

> Where were they?
>
> They were by my bed all the time!

FORMS					
Statements			**Yes/No questions**		
I	was	there.	Was	I	there?
He				he	
She	was not			she	
It				it	
We	were	at home.	Were	we	at home?
You				you	
They	were not			they	

Wb questions   **Full answers**

What was that noise?   It was an animal.
Where were they?   They were at home.

Short forms: was not = wasn't   were not = weren't

Use the past simple of *be* for any state.

Age: The boys **weren't** 15. They **were** 16.
Description: She **was** beautiful with fair hair.
Height: He **was** only 1 metre 50 when he was 13.
Weight: I **was** 80 kilos last week.   How heavy **was** the parcel?
Feelings: **Were** you sad at the end of the holiday?
Distance: How far **were** they from the sea?
Size: The house **was** about 2,000 square metres.
Price: **Was** that watch expensive?
Time: What time **was** your lesson yesterday?

Use the past simple of *be* in *there was/there were*.
- ● **Was there** a big match on Saturday?
- ○ Yes, and **there were** thousands of fans at the match.

Use *Yes/No* questions to check information. Form them like this.
> She **was** clever. → **Was** she clever?
> The students **were** in Room 1. → **Were** the students in Room 1?

You can answer *Yes/No* questions with short answers.
- ● **Was** she clever?   ○ Yes she **was**.
- ● **Were** the students in Room 1?   ○ No, they **weren't**.

We always use full forms in *Yes* answers, when the verb is the last word.
> Yes, I **was**.   Yes, he **was**.   Yes, they **were**.

We usually use short forms in *No* answers.
> No, she **wasn't**.   No, we **weren't**.

Use *Wh* questions to get more information.
- ● Who **was** she?   ○ Her name **was** Pam Woods.
- ● Where **was** she?   ○ She **was** in Room 1.

تستخدم صيغ الماضي من فعل be للتعبير عن اي من الحالات المبينة في الامثلة.

ويستخدم الماضي من فعل be في صيغتي there was و there were.

وتستخدم الاسئلة التي يجاب عنها بِ «نعم» او «لا» للتأكد من المعلومات، وتتكون كما هو وارد في الامثلة.

ويمكن الاجابة بطريقة مختصرة عن الاسئلة التي يجاب عنها بِ «نعم» او «لا».

وتستخدم الصيغ الكاملة دائماً، عند الاجابة بِ «نعم»، عندما يكون الفعل آخر كلمة في الجملة.

تستخدم عادة الصيغ المختصرة عند الاجابة بِ «لا».

وتستخدم أدوات الاستفهام التي تبدأ بحرفي (wh) للحصول على مزيد من المعلومات.

Exercises

1 Complete the statements and questions.

Example: ● How old _were_ you in 1989?
○ I _was_ 13.

1 It _____ late, and the children _____ tired.

2 The Johnson brothers _____ at the same college. Rod _____ a medical student, and Harry and Tony _____ law students.

3 We _____ 30 minutes early for the party and there _____ nobody there. The room _____ empty!

4 ● How long _____ you and your wife in Cairo?
○ I _____ there for three years, but she _____ there for only two.

2 Complete the conversation.

Two friends meet after a party.

Jenny: We _were_ sad that you _weren't_ at the party.

Robin: I [1]_____ sorry to miss it too. [2]_____ it a good one?

Jenny: Yes, it [3]_____ There [4]_____ a lot of old friends there. Where [5]_____ you and the family?

Robin: Dad [6]_____ away on business, and Mum [7]_____ very well. And my brothers [8]_____ back from holiday. They [9]_____ still away.

3 Read. Then write questions and answer them.

Example: (When/they/at the house)
● _When were they at the house?_
○ _Last night._

We saw a lovely house yesterday. We were there last night. It was about 100 years old, and we wanted to buy it immediately. There were four bedrooms upstairs. Downstairs, there was a beautiful dining-room, and the living-room was very big – 12 x 5 metres. The kitchen at the back of the house was large too, and very modern. Outside there was a beautiful garden with a stream. We loved the house! The only problem was the price. It was £200,000!

1 (How old/the house)
● _____
○ _____

2 (How many bedrooms)
● _____
○ _____

3 (How big/the living-room)
● _____
○ _____

4 (Where/the kitchen)
● _____
○ _____

5 (What/outside)
● _____
○ _____

6 (What/the only problem)
● _____
○ _____

7 (How much/the house)
● _____
○ _____

4 Complete the statements.

Example: Maria _wasn't_ good at English at school, but she _'s_ excellent now.

1 Go and see the old city. There _____ thousands of old buildings there. Some of them _____ over 500 years old.

2 Simon _____ at home yesterday, but he _____ there now.

3 We _____ wrong to leave the main road. Now we _____ lost!

4 The children _____ tired after the party, but I _____ nearly asleep.

5 Alan _____ at work yesterday, but he _____ at home today. Here _____ his phone number. You can call him.

21

8 Past continuous

It was raining again.

They looked out of the window. It was raining again.

FORMS

Statements

I	was	looking.
He		
She	was not	
It		
We	were	running.
You		
They	were not	

Yes/No questions

Was	I	looking?
	he	
	she	
	it	
Were	we	running?
	you	
	they	

Wb questions

What was she doing?
Where were they sitting?

Full answers

She was reading.
They were sitting in the garden.

Short forms: was not = wasn't   were not = weren't

Form the past continuous with *was, were* + main verb + *ing*. (See Unit 21 for information about *be* as a main verb and auxiliary verb.)

> *I **was reading** all last night.   What **were** you **doing** at 2.00?*

Remember the spelling rules with *ing*. (See Unit 4.)

> *move → moving, stop → stopping, die → dying*

Use the past continuous for things which were continuing at a certain moment in the past.

> ● *What **were** you **doing** at 12.00?*   ○ *I **was going** home for lunch.*

Use the past continuous for emphasizing that something was continuing for a long time – often something unwanted.

> *The baby **was crying** all night.*

Use the past continuous for things which were continuing (a continuing action) when something else suddenly happened (a short action).

a short past action/event
(past simple)

now

a continuing action/event (past continuous)

When the two actions are in one sentence, use the connectors *when, as* or *while* to join the two sentence parts.

> *Jenny **was reading when** Ann **phoned**.*
> *The truck **hit** my car **as** I **was turning**.*
> *The policeman **arrived while** we **were having** dinner.*

Do not confuse these two different ideas.

> *When Tom **arrived**, we **were having** tea. (Tea was continuing.)*
> *When Tom **arrived**, we **had** tea. (Tom arrived. Then tea started.)*

Some verbs usually take the past simple and not the past continuous. (See Unit 5 for a list of these.)

> *I **knew** what to do next.   Susan **didn't like** cold weather.*

يتكون الماضي المستمر من was او were + الفعل مضافاً له ing.

بجب مراعاة قواعد الاملاء عند اضافة ing لبعض الافعال (انظر unit 4).

يستخدم الماضي المستمر للتعبير عن الاحداث التي استمر حدوثها في وقت محدد في الماضي.

يستخدم الماضي المستمر للتأكيد على ان حدثاً ما قد استمر حدوثه طويلاً في الماضي... وغالباً ما يكون حدثاً غير مرغوب فيه.

يستخدم الماضي المستمر للتعبير عن حدث استمر حدوثه في الماضي (فعل مستمر) عندما تخلل حدوثه فعلٌ آخر بشكل مفاجئ (فعل مقتضب). ويوضح الرسم استمرارية الحدث من خلال الخط المتعرج، وكيف قاطع استمراريتَه حدثٌ آخر قصير تمثله العلامة السوداء في المنتصف.

عندما تحوي الجملة فعلين تستخدم كلمات الربط when او as او while لربط جزئي الجملة.

وعلينا ان نفرق بعناية بين الفكرتين المختلفتين اللتين تمثلهما الجملتان التاليتان.

وهناك مجموعة من الافعال التي تأتي عادة، في زمن الماضي البسيط وليس في الماضي المستمر. (انظر لائحة بهذه الافعال في unit 5).

Exercises

1 Write the verbs in the correct forms.

The Carter family all remember what they were doing when the last Californian earthquake happened.

Example: Sally: I _was cooking_ lunch for John. (cook)

1 John: I _____ my boss in New York. (call)

2 Ron and Sue: We _____ at the lake with Paul. (swim)

3 Tom: I _____ a football game on TV. (watch)

4 Ann and Carol: We _____ a Pepsi at the Corner Café. (have)

5 Flo: I _____ ready to go out with some friends. (get)

6 Tim and Bill: We _____ our bikes in the park. (ride)

2 Complete the questions and answers.

Examples: ● _Was_ Sally _cooking_ dinner? (cook)
○ No, she _wasn't_. She _was cooking_ lunch.
● What _were_ Ann and Carol _doing?_ (do)
○ They _were having_ a Pepsi at the Corner Café. (have)

1 ● Who _____ Ron and Sue _____ with? (swim)
○ They _____ with Paul.
● _____ at the swimming pool?
○ No, they _____ They _____ _____ at the lake.

2 ● _____ Tom _____ to the radio? (listen)
○ No, he _____ He _____ TV. (watch)
● What _____
○ He _____ a football game.

3 ● Where _____ Tim and Bill _____ their bikes? (ride)
○ They _____ their bikes in the park.

4 ● Who _____ John _____ (call)
○ He _____ his boss.

3 Write the verbs in the correct forms.

Examples: I _was making_ lunch when the earthquake _happened._ (make) (happen)
What _were the children doing_ at this time last week? (the children/do)

1 What _____ at this time yesterday? (you/do)

2 Why _____ along the street at 10.00 last night? (he/run)

3 She _____ home when her new car _____ (drive) (break down)

4 I _____ the window. (open) The sun _____ (shine)

5 They _____ in the garden when the phone _____ (work) (ring)

6 The storm _____ the boat as it _____ to reach the harbour. (hit) (try)

7 The plane _____ to land when it _____ (try) (crash)

4 Write the verbs in the correct forms.

When I _went_ out at 9.00 the sun _was shining._ (go) (shine) It [1]_____ a beautiful spring day and the birds in the park [2]_____ (be) (sing) I [3]_____ along the road beside the park when suddenly I [4]_____ my old friend, John. (walk) (notice) He [5]_____ football with his son in the park. (play) I [6]_____ to him and he [7]_____ round in surprise. (call) (look) Then he [8]_____ back and [9]_____ me to join them. (shout) (invite) Soon all of us [10]_____ _____ football together. (play) Then we [11]_____ to get some ice-creams. (stop) While we [12]_____ them, we [13]_____ to go to the lake and hire a boat. (eat) (decide) Then something terrible [14]_____ (happen) Just as I [15]_____ into the boat, it [16]_____ to move away, and I [17]_____ straight into the water between the boat and the shore. (get) (start) (fall) Hundreds of people [18]_____ , and they all [19]_____ (watch) (laugh) I [20]_____ really embarrassed! (feel)

23

9 Present perfect 1

I've washed the car.

Look, Dad! I've washed the car.

Great! It's really clean now.

FORMS

Statements

I / You / We / They	have	washed it.
	have not	
He / She / It	has	finished.
	has not	

Yes/No questions

Have	I / you / we / they	washed it?
Has	he / she / it	finished?

Wh questions

What have you done?
How long has the job taken?

Full answers

I have washed the car.
It has taken an hour.

Short forms: I/you/we/they have = I've, you've, we've, they've
he/she/it has = he's, she's, it's   have not = haven't
has not = hasn't

Form the present perfect with *have, has* + past participle. With regular verbs the past participle is the same as the past simple form – main verb + *ed*.

> *I've washed* the car. *I've* just *finished*.
> ● *Has* she *finished* dinner?   ○ No, she *hasn't*.

If the verb ends in *e*, add *d*.

> The train *has arrived*. There it is! Let's run.

If the verb ends in *y*, change the *y* to *ied*.

> Mary *has carried* the case for an hour. She's tired.

These are different.

> *say → said, pay → paid, lay → laid*

If the verb ends in a single consonant after a short vowel, double the consonant.

> The bus *has stopped*. We can get off now.

A lot of important verbs are irregular, and their past forms do not end in *ed*. The verbs *be, do* and *have* are all irregular. (See Unit 21 for information about *have* as a main verb and auxiliary verb.)

Infinitive	Past form	Past participle
be	*was/were*	*been*
do	*did*	*done*
have	*had*	*had*

Many common main verbs are irregular too. You have to learn these one by one. (See Appendix 1 for a list of these.)

Infinitive	Past form	Past participle
hit	*hit*	*hit*
make	*made*	*made*
speak	*spoke*	*spoken*
give	*gave*	*given*

يتكون المضارع التام من have أو has + التصريف الثالث للفعل. والتصريف الثالث للافعال القياسية هو نفس صيغة الماضي البسيط. وهو يتكون بإضافة ed إلى أصل الفعل.

واذا كان الفعل ينتهي بـ e يضاف إليه d فقط.

كذلك يبدل الحرف y اذا جاء في نهاية الفعل بـ ied.

والحال يختلف بالنسبة للافعال التالية:

اذا كانت نهاية الفعل حرفاً ثابتاً مسبوقاً بحرف متحرك قصير، يكتب الحرف الثابت مرتين.

هناك العديد من الافعال الهامة من النوع اللاقياسي التي لا تنتهي صيغة الماضي منها بـ ed، منها فعل be و do وhave، وكلها لا قياسية. (انظر unit 21 للمزيد من المعلومات حول فعل have كفعل رئيسي وكفعل مساعد).

وهناك العديد من الافعال الاساسية الشائعة من النوع اللاقياسي ايضاً والتي يجب تعلمها كل على حدة. (انظر لائحة بهذه الافعال في الملحق 1).

Use the present perfect when something happened in the past, and affects us now.

> Tom **has cleaned** the car. (So now it's really clean.)
> Ann **has broken** her arm. (So now she can't write.)

Use the present perfect when something started in the past and continues to the present. Look out for the words *yet* and *just*. *yet* means 'up to now'.

> ● **Have** they **repaired** the car **yet**?
> ○ No, they **haven't had** time **yet**. They're going to do it tomorrow.

just means 'only a very short time ago'.

> The water **has just boiled**. Would you like a cup of tea?
> Our new car **has just arrived**. Come and look.

We sometimes use *yet* and *just* together.

> ● **Have** you **finished** your homework **yet**?
> ○ Not **yet**. I've **just finished** question 1, but I **haven't finished** question 2. (I'm doing it now.)

Use *still ... not* for something that happens late.

> I started this last week and I **still haven't finished.**

Use *already* for something that happens early.

> It's only 8.00 in the morning and they**'ve already done** three hours work.

We sometimes use *still ... not* and *already* together.

> ● I suppose Joe **still hasn't started** work!
> ○ You're wrong. He**'s already finished**!

The *'s* short form can mean *is* or *has*, so check the main part of the verb. Study the different meanings.

> She**'s come** home. (*'s come* = has come)
> She**'s coming** home. (*'s coming* = is coming)

يستخدم المضارع التام للتعبير عن حدث وقع في الماضي وله أثر واضح في الحاضر.

يستخدم المضارع التام للتعبير عن حدث بدأ في الماضي واستمر حدوثه حتى الوقت الحاضر... وتستخدم في هذه الجمل كلمة yet (وتعني حتى الآن) وكلمة just.

وتعني كلمة just منذ برهة قصيرة فقط.

وتستخدم كلمتا yet و just معاً أحيانا في جملة واحدة.

ويستخدم التعبير اللغوي still ... not للتدليل على حدث تأخر الانتهاء منه.

وتستخدم كلمة already لتفيد معنى الانتهاء من عمل ما في وقت سابق.

وأحياناً تستخدم still ... not و already معاً في جملة واحدة.

قد تعني الصيغة المختصرة s' إما is أو has، الأمر الذي يتطلب التأكد من الجزء الخاص بالفعل الأساسي في الجملة. لاحظ فروق المعاني في الأمثلة التالية.

Exercises

1 Write the past participles.

Example: *buy* <u>bought</u>   *happen* <u>happened</u>
              meet <u>met</u>

1 *ask* _____
2 *be* _____
3 *choose* _____
4 *do* _____
5 *eat* _____
6 *find* _____
7 *give* _____
8 *have* _____
9 *invite* _____
10 *join* _____
11 *keep* _____
12 *leave* _____
13 *make* _____
14 *need* _____
15 *open* _____
16 *put* _____
17 *run* _____
18 *start* _____
19 *take* _____
20 *wake up* _____

Which verbs are irregular?
Which verbs can be main verbs and auxiliary verbs?

2 Complete the paragraph with verbs from Exercise 1 (including the examples).

Dear Mum,

Well, a lot of things have <u>happened</u> *since our move to Australia. Larry has* [1]_____ *a good job at a bank, and we have* [2]_____ *a small house outside town for $70,000. Peter and Sally have* [3]_____ *at their new school, and they're very happy there. Peter has* [4]_____ *the football team and Sally has* [5]_____ *a lot of good friends in her class. I have* [6]_____ *all the neighbours now, and they have* [7]_____ *very kind. In fact, our next-door neighbour has* [8]_____ *all of us to a barbecue lunch on Sunday.*

3 Write these verbs in the correct forms.

arrive, break, catch, get, paint, win

Example: *Tom* <u>has cleaned</u> *the car. Now it looks like new.*

1 *They _____ the TV. It doesn't work.*
2 *The police _____ the bank robbers. They're at the police station now.*
3 *Ann _____ the room. It's pink now.*
4 *My parents _____ Their car is outside.*
5 *Mark _____ the race. He's the new champion.*
6 *Dad _____ the tickets, so we can go in.*

4 Write statements with positive and negative forms.

Example: *(find/a job ✓) (find/a house ✗)*
            Alan <u>has found a job,</u> *but he* <u>hasn't found a house.</u>

1 *(join/the school drama group ✓) (join/the tennis club ✗)*
   Tony _____
   _____ but he _____
   _____

2 *(make/a cake ✓) (make/any sandwiches ✗)*
   Julie _____ but she
   _____

3 *(bring/their books ✓) (bring/their pens ✗)*
   The boys _____ but
   they _____

4 *(choose/the carpets for their new house ✓) (choose/any furniture ✗)*
   Ian and Sue _____
   _____ but they
   _____
   _____

5 *(wash/the car ✓) (wash/the children's bikes ✗)*
   I _____ but I
   _____
   _____

6 *(invite/Alan to the party ✓) (invite Joe ✗)*
   We _____
   but we _____

5 Write questions and and short answers.

Examples: *Lisa has cleaned her shoes. (boots) (Yes)*
● <u>Has she cleaned her boots too?</u>
○ <u>Yes, she has.</u>

Peter has eaten his lunch. (Bill) (No)
● <u>Has Bill eaten his lunch too?</u>
○ <u>No, he hasn't.</u>

1 *The boys have done their Maths homework. (French homework) (No)*
● _____
_____
○ _____

26

2 *Vicky has been busy all day. (Mark) (Yes)*
   ● _____
   _____
   ○ _____

3 *Barry has learnt to fly. (you) (Yes)*
   ● _____
   _____
   ○ _____

4 *Petra and I have brought our books. (Sally) (No)*
   ● _____
   _____
   ○ _____

6 Re-order the words to make questions.

Example: *(gone/where/girls/have/the)*
   Where have the girls gone?

1 *(lived/Emma/how long/London/has/in)*
   _____
   _____

2 *(late/come/you/why/so/have/home)*
   _____
   _____

3 *(my/what/you/have/with/shirt/done)*
   _____
   _____

4 *(the/has/Andy/where/put/bike)*
   _____
   _____

5 *(kilometres/you/how many/today/driven)*
   _____
   _____

7 Write the answers. Use *just* or *yet*.

Examples: ● *Is the TV working? (Yes) (mend/it)*
   ○ *Yes, I've just mended it.*

   ● *Have you seen your picture in today's newspaper? (No) (buy/one)*
   ○ *No, I haven't bought one yet.*

1 ● *Has Ruth moved? (Yes) (go to/Rome)*
   ○ _____

2 ● *Do you know the Smiths? (No) (not/meet/them)*
   ○ _____

3 ● *Does Bob like sweet things? (Yes) (buy/some chocolate)*
   ○ _____

4 ● *Are we going home now? (No) (not/finish/work)*
   ○ _____

5 ● *Have the boys had lunch? (No) (not/come/home)*
   ○ _____

6 ● *Have you got enough petrol? (Yes) (buy/some)*
   ○ _____

7 ● *Have you moved my books? (Yes) (put/them/in your case)*
   ○ _____

8 Write statements. Use *already* or *But . . . still . . . not.*

Examples: *Tom's boots are dirty. (clean/them ✗)*
   But he still hasn't cleaned them.
   Ann works very fast. (do/her Maths ✓)
   She's already done her Maths.

1 *I asked you to talk to Bill yesterday. (call/him ✗)*
   _____

2 *We're planning to go to Spain. (buy/the tickets ✓)*
   _____

3 *I asked you to get ready. (pack/your bag ✗)*
   _____

4 *She's saving for a CD player. (get/£50 ✓)*
   _____

5 *Number 33 is moving fast now. (do/300 kph ✓)*
   _____

6 *I write three weeks ago. (have/a reply ✗)*
   _____

FORMS

Present perfect + *for/since*

I have lived here	for 35 years. for a long time. for ages.
I haven't lived here	since I was young. since 1960. since yesterday.

Present perfect + number of times

- ● *Have you ever been back to Sydney?*
- ○ *Yes, I have been back three times.*

She has visited Spain	once or twice. four times this year. every year since 1985.

Present perfect + *for/since*

Use the present perfect when something started in the past and it continues to the present. We often use *for* and *since*. *for* shows how long something has continued. *since* shows when something started.

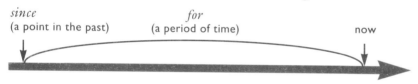

since   *for*
(a point in the past)   (a period of time)   now

*Karen **has been** a nurse **for 15 years**.* OR ***since 1980**.*

Present perfect + number of times

Use the present perfect when things have happened in a period of time that started in the past and continue to the present. We often use *ever* and *never* and time expressions such as *this year, this week, today, since 1960.*

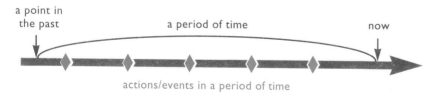

a point in
the past   a period of time   now

actions/events in a period of time

- ● ***Have** you **ever been*** back to Sydney? (In the 35-year period.)
- ○ *Three times.*
- ● ***Have** you **ever visited*** Scotland?
- ○ *Yes, I've **been** there many times.* OR *No, I've **never been** there.*

Study the different meanings of *been* and *gone*.

    *He's **been** to India. He went there last year.* (And now he's home again.)
    *He's **gone** to India. He's working in Calcutta.* (He's there now.)

يستخدم المضارع التام عندما نعبر عن فعل بدأ في الماضي واستمر حدوثه حتى الوقت الحاضر. وغالباً ما نستخدم في هذه الحالة كلمتي for و since. وتبين كلمة for الفترة الزمنية التي استغرقها الحدث، في حين تبين كلمة since نقطة بداية حدوث الفعل.

ويوضح الرسم عند السهم الاول نقطة البداية since، في حين تبين for الفترة الزمنية التي استغرقها حتى الوقت الحاضر (السهم الثاني).

ويستخدم المضارع التام للتعبير عن احداث حصلت خلال فترة زمنية بدأت في الماضي وتستمر حتى الوقت الحاضر. وغالباً ما نستخدم كلمتي ever و never اضافة إلى عبارات الدلالة الزمنية مثل this year..الخ.

ويوضح الرسم تعدد تكرار الحدث خلال فترة زمنية بدأت في الماضي كما يشير إلى ذلك السهم الأول، والى استمرارها حتى الوقت الحاضر كما يشير إلى ذلك السهم الثاني.

يجب التعرف من خلال الامثلة على اختلاف المعنى عند استخدام been و gone.

Exercises

1 Write statements.

Examples: *(Charlie/live/there/35 years)*
Charlie has lived there for 35 years.
(he/be/there/20 years old)
He's been there since he was 20 years old.

1 *(this land/belong to/Mr Hill/1950)*

_____

_____

2 *(Sally/have/the same car/five years)*

_____

_____

3 *(we/live/in this house/I was 25)*

_____

_____

2 Complete the questions and answers.

Example: ● *I live in London.*
○ *How long* _have you lived_ *there?*
● _Since_ *1985.* OR _For_ *ten years.*

1 ● *Nick and Sue have a Mercedes.*
○ *How long* _____ *it?*
● _____ *last month.*

2 ● *My brother works for IBM.*
○ *How long* _____ *for them?*
● _____ *three years.*

3 ● *The Carter family want to move house.*
○ *How long* _____ *to do that?*
● _____ *Mr Carter got a job in London.*

4 ● *Nick Ellis lives on a small island.*
○ *How long* _____ *there?*
● _____ *most of his life.*

3 Write negative answers for the questions.

Example: ● *When was the last time you had an ice-cream? (ages)* OR *(last week)*
○ _I haven't had an ice-cream for ages._ OR _since last week._

1 ● *When did Tim last see Susan? (three weeks)*
○ _____

_____

2 ● *When did the whole family last meet? (Claire's wedding)*
○ _____

_____

3 ● *When was the last time we had fish for dinner? (months)*
○ _____

4 Write questions. Use *ever* where possible. Then answer the questions.

Examples: *(you/stay/in Miami) (three times)*
● _Have you ever stayed in Miami?_
○ _Yes, I've stayed there three times._
(How often/he/stay/there) (once)
● _How often has he stayed there?_
○ _He's stayed there once._

1 *(you/study/English/before) (once)*
● _____

_____

○ _____

2 *(How many times/he/see/Superman) (seven times)*
● _____

_____

○ _____

3 *(they/try/Indian food) (a few times)*
● _____

_____

○ _____

4 *(How often/it/rain/today) (twice)*
● _____

○ _____

5 Complete the questions and answers.

Example: ● *Does Susan like sailing?*
○ *She loves it! She* _'s been_ *sailing every weekend this year. She* _'s gone_ *again this weekend.*

1 ● _____ *you ever* _____ *to Rome?*
○ *No, but my brother* _____ *just* _____ *there this week. He's there now.*

2 ● *Where's Alan?*
○ *He* _____ *to the bank to get some money.*

3 *Sue* _____ *never* _____ *to China.*

11 Present perfect or past simple

It has opened.   It opened last week.

Look! The new sports shop has opened.

Yes, I know. It opened last week.

CHAMPION SPORTS

NOW OPEN!

NOW OPEN!

CROSSCHECK

Present perfect

Use the present perfect when something happened in the past, but you do not know when.

> *The new sports shop **has opened**.*

Use the present perfect when something happened in the past, but it affects us now.

> *He's **broken** his leg.* (The leg is still broken.)

Use the present perfect when something started in the past and it continues to the present.

> *Mary **has lived** in London for seven years.* (And she still lives there now.)

Use the present perfect when something has happened in a period of time up to the present, eg *today, this year.*

> *She's **written** three letters today.*
> ***Have** you **had** exams this year?*

Use the present perfect to find out if something has happened, not when.

> ***Has** Peter **gone** home yet?*

We often start to talk about an event at an unstated time in the past.

> ● ***Have** you ever **visited** Japan?*
> ○ *Yes, I've **been** there three times.*

Past simple

Use the past simple when something happened completely in the past.

> *It **opened** last week.*

Use the past simple when something started and finished in the past and you know when.

> *He **broke** his leg last year.* (His leg is OK now.)

Use the past simple when something started and finished in the past.

> *Mary **lived** in London for seven years.* (But she doesn't live there now.)

Use the past simple when something happened in a period of past time, eg *yesterday, last year.*

> *She **wrote** five letters yesterday.*
> ***Did** you **have** exams last year?*

Use the past simple to find out when something happened.

> *When **did** Peter **go** home?*

We then fix the details of the event in the past with the past simple.

> ● *When **were** you last there?*
> ○ *I **stayed** there last summer.*

يستخدم المضارع التام للتعبير عن فعل حدث في وقت غير محدد في الماضي.

ويستخدم الماضي البسيط للتعبير عن فعل وقع وانتهى في الماضي.

يستخدم المضارع التام للتعبير عن فعل وقع في الماضي وما زالت آثاره حتى الوقت الحاضر.

ويستخدم الماضي البسيط للتعبير عن فعل بدأ وانتهى في وقت محدد في الماضي.

يستخدم المضارع التام للتعبير عن فعل بدأ في الماضي ويستمر حدوثه حتى الوقت الحاضر.

ويستخدم الماضي البسيط للتعبير عن فعل بدأ وانتهى في الماضي.

يستخدم المضارع التام للتعبير عن فعل حدث خلال فترة زمنية امتدت حتى الوقت الحاضر (اليوم أو هذا العام).

ويستخدم الماضي البسيط للتعبير عن فعل حدث في فترة زمنية انتهت في الماضي (أمس أو العام الماضي).

يستخدم المضارع التام للاستدلال عن وقوع فعل ما وليس عن زمن وقوعه بشكل محدد.

ويستخدم الماضي البسيط للاستدلال عن وقت حدوث فعل ما بشكل محدد.

غالباً ما نتحدث عن وقوع حدث ما في وقت غير محدد في الماضي.

ثم نعمل على تحديد تفاصيل هذا الحدث الماضي باستخدام الماضي البسيط.

Exercises

1 Write the verbs in positive, negative or question forms of the past simple.

Rob: *You know, last night <u>was</u> terrible. (be) I <u>locked</u> myself out of the house. (lock)*

Lyn: *Oh, no! What [1]_____ (you/do)*

Rob: *I [2]_____ round the house and I [3]_____ for an open window. (go) (look)*

Lyn: *[4]_____ one? (you/find)*

Rob: *There [5]_____ any on the ground floor, but there [6]_____ one upstairs. (not/be) (be)*

Lyn: *It's a pity you [7]_____ us. (not/call) You're always welcome to stay here.*

Rob: *Thanks, but I [8]_____ to give you any trouble. (not/want)*

Lyn: *So what [9]_____ after that? (you/do)*

Rob: *I [10]_____ the police. (phone)*

2 Write the verbs in positive, negative or question forms of the present perfect.

Tina and Bill are getting ready for school.

Example: Mum: *<u>Have you had</u> enough to eat? (you/have)*

Tina: *Thanks, Mum. I <u>'ve eaten</u> lots. (eat)*

Bill: *Well, I <u>haven't</u> . I'm still hungry.*

1 Tina: *Bill, where _____ my coat? (you/put)*

Bill: *I _____ your coat since last week. (not/see)*

2 Mum: *_____ your bag for school, Tina? (you/pack)*

Tina: *Yes, but I _____ my pencil case upstairs. (leave)*

3 Mum: *_____ you your lunch money, Bill? (Dad/give)*

Bill: *No, he _____ Can you give me some?*

4 Dad: *I _____ the car to the front door. (bring) Are you ready to go?*

Bill: *I am, but Tina _____ upstairs for her pencil case. (go)*

3 Write the past forms and past participles.

Examples: *write <u>wrote written</u>*

1 *ask* _____ _____
2 *be* _____ _____
3 *cut* _____ _____
4 *do* _____ _____
5 *find* _____ _____
6 *go* _____ _____
7 *have* _____ _____
8 *invite* _____ _____
9 *join* _____ _____
10 *keep* _____ _____

Which verbs are irregular?
Which verbs can be main verbs and auxiliary verbs?

4 Complete the statements and questions.

Examples: *Helen <u>has</u> never been to Canada.*
<u>Did</u> you spend much money yesterday?

1 *How long _____ Ann been at home?*
2 *I'm sure Peter _____ make a mistake.*
3 *Tom _____ finished work yet.*
4 *_____ anybody see the news at 1.00?*
5 *We _____ found the way, but we're trying.*
6 *_____ anybody seen my sweater?*
7 *When _____ the accident happen?*
8 *How many times _____ you seen that film?*

5 Write the verbs in the correct forms.

Mark is writing home to his parents in London.

6th November

Dear Mum and Dad,

Well, I <u>arrived</u> here in New York on 6th September, so I <u>'ve been</u> here for two months. (arrive) (be) I'm sorry I [1]_____ to you since last month, but life [2]_____ very busy. (not/write) (be) Classes [3]_____ and I [4]_____ a lot of things to do. (begin) (have) I [5]_____ you about Rod in my last letter. (tell) He [6]_____ me stay at his place since I first [7]_____ here. (let) (get) But, at last I [8]_____ a place of my own. (find) I [9]_____ the agreement with the owner last night, and he [10]_____ me a key. (sign) (give)

12 Present perfect continuous
I've been waiting for an hour.

Statements

I	have	been waiting.
You		
We	have not	
They		

He	has	been playing.
She		
It	has not	

Yes/No questions

Have	I	been waiting?
	you	
	we	
	they	

Has	he	been playing?
	she	
	it	

Wh questions

What have you been doing?
How long has he been waiting?

Full answers

I have been watching TV.
He has been waiting for an hour.

Short forms: I/you/we/they have = I've, you've, we've, they've
he/she/it has = he's, she's, it's   have not = haven't   has not = hasn't

We often use the present perfect continuous instead of the present perfect. We use it to emphasize that something has continued for a long time.

> **I've been waiting** for an hour!
> Tom **has been building** that boat since 1985. Will he ever finish?
> How long **have** you **been learning** English?

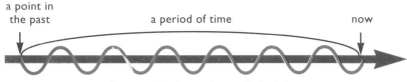

a continuing action/event in a period of time

We can use the present perfect continuous when something stops just before the present, but it affects us now.

> Look, the road is wet. It**'s been raining**.
> Bob **has been travelling** on business, but he's home now.

We can use the present perfect continuous when things have happened many times from the past to the present.

> We**'ve been going** to France for our holidays for ten years.
> How long **have** you **been going** to work by bicycle?

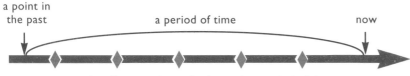

a continually repeating action/event in a period of time

We use many adverbs and other expressions of time to help emphasize 'how long', eg *for, since, lately, recently, all morning/day/week, the whole morning/day/week.* (See Unit 10 for the difference between *for* and *since*.)

> We**'ve been waiting** for an hour.   I**'ve been feeling** ill lately.
> We**'ve been working** since 6.00 this morning.

غالباً ما يستخدم المضارع التام المستمر عوضاً عن المضارع التام، وذلك للتأكيد على أن الحدث قد استمر لفترة طويلة من الزمن.

ويوضح الرسم بداية الفعل من نقطة في الماضي عند السهم الاول، واستمرار حدوثه طوال الفترة الزمنية حتى الوقت الحاضر (عند السهم الاخير).

ويمكن استخدام المضارع التام المستمر للتعبير عن حدث توقف قبل اللحظة الحاضرة ولكنه يؤثر فينا الآن.

ويمكن استخدام المضارع التام المستمر للتعبير عن الاحداث التي تكرر حدوثها من الماضي وحتى الوقت الحاضر.

ويوضح الرسم استمرار تكرار حدوث الفعل بين نقطة بدء حدوثه في الماضي، التي يشير اليها السهم الاول، طوال الفترة الزمنية حتى الوقت الحاضر، والتي يشير اليها السهم الاخير.

ويستخدم العديد من الظروف والتعبيرات الزمنية الاخرى للمساعدة في تأكيد طول الفترة الزمنية... مثل for و since و lately... الخ.

Exercises

1 Complete the answers.

Example: ● *Why are you so tired?*
○ *I 'νe been studying all night. (study)*

1 ● *Hello! Where have you been recently?*
○ *I _____ in London. (work)*

2 ● *Why are the children so dirty?*
○ *They _____ in the garden. (play)*

3 ● *I can't find my Walkman. Where is it?*
○ *John _____ it upstairs. (use)*

4 ● *Why haven't you washed the car yet?*
○ *I _____ jobs for Mum. (do)*

5 ● *Maria speaks very good English.*
○ *Yes. She _____ very hard. (study)*

2 Complete the answers.

Example: ● *Have the children been helping Mum?*
○ *No, they haven't been helping her. They 've been watching TV. (watch)*

1 ● *Has Tony been spending all his money?*
○ *No, he _____ it. He _____ it. (save)*

2 ● *Have we been going the wrong way?*
○ *No, we _____ the wrong way. We _____ the right way. (go)*

3 ● *Has Ann been doing her homework?*
○ *No, she _____ that. She _____ to her new CD. (listen)*

3 Complete the questions.

Examples: You meet an old friend who is now at college.
● *How have you been getting on at college? (you/get on)*

You ask about your friend's brother. He's recently started at a new school.
● *Has your brother been enjoying his new school? (your brother/enjoy)*

1 You meet a friend. You haven't seen her for a month.
● *What _____ recently? (you/do)*

2 You ask Tom's sister about him. He's been studying Spanish in Spain.
● *How _____ in Spain? (he/get on)*

3 You want to know about Tom's studies.
● *_____ a lot of Spanish? (he/learn)*

4 Your small brother's hands and mouth are dirty.
● *_____ chocolate? (you/eat)*

5 Someone tells you about some friends. They're working in London.
● *How long _____ there? (they/work)*

4 Write questions and answer them.

Examples: Joe is travelling round the world. He left at the end of last year OR six months ago.
● *What has Joe been doing recently?*
○ *He's been travelling round the world.*
● *How long has he been doing that?*
○ *Since the end of last year. OR For six months.*

1 Pam is looking for a new job. She started last month
● *What _____ recently?*
○ *_____*
_____
● *How long _____ that?*
○ *_____*

2 Nick and Andy are training for the London Marathon. They began three months ago.
● *What _____ recently?*
○ *_____*
_____
● *How long _____ that?*
○ *_____*

33

13 Past perfect and past simple
When they arrived the film had started.

When they arrived the film had started.

FORMS					
Statements			**Yes/No questions**		
I	had	started.	Had	I	started?
You				you	
He	had not			he	
She				she	
It				it	
We				we	
They				they	

Wb questions

What film had they gone to see?

What time had it started?

Full answers

They had gone to see
Superman 6.

It had started at 7.00.

Short forms: I/you/he/she/we/they had = I'd, you'd, he'd,
she'd, we'd, they'd   had not = hadn't

Form the past perfect with *had* + past participle.
> The film **had started** before we arrived.
> **Had** it **begun** before you arrived?

Use the past perfect for a past event before another past event. Use it to show the time connection between two events.

1st past action/event	2nd past action/event	
(past perfect)	(past simple)	now

> At the airport I couldn't find my passport. I'**d left** it at home.
> The rain **had** just **stopped**, so we decided to go out for a walk.
> I got to the party at 8.00. My friends **had** already **gone**.

The past perfect shows the end of one past event before the start of another past event. We can talk about these two events in one sentence. Use these words to connect the two sentence parts: *when, after, before, once, until, as soon as.*
> **When** the last person **had** finally **come**, the meeting started.
> Susan cried for ages **after** her brother **had gone**.
> We went out **as soon as** the rain **had stopped**.

Do not over-use the past perfect. Use the past simple for two events that happen quickly after one another.
> I **saw** Peter and I **said** hello.
> When I **got** home, I **sat** down and **turned on** the TV.

Note the difference in meaning between the following.
> When the Director **arrived**, the meeting **started**. (First the Director arrived and then the meeting started.)
> When the Director **arrived**, the meeting **had started**. (First the meeting started and then the Director arrived.)

يتكون الماضي التام من had + التصريف الثالث للفعل.

يستخدم الماضي التام للتعبير عن فعل سبق في حدوثه فعلاً آخر في الماضي... وهو بالتالي يبين العلاقة الزمنية بين الحدثين.

ويوضح الرسم الوقت الذي حدث فيه الفعل في الماضي وهو الماضي التام، ثم وقت وقوع الفعل الآخر الذي يأتي في الماضي البسيط.

ويبين الماضي التام نهاية فعلٍ ما في الماضي قبل بدء حدثٍ آخر في الماضي ايضاً. ويمكن جمع هذين الحدثين في جملة واحدة.

ويستدعي ذلك استخدام الكلمات التالية لربط جُزْءَي الجملة.

ويجدر التنويه بأهمية عدم التمادي في استخدام الماضي التام حيث يمكن استخدام الماضي البسيط للتعبير عن حدثين وقعا متتابعين بشكل سريع.

كذلك يجب ملاحظة الفارق في المعنى بين هذين المثالين.

Exercises

1 Write the verbs in the correct forms.

Example: *It was a strange house. Nobody ___had lived___ there for years. (live)*

1 *The town was empty. Everyone _____ (go)*

2 *The car wasn't there. A thief _____ it. (take)*

3 *The biscuit tin was empty. Tim _____ them all. (eat)*

4 *I didn't recognize old Mr Jarvis. He _____ a lot. (change)*

5 *We decided to buy a sofa which we _____ the weekend before. (see)*

6 *We went back to the shop to get the sofa, but somebody else _____ it. (buy)*

7 *I wanted to speak to Mr Jones, so I phoned his office. Unfortunately he _____ five minutes before. (leave)*

8 *Bob was late for football practice and they _____ without him. (start)*

2 Write the verbs in the correct forms.

Example: *We ___'d only been___ at home for a few minutes when the phone rang. (only/be)*

1 *I invited Pat, but she _____ to go out. (already/arrange)*

2 *They were amazed. They _____ such a beautiful place. (never/see)*

3 *Celia _____ dinner when the police called. (just/start)*

4 *Mrs Spear was worried. She _____ _____ her son's accident. (recently/hear about)*

5 *I phoned the garage, but they _____ _____ my car. (still/not/repair)*

6 *Tony wanted to buy a bike with the money, but Tina _____ it. (already/spent)*

7 *The Grant family _____ their house for a year when it burned down. (only/have)*

3 Write the verbs in the correct forms.

Example: *Alan ___had lost___ his key, so he ___broke___ a window to get in. (lose) (break)*

1 *I _____ at the party at 8.00, but my friends _____ (arrive) (go)*

2 *The horses _____ before we _____ the gate. (get away) (close)*

3 *Once we _____ the river, we _____ to move faster. (cross) (be able)*

4 *The manager _____ us all there until we _____ everything possible. (leave) (do)*

5 *They _____ because they _____ food and water. (turn back) (run out of)*

4 Join each pair of statements to make one statement. Use *when.*

Example: *We went out. We had breakfast.*
We ___went out when___ we'd had breakfast.

1 *We drove out of town. We loaded the jeep.*
_____
_____

2 *We stopped for a rest. We drove into the hills.*
_____
_____

3 *We started again. We had a good rest.*
_____
_____

4 *We stopped for the night. We were on the road for ten hours.*
_____
_____

5 *We started to cook dinner. We unpacked the jeep.*
_____
_____

6 *We went to sleep. We finished dinner.*
_____
_____

14 Future with *going to*

We're going to drive.

Use *going to* to explain future plans.
- ● What **are you going to do** on Saturday?
- ○ *I'm going to visit* my grandparents.

Use *going to* to talk about a decision to do something in the very near future.
I'm just going to make some salad. Then we can have dinner.
- ● *Dad, can you help me with my homework?*
- ○ *Sure, I'm just going to watch the news. I'll help you when it's finished.*

Use *going to* when it is clear that something must happen soon.
Look at the clouds. It's going to rain.
Listen to the car! It's going to break down!

Use *going to* with *go*, just like any other verb.
We're going to go to the cinema.

CROSSCHECK

Present continuous

We often use the present continuous to talk about future arrangements.
- ● *Are you doing anything tomorrow?*
- ○ *Yes, I'm seeing Sally. We're meeting at 3.00.*

going to

When we use *going to*, the arrangements sound more carefully planned.
- ● What **are you going to do**?
- ○ *First we're going to take a trip on the river. Then we're going to see a film.*

تستخدم صيغة going to لشرح الخطط المستقبلية.

وتستخدم صيغة going to للحديث عن قرار القيام بعملٍ ما في المستقبل القريب جداً.

تستخدم صيغة going to عند وجود علامات واضحة تدل على قرب حدوث شيءٍ ما.

تستخدم صيغة going to مع فعل go مثلما تستخدم مع اي فعل آخر.

غالباً ما يستخدم المضارع المستمر للتعبير عن خطط مستقبلية.

وعند استخدام going to فإن ذلك يوحي بان الخطط المستقبلية معدة بمزيد من الدقة.

Exercises

1 Complete the answers.

Example: ● *Have you had dinner yet? (later)*
   ○ *No, not yet. I 'm going to have it later.*

1 ● *Have you washed the car yet? (after lunch)*
   ○ *No, not yet. I _____*
   _____

2 ● *Has Tessa cleaned her shoes yet? (now)*
   ○ *No, not yet. She _____*
   _____

3 ● *Have the boys mended their bikes yet? (this evening)*
   ○ *No, not yet. They _____*
   _____

4 ● *Has the cat had its food yet? (in a minute)*
   ○ *No, not yet. It _____*
   _____

2 Write the verbs in positive or negative forms.

Example: Your local football team are in the cup final, but they're playing badly.
   ● *They 're going to lose. (lose)*
   ○ *They aren't going to win. (not/win)*

1 You're in the hills. There are black clouds.
   ● *It _____ (rain)*
   ○ *We _____ very wet. (get)*

2 Alan should be on his way to the airport to catch a plane, but he's still in bed.
   ● *He _____ there in time. (not/get)*
   ○ *He _____ his plane. (miss)*

3 Your car is very low on petrol, and you're still a long way from the petrol station.
   ● *We _____ petrol. (run out of)*
   ○ *We _____ the petrol station in time. (not/reach)*

4 Your friend is in a marathon race. He's very tired, but he's very near the end of the race.
   ● *He _____ now. (not/give up)*
   ○ *He _____ for sure. (finish)*

3 Write questions and short answers.

Example: *(we/be/late) (No)*
   ● *Are we going to be late?*
   ○ *No, we aren't.*

1 *(Sam/pass/his exams) (Yes)*
   ● _____
   _____
   ○ _____

2 *(your parents/take/you out) (No)*
   ● _____
   _____
   ○ _____

3 *(you/watch/TV this evening) (Yes)*
   ● _____
   _____
   ○ _____

4 *(Sally/buy/a newspaper) (No)*
   ● _____
   ○ _____

4 Write questions.

Example: ● *I'm planning to go on holiday.*
   ○ *(Where/you/go)*
   Where are you going to go?

1 ● *Ann has bought some lovely flowers.*
   ○ *(Where/she/put them)*

2 ● *The Smith family have sold their house.*
   ○ *(When/they/move out)*
   _____

3 ● *I'm making some cakes for the party.*
   ○ *(How many/you/do)*
   _____

4 ● *Bill is planning to go to the cinema.*
   ○ *(What/he/see)*
   _____

15 Future with *will*

People will live in space.

One day soon people will live in space.

OUR WORLD TOMORROW

Use *will* to express future facts.
>   Sam **will be** 20 next month.   The new road **will be** eight lanes wide.

Use *will* to predict something in the future – something that you know or believe will happen.
>   One day soon people **will live** in space.
>   Don't worry! I'm sure you**'ll pass** your exams.

Use *will* to say what you decide to do at the time of speaking.
>   I've left the window open. I**'ll go back** and **close** it.

Use *will* to offer, promise or threaten to do something.
>   That looks heavy. I**'ll help** you.   I promise I **won't be** late.

Use *will* to ask somebody to do something and to agree or refuse to do it.
> ● **Will** you **post** this card for me? ○ Yes, I**'ll post** it on my way home.

We use *will* to predict the future, so we often use it with words such as *sure, certain, probably, definitely* and *certainly*. Note that the *ly* words change position in *will* and *won't* sentences.
>   He**'ll definitely love** Rome. He **probably won't want** to come home.

Do not use *will* to express plans and arrangements.
>   I can't see you tomorrow as I**'m visiting/going to visit** my parents. (not *will visit*)

will often goes with verbs like *expect, think* and *know*.
>   I **expect** I**'ll be** late home tonight.
>   I **don't think** he**'ll agree** to the idea.

We sometimes use *shall/shall not (shan't)* instead of *will/will not*, but only with *I* or *we*. We usually use it for suggestions, offers and asking for instructions or suggestions.
>   You look terrible! **Shall** we **call** a doctor?
>   I've finished this job. What **shall** I **do** next?

تستخدم will للتعبير عن الحقائق المستقبلية.

وتستخدم will للتنبؤ بحدوث شيء في المستقبل. هنا يكون الشخص عارفاً او معتقداً بان هذا الشيء سوف يحدث.

وتستخدم will عند تقرير القيام بعمل ما في لحظة التكلم.

وتستخدم will عند التطوع بالقيام بعمل ما، وعند الوعد او التهديد بعمل ما.

وتستخدم will عند طلب عمل ما من شخص معين وعند الموافقة او رفض القيام بهذا العمل.

تستخدم will للتنبؤ بالمستقبل، لذلك فهي غالباً ما تستخدم مع كلمات مثل sure .... الخ. ويلاحظ ان الكلمات التي تنتهي بـ ly تغير موقعها في الجمل التي تستخدم فيها will او won't.

يجدر عدم استخدام will للتعبير عن الخطط والترتيبات.

تستخدم will عادةً مع الافعال expect وthink وknow.

تستخدم shall او shall not (shan't) احياناً عوضاً عن will وwill not وذلك مع الضميرين I وwe فقط. وهي تستخدم للتعبير عن الاقتراحات وعن التطوع بعمل ما، او عند طلب تعليمات او اقتراحات.

Exercises

1 Write the verbs in positive or negative forms.

Examples: *The film <u>will start</u> at 8.00. (start)*
It <u>won't finish</u> until 11.00. (not/finish)

1 *I've hidden the presents, so the children*
_____ them. (not/find)

2 *The bridge _____ the river here. (cross)*

3 *The road _____ until next year. (not/open)*

4 *Ask the boys. They _____ the job for you. (do)*

5 *Paul _____ 20 until next year. (not/be)*

2 Complete the offers and promises with positive or negative forms of these verbs.

be, buy, close, forget, look after, lose, make, wash

Example: ● *Please look after my jewellery.*
○ *Don't worry. I <u>'ll look after</u> it.* OR
○ *Don't worry. I <u>won't lose</u> it.*

1 ● *We haven't got any milk.*
○ *All right. I _____ some at the shop.*

2 ● *Be sure to get there on time.*
○ *Don't worry. I _____ late.*

3 ● *The car is very dirty.*
○ *OK. I _____ it.*

4 ● *Look, the windows are open.*
○ *All right. I _____ them.*

5 ● *Try to get everything right this time.*
○ *No problem. I _____ any mistakes.*

6 ● *Remember to take this letter and post it.*
○ *Don't worry. I _____ it.*

3 Complete the answers with these verbs. Use the correct pronouns.

be, carry, cut, get, give, phone

Example: ● *Please give your parents a call.*
○ *Yes, I <u>'ll phone</u> them now.*

1 ● *Is Simon at work now?*
○ *No, not yet. _____ to the office at 9.00.*

2 ● *I'm thirsty.*
○ *Ask Sue. _____ you a Pepsi.*

3 ● *This case is very heavy.*
○ *Give it to me. _____ it for you.*

4 ● *Dad's very late.*
○ *Don't worry. _____ home soon.*

5 ● *We need some wood for the fire.*
○ *OK. _____ some pieces now.*

4 Write questions and short answers.

Example: *(Joe/win/the competition) (No)*
● *<u>Will Joe win the competition?</u>*
○ *<u>No, he won't.</u>*

1 *(Ann/be/ten next week) (Yes)*
● _____
○ _____

2 *(the boys/like/their new school) (No)*
● _____
○ _____

3 *(Mr Hall/arrive/tonight) (Yes)*
● _____
○ _____

4 *(next term/start/on 15th April) (No)*
● _____
○ _____

5 Write the verbs in the correct forms.

Luke and his friends are planning a class river trip.

Luke: *Here's my idea. We <u>'ll take</u> some boats and go up the river. (take)*

Andy: *OK, but how much <u>will it cost</u>? (it/cost)*

Luke: *I don't know. I* [1]_____ *the boat company and ask. (phone) But I'm sure it* [2]_____ *too expensive. (not/be)*

Andy: [3]_____ *to go? (everybody/want)*

Luke: *Yes, I'm sure they* [4]_____

Tony: *What* [5]_____ *to take? (we/need)*

Luke: *We* [6]_____ *take a picnic. (have to)*

Andy: [7]_____ *raincoats? (we/need)*

Luke: *No, we* [8]_____ *Don't worry. The TV weatherman says we* [9]_____ *a lovely day tomorrow, and he promises it* [10]_____ *(have) (not/rain)*

16 Future continuous

I'll be swimming.

Just think! At this time tomorrow, I'll be swimming in the Indian Ocean.

FORMS

Statements

I	will be	swimming.	
You			
He	will not be		
She			
It			
We			
They			

Yes/No questions

Will	I	be swimming?
	you	
	he	
	she	
	it	
	we	
	they	

Wh questions

What will she be doing?
Where will he be swimming?

Full answers

She will be working.
He will be swimming in the sea.

Short forms: I/you/he/she/it/we/they will be = I'll be, you'll be, he'll be, she'll be, it'll be, we'll be, they'll be   will not be = won't be

---

Use the future continuous to say that something will be continuing at a certain point in the future.

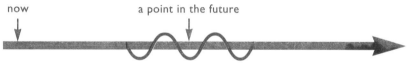

now

a point in the future

a continuing action/event happening at a point in the future

- What **will** you **be doing** in five years?
- ○ **I'll be travelling** round the world.

Use the future continuous to show that something will continue for a long time.

> There's so much to do! We**'ll be working** all day.
> We're having a party tomorrow evening, so we**'ll be cooking** all afternoon.

These uses of the future continuous are similar to uses of other continuous tenses. Compare the following.

> It's 9.00 now. Harry **is watching** TV.
> At 9.00 yesterday he **was watching** TV too.
> At 9.00 tomorrow he**'ll be watching** TV again.

Use the future continuous to talk about something that is already arranged.

- Will you be free after school?
- ○ No, **I'll be playing** basketball then.

This use is like the present continuous for future arrangements and *going to* for expressing plans.

I'll be calling	at the supermarket on my way home. Can I
I'm calling	get you anything?
I'm going to call	

يستخدم المستقبل المستمر لبيان أن حدثاً سوف يكون مستمراً في وقت محدد في المستقبل.

ويوضح الرسم النقطة المستقبلية (السهم الثاني) التي سيكون الحدث عندها مستمراً، في حين يشير السهم الأول الى الوقت الحالي.

ويستخدم المستقبل المستمر ليبين ان الحدث سيستمر لفترة طويلة.

وتشبه هذه الاستخدامات لزمن المستقبل المستمر استخدامات الازمنة المستمرة الاخرى كما توضح الامثلة التالية:

يستخدم المستقبل المستمر للتعبير عن فعل تمّ التخطيط لحدوثه.

واستخدامه هذا يشبه استخدام المضارع المستمر عند التعبير عن ترتيبات مستقبلية، ويشبه استخدام going to عند التعبير عن خطط.

40

Exercises

1 Read. Then answer the question. Use these verbs.

do, have, learn, study

John's timetable

9.00	9.45	10.30	11.15	12.00	12.45
Science	Art	French	Maths	English	Lunch

What will John be doing at these times?
9.30, 10.00, 10.45, 11.20, 12.20, 1.05

Example: *At 9.30 he'll be having Science.*

1 _____

2 _____

3 _____

4 _____

5 _____

2 Read Jack's and Lisa's diary pages for next week. Then complete the conversation.

	Jack Hill	Lisa Bell
Mon. 1	Morning – Talk to customers from Japan.	Afternoon – Meet the Sales Manager.
Tues. 2	Morning – Visit the factory.	Afternoon – Have meetings with the sales team.
Wed. 3	Show visitors round London all day.	–
Thur. 4	–	Spend the day in Paris.
Fri. 5	–	–

Company directors Jack and Lisa need to have a meeting next week, but when?

Lisa: *Can we meet on Monday morning?*

Jack: *No, sorry. I'll be talking to customers from Japan. Are you free on Monday afternoon?*

Lisa: *I'm afraid not. I¹_____ Are you free on Tuesday morning?*

Jack: *No, I'm afraid not. I²_____ Can we meet on Tuesday afternoon?*

Lisa: *No, sorry. I³_____ Are you free on Wednesday?*

Jack: *No, sorry. I⁴_____ Are you free on Thursday?*

Lisa: *I'm afraid not. I⁵_____ Can we we meet on Friday?*

Jack: *Yes, I'm free then.*

3 Read. Then write questions and answer them.

Roger Barnes is a traveller. On his next trip he will be travelling round the world by bicycle. He will be flying to Florida next Monday. Then he will be riding across America on his bike for the next two months. He will be arriving in California in ten weeks. From there he will be going up the west coast to Alaska. Then he will be crossing to Asia by ship.

Example: *(How/he/travel/round/the world)*
- ● *How will he be travelling round the world?*
- ○ *By bike.*

1 *(When/he/fly/Florida)*
- ● _____
- ○ _____

2 *(How long/he/ride/across America)*
- ● _____
- ○ _____

3 *(Where/he/arrive/in ten weeks)*
- ● _____
- ○ _____

4 *(Where/he/go/from there)*
- ● _____
- ○ _____

17 Future perfect

We'll have done it by 4.00.

Form the future perfect with *will* + *have* + past participle.
> *We'll **have cleaned** it by 4.00.*
> *We'll **have done** it before closing time.*

Use the future perfect to say that something will happen *before* or *by* a future time. In the negative we often use *not ... until/till*.

an action/event before a point in the future

now   a point in the future

> *The new manager **will have started** work **before/by** 1st May.*
> *The new manager **won't have met** all the staff **before/by** 1st May.*
> *The new manager **won't have met** all the staff **until/till** 30th May.*

Do not use *until/till* after a positive future perfect form. Use *before* or *by*.

Yes/No questions are unusual in the future perfect. *Wh* questions in the future perfect are very unusual.

> ● *We need to arrange a meeting for tomorrow afternoon. **Will** you **have had** your lunch by 1.30?*
> ○ *Yes, I **will**.*
> ● *Good. Let's have the meeting then.*

We often use the future continuous to say that something will be happening at a certain time in the future. We use the future perfect to say that something will happen before a certain time in the future. Compare the following.

> *I'll **be doing** the work at midday.*
> *I'll **have done** the work by 1.00.*

يتكون المستقبل التام من will + have + التصريف الثالث.

يستخدم المستقبل التام للتعبير عن فعل سوف يحدث قبل او مع حلول وقت معين في المستقبل، وغالباً ما تستخدم not في حالة النفي بالإضافة إلى كلمة until او till.

ويوضح الرسم وقت حدوث الفعل المستقبلي بين الوقت الحاضر الذي يشير اليه السهم الاول، وبين نقطة زمنية محددة في المستقبل يشير اليها السهم الثاني.

لا تستخدم اي من كلمتي until او till في حالة الإثبات بل تستخدم كلمتا before او by.

يندر استخدام الاسئلة التي يجاب عنها بـ «نعم» او بـ «لا» في زمن المستقبل التام، اما الاسئلة التي تبدأ باداة استفهام، فإن استخدامها في هذا الزمن نادر جداً.

غالباً ما يستخدم المستقبل المستمر للتعبير عن فعل سوف يحدث في وقت محدد في المستقبل. ويستخدم المستقبل التام للتعبير عن فعل سوف يتم قبل وقت معين في المستقبل.

ويتضح الامر من خلال مقارنة الامثلة.

Exercises

1 Read. Then write statements.

Tessa Black is 16. She wants to be a famous writer. These are her ambitions.

By the age of:

18 – sell some short stories
20 – write a book of short stories
25 – produce a play in London
30 – publish a best-seller novel
35 – win an important international prize
40 – make a lot of money

Example: *By the age of 18, she hopes she 'll have sold some short stories.*

1 *By the age of 20, she hopes she* _____

_____

2 *By the age of 25, she hopes she* _____

_____

3 *By the age of 30, she hopes she* _____

_____

4 *By the age of 35, she hopes she* _____

_____

5 *By the age of 40, she hopes she* _____

_____

2 Write the verbs in positive or negative forms.

Example: ● *Could you record the 9.00 news?*
○ *All right. I 'll have mended the video by then. (mend)* OR
○ *I'm sorry. I won't have mended the video by then. (not/mended)*

1 ● *Could I have the report by 5.00, please?*
○ *I'm afraid I* _____
it by then. (not/finish)

2 ● *Let's buy the red sofa which we saw.*
○ *The shop* _____ *it by the time we get there. (sell) It was very cheap.*

3 ● *Ask everyone to come here at 6.00.*
○ *I'm sorry, but they* _____ *by 6.00. (go)*

4 ● *Will she know the results by the 15th?*
○ *Yes, she* _____ *them before then. (get)*

5 ● *Will Alex bring a present to the party?*
○ *No, he* _____ *time to get one. (not/have)*

3 Read. Then complete the questions and answer them.

This is a schedule for building a house.

	Schedule
Finish putting up the walls	10/6
Finish putting on the roof	20/6
Finish putting in the windows	12/7
Finish fitting the doors	29/7
Finish doing the wiring	6/8
Finish laying the floors	18/8
Finish plastering the walls	10/9
Finish painting the house	25/9

Example: ● *What will they have finished by 15/6?*
○ *They'll have put up the walls, but they won't have put on the roof.*

1 ● _____
by 15/7?
○ _____

_____

_____

2 ● _____
by 15/8?
○ _____

_____

_____

3 ● _____
by 15/9?
○ _____

_____

_____

18 Future review

I'll be 18 next week.   I'm going to have a party.

I'll be 18 next Sunday, so I'm going to have a party. Please come, everyone!

All of these ways of talking about the future are correct grammatically, and they all give the same information. But each one shows that the speaker is thinking about the information in a different way. Different future forms are correct in different situations.

The party will start at 6.00.   It's starting at 6.00.
It'll be starting at 6.00.   It starts at 6.00.
It's going to start at 6.00.   It'll have started at 6.00.

CROSSCHECK

will

Use *will* to express things that you know or believe will happen.
*Susan **will be** 18 next Sunday.*

Use *will* to say what you decide to do at the time of speaking.
*I know! I'll **have** a party!*

Use *will* to offer, promise or threaten. Use *will* to request or refuse to do it.
● *I'll **pay** you £100 to do the job.*
○ *All right. I'll **do** it tonight.*

Present simple

Use the present simple for facts about future events and times.
*The party **starts** at 6.00.*
*Susan's school **finishes** next Thursday.*
*When **does** school **start** next term?*

will

Use *will* to express a complete action in the future.
*The party **will start** at 6.00.*

Future perfect

Use the future perfect for an action that will be complete before a certain point in the future.
*Don't worry! The party **will have finished** long before midnight.*

going to

Use *going to* when it is clear that something must happen soon.
*That's a big shopping list. It's **going to be** an expensive party!*

Use *going to* when you explain future plans.
*I'm **going to make** a huge cake.*

Present continuous

Use the present continuous for future plans.
*She's **having** a big cake.*
*Susan **is having** a party next Sunday.*
*All her friends **are coming** to the party.*

Future continuous

Use the future continuous for something continuing in the future.
*They'll **be dancing** for hours.*

Future continuous

Use the future continuous for something continuing at a certain point in the future.
*At lunchtime next day they'll still **be cleaning up** after the party!*

نستخدم will للتعبير عن الافعال التي نعرف او نعتقد بانها ستحدث.

وتستخدم going to عندما يكون واضحاً بان شيئاً سوف يحدث حالاً.

تستخدم will للتعبير عمّا نقرر عمله في لحظة التكلم.

وتستخدم going to لعرض الخطط المستقبلية.

تستخدم will عند تقديم عرض معين وعند الوعد او التهديد بالقيام بعملٍ ما. وتستخدم will ايضاً لطلب القيام بعملٍ ما او لرفض القيام به.

يستخدم المضارع البسيط للتعبير عن حقائق تتعلق بأحداث وأوقات مستقبلية.

ويستخدم المضارع المستمر للتعبير عن خطط مستقبلية.

تستخدم will للتعبير عن حدث متكامل في المستقبل.

ويستخدم المستقبل المستمر للتعبير عن فعل سوف يستمر حدوثه في المستقبل.

ويستخدم المستقبل التام للتعبير عن حدث سوف يكتمل قبل حلول وقت معين في المستقبل.

Exercises

1 Write the verbs in future forms. Use *going to* or *will*.

Example: ● We *'re going to run out of* milk soon. (run out of)

○ I *'m going to get* a newspaper, so I *'ll buy* some milk too. (get) (buy)

1 ● Slow down! We _____ (crash)

○ Don't worry. We _____ all right. (be) I promise.

2 ● _____ out this evening? (we/eat)

○ Yes, we _____ to the Café de Paris. (go)

3 ● What would you like – tea or coffee?

○ I _____ some coffee, please. (have)

4 ● The phone is ringing. _____ it, please? (you/answer)

○ Yes. It _____ Harry. (probably/be)

5 ● You _____ 18 soon, so _____ _____ school? (be) (you/leave)

○ Yes, I _____ engineering at college. (study)

6 ● What time _____ ? (the meeting/start)

○ At 6.00 exactly, so be there on time.

● I _____ late. (not/be) I promise.

2 Write the verbs in present tense forms for future meanings.

Examples: The Stone family *are going* to Cyprus for their holidays. (go)

Their train *leaves* at 18.15. (leave)

1 They _____ a train to the airport. (take)

2 It _____ the airport at 19.45. (reach)

3 They _____ with KLM. (fly)

4 The plane _____ at 21.30. (take off)

5 It _____ in Cyprus at 00.30. (arrive)

6 The family _____ in a villa near the beach. (stay)

3 Write the verbs in future forms. Use *will* or the future continuous.

Example: ● *Will you be* at home at 5.00? (you/be)

○ No, I *won't*. I *'ll be playing* tennis then. (play)

1 ● At this time tomorrow, I _____ to Australia. (fly) What _____ _____ (you/do)

○ I _____ here, as usual. (work)

2 ● Do you think she _____ her exams? (pass)

○ I don't know. She certainly _____ very well if she doesn't work harder. (not/do)

3 ● What time _____ home from college? (Sam/be)

○ At lunchtime. I expect you and Sam _____ _____ a lot to talk about. (have)

● Yes, I expect we _____ all afternoon. (talk)

4 ● Hurry up, or we _____ here all day. (wait)

○ Don't worry. I _____ everything ready in five minutes. (have)

4 Write the verbs in future forms. Use the future perfect or future continuous.

Example: By this time next week, I *'ll have left* London, and I *'ll be travelling* to Africa. (leave) (travel)

1 By the time they finish the new offices, 2,000 builders _____ 30 million bricks. (lay)

2 In two months from now, 1,000 people _____ _____ in the new offices. (work)

3 Don't worry. Your washing machine _____ _____ again in a minute. (work)

4 I _____ my exams in June. (take)

5 By this time next year, I _____ school, and I _____ as a pilot. (leave) (train)

6 ● Could you come soon after 5.00? The others _____ _____ between 5.00 and 5.30. (arrive)

○ I'm sorry, but I _____ work by then. (not/finish)

19 *have* and *have got*

He has a huge pack.   *He's got a huge pack.*   *He's having a rest.*

He's got a huge pack.
He's having a rest.

have and *have got* for possession

have			*have got*		
Present					
I	*have* *do not have*	*a huge pack.*	*I*	*have got* *have not got*	*a huge pack.*
He	*has* *does not have*		*He*	*has got* *has not got*	
Past					
I	*had*	*a huge pack.*	*I*	*had*	*a huge pack.*
He	*did not have*		*He*	*did not have*	

have for an action

He is having a rest.   *He is having a Pepsi.*

Short forms: *I/you/we/they have got = I've got, you've got, we've got, they've got   he/she/it has got = he's got, she's got, it's got   have not got = haven't got   has not got = hasn't got*

have and *have got*

We use both *have* and *have got* to mean 'own' or 'possess'. Both forms are usually possible, but *have got* is less formal than *have*.
> **Does** he **have** a pack?   **Has** he **got** a pack?

We use *have* (own) in simple tenses, and not continuous tenses, eg present simple, not present continuous.
> ● **Do** you **have** any fruit juice?   ○ No, I **don't**. I only **have** Pepsi.

The verb form *have got* is the present perfect form of *get*, but the meaning is present.
> ● **Have** you **got** any coins?   ○ No, I **haven't**. I've only **got** notes.

Auxiliary verb *have* and main verb *have* often go together. Auxiliary verb *have* often shortens, but main verb *have* does not shorten. (See Unit 21 for more information about *have* as a main verb and auxiliary verb.)
> *He's* **had** that car for 11 years.   They've **had** that house since May.

When we use the past simple, we usually use the form *had*, not *had got*. When we use the present perfect, we always use the form *had*.
> *He bought that car 11 years ago. He's* **had** it for 11 years.

have for an action

We use this form of *have* in continuous tenses as well as simple tenses.
> *He's* **having** a rest now.   He **has** a swim every day.

We use this form of *have* in a lot of very useful expressions. These are the most common.
> *have a swim/wash/bath/shower   have a walk/run/ride*
> *have (a cup of) coffee/tea   have breakfast/lunch/dinner*
> *have a meal/snack/break/rest   have a look*
> *have a talk/chat/discussion/fight/an argument*

يمكن استخدام صيغتي have و have got للتعبير عن الملكية وتكون الصيغتان ممكنتين عادة، ولكن have got اقل رسمية من have.

وتستخدم have بمعنى الملكية، مع الازمنة البسيطة وليس مع الازمنة المستمرة، اي مع المضارع البسيط، وليس مع المضارع المستمر.

وصيغة have got عبارة عن فعل get في زمن المضارع التام، ولكن المعنى الذي تعبر عنه هو المضارع.

غالباً ما يستخدم فعل have كفعل مساعد وكفعل اساسي في جملة واحدة. وغالباً ما يصير الى استخدام الصيغة المختصرة للفعل المساعد ولكن ليس للفعل الاساسي (انظر unit 21 للمزيد من المعلومات عن have كفعل اساسي وفعل مساعد).

اما في الماضي البسيط فتستخدم had وليس had got.. وتستخدم had بشكل دائم مع المضارع التام.

تستخدم هذه الصيغة من have مع الازمنة المستمرة وكذلك مع الازمنة البسيطة.

كما تستخدم صيغة have في الكثير من التعبيرات اللغوية المفيدة، وهذه اكثرها شيوعاً.

Exercises

1 Write the correct forms of *have got*.

Example: ● _Have you got_ any free time later? *(you)*
○ _No, I haven't got_ a minute. Sorry.

1 ● _____ any coins for the phone?
(you)
○ No, sorry. I _____ any money at all.
Ask Tom. I think he _____ some.
● No, he _____ any. I've already asked
him.

2 ● What does your brother look like?
○ He's tall and he _____ red hair.
● _____ a moustache? *(he)*
○ No, he _____ You're thinking of someone else.

2 Write the correct forms of *have*.

Example: ● _Do you have_ any free time later? *(you)*
○ _No, I don't have_ a minute. Sorry.

1 ● _____ any stamps for this letter?
(you)
○ No, sorry. I _____ any stamps at all.
Ask Sue. I think she _____ some.
● No, she _____ any. I've already
asked her.

2 ● What does your sister look like?
○ She's thin and she _____ dark hair.
● _____ glasses? *(she)*
○ No, she _____ You're thinking of someone else.

3 ● _____ a bike when you were
young? *(you)*
○ Yes, I _____ , but it was very heavy. I _____
_____ a good bike until I was 15. That was a
great bike. It _____ a special light-weight frame.

4 ● Alan, what kind of car _____
(you)
○ I _____ one. I walk everywhere. I
_____ one for three years. I sold it.
● What kind of car _____ *(you)*
○ It was a Toyota.

5 ● Nick, _____ a holiday home in Spain.
○ Lucky man! How long _____ it? *(he)*

● I think he _____ it since 1989. But it's sad
because he _____ much time to
go there these days.

3 Write the correct forms of *have* and *have got*. Use *have got* where possible.

Example: Ann _has got_ a new TV. She _'s_ only _had_
it for a week.

Tom and Sue [1]_____ an old French car. It
[2]_____ a very big engine, so it doesn't go
very fast. Tom and Sue don't mind though. They love it.
In fact, they [3]_____ a name for it – Harold.
They [4]_____ the car for eight years, and it's the
only car they [5]_____ ever _____ Before that, they were
students. They were very poor and they [6]_____
_____ a car. They only [7]_____ bicycles. Now they
[8]_____ enough money for a new car, but they
don't want to change. They're happy with the car that
they [9]_____ , even though it [10]_____ some
engine problems in the last few months.

4 Write the correct forms of these expressions.

have breakfast, have a chance, have a chat, have coffee,
have a game, have a look, have lunch, have a rest,
have a run, have a swim, have time

Don and Lyn Blake work hard all week, so at the
weekend they like to relax. They _have breakfast_ at
9.00 instead of 7.30. Then Don [1]_____
_____ at the newspaper and Lyn often [2]_____
_____ with her mother on the phone. They never
[3]_____ to do much shopping in the
week, so they go to the supermarket and do the week's
food shopping. After that they usually
[4]_____ in a café. Then they go to the
sports centre together. Lyn usually
[5]_____ of tennis with a friend, while
Don [6]_____ in the indoor pool. When
they go home, they are hungry, so they
[7]_____ and then they
[8]_____ because they are tired. Later
Don often [9]_____ round the park and
Lyn [10]_____ to write all her letters.

20 Review: main verb forms
talk, talked, talked, talking, talks

FORMS

1	Infinitive form:	*look*	*fall*
2	The *s* form:	*looks*	*falls*
3	Past form:	*looked*	*fell*
4	Past participle:	*looked*	*fallen*
5	Present participle: (the *ing* form)	*looking*	*falling*

Only use the *s* form with the 3rd person singular of the present simple. (See Unit 2 for the *s/es* difference.)

> He **talks**.   She **crashes**.   It **falls**.

تضاف s مع ضمائر المفرد الغائب في زمن المضارع البسيط فقط.

The past and past participle forms of regular verbs are the same.

> *talked, talked   crashed, crashed*

لا يختلف شكل تصريف الفعل القياسي في حالة الماضي عنه في حالة التصريف الثالث.

With irregular verbs they are often different. (See Appendix 1 for a list of common irregular verbs.)

> *fell, fallen   took, taken*

ولكن في حالة الافعال اللاقياسية، فهما غالباً ما يختلفان. (انظر لائحة بالافعال اللاقياسية الشائعة في الملحق 1).

Use the verb forms as follows.

Forms	Uses	Examples
1 **Infinitive form**	Infinitive	*He tried to **stop**.*
	Imperative	***Look** at me!*
	Future with *will*	*He**'ll hurt** himself.*
	Present simple	*Children **make** mistakes.*
2 **The *s* form**	Present simple (3rd person)	*That boy often **makes** mistakes.*
3 **Past form**	Past simple	*He **crashed**. He **fell** off.*
4 **Past participle**	Perfect tenses (present, past, future)	*He**'s damaged** his bike.* *He crashed just after the boy **had warned** him.* *We**'ll have finished** by 3.00.*
5 **Present participle** (the *ing* form)	Continuous tenses (present, past, present perfect, future)	*The boy **is talking** to an adult.* *He **was going** too fast when he crashed.* *He**'s been crying** ever since he crashed.* *His arm is broken. He **won't be riding** a bike again for a long time!*

وتستخدم صيغ الافعال كما هو مبين في الامثلة.

We use different forms of the auxiliary verbs *be, do* and *have* with main verbs.

> *be → am, is, are, was, were, been, being*
> *do → do, does, did   have → have, has, had, having*

تستخدم تصاريف مختلفة للافعال المساعدة be و do و have مضافة إلى الفعل الاساسي.

Together, auxiliary verbs and main verbs form the verb structure of a sentence. Verb structures add extra information to the meaning of the main verbs, including information about the time of the action – present, past or future. (See Unit 21 for more about auxiliary verbs.)

> *I**'m riding** a bike.*   ***Did** you **know** that boy?*
> ***Have** you **hurt** yourself?*

ويكوّن الفعل المساعد مع الفعل الاساسي تركيبة الفعل في الجملة التي تضيف معلومات اخرى إلى معنى الفعل الاساسي في الجملة، بما فيها معلومات عن زمن حدوث الفعل ـ في المضارع أوالماضي أو المستقبل. (انظر unit 21 للمزيد عن الافعال المساعدة).

Exercises

1 Write the verbs in the present simple.

Example: ● *Where does Ann* <u>*live?*</u> *(live)*
○ *She* <u>*lives*</u> *in New York. (live)*

1 ● *Do you _____ Joe Lee? (know)*
○ *Yes, he _____ a BMW, doesn't he? (drive)*

2 ● *When does the film _____ (start)*
○ *It _____ at 7.45. (begin)*

3 ● *Ann doesn't _____ watching TV in the morning.*
(like)
○ *No, but she _____ it a lot in the evening.*
(watch)

4 ● *What does Peter _____ for lunch? (have)*
○ *He usually _____ a sandwich. (have)*

2 Write the verbs in the present simple or present continuous.

Examples: *Steve always* <u>*comes*</u> *at 8.00. (come)*
Look! He <u>*'s coming*</u> *now. (come)*

1 *Helen _____ work at 5.00 most days. (finish)*
2 *Quiet! I _____ to the news. (listen)*
3 *I _____ I'm not late. (hope)*
4 *What _____ with those bits of wood?*
(he / make)
5 *How _____ to school every morning?*
(she / go)
6 ● *_____ the film?*
(you / enjoy)
○ *No, not really. Let's go home.*

3 Write the infinitive, past form and past participle of these irregular verbs.

cost, cut, earn, get, give, hit, let, make, pay, read, ride, see, take, wear

Infinitive	Past form	Past participle
Verbs with no change		
cost	_____	_____
_____	_____	_____
_____	_____	_____
_____	_____	_____
_____	_____	_____

Infinitive	Past form	Past participle
Verbs with one change		
learn	_____	_____
_____	_____	_____
_____	_____	_____
_____	_____	_____

Infinitive	Past form	Past participle
Verbs with two changes		
ride	_____	_____
_____	_____	_____
_____	_____	_____
_____	_____	_____

4 Write the verbs in the past simple.

Example: ● *Who did you* <u>*see*</u> *at the party? (see)*
○ *I* <u>*saw*</u> *Ann and Steve. (see)*

1 ● *Did Mary _____ herself? (cut)*
○ *Yes, she _____ her hand with a knife. (cut)*

2 ● *Did you _____ any cakes? (make)*
○ *Yes, I _____ two. (make)*

3 ● *Did Tom _____ my bike? (ride)*
○ *No, he didn't _____ yours. (ride) He _____*
his own. (ride)

4 ● *Why did you _____ him go? (let)*
○ *I didn't _____ him go. (let) He _____ me and*
_____ away. (hit) (get)

5 Write the verbs in the present perfect.

Example: ● *What have they* <u>*done?*</u> *(do)*
○ *They've* <u>*taken*</u> *the old car. (take)*

1 ● *What have the children _____ (do)*
○ *They've _____ these models. (make)*

2 ● *Has Bob _____ the report yet? (see)*
○ *No, I haven't _____ it to him yet. (give)*

3 ● *Have you _____ the list of verbs yet? (read)*
○ *Yes, but I haven't _____ them yet. (learn)*

4 ● *Ow! I've _____ myself! (hit)*
○ *Yes, and you've _____ yourself too. (cut)*

21 Review: auxiliary verb forms
be, do, have

The forms of main verbs help to form verb structures. (See Unit 20.)

1	2	3	4	5
look	looks	looked	looked	looking
know	knows	knew	known	knowing

تساعد تصاريف الأفعال الأساسية على تكوين التراكيب الفعلية.

The auxiliary verbs *be*, *do* and *have* also help to form verb structures.

be → am, is, are, was, were, been, being
do → do, does, did
have → have, has, had, having

كذلك تساعد الأفعال المساعدة *be* و *do* و *have* على تكوين التراكيب الفعلية أيضاً.

Together, auxiliary verbs and main verbs form verb structures. Verb structures add extra information to the meaning of the main verb, including information about the time of the action – present, past or future.

وبالتالي فإن التراكيب الفعلية تتكون من الأفعال المساعدة والأساسية معاً. وتضيف التراكيب الفعلية معلومات إضافية لمعنى الفعل الأساسي في الجملة. وذلك فيما يتعلق بزمن حدوث الفعل مضارعاً كان أم ماضياً أم مستقبلاً.

	Auxiliary	**Main**	
John	**is**	**talking**,	*so please listen.*
Peter	**has**	**found**	*his bag.*
Lyn	**didn't**	**answer**	*the question.*

Use auxiliaries with *not (n't)* to form negative questions. These *Yes/No* question forms show surprise.

> **Isn't** he winning the match? (He was champion last year!) ·
> **Don't** you like the food? (Most people love it!)
> **Haven't** you heard of her before? (She's famous!)

وتستخدم الأفعال المساعدة مع أداة النفي (*n't*)/*not* لتكوين صيغة الاستفهام المنفي – والأمثلة هذه للأسئلة التي يجاب عنها بنعم أو بلا تفيد حالة الدهشة.

These *Wh* question forms ask about a non-action. *Why* questions are the most common type of negative *Wh* questions.

> **Why aren't** you going? (You aren't going. Why not?)
> **What didn't** we do? (We didn't do something. What?)
> **Who haven't** we called? (We haven't called somebody. Who?)

الأمثلة التالية للأسئلة التي تبدأ بأداة استفهام تسأل عن حالة امتناع وقوع الحدث... وتعتبر الأسئلة التي تبدأ بكلمة *Why* أكثر شيوعاً بين الأسئلة التي تبدأ بأداة استفهام والتي تفيد الامتناع.

Use auxiliaries to form tag questions. Tag questions can check information. (See also Unit 25.) They expect the listener to agree. Use a falling tone (➘).

> You're coming later, **aren't** you? ➘

> You live in Liverpool, **don't** you? ➘

> You **haven't** read the book, **have** you? ➘

وتستخدم الأفعال المساعدة لتكوين أسئلة النهاية التي تهدف إلى التحقق من معلومة ما، وتستخدم بحيث تأتي استجابة المستمع المتوقعة بالموافقة.
وهذه الحالة التي يشار إليها باستخدام السهم النازل الذي يفيد انخفاض نغمة الصوت.

Tag questions can also be like a real question. The speaker does not know for sure. Use a rising tone (➚).

> You're coming later, **aren't** you? ➚

ويمكن أن يعمل سؤال النهاية عمل السؤال الحقيقي، وهنا لا يكون السائل متأكداً من الاستجابة وبالتالي يستخدم السهم الصاعد الذي يفيد ارتفاع نغمة الصوت.

The tag question is usually the opposite (positive/negative) of the main verb.

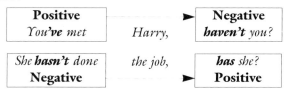

Positive		Negative
You've met	*Harry,*	*haven't* you?

Negative		Positive
She *hasn't* done	*the job,*	*has* she?

يأتي سؤال النهاية في الغالب عكس حالة الفعل الأساسي في الجملة... فإذا كان الفعل مثبتاً جاء سؤال النهاية منفياً، والعكس صحيح، إذا جاء الفعل الأساسي منفياً جاء سؤال النهاية مثبتاً.

Use auxiliary forms in short answers, and do not repeat the main verb. Use them to reply to ordinary *Yes/No* questions and to tag questions.
- ● *Are* you *looking* for your bag?   ○ *Yes, I am.*
- ● *Do* you *know* where it is?   ○ *No, I don't.*
- ● *Have* you *found* it yet?   ○ *Yes, I have.*
- ● *You're* worried, *aren't* you.   ○ *Yes, I am.*
- ● *You haven't* found it, *have* you?   ○ *No, I haven't.*

وتستخدم الأفعال المساعدة عند الإجابات القصيرة ولا يتكرر ذكر الفعل الأساسي. كذلك تستخدم الأفعال المساعدة عند الإجابة على الأسئلة التي يجاب عنها بنعم أو بلا وكذلك في أسئلة النهاية.

Use auxiliary forms with *So, Nor* and *Neither.* Be very careful – the word order looks like a question. (See also Unit 28.)
- ● *I'm tired.*   ○ *So am I.*
- ● *He doesn't work hard.*   ○ *Nor does she.*
- ● *We haven't finished.*   ○ *Neither have they.*

تستخدم الأفعال المساعدة مع *So* و *Nor* و *Neither*. وتجدر الملاحظة هنا بأن ترتيب الكلمات في الجملة يتغير بحيث تبدو وكأنها جملة استفهامية.

Use auxiliary forms for special emphasis in reply to another speaker's words.
- ● *Please read it.*   ○ *I am reading it.*
- ● *You didn't finish.*   ○ *Actually I did finish.*
- ● *We haven't studied Unit 3.*   ○ *We have studied it.*

وتستخدم الأفعال المساعدة للتأكيد وذلك عند الإجابة رداً على كلام من شخص آخر.

be, do and *have* are not only auxiliary verbs. They can also be main verbs. We can use *be, do* and *have* (auxiliary) with *be, do* and *have* (main) in the same sentence.

إن الأفعال *be* و *do* و *have* ليست أفعالاً مساعدة فقط ولكنها أساسية أيضاً. ويمكن استخدام أي منها كفعل مساعد وأساسي في الجملة نفسها.

Use *be* as an auxiliary with a main verb.
   We were writing letters.   *Is he eating lunch?*

ويستخدم فعل *be* كفعل مساعد مع الأفعال الأساسية.

Use *be* as a link verb with a noun or adjective.
   Is she a doctor.   *They were clever.*

ويستخدم فعل *be* كفعل ربط بين الأسماء والصفات.

Use *be* as an auxiliary with *be* as a main verb.
   Why are you being so stupid? (behaving stupidly)

ويستخدم *be* كفعل مساعد وكفعل أساسي في الجملة نفسها.

Use *do* as an auxiliary with a main verb in questions and negative statements.
   Do you like football?   *She doesn't want to leave.*

ويستخدم *do* كفعل مساعد مع فعل أساسي في الجمل الاستفهامية وفي الجمل المنفية.

Use *do* as a main verb.
   Is he doing his homework?   *I did my exercises.*

ويستخدم *do* كفعل أساسي أيضاً.

Use *do* as an auxiliary with *do* as a main verb in questions and negative statements.
   Does he do his homework every day?   *I didn't do my exercises.*

ويستخدم *do* كفعل مساعد وكذلك كفعل أساسي في الجملة الاستفهامية نفسها وفي الجمل المنفية أيضاً.

Use *have* as an auxiliary with a main verb.
   Have you finished yet?   *When I arrived it had started.*

ويستخدم *have* كفعل مساعد مع فعل أساسي آخر.

Use *have* as a main verb.
   When are you having lunch?   *I had a rest.*

كما يستخدم *have* كفعل أساسي في الجملة.

Use *have* as an auxiliary with *have* as a main verb.
   Have you had this car for long?   *Ann has had her lunch.*

وكذلك يستخدم *have* كفعل مساعد وكفعل أساسي في الجملة نفسها.

Exercises

1 Write the correct forms of *be*.

Example: *Lyn* _was_ *working all day yesterday.*

1 *I _____ taking Ann home next week.*

2 *Look! Where _____ Ed going with my bike?*

3 *We _____ flying to Japan at this time tomorrow.*

4 *Alan _____ staying in London since last month.*

5 *What _____ you doing at 9.00 last night?*

6 *At last, you're here! I _____ waiting for hours.*

7 *_____ you doing anything at the moment?*

8 *I _____ phoning Pam when Tom arrived.*

2 Write the correct forms of *do*.

Example: ● _Does_ *Peter Speak German?*
○ *He* _doesn't_ *speak much, but he can read a little.*

1 ● *How _____ you play this game?*
○ *I'm not sure. We _____ have any instructions.*

2 ● *_____ you want to go home, Sue?*
○ *No, I _____ want to go home just yet.*

3 ● *When _____ you get home last night?*
○ *I _____ go home. I stayed at a hotel.*

4 ● *Why _____ he keep looking at us?*
○ *I _____ know. I'll tell him to stop.*

5 ● *_____ you say much at the meeting?*
○ *No, I _____ say anything. I kept quiet.*

6 ● *_____ Fred play tennis?*
○ *No, he _____ , but he plays football.*

3 Write the correct forms of *have*.

Example: ● *How much* _has_ *Andy written?*
○ *He* _hasn't_ *written much. Just a page.*

1 ● *_____ the trucks crossed the river yet?*
○ *No, they _____ because we _____ built a bridge yet.*

2 ● *Why were you so angry with Bob?*
○ *Because he _____ done the work.*

3 ● *_____ you found your shoes yet?*
○ *I _____ found one, but I _____ found the other one. I don't know where it is.*

4 ● *Why did he come late?*
○ *Because he _____ noticed the time.*

5 ● *Will their car be ready by 5.00?*
○ *Oh, yes. We _____ finished before then.*

6 ● *How long _____ Fred lived here now?*
○ *He _____ been here for five years.*

7 ● *I need your report by Friday.*
○ *I'm sorry. I _____ finished it by then.*

8 ● *Why didn't the boys have any money?*
○ *Because they _____ spent it all on sweets.*

4 Re-order the words to make negative questions.

Examples: *(job/didn't/the/finish/you)*
Didn't you finish the job?
(job/didn't/the/finish/you/why)
Why didn't you finish the job?

1 *(Paul/home/hasn't/come/yet)*

_____

2 *(they/the/call/didn't/police/why)*

_____

_____

3 *(enjoying/film/aren't/you/the)*

_____

4 *(you/agree/don't/why/me/with)*

_____

5 *(Rosie/the/isn't/wedding/going/to)*

_____

_____

6 *(questions/they/yet/answered/which/haven't)*

_____

7 *(you/go/have to/home/now/don't)*

_____

_____

8 *(parts/don't/have to/we/which/learn)*

_____

_____

5 Write tag questions.

Examples: *They're going to crash,* <u>*aren't they?*</u>
You didn't finish, <u>*did you?*</u>

1 *You haven't understood,* _____

2 *He likes her,* _____

3 *They were angry with you,* _____

4 *You don't know Tony,* _____

5 *He arrived late,* _____

6 *They've done the shopping,* _____

7 *Alan doesn't like travelling,* _____

8 *Ann was studying last night,* _____

9 *You aren't enjoying this,* _____

10 *Nick didn't get home until midnight,* _____

6 Agree with the first speaker.

Examples: ● *I'm hungry. (I)*
　○ <u>*So am I.*</u>
　● *She didn't like the film. (he)*
　○ <u>*Neither/Nor did he.*</u>

1 ● *They don't understand the question. (we)*
　○ _____

2 ● *Peter likes the new teacher. (Alan)*
　○ _____

3 ● *I've never been to India before. (I)*
　○ _____

4 ● *Sam didn't do his homework. (Lisa)*
　○ _____

5 ● *Sue has called her parents. (her brothers)*
　○ _____

6 ● *We aren't going to buy the book. (she)*
　○ _____

7 ● *I'd never seen such a lovely place. (we)*
　○ _____

8 ● *The car broke down again yesterday. (the van)*
　○ _____

9 ● *You aren't telling the truth. (you)*
　○ _____

10 ● *Kate has been to America. (Andy)*
　○ _____

7 Write questions and answers with *do, have* and *be* as main verbs. Use a) the present continuous, b) the past simple and c) the present perfect.

Examples: (● *Which question / you / do*)
　(○ *we / do / number 2*)
　a) ● <u>*Which question are you doing?*</u>
　　○ <u>*We're doing number 2.*</u>
　b) ● <u>*Which question did you do?*</u>
　　○ <u>*We did number 2.*</u>
　c) ● <u>*Which question have you done?*</u>
　　○ <u>*We've done number 2.*</u>

1 (● *What / you / have / for lunch*)
　(○ *we / have / chicken*)
a) ● _____
　　_____
　○ _____
b) ● _____
　　_____
　○ _____
c) ● _____
　　_____
　○ _____

2 (● *How much work / he / do*)
　(○ *he / do / ten hours*)
a) ● _____
　○ _____
b) ● _____
　○ _____
c) ● _____
　○ _____

3 (● *Why / they / be / so slow with their work*)
　(○ *because they / be / careful*)
a) ● _____
　　_____
　○ _____
b) ● _____
　　_____
　○ _____
c) ● _____
　　_____
　○ _____

53

22 Short form or full form
I'm angry!   *I am angry!*

FORMS					
Short forms			**Full forms**		
be			*be*		
I'm	*you're*	*he's*	*I am*	*you are*	*he is*
I'm not	*you aren't*	*he isn't*	*I am not*	*you are not*	*he is not*
	you're not	*he's not*			
I wasn't	*you weren't*		*I was not*	*you were not*	
do			*do*		
I don't	*he doesn't*	*they didn't*	*I do not*	*he does not*	*they did not*
have			*have*		
I've	*he's*	*I'd*	*I have*	*he has*	*I had*
I haven't	*he hasn't*	*I hadn't*	*I have not*	*he has not*	*I had not*
will			*will*		
I'll	*we won't*		*I will*	*we will not*	
would			*would*		
he'd	*you wouldn't*		*he would*	*you would not*	

's can mean *is* or *has*, so check the main part of the verb.
    She's coming home. (*'s* = *is*)   *She's come home.* (*'s* = *has*)

Do not confuse *it's* and *its*.
    It's *going to sleep.* (**It's** = It is)
    The cat is closing **its** *eyes.* (***its*** = pronoun)

Also, do not confuse the possessive *'s* and *'s* meaning *is*.
    This is Alan's hat. (*'s* = possessive)   *Alan's at home.* (*'s* = *is*)

'd can mean *had* or *would*, so check the main part of the verb.
    They'd finished by 12.00. (*'d* = *had*)

CROSSCHECK

Short forms

Use short forms for normal speaking.
    They're trying to finish early.

Use short forms for ordinary statements.
    ● *He isn't working.*

Use short forms for informal writing, eg a letter to a friend.
    Dear Sally,
    We're having a great holiday.

Full forms

Show strong feeling with full forms and stress.
    I am sad you have to go away!

Use full positive forms with stress to correct statements.
    ○ *Oh, yes, he is working!*

Use full forms to ask questions and at the end of sentences.
    ● *Are they working hard?*
    ○ *Yes, they are.*

Use full forms for most writing, eg a business letter or a report.
    Dear Sir,
    We are pleased to inform you ...

يمكن ان تكون 's اختصاراً لـ is او لـ has، وللتأكد يجب الرجوع الى الفعل الاساسي في الجملة.
ويجب عدم الخلط بين it's وبين its.

كما يجب عدم الخلط بين 's التي تفيد الملكية وبين الاخرى التي تعني is.
كذلك فإن 'd تأتي اختصاراً لـ had وكذلك للـ would الامر الذي يتطلب التعرف على جزء الفعل الاساسي في الجملة.
تستخدم الصيغ المختصرة في الحديث العادي في حين تستخدم الصيغ الكاملة للتعبير عن المشاعر التي تتسم بالقوة... وكذلك فإنها تستخدم للتأكيد.

وتستخدم الصيغ المختصرة في الجمل الخبرية العادية.
وتستخدم الصيغ المثبتة الكاملة مع النبرة (stress) لتصحيح الجمل الخبرية.
وتستخدم الصيغ الكاملة لتكوين الجمل الاستفهامية وكذلك عندما تأتي في نهاية الجملة.
تستخدم الصيغ المختصرة للكتابة غير الرسمية، رسالة الى صديق مثلاً.
وتستخدم الصيغ الكاملة في الكتابة بشكل عام مثل كتابة الخطابات الرسمية والتقارير.

Exercises

1 Write the short forms.

Example: (I have) _I've_ been here all day.

1 (You are) _____ right.

2 (He has) _____ hurt his leg.

3 (I am) _____ 18 next month.

4 (What is) _____ her name?

5 (We will) _____ be late.

6 If (he is) _____ wrong, (he will) _____ lose all his money.

7 If you were on that plane, (you would) _____ be half-way to India now.

8 If (she had) _____ gone to the interview, (she would) _____ have got the job.

9 (They have) _____ finished their lunch.

10 (I would) _____ like a cup of tea, please.

2 Write the negative short forms.

Example: Mary _hasn't_ eaten since yesterday.

1 I _____ like coffee. I never drink it.

2 She _____ singing at the moment.

3 Peter _____ seen Tom for ages.

4 We _____ be late again tomorrow.

5 _____ watch the film, Sam. I saw it at the cinema and I _____ enjoy it.

6 I _____ going to eat at that restaurant again.

7 This engine _____ much use. It _____ work properly.

8 If you _____ called me yesterday morning, I _____ have woken up in time.

9 Mike and Sue _____ been to Malta before. This is their first time.

10 Joe _____ at school yesterday because he felt sick.

3 Write the positive or negative short forms.

Tom is worried about his friend, Ben.

Tom: What's wrong, Ben? You _don't_ look well.

Ben: I ¹_____ feel very well either. I ²_____ ill.

Tom: What ³_____ the matter exactly?

Ben: Oh, I ⁴_____ got a headache and I feel bad.

Tom: You ⁵_____ better see the doctor.

Ben: I ⁶_____ like to do that, but I ⁷_____ got any time. I ⁸_____ going to an important meeting this morning.

Tom: ⁹_____ be stupid. You ¹⁰_____ ill, so if you go to the meeting, you ¹¹_____ be able to work properly. Can Roger go instead of you?

Ben: He ¹²_____ really know enough about the project, but perhaps he can. I ¹³_____ call him and ask him.

Tom: Good. I know he ¹⁴_____ say yes. And then we ¹⁵_____ go to the doctor together.

Ben: Thanks. That ¹⁶_____ really kind of you.

4 Write the full forms.

The bank manager has written an unpleasant letter to a customer.

Dear Mr Morton,
(I'm) _I am_ writing to you about your company's latest sales figures, which (we've) ¹_____ recently received.

As you say in your letter, the figures (aren't) ²_____ good and they (don't) ³_____ seem to be improving. Your figures have been showing losses for three years, and (I'm) ⁴_____ very sorry to say that (they're) ⁵_____ still showing large losses. As a result, you (won't) ⁶_____ be surprised to know that (we're) ⁷_____ getting very worried about the business loan which you (haven't) ⁸_____ yet been able to start repaying.

5 Write the full forms.

The letter from the bank continues.

Until your latest sales report, (we'd) ¹_____ hoped (you'd) ²_____ succeed, but (it's) ³_____ clear now that the company will soon have to close. Our accountant is still studying your sales figures, but (he's) ⁴_____ decided that we must now close your loan account with this bank. (He's) ⁵_____ sending you a copy of his report in tomorrow's post. (I'd) ⁶_____ like to suggest that we meet early this week.

Question forms 1

Are you from Japan?

FORMS

Yes/No questions

- ● *Is he from Japan?*
- ○ *Yes, he is./No, he isn't.*

- ● *Was she a doctor?*
- ○ *Yes, she was./No, she wasn't.*

- ● *Have we finished?*
- ○ *Yes, we have./No, we haven't.*

- ● *Can they understand?*
- ○ *Yes, they can./No, they can't.*

Use *Yes/No* questions to check information.
- ● *Is he from America?*
- ○ *Yes, he is./No, he isn't.*
- ● *Does the film start at 7.30?*
- ○ *Yes, it does./No, it doesn't.*

Form questions from statements in the following ways.
With one auxiliary verb, do this.
> *They can* understand. → *Can they* understand?
> *He is* working. → *Is he* working?
> *They were* reading. → *Were they* reading?

With two auxiliary verbs (eg *has been, is going to*), do this.
> *He has been* working hard. → *Has he been* working hard?
> *He is going to* work hard. → *Is he going to* work hard?

With no auxiliary verbs, add *do* or *does* in the present simple and add *did* in the past simple. In the present and past simple, use only the infinitive form of the verb.
> *I know* her. → *Do I know* her?
> *He knows* her. → *Does he know* her?
> *He knew* her. → *Did he know* her?

Form *Yes/No* questions with *will* and modal auxilary verbs + infinitive.
> *Will* he *win*?
> *Can* she *speak* French?
> *Must* you *go*?

Use auxiliaries with *not (n't)* to form negative questions. These *Yes/No* questions show surprise.
> *Isn't* he winning the match? (He was champion last year!)
> *Don't* you like the food? (Most people love it!)
> *Haven't* you heard of her before? (She's famous!)

تستخدم الاسئلة التي يجاب عنها بِ «نعم» أو «لا»، للتأكد من المعلومات.

كوّن اسئلة من جمل خبرية تحتوي على فعل مساعد واحد، يجري تقديمه على الفاعل.

عندما تحتوي الجملة على فعلين مساعدين يقدم الاول على الفاعل.

عندما لا تحتوي الجملة على فعل مساعد تضاف do او does في زمن المضارع البسيط، وتضاف did في زمن الماضي البسيط. وتستخدم صيغة المصدر فقط من الفعل الاساسي مع المضارع البسيط ومع الماضي البسيط.

يتكون السؤال الذي يجاب عنه بِ «نعم» أو «لا»، باستخدام will والافعال المساعدة الدالة على صيغة الفعل الاصلي المستعمل معها + المصدر من الفعل الاساسي.

تستخدم الافعال المساعدة مع not/ n't لتكوين صيغة النفي من الجمل الاستفهامية... وهنا تأتي الاسئلة التي يجاب عنها بنعم او بلا لتعبر عن الدهشة.

Exercises

1 Write questions from the statements.

Examples: *Ed speaks French. (German)*
  Does Ed speak German too?
She's having a piano lesson. (he)
  Is he having a piano lesson too?

1 *Bob likes basketball. (football)*

   _____

2 *Sally is good at cooking. (Lucy)*

   _____

3 *The boys have had dinner. (Dad)*

   _____

4 *Jim cooked some vegetables. (meat)*

   _____

5 *We're going out tonight. (you)*

   _____

2 Write questions from the statements.

Example: *Rob can speak Japanese. (you)*
  Can you speak Japanese too?

1 *I have to go now. (he)*

   _____

2 *She must finish the report. (letters)*

   _____

3 *He can run fast. (swim fast)*

   _____

4 *We should train every morning. (evening)*

   _____

5 *We'll have to write to all our relatives. (friends)*

   _____

   _____

3 Re-order the words to make questions.

Examples: *(be / married / Liz and Bill)*
  ● *Are Liz and Bill married?*
  ○ *Yes, they are.*
  (in London / live / they)
  ● *Do they live in London?*
  ○ *No, they don't. They live in Manchester.*

1 *(for long / be / married / they)*
  ● _____

  ○ *Yes, they've been married for eight years.*

2 *(move / at that time / to Manchester / they)*
  ● _____

  ○ *No, they moved there a year later.*

3 *(they / any children / have got)*
  ● _____

  ○ *Yes, they have got one son and one daughter.*

4 *(go / the children / to school)*
  ● _____

  ○ *The boy does, but the girl is still too young.*

5 *(soon / she / school / start)*
  ● _____

  ○ *Yes, she's starting school in September.*

4 Write negative questions.

Example: ● *I'm tired. I want to stay at home.*
  ○ *Really? (you / not / want to meet Sue)*
  Really? Don't you want to meet Sue?

1 ● *Don't buy that car.*
  ○ *Why? (it / not / be / a good one)*

  _____

2 ● *Let's take the train, not the plane.*
  ○ *Really? (you / not / like / flying)*

  _____

3 ● *Rod is working at the bank.*
  ○ *Why? (he / not / go / to college yet)*

  _____

4 ● *The children are starting another game on the computer.*
  ○ *Really? (they / not / go / to bed soon)*

  _____

5 ● *Pam has just bought a new pen.*
  ○ *Why? (she / not / buy / one yesterday)*

  _____

   _____

24 Question forms 2
Where are you going?

> Where are you going?

> I'm going to London.

Wb questions
- ● *Where is he going?*
- ○ *He is going to London.*

- ● *How is he travelling?*
- ○ *He is travelling by plane.*

- ● *What are they doing?*
- ○ *They are talking.*

- ● *Why are they travelling?*
- ○ *They are travelling because they have business in the UK.*

Use *Wh* questions to get more information.
- ● *Where is he going?*
- ○ *To London.*
- ● *What does he do?*
- ○ *He works for IBM.*

Form questions from statements in the following ways.
First use a question word.
> *Where, When, Why, What, Who, Whose, Which, How, How much, How many, How old, etc*

Then change the subject and the auxiliary verb.
> *Where **are we** going?*
> *What **has she** been doing?*
> *How **does he** like the town?*
> *Why **did they** leave?*

Who and *What* can ask about the subject or the object of an action.
> *A car hit the cat.* → ● ***What hit** the cat?* (subject) ○ ***The car** hit the cat.* OR ● ***What did** the car **hit**?* (object) ○ *The car hit **the cat**.*
> *Tim called Ken.* → ● ***Who called** Ken?* (subject) ○ ***Tim** called Ken.* OR ***Who did** Tim call?* (object) ○ *Tim called **Ken**.*

Use auxiliaries with *not (n't)* to form negative questions. Use *Wh* questions to ask about a non-action. *Why* questions are the most common.
> ***Why aren't** you going?* (*You aren't going. Why?*)
> ***What didn't** we do?* (*We didn't do something. What?*)
> ***Who haven't** we called?* (*We haven't called somebody. Who?*)

تستخدم الاسئلة التي تبدأ بأداة استفهام للحصول على معلومات اضافية.

تتكون الاسئلة من الجمل الخبرية باستخدام إحدى ادوات الاستفهام كما هو مبين.

ثم يوضع الفعل المساعد قبل الفاعل.

اداتا الاستفهام who و what تسألان عن الفاعل او عن المفعول به.

تستخدم الافعال المساعدة مع اداة النفي not/n't لتكوين اسئلة منفية. وتستخدم الاسئلة المنفية التي تبدأ باداة الاستفهام، لتفيد انعدام وقوع الحدث.. واكثر هذا النوع شيوعاً هو الذي يبدأ بأداة الاستفهام why.

Exercises

1 Write the question words.

Example: ● _When_ did Liz and Bill get married?
○ _Eight years ago._

1 ● _____ do they live?
○ _In Manchester._

2 ● _____ parents live with them?
○ _Bill's._

3 ● _____ have they lived in Manchester?
○ _For seven years._

4 ● _____ children have they got?
○ _Two. A son and a daughter._

5 ● _____ one is older?
○ _Their son. He's seven._

6 ● _____ is their daughter going to start school?
○ _This year._

7 ● _____ do they live in Manchester?
○ _Because Bill has got a good job there._

8 ● _____ does he do?
○ _He's an engineer._

2 Re-order the words to make questions. Then write true answers about yourself.

Example: _(your/what's/name)_
● _What's your name?_
○ _My name's ..._

1 _(you/are/how/old)_
● _____
○ _____

2 _(your/address/what's)_
● _____
○ _____

3 _(father/do/does/your/what)_
● _____
○ _____

4 _(got/and/brothers/have/how many/you/sisters)_
● _____

○ _____

5 _(you/learning/why/are/English)_
● _____
○ _____

3 Write negative questions.

Example: _We didn't finish something. (What)_
What didn't we finish?

1 _Tom hasn't answered my letter. (Why)_
_____
_____

2 _We haven't done something. (What)_
_____

3 _They won't be able to go on holiday. (Why)_
_____

4 _We didn't go somewhere. (Where)_
_____

5 _Ann isn't going to go out tonight. (Why)_
_____

6 _I don't like this television programme. (Why)_
_____
_____

4 Write questions with _Who_ or _What_.

Example: _Somebody called the manager._
Who called the manager?
The customer called somebody.
Who did the customer call?

1 _Somebody called the police._
_____

2 _Something went wrong._
_____

3 _Bob found something by the door._
_____

4 _Tom phoned somebody._
_____

5 _The car ran over something._
_____

6 _Somebody saw Peter._
_____

7 _Julie ate something._
_____

25 Tag questions

Alan is finishing college soon, isn't he?

> Alan is finishing college soon, isn't he?
>
> Yes, he is.

The tag question is usually the opposite (positive/negative) of the main verb.

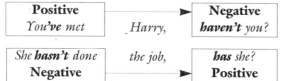

| **Positive** | | **Negative** |
| *You've met* | *Harry,* | *haven't you?* |

| *She hasn't done* | *the job,* | *has she?* |
| **Negative** | | **Positive** |

With one auxiliary verb, use the opposite auxiliary form, eg *is → isn't*.

With two auxiliary verbs, use the opposite of the first auxiliary, eg *will have → won't have*.

With no auxiliary verbs, in the present and past simple, use a form of *do* (main verb → *don't, doesn't* or *didn't*). *have to* and *need to* also work like this.

Tag questions are not ordinary questions. We can use them to check information. They expect the listener to agree. Use a falling tone (➘).

> *You're 18, **aren't** you?*   *You live in Liverpool, **don't** you?*

We can also use this type of tag question to help a conversation.
> ● *It's a good film, **isn't** it?*   ○ *Yes, it's great. The acting is wonderful.*

Tag questions can be more like ordinary questions – the speaker does not know something for sure. Use a rising tone (➚).

> *You're 18, **aren't** you?*   *You live in Liverpool, **don't** you?*

Note the negative tag after *I am*.
> *I'm late, **aren't** I?*

يأتي سؤال النهاية عادةً مخالفاً لحالة الفعل الاساسي في الجملة من حيث كونه مثبتاً او منفياً.

عند احتواء الجملة على فعل مساعد واحد يأتي سؤال النهاية مخالفاً له ... (is تصبح isn't).

وعند احتواء الجملة على فعلين مساعدين نعكس حالة الأول منهما (will have تصبح won't have).

وعند خلو الجملة من الافعال المساعدة في زمني المضارع البسيط والماضي البسيط نستخدم تصريفات do كفعل اساسي (don't و doesn't و didn't) ويعامل فعلاً have to و need to بالطريقة نفسها.

ولا تعتبر اسئلة النهاية اسئلة عادية، فهي تستخدم للتحقق من المعلومات بحيث نتوقع من المستمع الموافقة باستخدام نغمة الصوت المنخفضة التي يشار اليها بالسهم النازل.

ويمكن استخدام هذا النوع من الاسئلة ليعين على الحوار اثناء الحديث.

ويمكن ان تعمل اسئلة النهاية مثل عمل الاسئلة العادية تقريباً، وذلك حين لا يكون المتكلم متأكداً من معلومة معينة...

وهنا تستخدم نغمة صوتية مرتفعة يشار اليها بالسهم الصاعد.

وتجدر ملاحظة كيفية استخدام سؤال النهاية مع I am وهي كما هو موضح في المثال.

Exercises

1 Write tag questions.

Examples: *It's hot today,* <u>*isn't it?*</u>
He won't be working late, <u>*will he?*</u>

With one auxiliary and most modal verbs

1 *You'll be at home tonight,* _____

2 *The letter hasn't arrived yet,* _____

3 *They're doing the shopping,* _____

4 *It rained last night,* _____

5 *She isn't at home now,* _____

6 *Peter wasn't working yesterday,* _____

7 *Barry can't come to the party,* _____

8 *He should finish by 5.00,* _____

9 *We needn't pay now,* _____

10 *She might arrive tomorrow,* _____

With two auxiliaries

11 *He'll be working all day,* _____

12 *You haven't been listening to me,* _____

13 *The boys will have gone by 4.00,* _____

14 *The window hasn't been mended,* _____

15 *Your book isn't being printed yet,* _____

16 *Tony's car was being serviced yesterday,* _____

With no auxiliaries and with modal auxiliaries *have to* and *need to*

17 *Bob owns all his land,* _____

18 *You forgot to post the letters,* _____

19 *You need to ask the boss,* _____

20 *Mary had to sell the house,* _____

2 Write tag questions.

You're interviewing the famous film star, Rocky Reed.

Example: *Mr Reed, you've made nearly 40 films,*
<u>*haven't you?*</u>

1 *Your last film earned $30 million,* _____

2 *Your early films weren't so successful,* _____

3 *You're going to make your next film in Mexico,*

_____

4 *You don't like being away from your home and family,*

_____

5 *Your wife isn't interested in films,* _____

6 *You've got four children,* _____

7 *They won't be going into the film industry,*

_____

These tag questions check information. Mark the tags with a falling tone (⬊).

3 Write tag questions.

You're at a party.

Example: *It's a lovely house,* <u>*isn't it?*</u>

1 *The food is wonderful,* _____

2 *There aren't many people here yet,* _____

3 *Bob and Celia aren't coming,* _____

4 *I haven't seen you since last year,* _____

5 *You met my wife at the last party,* _____

6 *We'll be seeing you next week,* _____

These tag questions encourage the listener to speak. Mark the tags with a falling tone (⬊).

4 Write tag questions.

Lucy and her daughter, Emma, are going to the airport. Emma is very worried, but Lucy is calm.

Emma: *Mum, you didn't forget to bring the passports,*
<u>*did you?*</u>

Lucy: *Don't worry. I told you I'd brought them,*
¹ _____

Emma: *Yes, that's right. I forgot. And you've got the tickets,* ² _____

Lucy: *Yes, don't you remember? They were on the table with the passports,* ³ _____

Emma: *Yes, I suppose so. But Mum, what's the time? We're going to be late,* ⁴ _____

Lucy: *Calm down, Emma. It's 10.30 now and the flight doesn't leave until 12.30,*
⁵ _____ *And we only have to go another 30 kilometres,* ⁶ _____

Emma: *I guess you're right.*

Lucy: *Well, then, there's nothing to worry about,*
⁷ _____

Emma is unsure. Mark her tags with a rising tone (⬈).

Lucy is sure. Mark her tags with a falling tone (⬊).

26 Short answers

Yes, I am.   No, I can't.

A short answer can be a *Yes* or a *No* answer. The verb in the answer matches the verb in the question.

- **Is the room** *on fire?*
- *Yes,* **it is**.
- **Can you** *see the boy now?*
- *No,* **I can't**.

We always use full forms in *Yes* answers, when the verb is the last word.

Yes, **I am**.   *Yes,* **it is**.   *Yes,* **I can**.

We usually use short forms in *No* answers.

No, it **isn't**.   *No,* **I can't**.   *No, they* **didn't**.
(But *No,* **I'm not**.)

Here are some more examples.

Present
- *Are they at home?*   ○ *Yes,* **they are**./*No,* **they aren't**.
- *Is Ann going home?*   ○ *Yes,* **she is**./*No,* **she isn't**.
- *Do you like Italian food?*   ○ *Yes,* **I do**./*No,* **I don't**.

Perfect
- *Has Peter posted the letter?*   ○ *Yes,* **he has**./*No,* **he hasn't**.
- *Had the film started by 8.00?*   ○ *Yes,* **it had**./*No,* **it hadn't**.

Past
- *Were the children at home?*   ○ *Yes,* **they were**./*No,* **they weren't**.
- *Was the cat eating?*   ○ *Yes,* **it was**./*No,* **it wasn't**.
- *Did you see Susan last night?*   ○ *Yes,* **I did**./*No,* **I didn't**.

Future
- *Are we going to be late?*   ○ *Yes,* **we are**./*No,* **we aren't**.
- *Will Joe be at home tonight?*   ○ *Yes,* **he will**./*No,* **he won't**.

In conversation, we often give extra information after a short answer. This helps the conversation to continue.

- *Do you know Helen?*
- ○ *Yes, I do.* **I've known her for years**.
- *Have you finished work yet?*
- ○ *No, I haven't.* **I still have to write a report**.

يمكن ان تكون الاجابات المختصرة إجابات كاملة بـ «نعم» أو «لا». ويكون الفعل في الاجابة نظيراً للفعل في السؤال.

وتستخدم الصيغ الكاملة دائماً، عند الاجابة بـ «بنعم» وعندما يكون الفعل آخر كلمة في الجملة.

وتستخدم الصيغ المختصرة عادة، عند الاجابة المنفية بـ «لا».

واليك مزيداً من الامثلة توضح الافكار السابقة الذكر.

غالباً ما يعطى مزيد من التفاصيل بعد الاجابات القصيرة اثناء الحوار وهذا يساعد على استمرار المحادثة.

Exercises

1 Complete the answers.

Some people are talking at a wedding party.

Example: ● *Are you a member of the family?*
○ *No, <u>I'm not.</u> I'm a friend.*

1 ● *Have you met Tony?*
○ *No, _____ Hello.*

2 ● *Do you know Mary?*
○ *Yes, _____ We're old friends.*

3 ● *Are you from London?*
○ *No, _____ . I'm from Liverpool.*

4 ● *Should we go and get some food now?*
○ *Yes, _____ It's in the next room.*

5 ● *Would you like some more wedding cake?*
○ *Yes, _____ It's delicious.*

6 ● *Are there any more sandwiches?*
○ *No, _____ They're all gone.*

7 ● *Have you known Susie for long?*
○ *No, _____ But I know Ian well.*

8 ● *Is Ian going to give a speech?*
○ *Yes, _____ He's standing up now.*

9 ● *Can you hear what Ian is saying?*
○ *No, _____ It's too noisy.*

10 ● *Did you enjoy the wedding?*
○ *Yes, _____ It was lovely.*

11 ● *Must you go already?*
○ *Yes, _____ . I'm sorry.*

2 Complete the answers in the game, *Who am I?*

The answer to 10 is *Yes, <u>I was.</u>*

1 ● *Are you alive?*
○ *No, _____*

2 ● *Have you died recently?*
○ *No, _____*

3 ● *Were you a woman?*
○ *No, _____*

4 ● *Did you come from Britain?*
○ *No, _____*

5 ● *Were you European?*
○ *Yes, _____*

6 ● *Were you a soldier?*
○ *Yes, _____*

7 ● *Did you lead your country?*
○ *Yes, _____*

8 ● *Were you like a king?*
○ *Yes, _____*

9 ● *Did you live about 200 years ago?*
○ *Yes, _____*

10 ● *Were you Emperor Napoleon of France?*
○ *Yes, _____*

3 Write true short answers about yourself.

Example: ● *Are you studying English?*
○ <u>*Yes, I am.*</u>

1 ● *Are you a full-time student?*
○ _____

2 ● *Do you ever speak English outside class?*
○ _____

3 ● *Is English a difficult language to learn?*
○ _____

4 ● *Are you learning any other language?*
○ _____

5 ● *Do most people learn English in your country?*
○ _____

6 ● *Do a lot of people in your country use English in their work?*
○ _____

7 ● *Do you think you will use your English in the next year?*
○ _____

8 ● *Will you travel abroad in the next year?*
○ _____

9 ● *Have you ever been to Britain or the USA?*
○ _____

10 ● *Would you like to visit an English-speaking country?*
○ _____

Indirect forms
Could you tell me what time it is?

Indirect questions are a polite form, and we often use them to ask for information or opinions. There are several common ways of starting indirect questions.

> *Could you tell me ...?   Do you know ...?*
> *Do you have any idea ...?   Can you tell me ...?*

A *Wh* question continues like this.

> *Could you tell me* **what** (or **when**, **where**, **why**, **how**, etc) *...?*

A *Yes/No* question continues like this.

> *Do you know* **if** (or **whether**) *...?*

The following subjects and verbs are not in question form. They are like subjects and verbs in a statement.

> *Could you tell me what time* **it is**?   *Do you know if* **he went**?

Be careful about *do, does* and *did*. We use them in ordinary present simple and past simple questions, but not in indirect questions.

> *What* **does** *the bank* **close**? → *Could you tell me what time the bank* **closes**?
> **Did** *the bank* **close** *at 4.30?* → *Can you tell me if the bank* **closed** *at 4.30?*

We can use indirect forms in statements too.

I know/don't know	*what time it is.*
I can/can't tell you	*when the bank closes.*
I've no idea	*if the bank opens late.*
I wonder	*whether it's open now.*

Indirect forms are similar to reported forms. (See Unit 47.)

> *Where* **can I get** *some stamps?* → ***Do you know where I can get*** *some stamps?* OR ***He wants to know where he can get*** *some stamps.*

We often use the form *Do you think ...?* to ask for an opinion.

> ***Is it*** *going to rain?* → ***Do you think it is*** *going to rain?*

A *Yes/No* question does not take *if* or *whether*.

> ***Do you think she went*** *home?*   ***Do you think she was*** *angry?*

The question word is at the beginning in a *Wh* question.

> ***Where*** *do you think she went?*
> ***How long*** *do you think he'll stay?*

تعتبر الاسئلة غير المباشرة اسلوباً متأدباً في اللغة وغالباً ما تستخدم بغرض الوصول الى معلومات او آراء. وهناك العديد من الطرق الشائعة لبدء هذا النوع من الاسئلة.

ويجري طرح السؤال الذي يبدأ بأداة استفهام في هذا السياق كما هو مبين.

كما يجري طرح السؤال الذي يجاب عنه بِـ «نعم» أو «لا»، كما هو مبين.

الفاعل والفعل فيما يلي، ليسا في صيغة السؤال، بل مثل الفعل والفاعل في الجملة الخبرية.

وتجدر الملاحظة بان استخدام do و does و did يكون في الاسئلة العادية في زمني المضارع البسيط والماضي البسيط ولكن ليس في الاسئلة غير المباشرة.

يمكن استخدام صيغ الاسئلة غير المباشرة مع الجمل الخبرية ايضاً.

وتشبه صيغ الاسئلة غير المباشرة صيغ الكلام غير المباشر (انظر unit 47).

غالباً ما تستخدم صيغة ?...Do you think للاستفسار عن وجهة نظر ما.

ولا تتطلب الاسئلة التي يجاب عنها بِـ «نعم» أو «لا»، استخدام if او whether.

وتستخدم اداة الاستفهام في بداية الجملة الاستفهامية التي تبدأ بها.

Exercises

1 Write indirect questions with *Wh* forms.

Example: *What time is it? Can you tell me?*
Can you tell me what time it is?

1 *What date is it today? Do you know?*

2 *When is Ann coming home? Could you tell me?*

3 *Why has Tom gone? Do you have any idea?*

4 *How long will you be away? Can you say?*

5 *Where have they gone? Can you tell me?*

2 Write indirect questions with *Yes/No* forms.

Example: *Is the shop open? Can you tell me?*
Can you tell me if/whether the shop is open?

1 *Have they had lunch? Do you know?*

2 *Will you be home tonight? Can you say?*

3 *Are the team going to win? Do you have any idea?*

4 *Are we having a test this week? Can you tell us?*

3 Write indirect questions with *do/did* forms.

Example: *Did they leave at 1.00? Do you know?*
Do you know if/whether they left at 1.00?

1 *Does Tom go to school? Can you tell me?*

2 *Did the ring cost a lot? Can you say?*

3 *Do they play tennis? Do you have any idea?*

4 *When did the bus go? Could you tell us?*

5 *How does the engine work? Do you know?*

6 *Where do they always go? Can you tell me?*

4 Write indirect questions with ... *do/Do you think* ... ?

Examples: *Will it rain?*
Do you think it'll rain?
When did he go?
When do you think he went?

1 *Why does he arrive late?*

2 *Are they going to finish today?*

3 *How far did they walk?*

4 *Have we made a mistake?*

5 *Where will you live when you go to college?*

So am I.   Neither/Nor do I.   *I think so.   I'm afraid not.*

So and **Neither/Nor**

Positive	**Negative**
● *I'm thirsty.*	● *I don't understand.*
○ *So am I.*	○ *Neither/Nor do I.*

so and **not**

Positive	**Negative**
● *Is there any milk?*	● *Do you understand?*
○ *I think so.*	○ *I'm afraid not.*

So and Neither/Nor

So follows a positive statement. *Neither* or *Nor* follow a negative statement.

- ● *I'm hungry.*   ○ **So** *am I.*
- ● *I'm not hungry.*   ○ **Neither/Nor** *am I.*

The next word is a verb. It matches the verb in the first statement. It may be a form of *be*, *do* or *have*, or it may be a modal verb, eg *can*, *should*, *ought to*.

- ● *I'm thirsty.*   ○ *So* **am** *I.*
- ● *I* **can't** *do it.*   ○ *Neither* **can** *we.*

do or *does* follow a positive present simple statement. *did* follows a positive past simple statement.

- ● *She* **likes** *TV.*   ○ *So* **does** *he.*
- ● *He* **watched** *the news.*   ○ *So* **did** *she.*

The subject comes after the verb.

    So am **I**.   *Neither did* **we**.   *So will* **they**.

Use these forms to agree with another speaker's statement. Compare the replies.

● *I often go out on Saturday.*	● *He didn't arrive on time.*
○ *I often go out on Saturday* **too**.	○ *We* **didn't** *arrive on time* **either**.
OR **So do I.**	OR **Neither did we.**

so and not

You can use *so* after *hope*, *think*, *believe*, *expect*, *suppose*, *guess* and *be afraid*. Verb + *so* shows a positive feeling.

- ● *Is this answer right?*   ○ *I* **hope** *so.* OR *I* **think** *so.*

There are two negative forms – positive + *not* and negative + *so*.

- ● *Perhaps the bus isn't coming.*   ○ *I* **guess** *not.* OR *I'm* **afraid not**.

- ● *Are you going to be rich?*   ○ *I* **don't** *imagine so.*

With *believe*, *expect* and *suppose*, we can use either positive + *not* or negative + *so*.

- ● *Is Tom arriving tomorrow?*
- ○ *I* **believe not**. OR *I* **don't** *believe so.*

تتبع كلمة so جملة خبرية مثبتة، أما neither او nor فيتبعان جملة خبرية منفية.

الكلمة التي تلي أياً من هذه الكلمات تكون فعلاً يماثل الفعل المستخدم في الجملة الخبرية الاولى، ويمكن ان تكون احد تصاريف be او do او have او أحد الافعال المساعدة الناقصة مثل can.. الخ.

وتتبع do او does جملة خبرية مثبتة في زمن المضارع البسيط. في حين تتبع did جملة خبرية مثبتة في زمن الماضي البسيط.

ويأتي الفاعل بعد الفعل.

وتستخدم هذه الصيغ للموافقة على ما يقوله المتحدث. ويتضح الامر من خلال مقارنة الاجابات المبينة.

ويمكن استخدام so بعد الأفعال المبينة. ويدلّ استخدام الفعل + so على مشاعر ايجابية.

هناك صيغتان للنفي: فعل مثبت + not وفعل منفي + so. عند استخدام اي من الافعال الثلاثة المبينة يمكن استخدام الصيغة المثبتة متبوعة بـ not او الصيغة المنفية متبوعة بـ so.

Exercises

1 Complete the conversation. Use *So ...* or *Neither/Nor ...*

Two people on a train journey are talking.

Examples: Tony: *I'm travelling to Glasgow.*
Nick: *So am I.*
Tony: *I don't like long journeys much.*
Nick: *Neither/Nor do I.*

Tony: *I don't come from Glasgow.*
Nick: ¹_____ . *I'm from London.*
Tony: ²_____ . *I'm going to a meeting.*
Nick: ³_____ *You know, I had to get up at 6.30 this morning to catch this plane.*
Tony: ⁴_____ . *I didn't enjoy that at all.*
Nick: ⁵_____ . *I wanted to have the meeting in London.*
Tony: ⁶_____ . *I couldn't understand why they didn't want a meeting in London?*
Nick: ⁷_____ . *I was told I had to go to the Head Office in Glasgow.*
Tony: ⁸_____ *Where's your meeting?*
Nick: *It's at Northern Technical.*
Tony: ⁹_____ *That's amazing. What time does your meeting start? Mine starts at 10.00.*
Nick: ¹⁰_____ *That's even more strange! My meeting is about their new steel pipe project.*
Tony: ¹¹_____ *Tell me, who are you meeting?*
Nick: *Dr Tony Blair.*
Tony: *That's me!*

2 Look at the table. Then complete the statements.

	Ken	Sally	Ted	Claire
Tennis	✗	✗		
Judo	✗			✗
Swimming		✗	✗	
Computer games			✗	✗

Examples: Ken does judo, and *so does Sally.*
Ted can't play tennis, and *neither/nor can Claire.*

1 *Sally isn't interested in judo, and* _____ _____

2 *Ken is very good at tennis, and* _____ _____

3 *Ted loves playing computer games, and* _____ _____

4 *Sally hates computer games, and* _____ _____

5 *Sally can swim very well, and* _____ _____

6 *Ken can't swim at all, and* _____ _____

3 Complete the answers.

Examples: ● *Does the bank open on Saturday morning?*
○ *I think so.* (think) *Most big banks do.*
● *I think it's going to snow.*
○ *I hope not.* (hope) *I haven't got a coat.*

1 ● *Will Tessa get home late again tonight?*
○ _____ (expect) *She usually gets home late.*

2 ● *I think they're going to build the new road.*
○ _____ (suppose) *Everybody says they are.*

3 ● *Are you going to wear the blue shirt?*
○ _____ (not/think) *I don't like it any more.*

4 ● *Do you think Alex passed her exam?*
○ _____ (be afraid) *She didn't do any work.*

5 ● *I don't think Tom is coming.*
○ _____ (guess) *He should be here by now.*

6 ● *I wonder if we'll get to the shop in time.*
○ _____ (think) *It doesn't close until 6.00.*

29 Modal auxiliary verbs 1

can, could, be able to   can't have, could have, couldn't have

Help! I can't swim!

FORMS

can

The sea is warm now. We can go swimming.
Mary can swim very well.
The child cannot swim.

could and **be able to**

Mary could swim when she was five.
She was able to swim 100 metres when she was six.
The other day a child fell in the sea. He could not swim, but Mary was able to rescue him.

can

Use *can* to express ability and possibility in the present and future. The negative form is one word – *cannot*. The short form is *can't*.

> *She **can swim** very well.   It's warm, so we **can go** swimming.*
> *The boy **cannot swim**.   Help! I **can't swim**.*

could

Use *could* to express ability and possibility in the past.

> *She **could swim** when she was five.*
> *It was warm, so we **could go** swimming.*

Use *could not (couldn't)* for an impossible action in the past.

> *He was underwater. He **couldn't breathe**.*

Use *could* for an action in the past with these verbs: *feel, hear, see, smell, taste, remember, understand.* (For most other verbs see below.)

> *I **could hear** his call for help.   I **could see** that he needed help.*

be able to

You can use *be able to* for ability and possibility in the present and past, but it is more formal than *can* and less common.

> *She**'s able to swim** ten kilometres.*

Use *be able to* instead of *can* in the present perfect.

> *I've had some free time, so I**'ve been able to write** some letters.*

Use *be able to* instead of *could* for a past action with most verbs.

> *We had some free time, so we **were able to look** round town.*

can't have, could have and couldn't have

Use *can't have* or *couldn't have* when something was impossible in the past. (See also Unit 34.)

> *He **can't/couldn't have been** in Tokyo yesterday. I saw him in London.*

Use *could have* to talk about a missed opportunity in the past.

> *You **could have visited** Ann in hospital. Why didn't you?*

We often use *could have* when something was possible in the past.

> *The thief **could have entered** through the door or the kitchen window. We don't know which.*

تستخدم can للتعبير عن القدرة وعن الاحتمالية في الحاضر والمستقبل.. وتنفى في كلمة واحدة cannot وتختصر على شكل can't.

تستخدم could للتعبير عن القدرة وعن معنى الاحتمال في الماضي.

وتستخدم could not (couldn't) للتعبير عن استحالة وقوع حدث في الماضي.

تستخدم could مع حدثٍ ما في الماضي مصحوبةً باحد الافعال المبينة.

وتستخدم be able to للتعبير عن القدرة ومعنى الاحتمال في زمني المضارع والماضي ولكنها تعتبر اكثر رسمية من can واقل شيوعاً.

وتستخدم be able to عوضاً عن can مع زمن المضارع التام.

وتستخدم be able to عوضاً عن could مع معظم الأفعال في الماضي.

تستخدم صيغتا can't have وcouldn't have للتعبير عن استحالة وقوع الحدث في الماضي.

وتستخدم could have للتعبير عن ضياع فرصة امكانية عمل شيء ما في الماضي.

وغالباً ما تستخدم could have عند توفر إمكانية القيام بعملٍ ما في الماضي.

Exercises

1 Complete the statements. Use *can* or *can't* and these verbs.

catch, go, hear, see, walk

Example: *Please speak up. I* <u>*can't hear*</u> *very well.*

1 I _____ Lucy now. Look!

2 I've finished, so I _____ home.

3 Tim is only a baby. He _____ yet.

4 You _____ me! I'm too fast for you.

2 Complete the statements. Use *can/can't* or *could/couldn't*.

Example: *I* <u>*can*</u> *speak French well now, but I* <u>*couldn't*</u> *speak it at all five years ago.*

1 Poor old Mr Black _____ play football now, but he _____ play well when he was young.

2 Sally _____ read now, but she _____ read at all when she was five.

3 I _____ understand the game last time, and I still _____ understand now. It's very difficult.

4 Fifty years ago, you _____ buy a house for £500, but you certainly _____ do that now.

3 Complete the statements. Use *could* and choose from these verbs.

feel, hear, remember, see, smell, taste, understand

Example: *I woke up suddenly. I* <u>*could smell*</u> *something burning downstairs.*

1 The waterfall was huge. You _____ _____ the noise a kilometre away.

2 I thought about the girl. I _____ _____ her face, but not her name.

3 Ann _____ the words, but she still wasn't sure what the French girl wanted.

4 I _____ the rain running down my neck. It was horrible.

4 Complete the statements. Use *could* or *be able to*. Use *could* where possible.

Example: *The door was open, so we* <u>*were able to*</u> *go straight in.*

1 Lucy _____ hear somebody outside.

2 Lisa _____ read when she was four.

3 The police _____ stop the two men.

4 The plane crashed, but the pilot _____ get out.

5 Dan _____ see the mountains 20 kilometres away.

5 Complete the story. Use *can/can't* or *could/couldn't* or *be able to*.

Luckily, we <u>*were able to*</u> *hire a four-wheel drive vehicle quite easily. Next day we started early, and we* [1] _____ *travel fast across the open country. Later we climbed into the hills and stopped for a rest. From there, we* [2] _____ *look back across the flat land to the city. Maria pointed. 'Look, Rod,' she said. 'You* [3] _____ *still see the castle.' Rod looked, but he wasn't wearing his glasses and he* [4] _____ *see it. 'Let's go,' I said. 'If we hurry, we may* [5] _____ *reach the valley by 6.00. Later we ran into some deep mud. 'It's no good,' I said. 'We* [6] _____ *go forward or back.' Then we got out and pushed. In the end we* [7] _____ *move the vehicle, but we were covered in mud. Rod and I looked at ourselves and laughed, but Maria was upset. She* [8] _____ *see what was funny at all.*

6 Complete the statements. Use *can't have* or *could have*.

Example: *Peter* <u>*can't have*</u> *bought a car. He hasn't got any money.*

1 You _____ finished already. Nobody can work as fast as that.

2 Lucy _____ gone to the party, but she decided to stay at home.

3 Ed _____ been at the restaurant because I was there and I didn't see him.

4 We don't know how Steve went, but he _____ by train or bus.

69

30 Modal auxiliary verbs 2

can, could, would, may

Could you be quiet, please?

can, could, would and **may**

Bob, can you answer the phone for me?
Could you meet me at 4.00, please?
Miss Evans, would you book me a flight to New York, please?
Can I use your pen, Ann?
May I speak to Mr Evans, please?
● *Could I borrow the car tonight, Dad?*
○ *Yes, of course you can. You can have the car keys now. Here you are.*

Can/Could/Would you ...?

Use these verbs for requesting + 2nd or 3rd person.

> *Can you help me for a moment?* (informal)
> *Could you give me your name, please, Sir?* (polite/formal)
> *Would guests kindly leave their rooms by midday?* (more formal)

تستخدم هذه الافعال لصيغة الطلب + ضمير المخاطب او المفرد الغائب.

Can/Could/May I ...?

Use these verbs for requesting + 1st person.

> *Can I borrow your pen for a second?* (informal)
> *Could I have your phone number, Sir?* (polite/formal)
> *Ladies and gentlemen, may I have your attention, please?* (more formal)

تستخدم هذه الافعال لصيغة الطلب + ضمير المتكلم.

Yes, you can/may.

Use these verbs for permission.

> ● *Could I borrow some money, Sam?*
> ○ *Yes, of course you can. How much?* (informal/formal)
> ● *Could I talk to the King, please?*   ○ *Yes. You may see him at 10.00 tomorrow.* (very formal/old-fashioned)

تستخدم هذه الافعال للتعبير عن منح الاذن.

When we refuse permission, we do not usually use the negative of *can* or *may*.

> ● *Can I borrow your jacket tonight?*
> ○ *No, I'm sorry. I need it tonight.*

عند الرفض لا نستخدم عادة نفي can او may.

If we use *cannot (can't)* or *may not*, it shows very strong feeling.

> ● *Dad, could I have this week off school?*
> ○ *No, you certainly can't!* OR *No, you most certainly may not!*

وعند استخدام صيغة النفي cannot (can't) او may not فانها تدل على الرفض الشديد.

can/may

Use these verbs for offering.

> *You can ride my bike if you want.* (informal)
> *Can I help you, Mr Hill?* (informal)
> *Good morning, Barclays Bank. How may we help you?* (more formal)
> *Regular customers may open a monthly account if they wish.* (more formal)

تستخدم الافعال المبينة لعرض شيء على الآخرين.

Exercises

1 Complete the requests with suitable modal verbs.

Example: You're speaking to an old friend.
Ed, _can_ you pass the dictionary?

1 You're speaking to an old friend.
Ed, _____ you tell me what this means?

2 You're speaking to a foreign visitor at your firm.
_____ you come with me, Mr Hoffman?

3 A stewardess is speaking to the passengers.
_____ all passengers kindly return to their seats?

4 You're speaking to an old friend.
Jim, _____ I use your bike for ten minutes?

5 You're speaking to a foreign visitor at your firm.
_____ I have your name, Sir?

6 A stewardess is speaking to a passenger.
_____ I take your cup, if you've finished?

2 Complete the requests with suitable modal verbs.

Example: A stewardess wants all passengers to fasten their seat belts.
Would all passengers kindly fasten their seat belts?

1 You want to borrow your friend's book.
_____

2 You want your friend to lend you his pen.
_____

3 You want to know the company visitor's address.
_____

4 You want the company visitor to take a seat for a moment.
_____

5 A stewardess wants to put a passenger's bag away.
_____

6 A stewardess wants all passengers to remain in their seats until the plane stops.
_____
_____
_____

3 Write the answers. Use *Yes, you can ...* or *No, you can't ...*

Example: ● *Can I turn right here?*
○ _No, you can't turn right here._ It says NO ENTRY.

1 ● *Can I go now?*
○ _____ The lights are green.

2 ● *Can I park here?*
○ _____ It says NO PARKING.

3 ● *Can I pass this bus?*
○ _____
There are no cars coming.

4 ● *Can I turn round here?*
○ _____
It's dangerous.

4 Complete the conversation. Use suitable modal forms for requesting, permitting and offering.

Simon Bell has brought a German businessman, Franz Hoffman, home for dinner.

Simon: *Come in, Franz. Can I take your coat for you?*
Franz: *Thanks very much.*
Simon: *Now, 1_____ you like to meet the family?*
Franz: *Please.*
Simon: *This is my wife, Carol, and these are the children– Luke and Lisa.*
Carol: *It's nice to meet you Mr Hoffman.*
Franz: *And it's very good to meet you too. But one thing. 2_____ you just call me Franz?*
Carol: *Yes, of course. Now 3_____ you all come and eat? Dinner's getting cold.*

Ten minutes later

Simon: *4_____ you pass the salt, please?*
Carol: *Yes, of course. Here you are.*
Lisa: *Dad, 5_____ you help me with my German homework after dinner?*
Simon: *No, I 6_____ My German isn't very good.*

> *You look really tired! I think you should stop now. You ought to go to bed.*

should and *ought to*

These are nearly the same, but *ought to* is a little stronger and more formal. Use *should* and *ought to* for advising the right thing to do in a particular situation.

> *That hat looks terrible, Tom! You **should try** this one.*
> *You look very ill, Mr Jones. I think you **ought to see** the doctor.*

Also use *should not (shouldn't)* and *ought not to (oughtn't to)* for advising what not to do.

> *You **shouldn't wear** those shoes, Tom. They're not very nice.*
> *You **oughtn't to work** today. Really! Please go and see the doctor.*

Use *should* and *ought to* for saying what is always the right or wrong thing to do.

> *Parents **should teach** their children to be polite.*
> *People **oughtn't to play** loud music at night.*

Use *should* and *ought to* for saying what is wrong and what is necessary.

> *Excuse me. The bill **shouldn't be** £5.50. It **ought to be** £3.70.*

had better

had better ('d better) is like *should* and *ought to* (first use) for advising the right thing to do in a particular situation.

> *That hat looks terrible, Tom! You**'d better try** this one.*
> *You look very ill, Mr Jones. I think you**'d better see** a doctor.*

Also use *had better not ('d better not)* for advising what not to do.

> *You**'d better not wear** those shoes.   You**'d better not work** today.*

You cannot use *had better* for the other uses of *should* and *ought to*. But *had better* can be much stronger than *should* or *ought to*. It can be a threat.

> *You**'d better work** a lot harder, or you're going to lose your job!*
> *You**'d better not say** that again, or I'll be angry!*

should (not) have and *ought (not) to have*

Use these past forms when somebody did the wrong thing.

> *Tom crashed the car. He **shouldn't have driven** so fast. OR He **should have driven** more slowly.*
> *Susie has broken all the plates. She **ought to have been** more careful. OR She **oughtn't to have carried** so many.*

هناك تشابه كبير في استخدام الصيغتين، الا ان ought to تعتبر اكثر قوة ورسمية. وتستخدم الصيغتان لتقديم النصح في مواقف معينة.

تستخدم الصيغتان ايضاً في صيغة النفي وذلك للنهي عن القيام بعملٍ ما.

تستخدم should و ought to للتعبير عن عمل يتصف دائماً بالصواب او الخطأ.

تستخدم should و ought to للتعبير عن الشيء الخطأ وكذلك عن الشيء الضروري.

ويشبه استخدام had better ('d better) استخدام should و ought to الاول وذلك بغرض تقديم النصح في ما يجب عمله في مواقف معينة.

وتستخدم had better not او اختصارها، للنهي عن القيام بعمل ما.

لا يمكن استخدام had better مثل الاستخدامات الاخرى لـ should او لـ ought to ولكن had better يمكن ان تكون اقوى منهما. وقد يفيد استخدام had better مفهوم التهديد.

تستخدم صيغة الماضي should (not) و(not) ought عند قيام شخص ما بعمل خطأ.

Exercises

1 Complete the conversation. Use *should* or *ought*.

Eve and Sam are getting ready for a party.

Eve: *What time __should__ we go?*

Sam: *We __ought__ to leave here at 7.30. And it's 6.30 now, so we ¹_____ to hurry now. What do you think I ²_____ wear?*

Eve: *I think you ³_____ to wear a jacket and tie. Do you think I ⁴_____ wear my red dress?*

Sam: *Yes, you ⁵_____ It looks very good.*

2 Complete the conversation. Use *should/shouldn't* or *ought/oughtn't*.

Tina and Steve are going to visit his parents.

Tina: *Do you think we __should__ go by train?*

Steve: *No, we __oughtn't__ to do that. We'll have too much to carry. We ¹_____ to go by car.*

Tina: *Well, OK, but we ²_____ to take too much. We're only going for two days.*

Steve: *All right, but I think we ³_____ take some warm clothes. The weather may be cold. And ⁴_____ we to take some toys for the children? They may be bored.*

Tina: *No, we ⁵_____ do that. I think we ⁶_____ just take one or two books for them to read. Now what time do you think we ⁷_____ leave?*

Steve: *Well, it takes five hours by car, so we ⁸_____ to leave here after 2.00.*

3 Complete the statements. Use *had better* or *had better not*.

Example: *You __'d better not__ play with those matches. They're dangerous.*

1 *You look ill. You _____ see a doctor.*

2 *Ed has got a lot of homework to do. He _____ _____ go out this evening.*

3 *We've only got a little food. We _____ _____ waste it.*

4 *The children are tired. They _____ go to bed.*

4 Give advice.

Example: ● *I'm overweight. (should/not/eat/so much)*
○ *You shouldn't eat so much.*

1 ● *I'm unfit. (ought/do/more exercise)*
○ _____

2 ● *I've got a bad toothache. (better/see/a dentist)*
○ _____

3 ● *I've got a lot of work to do. (should/not/watch/TV/so much)*
○ _____
_____

4 ● *I've got a huge phone bill. (ought/not/use/the phone/so much)*
○ _____
_____

5 ● *It's still raining. (better/not/go out/yet)*
○ _____

6 ● *It's nice and sunny now. (should/go/to the beach)*
○ _____

5 Write the replies.

Example: ● *Andy felt really ill this morning. (ought/not/go/to work)*
○ *He oughtn't to have gone to work.*

1 ● *Tim was ill this morning. (should/go/to the doctor)*
○ _____
_____

2 ● *The boys got wet in the rain. (should/not/play/outside)*
○ _____
_____

3 ● *We're on the wrong road. (ought/turn/left/the traffic lights)*
○ _____
_____

4 ● *Maria doesn't like her new jacket. (ought/not/buy/it)*
○ _____
_____

32 Modal auxiliary verbs 4
must, have to

Speech bubbles:
- *Please! You must come quickly, Doctor!*
- *I have to go and see old Mr Clay.*

FORMS

must

You must help my husband! Please! Stop those boys! They must not play with that knife!

have to

Dr Bell often has to visit people. I have to go now. He had to visit Mr Clay last night.

We use *must* and *have to* for saying something is necessary now or very soon.

    *It's late. You **must stop** work and **go** to bed now, Tom.*

● ***Must** you **drive** so fast?*
○ *Yes, or we'll miss the plane.*
    *He **has to start** work at 8.00 tomorrow.*
    *I **have to go**. My boss is calling me.*

Use *have to* for other times. (*have to* has tenses, but *must* does not.)

● *Did you **have to work** late?* ○ *Yes, we **had to stay** until midnight!*
● *Has Ann **had to go** to hospital?* ○ *Yes, she has. She's very ill.*
    *We can't finish now. We'll **have to come back** next week.*

We often use *have got to* instead of *have to*. Use *have got to* in conversation. Use it for saying something is necessary now or very soon.

    *I've **got to go** or Dad will be angry.*

● ***Have** we **got to do** all this?*
○ *Yes, you **have**. It's part of the job.*

CROSSCHECK

must

Use *must* when the speaker feels a strong need inside.

    *Quick! We **must run** for the bus!*
    *You **must come** quickly, Doctor!*

must not

Use *must not* for necessity not to do something. Use the short form *mustn't* in conversation. (Do not pronounce the *t* in the middle.)

    *Stop! You **mustn't drink** that! It'll make you ill.*

We often use *can't* like *mustn't*.

    *You **can't hold** the ball. It's against the rules.*

have to

Use *have to* when the speaker expresses a need from outside, eg from a boss or teacher or parent.

    *I **have to go** and see old Mr Clay.*
    *I **have to do** some Maths for Mr Davis.*

not have to

Use *not have to* for no necessity to do something. (See Unit 33 for information on *didn't need to* and *didn't have to*.)

    *You **don't have to take** the exam if you don't want to.*

تستخدم must او have to للقول بان شيئاً ما ضروري الآن او في اسرع وقت.

وتستخدم have to للتعبير عن ظروف اخرى. وتجدر الملاحظة ان have to تُصَرّف حسب الازمنة ولكن must لا تُصَرّف.

غالباً ما تستخدم صيغة have got to بديلاً من have to. وتستخدم have got to اثناء المحادثة وذلك للدلالة على ان شيئاً ما ضروريٌ الآن، او في القريب العاجل.

تستخدم must عندما يشعر المتحدث ' بحاجة داخلية ملحة. وتستخدم have to عندما يعبر المتحدث عن حاجة خارجة عن نطاقه (من قبل رئيس او مدرس او والد).

تستخدم must not للتعبير عن ضرورة عدم القيام بعمل ما. وتستخدم الصيغة المختصرة mustn't اثناء الحوار والنقاش (حرف t الواقع في وسطها لا يُنطق) وتستخدم not have to عند عدم وجود ضرورة للقيام بعمل ما. (انظر unit 33 لمعلومات حول didn't need to و if you don't want to).

غالباً ما تستخدم can't مثل استخدام mustn't.

Exercises

1 Complete the questions with *have to.*

Example: *Paul has had to buy a car.*
       Why <u>has Paul had to buy a car?</u>

1 *Paul has had to pay a lot of money for it.*
  How much _____
  _____

2 *Emma will have to go to London soon.*
  When _____
  _____

3 *The Smith family had to go last week.*
  Where _____
  _____

4 *Ann has to change all her plans.*
  Why _____
  _____

5 *Ed and Sue have had to live in the flat for years.*
  How long _____
  _____

2 Complete the statements. Use *must* or *have to.*

Examples: *He said, 'You must finish by 5.00, Ann.'*
        So Ann <u>has to finish by 5.00.</u>
        The children have to go to bed now.
        Mum said, 'You <u>must go to bed now, children.'</u>

1 *Old Mr Robbins has to rest for a week.*
  The doctor said, 'You _____
  _____

2 *The bill says they must pay immediately.*
  So they _____

3 *We have to check in one hour before the flight.*
  The air tickets say: 'Passengers _____
  _____

4 *The hotel sign says: 'All guests must complete a registration form.'*
  So all guests _____
  _____

5 *Jimmy has to be home by 6.00.*
  His mother said, 'You _____

6 *The policeman said, 'You must go to the police station, Mr Reece.'*
  So Mr Reece _____
  _____

3 Complete the statements. Use *must* or *have to.*

Examples: *We <u>had to</u> work all day yesterday.*
        The fireman said, 'Quick! You <u>must</u> leave the building immediately.'

1 *I _____ read Ian York's new book. I love his writing.*

2 *Alan _____ go to the shop for some milk. Do you want anything?*

3 *You _____ listen to what I tell you. It's very important.*

4 *Last week we _____ wait for hours at the airport because of bad weather.*

5 *We really _____ buy a new TV. This old one is terrible.*

6 *Our new trainer is tough. We _____ run ten kilometres every morning.*

7 *This job looks interesting. I _____ ask for an application form.*

4 Complete the statements. Use *mustn't* or *not have to.*

Examples: *You <u>don't have to</u> buy a new pen. You can use mine.*
        Bob <u>mustn't</u> go out. He's ill.

1 *You _____ be late or you won't get into the cinema.*

2 *Students _____ wear a uniform at this school.*

3 *You _____ talk like that. It's rude.*

4 *I _____ be late home. I've got a lot of homework to do.*

5 *Ruth _____ go to work tomorrow. She's on holiday.*

6 *I _____ eat it if I don't want to.*

33 Modal auxiliary verbs 5

needn't, mustn't, didn't need to, needn't have

> You needn't run. The bus isn't here yet.

> You mustn't cross the road. The lights are red.

FORMS

needn't and mustn't

We **needn't** buy any food. We've got lots.
I **mustn't** forget his phone number. I have to phone him tonight.
She **doesn't need to** do any housework. She's got a maid.

didn't need to and needn't have

I **didn't need to** buy any meat as there was some in the fridge.
I **needn't have** gone to the meeting. Nobody else was there!

CROSSCHECK

needn't

Use *need to* (or *have to*) for saying something is necessary.

> Come on! We **need to hurry**.

Use *need not* (or *not need to/not have to*) for no necessity to do something.

> We **needn't go** to the cinema to see it. We can get the video.
> We **don't need to buy** the video. We can rent it.
> We **don't have to rent** it. We can borrow it from Peter.

didn't need to

Use *didn't need to* (or *didn't have to*) + infinitive when something was not necessary.

> She's very clever, so she **didn't need to work** for the test.

didn't need to (or *didn't have to*) usually means that an action was not necessary, so it did not happen.

> Tom **didn't need to arrive** until 8.00, but he was there at 7.00. He likes being early.

But we can use it when an action was not necessary, but it still happened – like *needn't have*.

> You **didn't have to pay** him any money. He was happy to work for nothing.

mustn't

Use *must* for saying something is necessary.

> We **must get** there by 11.00.

Use *mustn't* for necessity not to do something.

> You **mustn't play** with that knife. You'll cut yourself.
> You **mustn't cross** the road when the lights are red.

needn't have

Use *needn't have* + past participle when something happened, but it was not necessary.

> Poor Sam **needn't have worked** so hard for the test. It was cancelled!

تستخدم need to (أو have to) للقول بان شيئاً ما ضروري.

وتستخدم must للتعبير عن ضرورة القيام بعملٍ ما ايضاً.

تستخدم need not او not need to او not have to عند انتفاء ضرورة القيام بعمل ما.

وتستخدم mustn't للتعبير عن ضرورة عدم القيام بعمل ما.

تستخدم didn't need to (أو didn't have to) + مصدر عند التعبير عن ان القيام بعمل لم يكن ضرورياً.

وتستخدم needn't have + التصريف الثالث للفعل للتعبير عن حدث حصل ولكنه لم يكن ضرورياً.
يعني استخدام didn't need to (او didn't have to) عادةً ان القيام بعملٍ مّا لم يكن ضرورياً، ولهذا فهو لم يحصل.

ولكن يمكن ان تُستخدم ايضاً للتعبير عن ان القيام بعملٍ مالم يكن ضرورياً ولكنه حدث رغم ذلك.

76

Exercises

1 Complete the statements. Use *needn't* or *mustn't*.

Examples: *We needn't hurry. We've got lots of time.*
We mustn't swim here. It's dangerous.

1 *Don't you like it? Well, you _____ drink it if you don't want to.*

2 *Listen! You _____ be late again or you'll be in bad trouble.*

3 *You _____ make so much noise. This is a library.*

4 *You _____ finish the report today, but please can I have it tomorrow?*

5 *Children _____ play with knives. They're dangerous things.*

6 *Ann _____ stay. Carol can do everything.*

2 Re-order the words to make positive and negative statements and questions.

Examples: *(there / he / go / to / have / doesn't)*
He doesn't have to go there.
(need / what / buy / we / do / to)
What do we need to buy?

1 *(work / to / I / late / have)*
_____

2 *(they / go / to / where / have / do)*
_____

3 *(she / need / go / does / to / so soon)*
_____

4 *(tomorrow / you / do / to / have / work)*
_____

5 *(need / I / homework / don't / do / my / to)*
_____

6 *(learn / why / to / they / French / do / need)*
_____

3 Complete the conversation. Use *need to, needn't* or *mustn't*.

Neil is telling his parents about his school trip to France.

Neil: *On the day we go I need to be at school at 7.45. The bus goes at 8.00.*

Mum: *What clothes do you need to take with you?*
¹_____ wear your school uniform? (you)

Neil: *No, we ²_____ do that. We can wear our ordinary clothes. We also ³_____ take clothes for outdoor activities – jeans, boots and anoraks. You ⁴_____ look at this list of clothes and equipment and this letter from school.*

Dad: *How much is it going to cost?*

Neil: *It's £200, but you ⁵_____ pay it all yet. The letter says you only ⁶_____ pay half now.*

Dad: *Good. We ⁷_____ spend too much now because we haven't got much money this month. How soon ⁸_____ give the school the first £100? (we)*

Neil: *I ⁹_____ take it by next weekend.*

Mum: *It sounds great fun.*

Neil: *Yes, but they've made a special rule. As soon as we get on the bus we ¹⁰_____ speak English any more. We can only speak French for a whole week!*

4 Complete the statements. Use *didn't need to* or *needn't have*.

Examples: *I needn't have gone to the meeting. Nobody else was there.*
Yesterday was a holiday, so I didn't need to go to work.

1 *At my school we _____ wear a uniform. People just wore their ordinary clothes.*

2 *They _____ worked so hard. Nobody even noticed all the work they did.*

3 *We _____ hurried. Everybody else was late too.*

4 *Sally _____ buy a coat. Her brother gave her a very nice one.*

5 *I _____ send the money. Mr Brant came for it.*

6 *You _____ written to them. I'd already told them your answer.*

34 Modal auxiliary verbs 6

may, might, could, may be, must be, can't be, may have, must have, can't have

may, might and could

Use *may* or *might* to say something is possible in the future.
> *The score is 3-3, so either side **may/might win**.*

Use *could* to say something is possible, but not likely.
> *The score is 3-1 against City. They **could win**, but I don't think so.*

may not and *might not* mean something negative is possible.
> *I'm very busy, so I **may not/might not have** time to go to the match.*

cannot (can't) and *could not (couldn't)* mean something negative is impossible.
> *City **can't/couldn't win** against Rangers. Rangers are too good.*

may be, might be, must be and can't be

Use *may be* or *might be* when something is not certain in the present.
> *Bill isn't in his office. He **may be** in Room 303, or he **might be seeing** Mr Bell.*

must be and *can't be* are opposites. Use them when something is certain in the present. *must be* means certain (negative).
> *Look at that car! It **must be doing** 250 kph. The driver **must be crazy**.*
> *This boy says he's 16, but he looks so young. He **can't be telling** the truth. He **can't be** more than 14.*

may have, must have and can't have

Use these (and *might have* or *could have*) when something is certain or uncertain in the past.
> *Jerry **must have left** his bag somewhere because he hasn't got it now.*
> *He **can't have left** it at school because he's checked and it isn't there.*
> *He **may have left** it somewhere on the way home.*

تستخدم may او might للقول بان شيئاً ما ممكن في المستقبل.

وتستخدم could للتعبير عن امكانية حدوث شيء ما، ولكن حدوثه امر مستبعد.

ويعني استخدام may not و might not وجود احتمال بنفي شيء ما.

ويعني استخدام cannot (can't) و could not (couldn't) أستحالة حدوث شيء سلبي.

تستخدم may be او might be عندما يكون الامر غير مؤكد في الوقت الراهن.

تأتي must be لتعني عكس can't be، ويستخدمان عندما يكون الامر مؤكداً في الوقت الراهن. ويفيد استخدام must be التأكد (السلبي).

تستخدم هذه الصيغ (أضافة الى might have او could have) عندما يكون شيءٌ ما مؤكداً او غير مؤكد في الماضي.

Exercises

1 Complete the statements. Use *may (not)/ might (not)*.

Example: *We're very late for the plane. We <u>may/might</u> miss it.*

1 *I _____ be late home tonight, so don't worry if I'm not back at the usual time.*

2 *Dr Jones _____ have time to see you, but I don't think so. Ask his secretary.*

3 *If we go on playing this badly, we _____ win the game.*

4 *I _____ catch the 9.00 train, but I'll probably get the one at 9.30.*

5 *We _____ have enough milk. Could you buy some, please?*

6 *I'll try and get a green sweater in town, but I _____ be able to find one.*

2 Write statements. Use *may (not) be/might (not) be, must be* or *can't be*.

Examples: ● *Do you know where Paul is?*
○ *(It's late, so he isn't at school.)*
      <u>He can't be at school.</u>
● *(Perhaps he's at home.)*
      <u>He may/might be at home.</u>
○ *(He's always with his friends in the evening.)*
      <u>He must be with his friends.</u>

1 ● *How old do you think Mr Lee is?*
○ *(I'm sure he isn't under 60.)*
_____

● *(Perhaps he's about 64 or 65.)*
_____

○ *(I know he's 65 because he's just retired from work.)*
_____
_____

2 ● *Is that Rod coming across the beach.*
○ *(I'm sure it's Julian because that looks like his jacket.)*
_____
_____

● *(Perhaps it isn't him. He's walking towards some other people.)*
_____
_____

○ *(I'm sure it isn't Rod. Rod is taller.)*
_____

3 Complete the conversation. Use *may be/ might be, must be* or *can't be* + present participle.

? = may be/might be, ✓ = must be, ✗ = can't be

Tina: *Do you know what Dave is doing?*

Nick: *I'm not sure. He <u>may/might be riding</u> his bike. (? ride)*

Tina: *No, he ¹_____ that. (✗ do) His bike is still in the garage.*

Nick: *Well, he ²_____ upstairs. (✗ play) The house is too quiet.*

Tina: *Oh, look. His baseball bat has gone. He ³_____ baseball in the park. (✓ practise)*

4 Complete the conversation. Use *may have/ might have, must have* or *can't have* + past participle.

? = may have/might have, ✓ = must have, ✗ = can't have

Dave: *Mum, have you seen my wallet in the dining-room?*

Tina: *No, you <u>can't have put</u> it there. (✗ put) I've just tidied the dining-room and I didn't see it.*

Dave: *And I ¹_____ it in the park because I didn't take my money. (✗ drop)*

Tina: *You ²_____ it upstairs in your bedroom. (? leave)*

Dave: *I'm not sure.*

Nick: *Wasn't your wallet in your jeans pocket yesterday?*

Tina: *And didn't you throw your jeans in the washing machine this morning?*

Dave: *Oh, so I ³_____ my wallet in the washing machine too. (✓ put) I'll have to hang my money out to dry!*

35 Modal auxiliary verbs 7: past forms

could, had to, needed to, may have, must have, can't have, could have, etc

FORMS

Grandad: *I could run 100 metres in ten seconds when I was young.*

Grandson: *Wow! You must have been the fastest in the country.*

Grandad: *Yes, I should have been in the Olympic team, but I was ill. I couldn't go.*

could, had to and needed to

Use *had to* and *needed to* to talk about past necessity and need. (*must* has no past form.) (See Units 32/33 for more information.)

> *I was late for the meeting. I **had to run**.*
> *We **needed to get** some milk, so I went to the shop.*

Use *could* and *could not* to talk about ability and possibility in the past.

> *I **could run** 30 kilometres when I was 20.*
> *He **couldn't swim** when he was five.*

Use *could not* for an action that did not happen.

> *I was so tired that I **couldn't walk** any more.*

We usually use *be able to* instead of *could* for a past action. But you can use *could* with verbs of feeling (*see, hear*, etc) and thinking (*remember, forget*, etc). (See Unit 29.)

> *After a long sleep, I **was able to get up** and **start** walking again.*
> *After a long while I **could see** a farm ahead of me.*

may have, must have and can't have

Use these (and *might have* or *could have*) when something seems certain or uncertain in the past. (See Unit 34 for more information.)

> ● *There's nobody at home. They **must have gone out**.*
> ○ *They **may have gone** to the beach.*
> ● *No. They **can't have done** that. Their car is still here.*

could have, should have and would have

Use these (and *ought to have* or *might have*) when somebody did something wrongly or differently.

> *You **could have called** earlier. Why didn't you?*
> *I'm sorry. I can't pay. I **should have brought** more money.*

would have is the same form as in Type 3 conditionals. (See Unit 45.) Use these negative forms in the same way: *should not have, ought not to have, would not have, need not have.* (See Units 31/33.)

> *We **would have visited** you, but we didn't know you were at home.*
> *He **shouldn't have shouted** at her. Look! She's crying now!*
> *You **needn't have gone** to town for a newspaper. You can get them near here.*

Compare *needn't have* and *didn't need to*.

> *I **didn't need to go** to work, so I stayed in bed.*

تستخدم had to و needed to للتعبير عن ضرورة وحاجة في الماضي. وتجدر الملاحظة بأنه لا توجد صيغة في الماضي لـ must. (انظر units 32/33 للمزيد من المعلومات).

وتستخدم could و could not للتعبير عن القدرة وعن الامكانية في الماضي.

وتستخدم could not للتعبير عن عمل لم يحدث.

تستخدم صيغة be able to عادةً عوضاً عن could عند التعبير عن حدث في الماضي. ويمكن استخدام could مع الافعال التي تتعلق بالحواس مثل (see و hear... الخ) وكذلك مع الافعال التي تتعلق بالتفكير مثل (remember و forget). (انظر unit 29).

تستخدم هذه الصيغ اضافة لـ might have او could have عندما يبدو شيءٌ ما مؤكداً او غير مؤكد في الماضي (انظر unit 34 للمزيد من المعلومات).

وتستخدم هذه الصيغ اضافة الى ought to have او might have عندما يكون الشخص قد اخطأ في عملٍ ما او ان يكون قد اتى بعمل مخالف.

ان صيغة would have هي نفسها صيغة النوع الثالث من الجمل الشرطية (انظر unit 45). وتستخدم الصيغ المنفية المبينة بالطريقة نفسها: مثل should not have ... الخ. (نظر units 31/33).

لاحظ الفرق بين صيغتي needn't have و didn't need to.

Exercises

1 Complete the story. Use past forms of *can*, *be able to*, *have to*, *need* or *need to*.

When Larry's boat hit a rock, he *didn't need to* look below. He ¹_____ hear the water rushing in, and he knew the boat was going down. He also knew he ²_____ get off the boat in two or three minutes. He ³_____ pull out the orange life-raft and he threw it quickly into the water, where it filled with air. Next, he ran to the cabin. He ⁴_____ collect as many things as possible – food, water medicine, a map, and so on. The only thing he ⁵_____ take was petrol – the life-raft had no motor. Soon water was coming into the cabin, and he ⁶_____ get out quickly. He looked round for the raft. He ⁷_____ see it! Then he did. It was ten metres away. Larry dropped his supplies on top of the cabin and jumped into the sea. He ⁸_____ get that raft! He reached it, climbed in and started rowing back for his supplies. As he rowed, he ⁹_____ see the boat sinking. He rowed harder. He ¹⁰_____ those supplies as much as the life-raft itself. He ¹¹_____ let those supplies go down with his boat.

Complete these possible endings.

But he ¹²_____ get there in time. He lost everything. OR

He got there just in time, and he ¹³_____ save everything.

2 Complete the conversation. Use *may have* (or *might have*/*could have*), *must have* or *can't have*.

Bob and Lucy are looking for their son, Joe, at the beach.

Bob: *He can't have gone into the water. He's still wearing his T-shirt and shorts.*

Lucy: *And he ¹_____ gone to the ice-cream van or the beach shop because he hasn't got any money.*

Bob: *He ²_____ gone to the beach shop just to look around.*

Lucy: *Yes, he ³_____ done that. He was asking me to buy a ball before. He's crazy about volleyball.*

Bob: *Talking about volleyball, there are some people playing volleyball over there, and there are some people watching. He ⁴_____ gone to watch the game. What do you think?*

Lucy: *You're wrong. He isn't watching. He's playing. He ⁵_____ gone and asked to join the game.*

3 Complete the conversation. Use *could have*, *would have* ('d have), *shouldn't have*, *should have*, *wouldn't have* or *needn't have*.

The Green family are coming back from a terrible holiday in the south of France. It rained all the time and it was very cold.

Mum: *Well, nobody could have guessed the weather would be so bad.*

Dad: *Yes, if we'd known about the weather, we certainly ¹_____ gone there.*

Tim: *We ²_____ taken our raincoats, rubber boots, hats, gloves and scarves.*

Jo: *And I ³_____ bought that new summer dress. I didn't wear it once. I'm so disappointed.*

Dad: *We ⁴_____ chosen a holiday in Greece as easily as the one in France. It ⁵_____ been the same price. In fact, I ⁶_____ chosen Greece except that we can all speak French, but not Greek.*

Mum: *We ⁷_____ listened to the travel agent. She said the weather was always wonderful in the south of France.*

Dad: *We ⁸_____ done better to stay at home and save our money.*

Mum: *Well, next year we'll go somewhere else – somewhere warm and dry.*

can, could, would, be able to, should, ought to, must, have to, etc

Ability (See Unit 29.)

*Most birds **can fly**.*
*Some people **can't swim**.*
*Ann **could write** when she was three.*
*I **was able to finish** the test in an hour.*

Requests, offers and permission (See Unit 30.)

***May I speak** to Mr Hill, please?*
***Could you keep** the noise down, please?*
***Would you post** this for me, please?*
***Would you like** a part-time job?*
● ***May I go** home early today?*
○ ***Yes**, of course **you can**.*

Advice (See Unit 31.)

*You **shouldn't eat** so much.*
*You **oughtn't to play** computer games so much.*
*You look tired. You**'d better go** home.*

Obligation and necessity (See Unit 32.)

*You **mustn't copy** his work. That's wrong.*
*At my new job I **have to start** at 9.00.*
*I've **got to go** now, or my parents will be angry.*
*You **can't walk** on the grass. Look! The notice says:*
'Keep off the grass.'
*If you want a licence, you **need to fill in** this form.*

Non-obligation (See Unit 33.)

You **needn't do** this work now. You can finish it tomorrow.
We **didn't have to work** at the weekend, but we wanted to help as much as we could.

Certainty and uncertainty (See Unit 34.)

He **might come**, but I don't think so.
She **definitely will/won't be** at the wedding.
They **could arrive** this evening, but I don't think so.
He **can't be** at the office. He never works this late.
He **must be visiting** a friend.

Past forms of modals (See Unit 35.)

We **should have gone** to school, but we went to the football match.
You **oughtn't to have used** the money. Now we haven't got any to buy food.
They **couldn't stay**. They **had to go** home.
Nobody answered the phone, so they **can't have been** at home. They **must have been** out.

Exercises

1 Complete the statements and questions. Use *can*, *can't*, *could*, *couldn't* or *be able to*.

Examples: *I'm tired. I _can't_ go on any longer.*
At last, we _were able to_ escape.

1 *I _____ understand the problem. _____ you?*

2 *Alex _____ already swim when he was three.*

3 *I tried to move, but I _____*

4 *You were near the accident, Mr Jones. _____ you see what happened?*

5 *In the end, we _____ save enough money to buy a car last year.*

6 *What happened when he got lost? _____ _____ find his way of the woods? (he)*

2 Write requests. (You can often give more than one answer.)

Example: A business caller wants to talk to the manager.
● *May I speak to the manager, please?*

1 A girl wants to borrow her friend's book.
● _____

2 A shop assistant offers to help a customer.
● _____

3 A manager asks his assistant to get the red file.
● _____

4 Somebody offers a friend a cup of tea.
● _____

5 A receptionist asks a business visitor his name.
● _____

6 Somebody asks a friend to lend him some money.
● _____

7 An office worker asks her boss for a day off next week.
● _____

8 A visitor asks if he can park his car outside the entrance.
● _____
_____

3 Give advice. (You can often give more than one answer.)

Examples: ● *I feel ill. (see the doctor)* OR *(not go to work today)*
○ *You'd better see the doctor.* OR *You oughtn't to go to work today.*

1 ● *I've got a terrible toothache. (go to the dentist)*
○ _____

2 ● *The boys have got a lot of work tonight. (not watch TV)*
○ _____

3 ● *I can't see very well. (get some glasses)*
○ _____

4 ● *My brother wants to make more money. (find a better job)*
○ _____

5 ● *Tom wants a good grade in Maths. (not miss the next test)*
○ _____

6 ● *Sam wants to play outside, but it's still raining. (not go out yet)*
○ _____

4 Complete the statements. Use *must*, *mustn't*, *have to* or *can't*.

Examples: Mary's new contract: *Employees _must_ work 38 hours a week*
Mary to her parents: *I _have to_ work 38 hours a week.*

1 Teacher to a new student: *Tony, you _____ come late again. You _____ always be here on time.*

2 Friend to Tony: *We _____ come to school late. If we do, we _____ stay behind for an hour after school.*

3 Notice on a beach: *DANGER! Visitors _____ remain close to the beach at all times. When the red flag is up, swimmers _____ leave the water.*

4 Swimmer to friend: *Look! The red flag is up. That means we _____ stay in the water. We _____ get out.*

5 **Complete the statements. Use the present form *needn't* and the present and past forms of *(not) need to* or *(not) have to*.**

Example: *There is a holiday next week, so we <u>don't have to</u> come to work.*

1 *You _____ go shopping. I've been already.*

2 *I _____ write a report last month. There was nothing to write about.*

3 *We _____ wear a uniform at work, but the boss always says we _____ dress smartly.*

4 *When I was at school, we _____ wear the school uniform until the last year, but in the last year, we _____ wear the uniform any more.*

5 *I _____ use the car again this week, so you can have it. But I _____ have it again by Monday morning.*

6 ● *How many questions did you _____ answer in the exam?*

   ○ *We _____ answer five questions.*

6 **Complete the conversation. Choose from *will, won't, could, may (not)* or *might (not)*.**

Two friends are waiting at the station for another friend, Ted, and for a train.

Tony: *I hope Ted isn't going to be late. The train <u>will</u> be here in a minute.*

Lisa: *Don't worry. Ted* [1]*_____ be here in a minute. He promised.*

Tony: *I don't know. He's often late. He* [2]*_____ get here, but he* [3]*_____ Look! The train is coming. It* [4]*_____ be here in a minute.*

Lisa: *You* [5]*_____ be right. But he still* [6]*_____ come. There's still a chance.*

Tony: *No. He* [7]*_____ get here in time now. It's too late. The train is here.*

Ted: *Hi, Tony. Hi, Lisa. I'm here.*

7 **Read Ann Green's diary for today. Then answer her colleague's questions. Use *can't be, may be* or *must be*.**

9.00 – 10.30	*visit GLA*
10.30 – 12.00	*travel to Birmingham*
12.00 – 1.00	*meet Stephen Fisher*
1.00 – 2.00	*have lunch with Eric Ross at the City Hotel or the Ritz Grill*
2.00 – 3.30	*travel to Liverpool or Manchester*

Examples: ● *What's she doing at the moment?* (It's 9.30.)
   ○ *She <u>must be visiting GLA</u>.*
   ● *Is she in Birmingham now?* (It's 11.15.)
   ○ *No, she <u>can't be in Birmingham</u>. She <u>must be travelling there</u>.*

1 ● *What's she doing now?* (It's 12.30.)
   ○ *She _____*

2 ● *Where's she having lunch?* (It's 1.15.)
   ○ *She _____ or she _____*

3 ● *Is she in Birmingham now?* (It's 2.45.)
   ○ *No, she _____ She _____*
   _____

8 **Complete the statements with past forms. Choose from these modals.**

could have, should have, ought to have, would have ('d have), can't have, couldn't have, shouldn't have, oughtn't to have, needn't have.

Examples: *Jean <u>needn't have</u> cooked so much. Nobody was very hungry.*

1 *I _____ said thank you, but I forgot.*

2 *They _____ crossed the desert. They had no water.*

3 *You _____ made your little brother cry.*

4 *We _____ taken our coats. It was warm.*

5 *I _____ given you the money if I'd known you needed it.*

37 Passive verb forms 1
Every bike is checked.

Every bike is checked before it leaves the factory.

Form the present simple passive with *am, is, are* + past participle, eg *am checked, is checked* and *are checked*. (See Appendix 1 for a list of common irregular participle forms.)

> **Active:** *Our workers **check** all the bikes.*
> **Passive:** *All the bikes **are checked** by our workers.*

Form the past simple passive with *was, were* + past participle eg *was made*, and *were made*.

> *The first bike **was made** 100 years ago.*
> *The first bikes **were made** 100 years ago.*

Form negative passives and passive questions like active sentences.

> ● ***Are** all these cars **sold** in Europe?*
> ○ *No, they **aren't**. Some cars **are sold** in America.*
> ● *How many **are sent** to America?*   ○ *About 500 a month.*

Use the passive to focus on the object of an active sentence, eg we are more interested in the cars than who built them – the agent.

> *The first plane **was built** by somebody nearly 100 years ago.*

You can leave out the agent if it is not important.

> *The first planes **were built** nearly 100 years ago.*

Sometimes, we use the passive because we do not know the agent.

> *The wheel **was invented** thousands of years ago.*

We often use the passive in technical English to explain how we do something. (Who does it is not important.)

> *The engines **are put** together in 85 separate steps.*

We often use the passive in formal English, eg in business agreements.

> *Under this agreement it **is understood** that both parties **are committed** to completing the project by 31st December, 1999.*

يتكون المضارع البسيط المبني للمجهول من am أو is أو are، إضافة للتصريف الثالث للفعل، مثلما هو موضح في الأمثلة. (انظر لائحة بصيغ التصريف الثالث للفعل اللاقياسية الشائعة، في الملحق رقم ١).

يتكون الماضي البسيط المبني للمجهول من was أو were إضافة إلى التصريف الثالث للفعل.

تتكوّن الجمل المبنية للمجهول النافية وكذلك الأسئلة المبنية للمجهول مثل الجمل المبنية للمعلوم.

تستخدم صيغة المبني للمجهول للتركيز على المفعول به في الجملة المبنية للمعلوم. ويوضح المثال أن اهتمامنا منصب على السيارة وليس على من صنعها.

ويمكن الاستغناء عن الفاعل عندما لا يضيف شيئاً إلى المعنى.

وأحياناً نستخدم صيغة المبني للمجهول لأن الفاعل غير معروف لدينا.

وغالباً ما تستخدم صيغة المبني للمجهول في المجال التقني لشرح كيفية عمل الأشياء حيث لامجال للاهتمام بالفاعل.

وغالباً ما تستخدم صيغة المبني للمجهول في اللغة الرسمية مثل الاتفاقات التي تتعلق بالأعمال التجارية.

Exercises

1 Write the verbs in the present simple passive.

The European Airbus A320 *is built* by a group of European aeroplane makers. (build) The nose of the plane [1]_____ by the French. (make) The body of the plane [2]_____ by the Germans. (produce) The wings [3]_____ by the British. (provide) Then of all the parts [4]_____ to one factory in France where the plane [5]_____ together. (brought) (put) The finished A320 planes [6]_____ to their customers. (deliver)

2 Write the verbs in the past simple passive.

One of the first flying machines *was designed* by Leonardo da Vinci. (design) The first real plane [1]_____ by the Wright brothers in 1903. (build) Planes soon became more common, and they [2]_____ in World War 1. (use) In 1919 letters [3]_____ across the Atlantic for the first time. (fly) Other ways of using planes [4]_____ too. (find) Passengers [5]_____ on regular flights, also in 1919. (carry) In the same year, the first international passenger flights [6]_____ between London and Paris. (begin) Airline services developed fast. In 1925 the first hot meals for passengers [7]_____ by a French airline. (provide) The first stewardess [8]_____ by an American airline in 1937. (employ)

3 Change the active statements into passive statements. Leave out the agents.

Example: *They didn't tell people about the plan.*
         People weren't told about the plan.

1 First the company built the new factory.

   _____

2 Then the engineers designed the new Superbike 2,000.

   _____
   _____

3 They didn't show the design to anyone.

   _____
   _____

4 People bought 1,000 in the first year.

   _____

4 Read. Then write questions and answers.

Examples: *(What/oil/need/for today)*
● *What is oil needed for today?*
○ *It's needed for modern transport and industry.*
(oil/know/in ancient times)
● *Was oil known in ancient times?*
○ *Yes, it was.*

Our modern world needs large amounts of oil for industry and modern forms of transport. But oil was first known and used thousands of years ago. In ancient times, it was burned in oil lamps for light at night. Boats were also covered with it to keep water out. It was also used as a surface for roads by the Chinese.

About 100 years ago, far more oil was suddenly needed as modern transport and industry developed. Oil wells were drilled and large amounts of oil were found in many parts of the world, including the Middle East and the USA.

Today, oil is less easy to find, but new supplies are still discovered. Nearly 50 million barrels of oil are pumped from the ground every day.

1 *(When/oil first/use)*
● _____
○ _____
   _____

2 *(it/burn/for light)*
● _____
○ _____

3 *(When/far more oil/need)*
● _____
○ _____

4 *(more oil/find/at that time)*
● _____
   _____
○ _____

5 *(How many barrels/oil/pump/every day now)*
● _____
   _____
○ _____
   _____

Passive verb forms 2

It's being checked.   It's been checked.   It can be checked.   Get it checked.

Tense forms

Form the different passive tenses like this.

Active	Passive
*They **check** everything.*	*Everything **is checked**.*
*They **checked** everything.*	*Everything **was checked**.*
*They **are checking** everything.*	*Everything **is being checked**.*
*They **were checking** everything.*	*Everything **was being checked**.*
*They **have checked** everything.*	*Everything **has been checked**.*
*They **had checked** everything.*	*Everything **had been checked**.*
*They **will have checked** everything.*	*Everything **will have been checked**.*

يتم تحويل أزمنة المبني للمجهول على أختلافها كما هو مبين:

Compare the different forms of *be* in continuous tenses and perfect tenses.

قارن بين صيغ تصاريف فعل be في الأزمنة المستمرة وفي الأزمنة التامة.

> *It **is being** finished.   They **are being** finished.*
> *It has **been** finished.   They have **been** finished.*

Future and modal passive forms

Use the following with *be* + past participle: *will, would, going to, can, could, may, might, must, should, have to, ought to*, etc.

تستخدم الأفعال المساعدة الناقصة المبينة هنا، مع فعل الكينونة be + التصريف الثالث.

Form the different future and modal passives like this.

Active	Passive
*They **will finish** everything.*	*Everything **will be finished**.*
*They **are going to finish** everything.*	*Everything **is going to be finished**.*
*They **must finish** everything.*	*Everything **must be finished**.*
*They **have to finish** everything.*	*Everything **has to be finished**.*

تتكون أزمنة المستقبل المبنية للمجهول على اختلافها وكذلك الأفعال المساعدة الناقصة في صيغة المبني للمجهول على النحو الذي توضحه الأمثلة.

have/get something done

Use this form when you give somebody else some work to do for you.
Form it with *have* or *get* + object + past participle.

> *I'm going to **have the car checked** by a mechanic.*
> *They **got the work done** for £10,000.*

تستخدم هذه الصيغة عند إسناد عمل ما إلى شخصٍ ما ليقوم به. وتتكون من have أو get + المفعول به + التصريف الثالث.

Use *had*, not *got*, in the present perfect.

> *We've **had the room decorated** and we've **had new curtains made** too.*

وتستخدم had عوضاً عن got في زمن المضارع التام المبني للمجهول.

Exercises

1 Write statements with verbs in continuous passive tenses.

Example: *The boy shouted for help. (he/carry/out to sea)*
He was being carried out to sea.

1 *We heard a noise and turned. (we/call/by somebody)*

2 *The towers are dangerous. (they/pull/down/next week)*

3 *The boss was angry. (the work/not/do/efficiently)*

4 *I didn't see little Ann yesterday. (she/look after/by Sue)*

5 *I haven't got my car. (it/service/at the garage)*

2 Write statements with verbs in perfect passive tenses.

Example: *I couldn't open the door. (it/lock/on the inside)*
It had been locked on the inside.

1 *The village is different now. (many new houses/build)*

2 *I managed to start the old car. (it/not/drive/for 20 years)*

3 *The bus has gone. (we/leave/behind)*

4 *We were angry about the plan. (we/not/tell/about it)*

3 Write the official rules.

Example: *Read this. It says we must pay bills within 30 days.*
Bills must be paid within 30 days.

At the library

1 *It says we can borrow up to five books.*

2 *It says we should return books on time.*

At work

3 *It says you must wear protective clothing at all times.*

4 *It says we mustn't eat food in the office.*

4 Write statements. Use *have/get* + object + past participle.

Example: *The door needs painting soon.*
Let's get the door painted soon.

1 *The window needs mending now.*
Let's _____

2 *These films need printing soon.*
Let's _____

3 *This wall needs rebuilding tomorrow.*
Let's _____

5 Change the active statements into passive statements. Leave out the agent if it is not important.

Examples: *The police are checking the house.*
The house is being checked by the police.
They haven't cleaned this room.
This room hasn't been cleaned.

1 *They built this castle in 1760.*

2 *Somebody was pulling Tony along the road.*

3 *Alan won't win the match. Jim will win it.*

4 *People should always read contracts before they sign them.*

5 *Bob has written a memo and the staff are reading it.*

39 Verb + *to* + infinitive or verb + *ing* form 1

I want to go.   I love going on the rides.

FORMS

Verb + *to* + infinitive

Mum: *I want to go home now. It's late.*
Tim: *Please, Mum! I want to stay.*

Verb + *ing* form

Mum: *We can't keep going round the fair.*
       It's expensive!
Tim: *But, Mum! I love going on the rides!*

CROSSCHECK

Verb + *to* + infinitive

Some verbs take this form. These are the most common.

> *agree, aim, appear, arrange, ask, attempt, can't afford, can't wait, choose, decide, expect, fail, happen, hesitate, hope, learn, manage, offer, plan, prepare, pretend, promise, refuse, seem, tend, threaten, train, want, wish*

> *I **agreed to go** with the others.*
> *We **aim to get** home by 9.00.*
> *Has Ed **promised not to spend** any more money?*

Verb + *ing* form

Some verbs take this form. These are the most common.

> *admit, avoid, can't face, can't help, can't stand, carry on, consider, delay, deny, detest, dislike, enjoy, fancy, finish, give up, imagine, involve, keep, keep on, mention, mind, miss, postpone, practise, put off, quit, regret, risk, suggest*

> *Steve **avoided seeing** Bob for months.*
> *Have you **finished writing** that letter?*
> *I **enjoy not getting up** early at the weekend.*

هناك مجموعة من الأفعال تتخذ صيغة الفعل to + + المصدر، وهذه قائمة بأكثرها شيوعاً.

وهناك مجموعة أخرى تتخذ صيغة الفعل مضافاً له ing. وهذه قائمة بأكثرها شيوعاً.

Some verbs take either a *to* + infinitive or an *ing* form, eg *continue, love* and *start*. (See Unit 40.)

> *It **continued to rain** all day.   It **continued raining** all day.*
> *Tom always **loves to win**.   Tom always **loves winning**.*
> *She **started to run**.   She **started running**.*

Some verbs take an object + *to* + infinitive, eg *ask, persuade* and *remind*. (See Unit 41.)

> *The manager **asked us to wait**.*
> *Tom **persuaded me to go**.*
> *Could you **remind me to call** Mr Hill at 4.00?*

Some verbs take a preposition + *ing* form, eg *think of* and *blame ... for*. (See Unit 42.)

> *We're **thinking of buying** a new car.*
> *I can't **blame her for leaving** that boring job.*

تتخذ بعض الأفعال إما to + المصدر أو إضافة ing إلى المصدر مثل أفعال continue و love و start. (انظر unit 40).

تتخذ بعض الأفعال المفعول به + to + المصدر مثل أفعال ask و persuade و remind. (انظر unit 41).

تتخذ بعض الأفعال حرف جر + مصدر مضافاً له ing مثل think of و blame... for. (انظر unit 42).

Exercises

1 Write these verbs in the correct forms.

climb, finish, get, give, learn, move, play, see, win

Example: *I've managed <u>to finish</u> the report in time.*

1 *Tom agreed _____ for our team.*

2 *Sandra refused _____ her son any more money.*

3 *I can't wait _____ my cousins again. They've been away for a long time.*

4 *Bob promised _____ here on time. He's late.*

5 *She's hoping _____ the competition.*

6 *My parents have decided _____ to a house in the country.*

7 *We're preparing _____ the mountain.*

8 *I've chosen _____ German this term.*

2 Write these verbs in the correct forms.

buy, crash, eat, lose, say, smoke, wait, walk, watch

Example: *Drive slowly. We don't want to risk <u>crashing</u> Dad's new car.*

1 *I can't stand _____ that TV programme.*

2 *They can't deny _____ the money. It's gone.*

3 *We've delayed _____ a car. We're short of money.*

4 *I enjoy _____ breakfast in the garden.*

5 *Don keeps on _____ he's clever, but he seems stupid to me.*

6 *Do you mind _____ here? Mr Price will be here soon.*

7 *I've given up _____ . I feel fitter already.*

8 *We'll have to carry on _____ We can't stop here.*

3 Write the verbs in the correct forms.

Jean: *I hate all these bills – gas, electricity, phone, the garage.*

Joe: *I detest <u>dealing with</u> them too. (deal with) But we can't afford <u>to pay</u> them any longer. (pay)*

Jean: *We seem ¹_____ all our money as fast as it comes in. (spend)*

Joe: *That's right. The bills keep on ²_____ (arrive)*

Jean: *Do you think we can afford ³_____ a holiday this summer? (have)*

Joe: *Maybe. If we try hard, I think we'll manage ⁴_____ enough. (save)*

Jean: *We should give up ⁵_____ (smoke) That would save a lot of money.*

Joe: *You're right. Anyway, where do you fancy ⁶_____ (go)*

Jean: *I've always wanted ⁷_____ Italy. (see) Would you mind ⁸_____ that? (do)*

Joe: *No, that's a good idea. And I suggest ⁹_____ in June. (go) I can get some free time then.*

Jean: *Fine. Let's plan ¹⁰_____ then. (go) I can imagine ¹¹_____ around the streets of Venice and Rome already! (walk)*

4 Complete the statements with negative forms.

Examples: *Are you sorry that you didn't pass the exam?*
Do you regret <u>not passing the exam?</u>
Please don't break the contract.
Please agree <u>not to break the contract.</u>

1 *Jean looks as if she doesn't mind what he said.*
Jean seems _____
_____

2 *Please don't make so much noise.*
Would you mind _____
_____

3 *'It's true. I don't have the money to repay Sam,' Tom said.*
Tom admitted _____
_____

4 *'I'm not going to go out with the others,' Suzie said.*
Suzie decided _____
_____

5 *'I'm not going to talk to Bill any more,' Ann said angrily.*
Ann threatened _____
_____

40 Verb + *to* + infinitive or verb + *ing* form 2
I started to race.   I started racing.

When did you start racing, Tony?

FORMS

Verb + *to* + infinitive or verb + *ing* form (no change of meaning)

Reporter: *When did you start racing?*
Driver: *I first started to race when I was 17.*

Verb + *to* + infinitive or verb + *ing* form (change of meaning)

Tony went on racing European Formula One cars for years. Later, he went on to race in the USA.

Verb + *to* + infinitive or verb + *ing* form (no change of meaning)

Some verbs can take either form with no change of meaning, eg *begin, start, continue, intend, propose* and *bother*.

> *It **began raining** at 10.00.   It **began to rain** at 10.00.*
> *I **intend visiting** my mother this weekend.*
> *I **intend to visit** my mother this weekend.*
> *Only 20 people **bothered coming** to the garden party.*
> *Only 20 people **bothered to come** to the garden party.*

Do not put two *ing* forms together.

> *People **were starting to leave** when the sun suddenly came out.*
> (not *leaving*)

These verbs also take the *ing* or the *to* + infinitive form: *like, love, hate, prefer.*

> *Tony **loves driving** fast.   Tony **loves to drive** fast.*
> *I **prefer drinking** tea.   I **prefer to drink** tea.*

Note the difference between *like* + *ing* and *like* + *to* + infinitive.

> *He **likes driving** classic racing cars.* (He enjoys this.)
> *He **likes to check** the oil and tyres before he drives anywhere.* (He thinks this is the right thing to do.)

Note the differences between *hate/would hate, like/would like, love/would love* and *prefer/would prefer.*

> *I **love** my mother and father very much.*
> *I'm really thirsty. I**'d love** a cup of tea.*
> *I always **prefer driving to going** by bus.*
> *I**'d prefer to drive** there tonight. The bus might be late.*

Some verbs can take either verb + *ing* form or object + *to* + infinitive with no change of meaning, eg *advise, allow, encourage, permit* and *recommend.*

> *Bill **advised doing** some exercise.*
> *Bill **advised me to do** some exercise.*
> *I **don't allow smoking** in my house.*
> *I **don't allow people to smoke** in my house.*

تأتي بعض الأفعال بأي من الصيغتين دون أن يتغير المعنى ... مثلا begin و start، الخ.

لا يمكن استخدام صيغتين من صيغ ing معاً.

تتخذ الأفعال المذكورة صيغة المصدر مضافاً له ing أو صيغة to + المصدر.

تجدر ملاحظة الفرق بين استخدام like + فعل مضاف له ing وبين استخدام صيغة like + to + المصدر.

تجدر ملاحظة الفروق في المعنى عند استخدام أفعال hate و love و prefer بمفردها وعند استخدامها مع would.

تأتي بعض الأفعال إما مع فعل مضاف له ing أو مع مفعول به + to + مصدر دون تغيير في المعنى .. ومنها الأفعال المذكورة.

Verb + *to* + infinitive or verb + *ing* form (change of meaning)

Some verbs can take either verb + *to* + infinitive or verb + *ing* form, but with a change of meaning.

تأتي بعض الأفعال إما مع فعل + *to* + مصدر أو مع فعل مضاف له *ing* ولكن بمعنى مختلف في كل صيغة.

CROSSCHECK

Verb + *to* + infinitive

remember/forget + *to* + infinitive (for necessary actions)

> Please **remember to buy** a newspaper.
> Please **don't forget to buy** some milk.

stop + *to* + infinitive (stop one thing and do something else for a short time)

> On our way home we **stopped to buy** some stamps.

try + *to* + infinitive (make a strong effort, do your best)

> We **tried to mend** the engine all night, but we failed.

mean + *to* + infinitive (1 plan to do something, 2 be required to do something)

1) I **meant to call** you, but I was busy.
1) I'm very sorry! I **didn't mean to hit** you.
2) You're **meant to sign** the papers here. Then they'll give you your money.

regret + *to* + infinitive (for showing you are sorry about what you are saying)

> We **regret to tell** you that Mr Briggs has died.

need + *to* + infinitive (has to do)

> Harry **needs to fly** to Cairo tonight as he has a meeting there tomorrow.

go on + *to* + infinitive (do something new after finishing another thing)

> She **went on to become** a famous artist.

Verb + *ing* form

remember/forget + verb *ing* (for memories of the past)

> I **remember climbing** that mountain in 1985.
> I'll never **forget reaching** the top. It was great!

stop + verb *ing* (end an action)

> Let's **stop fighting** and start talking.

try + verb *ing* (do something in a new way)

> I don't like the table here. Let's **try putting** it over there.

mean + verb + *ing* (one thing makes another thing necessary)

> I want to go to college, but that **means working** really hard.
> The bus has broken down. That **means waiting** for an hour for the next one.

regret + verb *ing* (for showing you are sorry about doing something)

> I **regretted leaving** my money at home. I needed it in town.

need + verb *ing* (for something that is necessary)

> Look at that dirty floor. It really **needs cleaning**.

go on + verb *ing* (continue doing)

> Sally **went on working** hard, even after her terrible accident.

يعني استخدام *remember* و *forget* + *to* + المصدر ضرورة القيام بشيء ما.

واستخدام الفعلين مع فعل آخر مضاف له *ing* بما يفيد استحضار الذكريات.

يعني استخدام صيغة فعل *stop* + *to* + مصدر التوقف عن القيام بعمل ما لبرهة قصيرة من أجل القيام بعمل آخر.

ويعني استخدام الفعل *stop* + فعل مضاف له *ing* بما يفيد التوقف عن القيام بعمل ما نهائياً.

يعني استخدام فعل *try* + *to* + المصدر القيام بجهد كبير

ويعني استخدام فعل *try* + الفعل مضافاً له *ing* القيام بعمل ما بطريقة جديدة.

يعني استخدام فعل *mean* + *to* + المصدر (١) التخطيط للقيام بعمل ما (٢) وجوب القيام بعمل ما.

أما استخدام فعل *mean* + فعل مضاف له *ing* فيعني ان أمراً ما يجعل أمراً آخر ضرورياً.

يبين استخدام فعل *regret* + *to* + مصدر الأسف على ما سيقال.

ويبين استخدام فعل *regret* + فعل مضاف له *ing* أسف المتحدث على ما بدر منه.

يبين استخدام فعل *need* + *to* + المصدر معنى الإلزام ووجوب القيام بالفعل.

ويبين استخدام فعل *need* + فعل مضاف له *ing* أن القيام بعمل ما أمر ضروري.

تستخدم صيغة *go on* + *to* + المصدر لتفيد القيام بعمل جديد يتلو أمراً آخر جرى الانتهاء منه.

ويفيد استخدام *go on* + فعل مضاف له *ing* استمرار القيام بعمل ما.

Exercises

1 Write these verbs in the correct forms.

ask, be, come, form, provide, take

Someone is making a speech.

Ladies and gentlemen,

Thank you for bothering to come to this meeting on a cold, wet December evening. I know most of us would prefer 1_____ at home. I don't intend 2_____ much of your time, but I have an important proposal to make. I'm proposing 3_____ a group of us to collect money for our local hospital. For many years, the hospital has continued 4_____ us all with a great service. Recently, though, the hospital has not been getting enough money for things such as children's toys. That's why the staff have started 5_____ for help from us, the local community.

2 Write the verbs in the correct forms.

Example: *Ed loves going on holiday. (go)*
Ed would love to go away this year. (go)

1 *Alan hates _____ early in the morning.*
(get up)

2 *Would you like _____ out to the cinema this evening? (go)*

3 *I like _____ that all the windows and doors are shut at night. (check)*

4 *We always prefer _____ in the sea to _____ in a pool. (swim)*

5 *Ben doesn't like _____ very much. (read)*

6 *Which would you prefer _____ tomorrow – stay at home or go out? (do)*

7 *I'd love _____ London and see Buckingham Palace. (visit)*

8 *When Emma was small, she loved _____ with her doll's house. (play)*

9 *Ann always likes _____ exactly where her children are. (know)*

10 *I'd hate _____ alone. (live)*

3 Write the verbs in the correct forms.

Tina: *Did you remember to post the letters and buy the new TV licence? (post)*

Bob: *Well, I remembered 1_____ the letters. (post) But I didn't get the licence.*

Tina: *Oh, no. You really forgot 2_____ the licence? (buy) I clearly remember 3_____ you to do that when you went out this morning. (ask)*

Bob: *Well, I don't remember 4_____ you. (hear) Perhaps I was too far away.*

Tina: *That's wrong. I remember you 5_____ , 'I'll get it on the way home.' (say)*

Bob: *Don't be silly. People don't forget 6_____ things like that. (say)*

Tina: *Well, you did. Anyway, please don't forget 7_____ it tomorrow. (get)*

Bob: *All right. I'll remember 8_____ that. (do) I promise.*

4 Write the verbs in the correct forms.

1 At a cleaners
Customer: *Can you try to clean this jacket for me, please? (clean) I've tried _____ these marks out, but I can't. (get)*

Assistant: *Have you tried _____ Vanish? (use) It's very good.*

2 At a hotel
Clerk: *Excuse me, Sir. Could you complete this form, please? It just means _____ your home address and _____ at the bottom. (write) (sign)*

Guest: *Oh, yes, of course. I meant _____ it when I arrived, but I had to make a quick phone call. (do)*

3 In an office
Manager: *This report needs _____ (correct)*

Secretary: *When would you like me to do it?*

Manager: *Oh, you don't need _____ it now. (do) Tomorrow is all right.*

5 Join each pair of statements to make one statement.

Example: *Bob didn't get the licence. He forgot.*
Bob forgot <u>to get the licence.</u>

1 *Ian said some terrible things to Emma. He didn't mean it.*
Ian didn't _____
_____
_____

2 *I thought I could develop a new kind of engine. I tried for years.*
For years I tried _____
_____
_____

3 *They say I had fights with other children. I don't remember them.*
I don't _____
_____
_____

4 *They shouldn't make so much noise late at night. They should stop.*
They should _____
_____
_____

5 *I hate telling you this, but your son has done badly in his exams. I regret that.*
I regret _____
_____
_____

6 *What about buying some things for dinner? Let's stop at this supermaerket.*
Let's _____
_____
_____

7 *Throw your work away and start again. That's what this mistake means.*
This mistake means _____
_____

8 *I'm sorry. I didn't telephone you this morning. I meant to.*
I'm sorry. I meant _____
_____
_____

9 *We should paint the dining-room. It really needs it.*
The dining-room really _____
_____

6 Write the verbs in the correct forms.

Alan Jones is talking to a careers adviser about starting a new career.

Adviser: *We need* <u>to work out</u> *a plan for your future. (work out) What have you done up to now?*

Alan: *Well, I tried* <u>working</u> *in a shop. (work) I also tried* [1]_____ *as an office worker. (train) But I've stopped now. I need* [2]_____ *something more interesting. (find)*

Adviser: *How long did you go on* [3]_____ *those jobs? (do)*

Alan: *For two years. Now what I need* [4]_____ *is to change completely. (do) I want to become a doctor.*

Adviser: *That's a very big change. It needs* [5]_____ *about. (think) First of all, it means* [6]_____ *a lot of exams. (pass) It's a pity you left school early. You must really regret* [7]_____ *without doing your final school examinations. (leave)*

Alan: *Yes, I do. I meant* [8]_____ *them. (take) But my dad suddenly got very ill, I regret* [9]_____ *(say) And I had to leave school and get a job to help support the family. Anyway, now I'm studying hard and I'm trying* [10]_____ *(catch up) If I do well enough in my exams next summer, I'll go on* [11]_____ *at medical college after that. (study)*

Adviser: *Well, I certainly hope you succeed.*

95

41 Verb + object + *to* + infinitive

Dad has invited us to stay.   He wants us to go.

Hi, Bob. Listen, Dad has invited us to stay with him.

Verb + object + *to* + infinitive

Some verbs take an object + *to* + infinitive, eg *cause, enable, force, get* (persuade), *instruct, invite, let, make, order, permit, persuade, remind, teach, tell* and *warn*.

> The officer **ordered his men to start**.
> I **told the children not to play** with matches.

After *let* and *make* use an infinitive without *to*.

> We **let students go** home at 4.00.   The boss **made us work** late.

Verb (+ object) + *to* + infinitive

Some verbs work with, and also without, an object, eg *ask, beg, expect, help, intend, mean* (intend), *want, (would) hate, (would) like, (would) love* and *(would) prefer*.

> She **asked to meet** the President.
> She **asked us to meet** the President.
> Steve **expects to pass** his driving test.
> Ann **expects everybody else to do** the work for her.

After *help* use either a *to* + infinitive or an infinitive without *to*.

> I **helped** (them) **to make** dinner.   I **helped** (them) **make** dinner.

The verbs *hate, like, love* and *prefer* can take all these forms.

> I **hate going**.   I **hate you going**.
> I **hate to go**.   I **hate you to go**.

Note the difference in meaning between forms of *like*.

> He **likes us visiting** him. (He enjoys this.)
> He **likes to call** him first. (He feels this is the right thing to do.)

These verbs can take an object + *to* + infinitive or the *ing* form: *advise, allow, encourage, permit, recommend*.

> We **don't allow people to smoke**.   We **don't allow smoking**.

After *suggest* do not use an infinitive or an object + infinitive. Use one of these forms.

> I **suggest going** to the park.   I **suggest (that) we go** to the park.

After *offer* and *promise* do not use an object + infinitive. Use one of these forms.

> I **promised Tim** a new book. (verb + object only)
> I **promised to buy Tim** a new book. (verb + *to* + infinitive only)
> I **promised (that) I would buy Tim** a book. (verb (+ *that*) + will/would)

تتطلب بعض الأفعال وجود مفعول به + to + مصدر، ومنها الأفعال المذكورة.

يستخدم مصدر الفعل بدون to بعد فعلي let وmake.

قد يأتي مفعول به مع بعض الأفعال وقد لا يأتي... ومثال ذلك الأفعال المبينة.

بعد فعل help يمكن استخدام to + المصدر كما يمكن استخدام المصدر بدون to أيضاً.

ويمكن أن تأتي الأفعال hate وlike وlove و prefer بأي من الصيغ المبينة.

وتجدر ملاحظة الفرق في المعنى بين صيغتي فعل like كما هو موضح في المثالين.

يمكن للأفعال التالية أن تتعدى إلى مفعول به + to + مصدر أو فعل مضاف له ing.

لا يجدر استخدام مصدر بعد فعل suggest ولا مفعول به + مصدر بل تستخدم أي من الصيغتين المبينتين.

ولا يجدر استخدام مفعول به + مصدر بعد فعلي offer و promise، بل يجب استخدام أي من الصيغ التالية المبينة.

Exercises

1 Complete the statements.

Example: 'Be careful, Steve!' John said.
John warned _Steve to be careful._

1 'Be quiet, Alan,' the teacher said.
The teacher told _____

2 The weather was bad and Ann said, 'Rob, don't drive so fast.'
Ann warned _____
_____

3 'Don't take photos,' the soldier said to me.
The soldier ordered _____
_____

4 Lucy always says to her son, 'Take your medicine after lunch.'
Lucy always reminds _____
_____

5 Nick said, 'Try this cake, everybody.'
Nick invited _____
_____

6 'Stop!' the policeman said to the man.
The policeman instructed _____

2 Join each pair of statements to make one statement.

Example: I went out last night. Bill persuaded me.
Bill persuaded _me to go out last night._

1 Tina didn't buy the dress. Suzie persuaded her.
Suzie persuaded _____
_____

2 The climbers turned back. The bad weather forced them.
The bad weather forced _____
_____

3 Our boat rolled over. A wave caused it.
A wave caused _____
_____

Be careful these are different!

4 You can buy now and pay later. This credit card lets you.
This credit card lets _____
_____

5 The boys ran five kilometres. The new trainer made them.
The new trainer made _____
_____

6 We didn't go out. Dad didn't let us.
Dad didn't let _____

3 Complete the statements.

Example: 'Can I listen, please?' Julie said.
Julie wanted _to listen._
'Listen, everybody,' Julie said.
Julie wanted _everybody to listen._

1 It would be great to buy that car.
I'd love _____

2 I'll be very angry if Tom gets the job.
I would hate _____

3 'Could you leave your cases there, Mrs Jones?' he said.
He asked _____
_____

4 Tony said, 'Can I see the contract, please?'
Tony asked _____

5 Our friends cut down a tree. We helped.
We helped _____
_____

6 You saw your present. We didn't want that yet.
We didn't mean _____
_____

4 Write the verbs in the correct forms.

Examples: I suggest _going_ home. (go)
I suggest we _go_ home. (go)

1 He doesn't allow people _____ in the river. (swim)

2 Our dentist likes everybody _____ a check-up every six months. (have)

3 The taxi driver offered _____ Lucy with her luggage. (help)

4 The doctor advised Bob _____ more exercise. (get)

5 I don't recommend you _____ that car. (buy)

6 I suggest you _____ to your teacher about the problem. (talk)

42 Verb/adjective + preposition + *ing* form
I dream of winning.   I'm bored with television.

FORMS

Verb/adjective + preposition (+ *ing* form)
Rick was thinking about the race.
He was bored with television.

Verb + preposition + *ing* form
He was dreaming of winning the race.

Verb + object + preposition + *ing* form
His boss accused him of wasting company time.

Adjective + preposition + *ing* form
Rick isn't very keen on working hard, but he's very enthusiastic about windsurfing.

Verb/adjective + preposition (+ *ing* form)

Some verbs and adjectives can take a preposition. If there is a verb after the preposition, it takes an *ing* form.

> *I'm thinking about the race.*
> *I'm bored with television.*
> *I don't feel like doing any more.*
> *I'm tired of working all the time.*

يمكن أن تأتي أدوات الجر مع بعض الأفعال والصفات. وإذا جاء فعل بعد أداة الجر يضاف له ing

Verb + preposition + *ing* form

Some verbs can take this form. These are the most common: *apologize for, approve/disapprove of, believe in, decide against, dream of, feel like, insist on, object to, rely on, think of, succeed in.*

> *I apologized for arriving late.   They don't approve of smoking.*
> *I decided against buying the car.   We can't rely on winning.*

We can also use *about + ing* with these verbs: *ask, complain, dream, speak, talk, think, wonder.*

> *I thought about going.   We talked about buying a car.*

Be careful about the different meanings of *think about* and *think of*.

> *I'm thinking about the problem.* (ideas going through your mind)
> *I'm thinking of going to Spain, but I'm not sure yet.* (ideas going through your mind about a future action)

تأتي بعض الأفعال مع أداة جر + فعل مضاف له ing . وهذه قائمة بأكثر هذه الأفعال شيوعاً.

يمكن استخدام about + فعل مضاف له ing مع الأفعال المذكورة.

وتجدر ملاحظة الفرق في المعنى بين think about وبين think of.

Verb + object + preposition + *ing* form

Some verbs can take this form. These are the most common: *accuse ... of, blame ... for, congratulate ... on, discourage ... from, forgive ... for, prevent ... from, stop ... from, punish ... for, suspect ... of, thank ... for, warn ... against.*

> *I blame Tom for causing the crash.   I thanked her for coming.*

يمكن أن تتخذ بعض الأفعال صيغة الفعل + مفعول به + أداة جر + فعل مضاف له ing.

وهذه قائمة بأكثر هذه الأفعال شيوعاً.

Adjective + preposition + *ing* form

Some adjectives can take this form. These are the most common: *annoyed at, bored with, capable of, enthusiastic about, excited about, fed up with, fond of, good/bad at, grateful for, guilty of, interested in, keen on, pleased about, tired of.*

> *Rick was annoyed at losing.   I'm good at dancing.*

يمكن أن تتخذ بعض الصفات صيغة الصفة + أداة جر + فعل مضاف له ing .. وهذه قائمة بأكثرها شيوعاً.

Exercises

1 Write the verbs in the correct forms and use these prepositions.

about, for, in, like, of, on, to

Example: *Tom tried nine times, but he never succeeded*
<u>*in winning.*</u> *(win)*

1 *Mike apologized _____ the vase.*
(break)

2 *He insisted _____ for a new one.*
(pay)

3 *We often wonder _____ house.*
(move) Is it a good idea?

4 *I object _____ out in this terrible*
weather. (go)

5 *What do you feel _____ today? (do)*

6 *We're thinking _____ a sports club*
next year. (join)

2 Join each pair of statements to make one statement.

Example: *She got the job. Her brother congratulated her.*
<u>*Her brother congratulated her on*</u>
<u>*getting the job.*</u>

1 *I'm going to win. You can't prevent me.*

_____

_____

2 *Ben broke the window. His father punished him.*

_____

_____

3 *Don't go sailing in this wind. I must warn you.*

_____

_____

4 *She hit my child. I can't forgive her.*

_____

_____

5 *He's left that terrible job. You can't blame him.*

_____

_____

6 *The dogs are fighting. We can't stop them.*

_____

_____

3 Write the adjectives and verbs in the correct forms.

Example: *The ship was* <u>*capable of crossing*</u> *the*
Atlantic in three days. (capable/cross)

1 *She's very kind. She isn't _____*
anybody. (capable/hurt)

2 *Are you _____ on*
holiday? (excited/go) It's very soon.

3 *I'm very _____ this village.*
(fond/visit) I love the old place.

4 *Which are you _____*
next year – Art or Music? (interested/study)

5 *Is Sam _____*
his exams? (pleased/pass) He got very good marks.

6 *We're _____*
the same music all the time. (fed up/hear)

7 *Tom is _____ (bad/cook) He*
always burns things.

4 Write the verbs in the correct forms.

Mary: *Do you remember the other night? We*
<u>*talked about going*</u> *away for a week. (talk/go)*
And we 1*_____*
_____ to Scotland for a week. (think/go)

Bill: *Yes, but we* 2*_____*
_____ that in the end. (decide/do) You
3*_____*
_____ Scotland as it's cold at this time
of year. (discourage/us/choose)

Mary: *That's right, but I mentioned the idea when I*
called Sheena in Edinburgh this evening. She's
4*_____ us*
again. (enthusiastic/see) She says we must come,
and she's really 5*_____*
_____ us Edinburgh.
(look forward/show)

Bill: *That's really nice of her. I must say I'm*
6*_____ all the*
time. Let's go. (tired/work)

Mary: *OK, I'll phone her and* 7*_____*
_____ us. (thank/her/ask) She'll
be very pleased.

43 Conditional forms: type 0 and type 1

If the wind is strong, the waves are dangerous.

FORMS

Type 0 conditionals

***If* + present simple,   present simple**

If the wind is strong,   the waves are dangerous.
OR *The waves are dangerous if the wind is strong.*

Type 1 conditionals

If* + present simple,   future with *will

If it's sunny tomorrow,   we'll go to the beach.
OR *We'll go to the beach if it's sunny tomorrow.*

Put a comma after the *If* part when it comes first.
If the wind is strong, the waves are dangerous.

Do not use a comma when the *If* part comes second.
We'll stay at home if it rains.

Type 0 conditionals

These express things which always happen. If one thing happens, then another thing always happens. This is similar to *When* + present simple, present simple.

> *If the wind **is** strong, the waves **are** dangerous.*
> *If you **shout** at her, she always **cries.***
> ***When** the wind **is** strong, the waves **are** dangerous.*
> ***When** you **shout**, she always **cries.***

We can also use *If* with instructions.

> *If Ann **phones**, please **take** a message.*
> *If your son still **feels** ill tomorrow, **call** me again.*

Type 1 conditionals

We also use *If* sentences to talk about a probable future action or condition. Both parts of the sentence are about the future, but the *If* part is in the present simple, not the future.

> *If it's sunny tomorrow, we'll **go** to the beach.*
> *If we **hurry**, we'll **catch** the bus.   If we **don't hurry**, we'll **miss** it.*

The *If* part of the sentence is about something which may or may not happen. The result – the other part of the sentence – follows from the *If* part.

If part	The result
If it's sunny, ...	*... we'll go to the beach.*
If it rains, ...	*... we'll stay at home.*
If we hurry, ...	*... we'll catch the bus.*
If we don't hurry, ...	*... we'll miss the bus.*

unless means *if not*.

> *I'll fail the test **unless I learn** these words. (if I don't learn)*

as long as and *provided (that)* mean *If* with a special emphasis.

> *You can borrow the car **as long as/provided (that) you bring** it back this evening. (if, and only if, you bring it back)*

يستخدم هذا النوع من الجمل الشرطية للتعبير عن الأحداث التي تقع بشكل دائم... فإذا حدث أمرٌ ما، يحدث امر آخر دائماً.

و هذا يشبه الصيغة التي تستخدم when + المضارع البسيط في الشطر الأول والمضارع البسيط في الشطر الثاني.

ويمكن استخدام if الشرطية لإعطاء التعليمات.

تستخدم جمل if الشرطية للتعبير عن احتمال حدوث فعل أو شرط مستقبلي. ويتعلق جزءا الجملة بالمستقبل رغم ان الجزء الشرطي الذي يحوي أداة الشرط if يكون في المضارع وليس في المستقبل.

يتعلق الجزء الشرطي الذي يحوي أداة الشرط if في الجملة بحدث يمكن أن يقع أو لا يقع. ويحدد الجزء الشرطي جواب الشرط في الجزء الآخر من الجملة والذي يأتي كنتيجة للجزء الشرطي.

كلمة unless تعني if not.

تعمل عبارة as long as وعبارة provided (that) عمل if الشرطية ولكن بما يفيد مزيداً من التأكيد.

Exercises

1 Complete the Type 0 conditionals. Use these endings.

it becomes ice.   it soon goes bad.
the machinery soon breaks down.   the oil light comes on.
the lights come on.   you get orange.

Example: *If you mix red and yellow, you get*
  orange.

1 *If the car needs oil, _____*

2 *If you cool water to 0°C, _____*

3 *If you don't keep food cool, _____*

4 *If you press this switch, _____*

5 *If the engineers don't check every month, _____*
  _____

2 Choose the correct form of the verbs.

Example: *If Ann doesn't call me, I'll call her.*
  (doesn't call/won't call)

1 *If the money _____ I'll put it in the bank.*
  (arrives/will arrive)

2 *Peter _____ us if he hears any news.*
  (tells/will tell)

3 *If you don't finish your homework, I _____*
  you watch TV. (don't let/won't let)

4 *You won't know what it tastes like if you*
  _____ it. (don't try/won't try)

5 *If the neighbours don't stop that noise, I*
  _____ the police. (call/'ll call)

6 *I'm sure Tom _____ you some money if you*
  ask him. (lends/will lend)

7 *If you shout like that again, Helen _____*
  to you. (doesn't listen/won't listen)

8 *If the climbers _____ down before the storm,*
  they'll be in great danger. (don't come/won't come)

3 Join each pair of statements to make one statement.

Example: *Tom may call. If so, I'll talk to him.*
  If Tom calls, I'll talk to him.

1 *The police may come. If so, they'll ask about Tom.*
  _____
  _____

2 *Enter the race. You'll probably win.*
  _____
  _____

3 *The party may go on till late. If so, we'll go home early.*
  _____
  _____

4 *Call the office at 2.00. Tony will be there.*
  _____
  _____

5 *Ann may not call. I'll be worried.*
  _____
  _____

6 *Finish the job today. Then you won't have to come*
  tomorrow.
  _____
  _____

4 Write the verbs in the correct forms.

Bob is reading the college newspaper.

Bob: *Look. Here's an advert for a water-ski weekend. If*
  we have a group of ten, we 'll get a special
  price. (have) (get)

Steve: *It sounds good. But I [1]_____ to go*
  if it [2]_____ in May. (not/be able) (be)

Bob: *No, the offer starts in June. We can go just after*
  the exams.

Steve: *Yes, if we [3]_____ to go then, everybody*
  [4]_____ (decide) (come) Let's ask
  some people. Ask Alan.

Bob: *Alan, [5]_____ us if we*
  [6]_____ a water-ski weekend in June?
  (you/join) (organize)

Steve: *If we [7]_____ just after the exams, we*
  [8]_____ a great time. (go) (have)

Alan: *OK, I [9]_____ if it [10]_____ too*
  expensive. (come) (be/not)

Steve: *There's a special group rate.*

Bob: *If we [11]_____ another seven people, it*
  [12]_____ just £30 each. (find) (cost)

Steve: *We'd better hurry. If we [13]_____ fast,*
  somebody else [14]_____ the offer and
  we [15]_____ the chance. (not/act) (take)
  (miss)

44 Conditional forms: type 2

If someone found him, he would have a huge meal.

What would you do if someone found us?

First, I'd have a huge meal.

FORMS

Type 2 conditionals

If + past simple,   *would + verb*

If someone found him,   *he would have a huge meal.*
OR *He would have a huge meal if someone found him.*

Put a comma after the *If* part when it comes first. Do not use a comma when the *If* part comes second.

In conversation we often use *'d* for *would* and *wouldn't* for *would not*, eg *I'd buy ... , He wouldn't buy ...*

Type 2 conditionals express future conditions which are not probable and present conditions which are not true.

> **If** *he* **won** *the prize, he'**d buy** some new clothes.* (But he probably won't win.)
> **If** *they* **had** *some money, they'**d stay** at a hotel.* (But they don't have any money.)

We use the past simple in the *If* part of the sentence. In the other part we usually use *would* (from *will*) + verb.

> **If** *he* **won** *£10,000, he* **would visit** *Rome.* (sure)

We also use *could* (from *can*) and *might* (from *may*).

> *... he* **could visit** *Rome.* (able to)   *... he* **might visit** *Rome.* (unsure)

We can make statements with *would*, *could* and *might*, but without the *If* part. The words *would*, *could* and *might* show that the statement is about something unlikely or impossible.

> ● *Let's invite Bill and Luke.*
> ○ *No, they hate each other. They'**d fight**.* (... if we invited them.)
> ● *I dream of going to Paris.*
> ○ *We* **could have** *a wonderful time there.* (... but it's only a dream.)
> ● *It's a pity Sally and Helen hardly ever meet.*
> ○ *Yes, they* **might become** *friends.* (... but they don't meet.)

We often give advice with Type 2 conditionals, and we can use these special expressions. Note the special form of *be* in Type 2 conditionals.

> **If I were you, I'd get** *a new job.*
> **If I were in your position, I'd tell** *the police what happened.*

wish and *If only*

We use the forms *wish + would/could* and *If only + would/could* to show that we want a change in the future (but we do not really expect the change to happen).

> *I* **wish** *that boy* **would do** *his work properly!*
> *I* **wish** *I* **could take** *a holiday, but I'm very busy.*
> **If only** *he'**d answer** the phone, but it just keeps ringing!*
> **If only** *the neighbours* **wouldn't make** *so much noise!*

We use the forms *wish + past* and *if only + past* to show that we want a change in the present (but we know it is impossible).

> *I* **wish** *things* **didn't cost** *so much.*
> **If only** *that man* **did** *his work properly, we* **wouldn't have to do** *the work all over again now.*

يعبر النوع الثاني من الجمل الشرطية عن شروط مستقبلية غير مرجحة وشروط حاضرة غير صحيحة.

يستخدم الماضي البسيط في الجزء الشرطي من الجملة، ويستخدم عادة would + فعل في الجزء الآخر.

وتستخدم ايضاً صيغة الماضي من can وهي could ، والماضي من may وهي might.

تستخدم الكلمات would و could و might في جمل خبرية بدون الجزء الشرطي الذي يضم if. وهذا يعني أن الجمل الخبرية تفيد أن وقوع الحدث أمر متوقع أو أنه مستحيل.

غالباً ما يستخدم النوع الثاني من الجمل الشرطية لإبداء النصح وذلك باستخدام الصيغ المبينة في الأمثلة، ويجدر ملاحظة الصيغة الخاصة من فعل be المستخدمة في هذا النوع.

تستخدم صيغة wish +would أو could وكذلك صيغة if only + would أو could للتعبير عن تمني حدوث تغيير مستقبلي ولكنه تغيير غير متوقع الحدوث.

تستخدم صيغتا wish + ماضٍ و if only + ماضٍ للتعبير عن التمني بأن يكون الحاضر مختلفاً مع العلم مسبقاً باستحالة ذلك.

Exercises

1 Write the verbs in the correct forms.

Examples: *If I* <u>had</u> *enough money, I'd buy that car.*
(have)
You <u>'d have</u> *enough money if you got a better job. (have)*

1 *If we _____ a bigger house, we could invite people to stay. (have)*

2 *I _____ out of business if we cut our prices. (go)*

3 *If I _____ my job, I wouldn't know what to do. (lose)*

4 *If we _____ the plan exactly, we'd never finish the job. (follow)*

5 *I think she _____ angry if I didn't invite her this evening. (be)*

6 *You _____ me if I told you the whole story. (not/believe)*

7 *If we decided to go to London, we _____ with my brother. (stay)*

8 *He's so good that I'd be very surprised if he _____ _____ into the team. (not/get)*

2 Write Type 2 conditionals.

Examples: *(we/be/surprised/Ann/come)*
<u>We'd be surprised if Ann came.</u>
(Tom/have/time/he/be/here)
<u>If Tom had time, he'd be here.</u>

1 *(Ann/be/pleased/Tom/call)*
_____
_____

2 *(you/not/visit/us again/we/be/very sad)*
_____
_____

3 *(I/get/fit quite fast/I/work out/at the gym)*
_____
_____

4 *(Barry/not/argue/so much/he/have/more friends)*
_____
_____

5 *(the team/win/more games/they train/harder)*
_____
_____

3 Write the verbs in the correct forms to complete the answers without *if*.

Example: ● *It'd be great if we had a million pounds.*
○ *Yes, we* <u>could do</u> *anything. (can/do)*

1 ● *Let's give Larry some money.*
○ *No, he _____ it all. (waste)*

2 ● *If you could change jobs, what would you do?*
○ *I _____ a film star. (become)*

3 ● *I don't want to go out tonight.*
○ *Why not? You _____ _____ yourself. (enjoy)*

4 ● *If I could, I'd love to travel through time.*
○ *But you _____ your friends and family again. (may/never/see)*

4 Write questions and answer them without *if*.

Example: *You might lose your money. (What/you/do) (go/to the police)*
● <u>What would you do if you lost your money?</u>
○ <u>I'd go to the police.</u>

1 *They might visit Turkey. (Where/they/stay) (stay/in cheap hotels)*
● _____
_____
○ _____

2 *We could complain at the Head Office. (Who/we/see) (talk/to the Sales Manager)*
● _____
_____
○ _____

3 *I might visit Scotland. (How/you/travel) (go/by car)*
● _____
_____
○ _____

4 *They could leave school now. (What/they/do) (get/jobs)*
● _____
_____
○ _____

45 Conditional forms: type 3

If he'd bought a present, she'd have been happy.

Yesterday was Mr and Mrs Carter's wedding anniversary. She remembered it, but he didn't. If he'd bought a present, she'd have been happy!

Type 3 conditionals express something past which was not true.

> *If he'd got a present, she'd have been happy.*
> (… but he didn't!)   (… and she was angry!)

Form Type 3 conditionals like this.

> *If he hadn't forgotten the present, she wouldn't have been angry.*
> (… but he did!)   (… and she was angry!)

In the *If* part of the sentence we use the past perfect. In the other part we usually use *would have* + past participle.

> *If he'd remembered to buy a present, …*
> *… she'd have been very pleased.* (sure)

But we also use *could have* and *might have*.

> *… he could have got it on the way home.* (possible)
> *… he might have decided to get some flowers.* (unsure)

We can make statements with *would have*, *could have* and *might have*, but without the *If* part. The words *would have*, *could have* and *might have* show that the statement is about something past and impossible.

> *I'm sorry that you didn't visit Harry. He'd have loved to see you.*
> (… if you'd visited him.)
> *I wanted to go to New York. We could have seen Manhattan.*
> (… if we'd gone to New York.)
> *He was stupid not to work. He might have passed his exams.*
> (… if he'd worked harder.)

wish and *If only*

We use the forms *wish* + past perfect and *If only* + past perfect to show that we would have liked a change in the past (but we know that it did not happen).

> *Most people wish they'd done a few things differently when they were younger.*
> *I wish I hadn't wasted so much time yesterday.*
> *If only they'd called the doctor immediately, they could have saved his life.*
> *If only we hadn't spent our money, we could have gone out last night.*

يستخدم النوع الثالث من الجمل الشرطية للتعبير عن أمرٍ ما في الماضي لم يكن حقيقياً.

تتشكل حالة النفي للنوع الثالث من الجمل الشرطية هكذا:

يستخدم زمن الماضي التام في الجزء الشرطي من الجملة في حين يكون جواب الشرط عادة مكوناً من would + have التصريف الثالث.

ولكن يمكن استخدام صيغتي could have و might have أيضاً.

ويمكن استخدام جمل خبرية مع would have و could have و might have دونما حاجة إلى استخدام الجزء الشرطي الذي يحتوي على if. وتبين تلك الصيغ أن الموضوع يتعلق بحدثٍ ماضٍ ومستحيل.

تستخدم صيغتا wish + ماضٍ تام و if only + ماضٍ تام لتبيان التمني لو أن تغييراً حدث في الماضي مع العلم بأن ذلك لم يحدث.

Exercises

1 Write the verbs in the correct forms.

Examples: If I _'d driven_ faster, I'd have arrived in time. (drive)

We _wouldn't have gone_ to the show if Alan hadn't recommended it. (not/go)

1 If you'd seen the film, you _____ it. (love)

2 If she _____ earlier, she'd have seen Pat. (go)

3 We wouldn't have noticed the house if you _____ it to us. (not/show)

4 If the weather _____ better yesterday, we'd have gone out. (be)

5 If she _____ some money, she _____ _____ enough for those shoes. (save) (have)

6 We _____ for help that night if we _____ desperate. (not/ask) (not/be)

2 Write Type 3 conditionals.

Examples: (you/come/to the party/you/enjoy/it)

If you'd come to the party, you'd have enjoyed it.

(we/be/very sad/John/not/marry/Suzie)

We'd have been very sad if John hadn't married Suzie.

1 (Jim/ask/us/we/lend/him our car)

_____

2 (I/not/write down/her phone number/I/forget)

_____

_____

3 (the car/not/crash/Tom/keep/to the speed limit)

_____

_____

4 (I/forget/to buy/Ann's present/you/not/remind/me)

_____

_____

3 Write Type 3 conditionals.

Example: The plane didn't crash because the pilot landed on a road.

If the pilot hadn't landed on the road, the plane would have crashed.

1 We didn't find the house as we didn't have a map.

_____

_____

2 The bus arrived late, so we didn't miss it.

_____

_____

3 They found the books when they opened the last box.

_____

_____

4 The tree didn't fall on the car, so the driver wasn't hurt.

_____

_____

_____

5 I got lost on the mountain because I didn't turn back.

_____

_____

4 Write answers without *if*.

Example: ● I wanted to go to New York. (we/can/see/the Manhattan skyline)

○ Yes, _we could have seen the Manhattan skyline._

1 ● It's a pity Tom's car broke down. (he/might/win/the race)

○ Yes, _____

_____

2 ● Why didn't she call the police? (they/can/catch/the thieves)

○ Yes, _____

_____

3 ● I should have taken the other road. (we/get/home an hour ago)

○ Yes, _____

_____

46 Reported speech 1: statements
He said (that) he was late.

FORMS

He said, 'I'm late.' → *He said (that) he was late.*

He said, 'I'll call you from New York.' → *He said (that) he would call us from New York.*

'I'm in New York now.' → *He says (that) he's in New York now.*

'I'm eating dinner here at my hotel.' → *He says (that) he's eating dinner there at his hotel.*

You can report a person's exact words in quotation marks (' ... '). This is common in stories.

> *He said, '**I'm late.**' '**What time is it?**' he asked.*

In conversation we usually express the speaker's idea in reported speech after a reporting verb such as *say, tell, shout* and *whisper*.

> *He **said** (that) he was late. He **told** us (that) he would call us.*
> *He **shouted** (that) ... She **whispered** (that) ...*

The reporting verb *say* is usually in the past. But it is sometimes in the present, eg when we report a telephone conversation as we listen.

> *He **says** (that) he's in New York now.*

After *say*, we do not usually mention the listener. After *tell* we always mention the listener.

> *He **said** he was working late.*
> *He **told me** he was working late.*

that after the reporting verb is formal. You can leave it out.

> *He **said that** he was tired. OR He **said** he was tired.*

There are word changes to show changes of person and place.

> *... call **you** from New York. → ... call **us** from New York.*
> *... **here** at **my** hotel. → ... **there** at **his** hotel.*

There are word changes to show time changes between the statement and reporting the statement.

> *He said, '**I'm** flying **tomorrow**.' → He said he **was** flying the **next day**.*

A main verb in the present simple, eg *call* or *calls*, changes to the past simple, *called*. Remember these other common verb changes.

> *am/is → was, are → were, have/has → had, have/has got → had,*
> *do/does → did, will → would, can → could, may → might*

Unlike *can* and *may*, these modal verbs do not change.

> *must, might, could, would, should, ought*

Remember these other common ways of showing time changes.

> *tomorrow → the next day/the day after*
> *yesterday → the previous day/the day before*
> *this Saturday → last Saturday/the following Saturday*

يمكن نقل حديث شخص ما بشكل حرفي بوضعه بين علامات تنصيص «....»، وهو أمر شائع في القصص.

وفي حالة الحوار فإننا عادة ما نعبر عن فكرة المتحدث بطريقة تقريرية بعد فعل تقريري مثل الأفعال المذكورة، أي بالتحويل إلى الكلام غير المباشر.

ويوضع فعل التقرير say عادة في الماضي ولكنه يأتي في المضارع احياناً، عند نقل محادثة تليفونية أثناء الاستماع إليها على سبيل المثال.

يغفل ذكر المستمع عادةً بعد فعل say ولكنه يذكر دائماً بعد فعل tell.

يعتبر استخدام that بعد فعل التقرير رسميا، ويمكن إغفال ذكرها.

وهناك تغييرات للكلمات لاظهار تغيير الشخص والمكان.

وهناك تغييرات للكلمات لاظهار تغيّر الزمن بين الجملة الخبرية المباشرة وبين الجملة المنقولة.

يتغير الفعل الأساسي في الجملة من المضارع البسيط إلى الماضي البسيط... تذكّر تغييرات الأفعال الشائعة المبينة.

لا تتغير صيغة الأفعال المساعدة الناقصة المذكورة وذلك على النقيض من فعلي can وmay.

تذكّر هذه الطرق الشائعة الاخرى التي تظهر تغيّرات الزمن.

Exercises

1 Report the telephone conversation.

Nick is in Australia and Alan is in Britain.

Nick: *It's hot here, and I'm sitting by our new pool.*
Alan: *It's really cold here, and we're sitting by our fire.*

They're telling their wives about the conversation.

Nick to Suzie: *Alan says <u>it's really cold there, and</u>*
_____

Alan to Celia: *Nick says* _____
_____
_____

2 Write the statements in reported speech. Use *He said …* and *He told me …*

You met an old school friend, Jim, last year

Examples: *'I've got a flat in London.'*
<u>*He said he had a flat in London.*</u>
'I'm visiting my parents this weekend.'
<u>*He told me he was visiting his*</u>
<u>*parents that weekend.*</u>

1 *'I'm working outside London this month.'*
_____
_____

2 *'I finished my college course a year ago.'*
_____
_____

3 *'I haven't been to see my parents for ages.'*
_____
_____

4 *'I arrived home with my family yesterday.'*
_____
_____

5 *'We're going to go back to London tomorrow.'*
_____
_____

6 *'We can't stay for long as I have to get back to work.'*
_____
_____
_____

7 *'We may come back next year. I don't know.'*
_____
_____
_____

8 *'I'll write soon and send you a photo of the family.'*
_____
_____

9 *'You should stay with us when you have time.'*
_____
_____

3 Write replies to the comments. Use *But you said …* and *But you told me …*

Example: ● *I'm going home. (stay/here)*

○ <u>*But you said you were staying*</u>
<u>*here.*</u>

1 ● *I don't like this music. (love)*
   ○ _____

2 ● *Tom has sold his bike. (not/sell)*
   ○ _____

3 ● *I'm not going to call her. (call)*
   ○ _____

4 ● *The film is on tomorrow. (today)*
   ○ _____

5 ● *They won the match. (lose)*
   ○ _____

6 ● *Lisa will be at home tomorrow. (tonight)*
   ○ _____

7 ● *They have sent me a present. (not/send/anything)*
   ○ _____

8 ● *The children can swim very well. (cannot/swim/at all)*
   ○ _____

Reported speech 2: questions

They asked if I was staying long.

FORMS

'Are you staying long?' → *They asked if I was staying long.*

'Did you have a good journey?' → *They wanted to know if I had had a good journey.*

'How are your parents?' → *They wanted to know how you were.*

'When will you go?' → *They asked when I would go.*

Reported questions usually start with *ask* or *want to know*.

> They **asked** how long I was staying.
> They **wanted to know** how you were.

Reported *Yes/No* questions need *if* or *whether*.

> They asked **if** I had had a good journey.
> They wanted to know **whether** I liked London.

Reported *Wh* questions need a question word, eg *how, when, what*, etc.

> They wanted to know **how** you were.
> They asked **what** I wanted to do.

The verb after *if* or *whether* or question word is not in question form. It is like a verb in a statement.

> They asked **if** I **was** hungry.
> They asked **what** I **wanted** to do.

Be careful about *do, does* and *did*. We use them in ordinary present and past simple questions, but not in reported questions.

> Where **do** you **want** to go? → They asked me where I **wanted** to go.
> How long **did** the journey **take**? → They asked me how the journey **had taken**.

The reported question form is similar to the form of indirect questions. (See Unit 22.)

> Why does he like London? → They wanted to know **why he likes London**. OR Could you tell me **why he likes London**?

The rules for word changes for change of person, place and time are the same as for reported statements. (See Unit 46.)

> *'How are you?'* → They asked how **I was**. (change of person)
> *'When will you get here?'* → They asked when I would get **there**. (change of place)
> *'Did you call yesterday?'* → They asked if I had called **the previous day**. (change of time)

تبدأ صيغة الاستفهام في الكلام غير المباشر عادةً بـ ask أو want to know.

يستدعي تحويل صيغ الأسئلة التي يجاب عنها بـ «نعم» أو «لا» إلى الكلام غير المباشر استخدام if أو whether. ويستدعي تحويل الأسئلة التي تبدأ بأداة استفهام مثل how و when، الخ... الاحتفاظ بأداة الاستفهام في الجملة غير المباشرة.

يوضع الفعل بعد if وبعد whether وكذلك بعد أداة الاستفهام، في صيغة الجملة الخبرية وليس في الصيغة الاستفهامية.

وتستخدم do و does و did في الجمل الاستفهامية العادية، في زمني المضارع والماضي البسيطين ولكنها لا تستخدم في الجمل الاستفهامية المحولة إلى الكلام غير المباشر.

تشبه الجمل الاستفهامية المحولة إلى الكلام غير المباشر صيغة الأسئلة غير المباشرة (انظر unit 22).

تتطابق قواعد تغيير الكلمات لتغيير الشخص والمكان والزمان مع قواعد تحويل الجمل الخبرية إلى الكلام غير المباشر. (انظر unit 46).

Exercises

1 Report the telephone conversation.

Nick is in Australia and Alan is in Britain.

Nick: *What are you and Celia doing this winter? Are you taking a skiing holiday again?*

Alan: *No, we're staying at home this year. Where are you and Suzie going for your holiday? Are you going to visit us again?*

They're telling their wives about the conversation.

Nick to Suzie: *Alan is asking where* _____

_____

_____ *He wants to know*

_____

Alan to Celia: *Nick is asking what* _____

_____ *He wants to know*

_____

_____

2 Write the *Yes/No* questions in reported speech.

You met your old school friend, Jim, last year.

Examples: Jim: *Are you still at college?*

Jim asked me whether I was still at college.

You: *Do you remember Joe?*

I asked him if he remembered Joe.

1 Jim: *Have you sold your terrible old car?*

_____

_____

2 Jim: *Do you still live with your parents?*

_____

_____

3 Jim: *Are you going to visit London soon?*

_____

_____

4 You: *Is there room for me to stay with you?*

_____

_____

5 You: *Can I have your phone number?*

_____

_____

6 You: *Did you meet your wife at college?*

_____

_____

3 Write the *Wh* questions in reported speech.

Some students are talking to a new French student.

Example: '*What subjects are you going to do?*'

They asked him what subjects he was going to do.

1 '*Where do you come from?*'

_____

_____

2 '*How long have you been in Britain?*'

_____

_____

3 '*Why did you decide to come here?*'

_____

_____

4 '*How long are you going to stay?*'

_____

_____

5 '*Where are you living?*'

_____

_____

4 Write the questions in reported speech.

At a language school

Example: A German student: *How can I renew my my passport?*

A German student asked me how he could renew his passport.

1 A Swedish student: *Do you know the way to the station?*

_____

_____

2 A Turkish student: *Can you help me find a flat?*

_____

_____

3 A Lebanese student: *Which is the best travel agency?*

_____

_____

48 Reported speech 3: orders, promises, etc
They told him to be quiet.

FORMS

Reported orders

'Be quiet!' → *They told him to be quiet.*

Reported requests

'Could you turn it down, please?' → *She asked him to turn it down.*

'Would you mind not making so much noise, please?' → *She asked him not to make so much noise.*

Reported orders, invitations, etc

tell, invite, remind, warn and *use* take *to* + infinitive after the object. In the negative form add *not* before the *to* + infinitive.

Subject	Verb	Object	to + Infinitive
They	**told**	*him*	**to be** *quiet.*
They	**warned**	*her*	**not to do** *it again.*

Reported promises, offers, etc

promise, offer, refuse, agree and *threaten* do not take an object before the *to* + infinitive. In the negative form add *not* before the *to* + infinitive.

Subject	Verb	to + Infinitive
He	**promised**	**to turn** *it down.*
They	**agreed**	**not to make** *so much noise.*

Reported suggestions, apologies, etc

suggest, apologize for, admit and *insist on* take an *ing* form.

Subject	Verb	ing form
Nick	**suggested**	**turning** *it down.*
They	**apologized**	**for making** *so much noise.*

With *suggest* it is possible to use this form.

> *Nick **suggested that they turn** it down.*

Other reporting verbs

Reporting verbs like *invite, promise, suggest, warn,* etc, tell us much more than the basic reporting verbs *say, tell* and *ask.* They express the speaker's aim – the type of communication that the speaker produced. In fact, the reporting verb can summarize some or all of the actual words that the speaker used. Similar reporting verbs include *accuse, complain, correct, deny* and *recommend.*

> The police to Mr Saunders: *'We have reason to believe that you took the car, Mr Saunders.'* → *The police **accused** Mr Saunders of taking the car.*
>
> A neighbour to a teenager: *'Do you have to make that terrible noise?'* → *The neighbour **complained** to the teenager about the terrible noise.*
>
> Mr MacLaren to a reporter: *'I'm sorry, but you've got my name wrong. It's M-a-c, not M-c.'* → *Mr MacLaren **corrected** the spelling of his name.*
>
> Mr Saunders to the police: *'I certainly didn't take the car.'* → *Mr Saunders **denied** taking the car.*

الأفعال التقريرية التالية tell و invite و remind و warn و use، تأخذ to + مصدر الفعل بعد المفعول به. وفي حالة النفي نأتي بأداة النفي not قبل المصدر مع to.

لا تتعدى الأفعال التقريرية promise و offer و refuse و agree و threaten، إلى مفعول به قبل المصدر مع to، وفي حالة النفي نأتي بأداة النفي not قبل المصدر مع to.

نأتي بالفعل مضافاً له ing عند استخدام الأفعال suggest و apologize for و admit و insist on.

من الممكن استخدام صيغة الفعل بدون ing مع الفعل التقريري suggest.

بعض الأفعال التقريرية مثل invite و promise و suggest و warn ... تفيدنا معلومات اكثر بكثير من الافعال التقريرية الأساسية say و tell و ask. فهي تعبّر عن غرض المتحدث وبالتالي نوعية المعلومات التي اعطاها المتحدث. في الواقع، يمكن للفعل التقريري ان يختصر بعض الكلمات التي استخدمها المتكلم، أو كلها. ومن الأفعال التقريرية المماثلة، accuse و complain و correct و deny و recommend.

Exercises

1 Put the direct speech into reported speech.

Example: 'Give me your books,' the teacher told us.
The teacher told us to give him/her our books.

1 'Could you open the door?' the girl asked me.

2 'Don't use this photocopier,' Carol instructed the new assistant.

3 'Come for dinner on Saturday,' Tom invited us.

4 'Don't be late for the party,' Celia reminded me.

5 'Could you please not make so much noise?' Ann asked everybody.

6 'Give your name to the receptionist,' Mrs Davis told Tony.

7 'Don't touch the red button,' Bob warned Emma.

8 'Remember to post the letters,' the manager reminded her assistant.

2 Report the conversation. Use these reporting verbs.

agree, offer, promise, threaten

Bill is always late for appointments. His sister, Jean, is tired of it.

Example: 'Can we meet outside the cinema?' Bill said.
'All right. Outside the cinema,' Jean agreed.
They agreed to meet outside the cinema.

1 'And can we meet at 7.30?' he said.
'Fine. 7.30,' she agreed.

2 'This time I'll be there on time,' he promised.

3 'I'm not going to wait for you if you're late,' she threatened.

4 'Look, if you like, I'll get there an hour early!' he offered.

5 'You don't need to do anything silly like that, but I'll leave if you aren't there at 7.30,' she threatened again.

6 'I won't be late. Believe me,' he promised.

3 Report the statements and questions. Use these reporting verbs.

admit, apologize for, insist on, suggest

Example: 'Let's do something exciting,' Bob suggested.
Bob suggested doing something exciting.

1 'Why don't we go parachuting?' Maria suggested.

2 'Good idea, but it's getting late. If we're going to go parachuting, we must go right now,' Barry insisted.

Later, 3,000 metres up in the sky ...

3 'I feel scared,' Barry admitted.

4 'I don't want to jump either. I'm sorry, Barry. I was stupid to suggest parachuting,' Maria apologized.

5 'Look we can't go back now. Even if you aren't going to jump, I am!' Barry insisted. 'Bye!'

49 Singular and plural

a girl, an apple, two boys, some chairs

FORMS

a

a girl, a table

an

an apple, an umbrella

number

two boys, five books

some

some chairs, some books

All the things in the picture are countable nouns – we can count them, eg *two boys*, *three chairs* and *five books*.

They have a singular form (for one), eg *boy*, and a plural form (for more than one), eg *boys*.

We can use *a/an* before the singular form. Use *a* before a hard sound (consonant), eg *a girl*, *a desk* and *a table* (but *an old table*).

Use *an* before a soft sound (vowel), eg *an apple*, *an orange* and *an olive* (but *a green olive*).

Compare *a hat* and *an hour*. Use *an* when the *h* is silent.

Compare *an umbrella* and *a university*. Use *a* when the *u* sounds like *you*.

Do not use a singular countable noun by itself. It needs a determiner. (See Unit 52 for more information about *a*, *an* and *the*.)

> I want **a book**.   I want **my book**.
> I want **that book**.   I want **the book** over there.

We use *a/an* to say what a thing or a person is.
- ● *What's that?*   ○ *It's **a map**.*
- ● *What's her job?*   ○ *She's **an actress**.*

If we talk about more than one thing or more than one person in this way, use the noun alone.
- ● *What are those?*   ○ *They're **maps**.*
- ● *What are their jobs?*   ○ *They're **actresses**.*

We can use the singular or the plural form to make general statements. In both these examples we mean 'all horses'.

> **A horse** is an animal with four legs.
> **Horses** are animals with four legs.

We often want to talk about more than one thing, but we do not know exactly how many. For this use *some*. (See Unit 55 for more information about *some* and *any*.)

> *I'd like a beefburger and **some fries**, please.*

Be careful. *fries* and *some fries*, etc, have different meanings.

> *I love **fries**.* (all fries, at any time, anywhere)
> *I'd like **some fries**.* (a number of fries now)

جميع الأشياء التي تحويها الصورة من نوع الأسماء التي يمكن عدها وبالتالي فهي الأسماء المعدودة.

وتأتي هذه الأسماء في صيغة المفرد مثل boy وكذلك في صيغة الجمع (لأكثر من واحد منها) مثل boys.

يمكن استخدام a/an قبل صيغة المفرد. تستخدم a قبل الأسماء التي تبدأ بحرف صامت (a girl) ولكن لاحظ (an old table).

تستخدم an قبل الأسماء التي تبدأ بحرف صائت (an apple) ولكن لاحظ (a green olive).

قارن بين a hat و an hour. وتستخدم an عندما يكون حرف h صامتاً.

تستخدم a قبل الكلمات التي تبدأ بالحرف u حين ينطق هذا الحرف yoo مثل كلمة university.

لا يستخدم اسم مفرد من النوع المعدود بمفرده بل مع محدد. (انظر unit 52 لمزيد من المعلومات عن a و an والـ the).

تستخدم a/an للتعبير عن ماهية الاسم إن كان شيئاً أو شخصاً.

عند الحديث عن الأشخاص أو الأشياء في صيغة الجمع نستخدم الاسم وحده، أي بدون a/an.

يمكن استخدام صيغتي المفرد والجمع في جمل خبرية عامة: والحديث في المثلين التاليين، هو عن النوع كله.

غالباً ما نتحدث عن أكثر من شيء واحد، ولكننا لا نعرف عدده بالتحديد، ولذلك نستخدم some. (انظر unit 55 لمزيد من المعلومات عن some و any).

يجدر الاشارة إلى أن معنى كلمة fries يختلف عن معناها في some fries.

112

Exercises

1 Write *a* or *an*.

Examples: *a girl* *an apple*

1 _____ *orange*
2 _____ *exercise*
3 _____ *newspaper*
4 _____ *aeroplane*
5 _____ *letter*
6 _____ *easy test*
7 _____ *magazine*
8 _____ *old car*
9 _____ *Italian*
10 _____ *good book*
11 _____ *united team*
12 _____ *unfriendly man*

2 Write *a*, *an* or *some* and choose from these words.

book / books, desk / desks, egg / eggs, glass / glasses, letter / letters, paint / paints, taxi / taxis, umbrella / umbrellas

Examples: *I'm reading a book about Japan.*
Let's put some desks in that classroom.

1 *Did you write _____ to Ann?*
2 *It's going to rain. Take _____ with you.*
3 *Get _____ and we'll start a picture.*
4 *The children want a drink, so can you get _____, please?*
5 *I usually have _____, toast and coffee for breakfast.*
6 *We're late. Let's take _____ to the airport.*

3 Write the correct present forms of *be* or *do*.

Examples: *Look. Some boys are coming.*
Does a lesson take 45 or 50 minutes?

1 _____ *some students live in college?*
2 _____ *a new car very expensive?*
3 *Two girls _____ helping the teacher.*
4 _____ *a computer disk take long to copy?*
5 *A secretary _____ typing the report.*
6 *A good dictionary _____ really useful.*
7 _____ *the children in bed?*
8 *The students _____ having lunch.*

4 Write *some* or nothing (✗).

Examples: *Liz and Joe are ✗ teachers.*
We've got some new CDs. Look.

1 *Could you get _____ oranges, please?*
2 *I love _____ apples. I eat about five a day.*
3 *I'm going to buy _____ shoes in the sale.*
4 *Everybody studies _____ languages at school.*
5 *You look hungry. Have _____ biscuits.*
6 *We found _____ old gold coins under a rock.*

5 Write alternative general statements.

Example: *A tractor is a farm vehicle.*
Tractors are farm vehicles.

1 *A college is a place to study.*
_____

2 *Large planes can carry very heavy loads.*
_____
_____

3 *Nowadays, a student needs to learn to use a computer.*
_____
_____

4 *Cars use more energy per person than trains or buses.*
_____
_____

6 Write *a*, *an*, *some* or nothing (✗).

At a jeweller's

● *Hello. Could I look at some rings, please? I want to buy a ring for my sister.*
○ *Certainly, Madam. Here are [1]_____ rings for ladies.*
● *These are all [2]_____ diamond rings, aren't they?*
○ *Yes, and they're [3]_____ top quality pieces. Look at this one. It's [4]_____ really lovely ring.*
● *Yes, but it's [5]_____ expensive one too.*
○ *Ah, but Madam, [6]_____ things are never cheap.*
● *Perhaps you're right. But could I look at [7]_____ other rings too? Could I see [8]_____ different types of stone?*
○ *Of course. Here's [9]_____ very nice one. This green stone is [10]_____ emerald.*

50 Irregular noun forms

clothes, scissors, news, team, sheep, etc

A few countable nouns are usually plural, so they take a plural verb. Learn these: *clothes, contents, thanks.*

> My **clothes** are in the cupboard.
> He opened the bag and poured the **contents** on the floor.
> I want to thank you. Many, many **thanks**!

هناك مجموعة من الأسماء المعدودة التي غالباً ما تأتي في صيغة الجمع ويأتي معها الفعل في صيغة الجمع أيضاً وذلك مثل *clothes* و *contents* و *thanks*.

Some countable nouns are always plural because they have two parts. Learn these: *scissors, jeans, trousers, shorts, glasses, binoculars.* We can make them singular by using *a pair of.*

> Where are my **scissors**?   Those are nice **jeans**!
> There's **a pair of glasses** on the table.

وهناك أسماء معدودة تأتي دائماً في حالة الجمع نظراً لأنها تتكون من شقين مثل *scissors*... الخ ويجري استخدامها في صيغة المفرد باستخدام *a pair of* معها.

A few countable nouns look singular because they have no *s*, but they are always plural and have no singular form. Learn these: *the police, cattle.* (Use these countable nouns for a singular form: *police officer, cow* or *bull.*)

> **The police** are looking for three men.
> Mr Giles has 200 **cattle** on his farm.

وهناك مجموعة من الأسماء المعدودة التي تبدو وكأنها في صيغة المفرد لأنها لا تنتهي بـ s في الجمع، ولكنها دائماً في حالة الجمع مثل *police* و *cattle*. وممكن استخدامها في صيغة المفرد بإضافات وتعديلات معينة مثل *police officer* و *cow*.

A few nouns look plural, but are not. Learn these: *athletics, news, mathematics, physics, gymnastics, the United States.*

> Here is the 9.00 **news**.
> **Mathematics** was the most difficult subject for me at school.
> **The United States** is 5,000 kilometres from east to west.

وهناك مجموعة من الأسماء تبدو في حالة الجمع ولكنها ليست كذلك مثل *athletics* و *news* الخ.

Group nouns are singular, but we often think of members of the group and use a plural verb. Learn these: *family, team, club, class, school, staff, committee, government.*

> My **family** are all angry with me.
> The **team** are very happy with the result of the match.
> The **club** are looking for young members to join the team.

تعامل أسماء المجموعات على أنها مفردة ولكنها عادة ما تعني الأفراد المكونين لها، وبالتالي نستخدم معها الفعل في حالة الجمع.

A few words are the same in the singular and the plural. Learn these: *sheep, fish, series, crossroads, species, headquarters, aircraft.*

> Mr Giles has 1,000 **sheep** on his farm.
> You only caught one **fish**, but I caught three **fish**!
> I saw three **aircraft** in five minutes.

وهناك مجموعة من الأسماء تأتي في حالتي الإفراد والجمع على نحو سواء... منها الأمثلة المذكورة.

A few plurals are irregular. (See Appendix 2 for special spelling rules.) Learn these: *child → children, man → men, woman → women, person → people, foot → feet, tooth → teeth.*

> I've got one **child**. My brother has got two **children**.
> One **man** was by the door, and there were three more **men** inside.
> My dentist filled one **tooth** and took two **teeth** out.

وهناك مجموعة من الأسماء التي تشذ عن قاعدة جمع المفرد العادية، منها ما هو مذكور.

Exercises

1 Complete the statements and questions with plural nouns.

Example: *Many __thanks__ for all your help.*

1 *Somebody has taken all Mrs Bell's money.*
The _____ are on their way here now.

2 *In the Old West in America, cowboys used to look after*
thousands of _____

3 *Open the can and empty the _____ into a large*
bowl.

4 *I'll cut your hair for you. Where are your _____*

5 *It's very cold in the mountains, so take some warm*
_____ with you.

6 *Where are my _____? I can't see without them!*

7 *You can't play for our football in jeans. You need some*
proper _____

8 *We get meat, milk and wool from _____*

2 Choose singular or plural present forms of *be* or *do*.

Examples: *Physics __is__ my best subject.*
__Do__ fish feel anything when we catch them?

1 *The news _____ very bad. Three people have died*
and hundreds have been injured.

2 *_____ this pair of glasses belong to you?*

3 *Sheep _____ really stupid animals!*

4 *_____ mathematics interesting?*

5 *Your trousers _____ too long. I'd better shorten the*
legs.

6 ● *Which _____ the biggest fish?*
○ *This one, I think.*

7 *The new science series on TV _____ very good.*

8 *Gymnastics _____ dangerous if you don't train*
carefully.

9 *_____ the United States have a prime minister or a*
president?

10 *Aircraft today _____ often able to fly 10,000*
miles or more.

3 Complete the statements with singular or plural irregular nouns.

Examples: *Two __men__ with beards came to the door.*
One __man__ spoke. The other said nothing.

1 *We've got two _____ . Pip is five and Lucy is four.*

2 *There's room for one more _____ in the taxi.*

3 *My left _____ hurts. I can't walk very well.*

4 *A normal adult human mouth contains 32 _____*

5 *This _____ really hurts. The dentist will have to*
take it out.

6 *This bus can carry 70 _____*

7 *In some countries _____ do the same jobs as men.*

8 *That _____ mustn't play in the road. It's*
dangerous. Let's stop her.

4 Complete the statements with the plural forms of these nouns. (Before you start, study Appendix 2.)

battery, knife, life, loaf, match, photo, potato, roof,
shelf, wife

Example: *Could you put the __shelves__ up here, please?*

1 *The children shouldn't play with _____ They*
might cut themselves.

2 *The children shouldn't play with _____ either.*
They might burn themselves.

3 *We eat _____ with every meal.*

4 *I've bought three _____ of bread.*

5 *Look. These are our holiday _____ This one*
shows our hotel.

6 *The men played golf and their _____ played a*
game of tennis.

7 *This radio runs on four 1.5 volt _____*

8 *When the ship sank, more than 1,500 people lost their*
_____

9 *The wind blew the _____ off several houses last*
night.

51 Countable and uncountable nouns

I'd like some olives.   *I'd like some olive oil.*

FORMS

Countable nouns

● *I'd like some olives, please.*
○ *How many would you like?*
● *Half a kilo, please.*

Uncountable nouns

● *And I'd like some olive oil, please.*
○ *How much would you like?*
● *A litre, please.*

CROSSCHECK

Countable nouns

We can count a thing like *an olive* or *three olives*. It has a singular and a plural form and goes with singular and plural verb forms.
> *These **olives are** very expensive.*

Countable nouns can go with other words, eg *some, any, the, this/these, my, many* and *a few*.
> *I'd like **some oranges**.*
> *Are there **any bottles**?*
> ***The glasses** are in the cupboard.*
> *Could I borrow **a few eggs**?*

We can count amounts of uncountable things by using expressions such as *a litre of/kilo of/can of/loaf of/carton of/bag of/bottle of/box of/ packet of/piece of/roll of*.
> ***Three cans of** Pepsi, please.*
> ***Two loaves of** bread, please.*

Uncountable nouns

We cannot count a thing like *olive oil*. We do NOT say *an olive oil* or *three olive oils*. We use a singular verb with an uncountable noun.
> *This **olive oil is** very good.*

Uncountable nouns can go with other words, eg *some, any, the, this, my, much* and *a little*.
> *I'd like **some orange juice**.*
> *Is there **any water**?*
> ***The salt** is in the cupboard.*
> *Could I borrow **a little milk**?*

These nouns are usually uncountable in English:
accommodation, advice, baggage, furniture, hair, health, information, knowledge, luggage, music, news, travel, trouble, work.
> *Excuse me. I need **some advice**.*
> *I'd like to listen to **some music**.*

Some nouns can be countable or uncountable. The countable form is an example or a part. The uncountable form means something in general or a material. Compare the following.

> *Football is a great **sport**!* (example)
> *It's made of large and small **stones**.* (parts of the wall)

> *I like **sport**.* (all sports)
> *The wall is made of **stone**.* (material)

Some nouns can be countable or uncountable, but the meaning is different. Compare the following.

> *Do you want a large **glass**?* (for drinking) OR *She wears **glasses**.* (for seeing)
> *Rob has a small **business**.* (a small company)

> *Windows are made of **glass**.* (material)
> *They want to do **business**.* (work together)

يمكن عدّ الأشياء مثل an olive أو three olives ، فهذا الاسم له صيغة مفرد وصيغة جمع، ويأتي مع الفعل في حالتي الإفراد والجمع أيضاً.

لا يمكن عدّ بعض الأشياء مثل olive oil واستخدام an/a أو مع عدد معها. بل صيغة المفرد من الفعل مع الاسم غير المعدود.

تستخدم الأسماء المعدودة مع كلمات اخرى مثل some... الخ.

ويمكن استخدام الأسماء التي لا تعد، مع كلمات أخرى مثل much... إلخ.

بإمكاننا أن نعد كميات من الأسماء غير المعدودة وذلك باستخدام تعبيرات مثل a litre of...إلخ.

وهذه قائمة بأسماء غير معدودة عادة، في اللغة الإنجليزية.

بعض الاسماء يمكن أن تكون معدودة أو غير معدودة. وتكون الصيغة المعدودة عبارة عن مثال أو جزء من الدلالة. أما الصيغة غير المعدودة فتعني شيئاً عاماً أو مادياً. لاحظ الأمثلة والفوارق فيها.

بعض الاسماء يمكن أن تكون معدودة او غير معدودة ولكن المعنى يختلف كما في الأمثلة.

Exercises

1 Write the kitchen things in two lists – countable and uncountable. Write the countable nouns in the plural.

apple	cheese	pea
apple juice	cooking oil	potato
banana	egg	rice
bean	milk	salt
biscuit	mineral water	soup
bread	olive	sugar
butter	onion	tea
carrot	orange	tomato

Countable nouns

1 _apples_____
2 _____
3 _____
4 _____
5 _____
6 _____
7 _____
8 _____
9 _____
10 _____
11 _____
12 _____

Uncountable nouns

13 _apple juice_____
14 _____
15 _____
16 _____
17 _____
18 _____
19 _____
20 _____
21 _____
22 _____
23 _____
24 _____

2 Write the nouns with or without _s_.

● We need some _things_ for dinner. (thing) For example, we haven't got any [1]_____ (meat)

○ Yes, and we've only got a few [2]_____ (vegetable)

● You're right. We'd better get some [3]_____ and [4]_____ (bean) (onion)

○ How much [5]_____ have we got? (rice)

● Only a little. And look, this [6]_____ is old. (bread) We should buy some more. And I'd like to get a few [7]_____ too. (bread roll)

○ These [8]_____ are going bad too. (tomato)

● Yes, and we must remember to buy a bottle of [9]_____ too. (olive oil)

○ OK. Now I'm going to write a [10]_____ , so we don't forget anything. (list)

3 Choose the correct words.

Examples: *I love this _music._ (music/musics)*
I want to buy _a_ newspaper. (a/some)

1 *My father gave me _____ good advice. (a/some)*

2 *Can you give me some _____ about your company? (information/informations)*

3 *I've got some _____ for a new book. (idea/ideas)*

4 *Here _____ the 9.00 o'clock news. (is/are)*

5 *Put all the _____ in the corner, so we can clean the floor. (furniture/furnitures)*

6 *I must go. I have to do _____ work now. (a/some)*

7 *I've got _____ job to do at home tonight. (a/some)*

8 *Where did you leave your _____ (luggage/luggages)*

9 *Helen has got long, dark _____ (hair/hairs)*

10 *Have you got _____ writing paper, please? (a/any)*

4 Match the two halves.

1	a packet of	a	kitchen paper
2	a carton of	b	cheese
3	a five-litre bottle of	c	matches
4	a roll of	d	cooking oil
5	three loaves of	e	tea
6	four cans of	f	bread
7	a box of	g	potatoes
8	a two-kilo bag of	h	Pepsi
9	a piece of	i	milk

1 _e_   I'd like _a packet of tea._
2 ___   I need _____
3 ___   I'd like _____
        _____
4 ___   I need _____
5 ___   I'd like _____
6 ___   I need _____
7 ___   I'd like _____
8 ___   I need _____
        _____
9 ___   I'd like _____

Larry saw an old woman.   The woman smiled.

FORMS

Yesterday, Larry saw *an* old woman in *the* park next to *the* bus station. She had *an* umbrella and *a* packet of sandwiches with her. *The* sun suddenly came out and *the* woman smiled. She sat down on *a* bench by *the* pond, and she put *the* umbrella on *the* bench beside her. She started to eat *the* sandwiches, and she threw *some* pieces of bread to *the* birds on the water. Half *an* hour later, she went, but she forgot *the* umbrella. Larry picked it up and went after her. He found her in *the* bus station. She was getting on *the* Number 26 bus to Old Town. She was really pleased. 'Stupid me!' she said. 'I nearly went home without it. Thank you for being such *an* honest person!'

a or an

Use *a* before a hard sound (consonant).

> *a bench, a packet, a sandwich, a woman*

تستخدم a قبل الكلمة التي تبدأ بحرف صامت.

Use *an* before a soft sound (vowel).

> *an old woman, an umbrella, an ice-cream, an egg, an apple*

تستخدم an قبل الكلمة التي تبدأ بحرف صائت.

But compare the following.

> *an umbrella* BUT *a university* (Use *a* when the *u* sounds like *you*.)
>
> *a hat, a house* BUT *an hour, an honest person* (Use *an* when the *h* is silent.)

عند مقارنة هاتين الكلمتين اللتين تبدآن بالحرف u نجد أننا نستخدم a عندما ينطق الحرف u وكأنه yoo، وتستخدم an قبل الكلمات التي تبدأ بالحرف h، وتستخدم a قبل الحرف h المنطوق.

a, an, some or the

Use *a* or *an* when you first mention something, eg *an old woman, an umbrella* and *a packet of sandwiches*.

> *Larry saw **an old woman**   She had **a packet of sandwiches**.*

تستخدم a أو an عندما تبدأ بذكر اسم ما كما هو مبين.

Use *some* for plural and uncountable nouns.

> *She threw **some pieces of bread**.   She threw **some bread**.*

وتستخدم some للأسماء في حالة جمع الاسماء غير المعدودة.

Use *the* when you mention something (singular, plural or uncountable) again. It is now old information. You already know, for example, about *the* woman and *the* packet.

> ***The old woman** smiled.   She opened **the packet**.*

تستخدم أداة التعريف the عند إعادة ذكر الاسم بغض النظر عن كونه في حالة المفرد أو الجمع، وبغض النظر عن كونه من النوع المعدود أو من النوع غير المعدود.

We do not always use *a* or *an* when we mention something new. We use *the* when we all know the thing, eg *the* sun and *the* sky.

> ***The sun** suddenly came out.   **The sky** was blue.*

لا نستخدم a أو an بشكل دائم عند ذكر شيء جديد، ونستخدم the عند ذكر شيء معروف لنا جميعاً مثل the sun.

More examples from nature: *the earth, the moon, the country(side), the air, the ground.*

وكذلك الحال عند ذكر امثلة من الطبيعة. ايضاً عند الحديث عن شيء محدد في بلد محدد.

More examples when you talk about a particular thing in a particular country: *the capital, the government, the army, the police.*

More examples when local people talk about particular local places.

> *... in **the park** next to **the bus station**.* (the only bus station in the local town)

وكذلك عندما يتحدث اناس محليون عن أماكن محلية محددة.

More examples when family members and friends talk about their things.

    *Let's do some work in **the garden** today.* (our particular garden)
    *Did you hear **the phone** ring?* (the only phone in our house)
    *I think **the boss** has gone home.* (our boss, the boss that we both work for)
    *You should see **the doctor**.* (your family doctor)

وكذلك عندما يتحدث أفراد العائلة والأصدقاء عن أشيائهم.

The speaker can point to something and use *the*. Compare the following.

    *She had **an umbrella**.*
    *Look. Whose is **the umbrella** on **the bench** over there?*

ويمكن أن يشير المتحدث إلى شيء ما مستخدماً *the*... لاحظ الأمثلة.

The speaker can give extra information to show which thing and use *the*.

    *She was getting on **the Number 26 bus**.*
    *She was getting on **the bus to London**.*
    *She was getting on **the bus outside the ticket office**.*

ويمكن للمتحدث أن يعطي معلومات إضافية ليوضح ماهية الشيء مستخدماً *the*.

Special uses of *a*, *an* and *the*

Numbers: We usually use *a* with these numbers.
    a hundred, a hundred and ninety-nine
    *(I've got about **a hundred**.* BUT *I've got exactly **one hundred**.)*
    a thousand, a thousand and ninety-nine
    (one thousand one hundred BUT *one thousand nine hundred and ninety-nine)*
    a million, a billion, a trillion

عادة ما تستخدم *a* مع الأرقام كما هو مبين.

Other quantities: We use *a* with other quantities such as *a month*, *a kilo*, *a litre*, *a dollar* and *a kilometre*.

وتستخدم *a* مع المدة الزمنية والكميات المبينة.

Rates: We can use *per* or *a/an* in the following.
    100 kilometres per hour OR *100 kilometres an hour*
    three dollars per kilo OR *three dollars a kilo*

وتستخدم كلمة *per* أو *an/a* كما هو مبين.

We use *the* to help talk about the position of things.
    *We live **in the middle of London/on the edge of town**.*
    *The house is **on the right/left**.*

وتستخدم *the* لتساعد على تحديد مواقع الأشياء.

Superlatives: A superlative adjective + noun needs *the* because there is only one (like *the sun* and *the moon*, etc).
    *It's **the fastest car** in the world.*
    *Question three was **the most difficult** in the whole exam.*
    *Leaving school early was **the worst mistake** he has ever made.*

وتستخدم *the* مع الدرجة الثالثة للصفة (أفعل التفضيل) لكونها الوحيدة من حيث درجة الصفة المستخدمة.

We also use *the* to talk about correct information.
    *What's **the time**, please?* (the correct time now)
    *Can you tell me **the way** to the cinema?* (the correct road)
    The right answer to Question 3 is ... (We also say *the wrong answer*.)

وتستخدم *the* أيضاً للحديث عن المعلومات الصحيحة والدقيقة.

Exercises

1 Write *a* or *an*.

Example: *I only had an apple for lunch.*

1   *Would you like _____ orange?*

2   *We planted about _____ hundred trees.*

3   *The car was travelling at 160 kilometres _____ hour.*

4   *Are we going to stop for _____ rest soon?*

5   *Slow down or we'll have _____ accident!*

6   *I've got _____ young son. He's only four.*

7   *When you work for _____ airline, you have to wear _____ uniform.*

8   *Alan was_____ honest person. He never told _____ lie in his life.*

2 Write *a, an* or *the*.

Example: At a leather goods shop

● *I want to buy a red, leather bag. Can you help me?*

○ *Yes, Madam. I think this is exactly the right bag for you.*

1   At a restaurant

● *I'd like [1]_____ table for three people, please.*

○ *Yes, of course. Please take [2]_____ table over there by the window.*

2   After shopping

● *I've bought [1]_____ book and [2]_____ magazine.*

○ *Is [3]_____ magazine for me?*

● *No. [4]_____ book is for you, but [5]_____ magazine. is for me.*

3   On the local radio news

● *Here's another piece of local news. There was [1]_____ bank robbery in central Oxford this afternoon. Police Inspector Ross, have you caught [2]_____ robbers yet?*

○ *No. We're looking for two men in [3]_____ orange BMW. [4]_____ driver of [5]_____ car is wearing [6]_____ green anorak. [7]_____ passenger is wearing [8]_____ old leather jacket.*

4   In a garden near home

● *Excuse me. I'm looking for [1]_____ small, black cat. It's run away from home.*

○ *Ah, yes. Look over there. Is that [2]_____ cat you mean?*

● *Yes, that's [3]_____ one. Thanks very much.*

5   In a street

● *Can you tell me [1]_____ way to Stanford Office Equipment?*

○ *Go along Charles Street for [2]_____ kilometre, and you'll come to [3]_____ big crossroads. Turn left there, and you'll see three big buildings on [4]_____ left. Stanford Office Equipment is [5]_____ building in [6]_____ middle.*

3 Write *a, an* or *the*.

1   A holiday postcard

I wrote a postcard to my friends at work when I was on holiday last month. It was only [1]_____ picture of [2]_____ hotel where I stayed, so it wasn't [3]_____ very special card, but I was angry. You see, [4]_____ card didn't reach [5]_____ office until [6]_____ week after I got back.

2   Two accidents in one day

Harry has got [1]_____ broken leg and [2]_____ broken arm. He got [3]_____ broken arm in [4]_____ car accident, but he got [5]_____ broken leg later. He was sitting in [6]_____ wheelchair and he was waiting for [7]_____ X-ray of [8]_____ broken bone. Unfortunately, he was waiting very near some stairs, and he moved [9]_____ wheelchair a little bit. One wheel went over [10]_____ edge of [11]_____ stairs, and that was how Harry's second accident happened. [12]_____ chair ran all [13]_____ way down [14]_____ stairs; Harry fell out of [15]_____ chair and into [16]_____ wall at [17]_____ bottom of [18]_____ stairs. [19]_____ doctors say Harry will have to stay in hospital for [20]_____ month!

4 Complete the paragraph with *the* and these words.

beach, birds, fields, hill, sand, sea, sky, sun, trees, waves, wind, world

I remember a wonderful day when I was very young. We left our holiday home early, and we walked down the hill for a swim at [1]_____ It was a beautiful summer morning. [2]_____ was shining, and [3]_____ was blue. [4]_____ were singing up in [5]_____ tall, green [6]_____ In [7]_____ wide, green [8]_____ to our left and right there were millions of flowers. They were all moving in ⁹_____ *gentle* ¹⁰_____ *Ahead of us, we could see* ¹¹_____ *blue and silver* ¹²_____ *and* ¹³_____ *fast, white* ¹⁴_____ *as they crashed onto* ¹⁵_____ *golden* ¹⁶_____ *For us,* ¹⁷_____ *was a perfect place that day.*

5 Write *a* or *the*.

Examples: a) *The boys always stop at* <u>the</u> *park on their way home from school.*

b) *The Town Council are thinking of building* <u>a</u> *new park.*

1 a) *John, _____ phone is ringing. Could you answer it, please?*

b) *My brother has got _____ phone in every room.*

2 a) *We used to visit our grandparents every summer. We loved _____ old house.*

b) *Mr Brook is rich. He's got _____ very big house.*

3 a) *It's warm now. Let's eat lunch in _____ garden.*

b) *We're going to move house. We want somewhere with _____ big garden.*

4 a) *Susan is training to be _____ doctor.*

b) *Jimmy is feeling very ill. Quick. Call _____ doctor.*

5 a) *Is Mr Bradley _____ good boss?*

b) *Where's _____ manager, please? I need to see her.*

6 a) *I'm going to pay this money in at _____ bank today.*

b) *Excuse me. Is there _____ bank near here?*

7 a) *Your train is at 1.00, so I'll take you to _____ station now.*

b) *Our town used to have _____ station, but it's closed now.*

8 a) *I go to _____ dentist every six months.*

b) *I wouldn't like to be _____ dentist. I think it's a horrible job!*

9 a) *Every old town in England has _____ town square.*

b) *I'll meet you in _____ town square at midday.*

10 a) *Could you get some stamps at _____ post office for me, please?*

b) *There's _____ post office in King Street.*

6 Write *a* or *the* and these words instead of the underlined words.

long letter, mountain, phone, police officer, postman, present, reporter, ship, vase

Examples: *He brings our post every morning.*

<u>The postman brings our post every morning.</u>

The plane crashed into <u>something</u>.

<u>The plane crashed into a mountain.</u>

1 *<u>Somebody</u> answered when I phoned the newspaper.*

_____

_____

_____

2 *Joe fell and knocked <u>something</u> over.*

_____

_____

_____

3 *<u>He</u> stopped me for driving too fast.*

_____

_____

_____

4 *<u>It</u> can travel from Britain to the USA in four days.*

_____

_____

_____

5 *When I was away, I bought <u>something</u> for my parents.*

_____

_____

_____

6 *I picked <u>it</u> up and called my sister.*

_____

_____

_____

7 *Sarah wrote <u>something</u> to her father.*

_____

_____

_____

53 Articles 2: general and specific

A plane is a beautiful thing.

General statements – singular

We can use a singular noun to make a general statement. *A plane* means 'any plane'. *The plane* means the type of thing called 'plane'.

  ***A plane** is a beautiful thing.* ***The plane** has changed our world.*

We can make general statements with plural nouns, eg *people*, and uncountable nouns, eg *life*. Compare the general statements (without *the*) and the specific statements (with *the*).

	General	**Specific**
Plural:	***People** fly every day.*	***The people** here are Dutch.*
	***Students** are usually poor.*	*Meet **the new students**.*
Uncountable:	*I like strong **curry**.*	*I enjoyed **the curry** last night.*
	*We need **water** to live.*	***The water** is hot now.*

Special expressions – *the* + things in groups

Groups in society: We often use *the* + adjective for groups in society, eg *the poor, the rich, the sick, the old* and *the young*.

  *The gap between **the rich** and **the poor** is getting wider.*

National groups: We use *the* with national and regional groups of people, eg *the Japanese, the French, the Germans, the Arabs* and *the Europeans*.

  ***The Japanese** and **the Germans** have worked hard to become rich.*

Geographical groups: Most country names do not take *the*, eg *Japan, France* and *Egypt*. But *the* is necessary for countries that are a group of smaller parts, eg *the Netherlands, the United Arab Emirates* and *the United States of America*.

Other groups of places also take *the* – islands, eg *the West Indies* and *the Seychelles*, but not single islands, eg *Madagascar*. Also mountains, eg *the Alps* and *the Himalayas*, but not single mountains, eg *Mount Everest*.

Regions: We talk about regions in different ways. Some are names with *the*, eg *the Far East, the Middle East, the Rift Valley, the Sahara Desert* and *the Nile Delta*. But names with direction + noun do not take *the*, eg *North America* and *South Korea*.

We can also talk about regions in this way.

  northern/southern/eastern/western Australia OR *the north/the south/the east/the west of Australia*

يمكن استخدام اسم مفرد لتكوين جملة خبرية عامة. فاستخدام a plane يعني أي طائرة. ولكن استخدام the plane يعني الشيء المسمى «طائرة». ويمكن تكوين جملة خبرية عامة باستخدام أسماء في حالة الجمع مثل peo-ple، وكذلك أسماء غير معدودة مثل life.

ويتضح الأمر عند مقارنة الأمثلة العامة بدون استخدام أل التعريف the، مع الأخرى التي تتصف بالتحديد والتي تستخدم معها أل التعريف the.

تستخدم صفات مسبوقة بـ the غالباً للدلالة على فئات من المجتمع مثل the poor، the young....إلخ.
وتستخدم the أيضاً مع مجموعات من الناس وطنية وإقليمية.

لا تستخدم the مع غالبية أسماء البلدان، ولكنها ضرورية مع أسماء البلدان التي تتكون من عدة أجزاء.

هناك مجموعات أخرى من الاماكن تقبل the ايضاً مثل الجزر، ولكن ليس الجزر المفردة، والجبال ولكن ليس الجبال المفردة.

وتسبق the أسماء المناطق الجغرافية مثل the Far east. ولكن أسماء المناطق الجغرافية المسبوقة بأحد الاتجاهات الجغرافية (North America) لا تسبقها the.

ويمكن أيضاً، الحديث عن المناطق الجغرافية كما في الأمثلة المبينة.

Rivers, etc: Rivers, canals, seas, gulfs, oceans and deserts all need *the*.

> **The (River) Mississippi** *flows into* **the Gulf of Mexico**.
> **The Panama Canal** *connects the* **Caribbean (Sea)** *and* **the Pacific (Ocean)**.

وتستخدم *the* مع أسماء الأنهار والقنوات والبحار والخلجان والصحارى.

Special expressions without and with articles

Places: We do not use *the* when we talk about normal activities that happen *at/to school*, *at/to work*, *at/to home*, and *in town*, *in bed*, *in hospital*, etc.

> *Ann is* **at school**.   *Bob's gone* **to bed**.

We use *the* when we talk about a specific building or place.

> **The school** *is opposite* **the hospital**.   *Tom was on* **the bed**.

لا تستخدم *the* عند الحديث عن النشاطات العادية التي تحدث في المدرسة أو في العمل أو في المنزل أو في المدينة أو في الفراش أو في المستشفيات... الخ.

وتستخدم *the* عند الحديث عن مبنى معين أو عن مكان محدد.

Time: We do not usually use *a*, *an* or *the* with most time words and phrases. But we use an article when we add something extra about these times. Compare the following.

> **New Year** *was on a Sunday*.   *We had* **a fantastic New Year**.
> *I came last* **week**.   *I came* **the week** *Tom was born*.

ولا تستخدم في العادة *a* أو *an* أو *the* مع أغلبية الكلمات أو أشباه الجمل التي تعبر عن الزمن. وتستخدم أحدها عند إضافة دلالات أخرى عن الزمن... لاحظ الأمثلة.

Remember these special expressions: *at night, during the night, on Saturday and Sunday, at the weekend, on Monday morning, in the morning*.

> *I woke up* **during the night**.
> *I was away* **on Saturday and Sunday**.
> *I was away* **at the weekend**.
> *I went out* **on Monday morning**.

من الأهمية تعلم التعبيرات المبينة وتذكرها بشكل جيد.

Meals: We do not usually use *a*, *an* or *the* with *breakfast*, *lunch*, *dinner* and *supper*. But we use an article when we add something extra about these meals. Compare the following.

> *I have* **breakfast** *at 8.00*.
> *I woke up at 9.00 and had* **a late breakfast**.
> *We had steak for* **dinner**.   *That was* **the best meal** *of my life!*

لا تستخدم *a* و *an* و *the* في الغالب مع أسماء الوجبات، ولكنها تستخدم عندما نضيف لأسماء الوجبات دلالات أخرى... لاحظ الأمثلة.

Transport: We do not use *a/an* or *the* when we talk about the method of transport. But we use an article when we talk about a specific plane, car, etc. Compare the following.

> *I came by* **plane**.   *I came on* **the 5.00 plane** *from Paris*.
> *She likes travelling by* **car**.   *It's* **a very comfortable car**.

لا تستخدم *a* و *an* و *the* عند الحديث عن وسائل المواصلات بشكل عام، ولكنها تستخدم عند الحديث عن واحدة محددة من الطائرات أو السيارات. لاحظ الأمثلة.

Entertainment: Note the use of articles in the following.

> *I watch* **TV** *a lot, but I never listen to* **the radio**.
> *We like going to* **the cinema**, *and we often go to* **the theatre** *too*.

لاحظ كيف تستخدم هذه الأدوات في الأمثلة المبينة.

Musical instruments: We use *the* to talk about playing instruments.

> *He plays* **the piano/the guitar/the drums**.

تستخدم the عند الحديث عن العزف على الالات الموسيقية.

Exercises

1 Match the objects and their uses.

1	A camera		a picking up food.
2	A pen		b holding papers.
3	A fork	is for	c taking phone messages.
4	A file		d taking pictures.
5	A diary		e writing.
6	A fridge		f keeping food cold.
7	An answering machine		g noting dates of meetings, etc.

1 _d_ _A camera is for taking pictures._

2 __ _____

3 __ _____

4 __ _____

5 __ _____

6 __ _____

7 __ _____

2 Match the people and their inventions.

1	Bell		a the electric lamp.
2	Otis		b the radio.
3	Marconi	invented	c the modern car tyre.
4	Biro		d the lift (or *elevator).
5	Edison		e the sewing machine.
6	Dunlop		f the ballpoint pen.
7	Singer		g the telephone.

*American English

1 _g_ _Bell invented the telephone._

2 __ _____

3 __ _____

4 __ _____

5 __ _____

6 __ _____

7 __ _____

3 Write true statements about these things. Use *I like*, *I don't like* or *I don't mind*.

black coffee, chocolate, fast cars, homework, long journeys, loud rock music, swimming, tennis

Examples: _I like chocolate._
I don't like long journeys.

1 _____

2 _____

3 _____

4 _____

5 _____

6 _____

4 Choose the correct words.

Examples: *All children like* _ice-cream._
(ice-cream/the ice-cream)
Did you enjoy _the film_ *last night?*
(film/the film)

1 *Peter is riding* _____ *which was ill last week.*
(horse/the horse)

2 *My brother visits* _____ *all over the world.*
(companies/the companies)

3 *Could you pass* _____ *, please? (salt/the salt)*

4 _____ *aren't here. Where are they?*
(Books/The books)

5 _____ *isn't the most important thing in the world. (Money/The money)*

6 *People can't live for long without* _____
(water/the water)

7 _____ *live in Africa and India.*
(Elephants/The elephants)

8 _____ *is ringing. Could you answer it, please?*
(Phone/The phone)

5 Complete the statements with *the* and these words.

old, poor, rich, unemployed, young

Example: <u>The rich</u> have to pay high taxes.

1 In the old days the government did very little to help
_____

2 These days _____ receive payments
while they are unable to work.

3 Today, _____ are living for longer
than ever before.

4 _____ have to learn from their
parents and their teachers.

5 _____ often use a dog or a stick to
help them find their way.

6 Write the names of the people.

Country	People
1 Australia	<u>the Australians</u>
2 Britain	_____
3 China	_____
4 Denmark	_____
5 Egypt	_____
6 France	_____
7 Indonesia	_____
8 Japan	_____
9 Kuwait	_____
10 Netherlands	_____
11 Portugal	_____
12 Spain	_____
13 Russia	_____
14 Turkey	_____
15 the United States	_____
16 Venezuela	_____

Now write the names of your country and your people.

_____

_____

7 Write *the* or nothing (✗).

Example: <u>The</u> Netherlands is a small country in
<u>✗</u> Europe.

1 _____ Mississippi is the longest river in _____ United
States.

2 _____ Lake Victoria is a beautiful lake in _____ east
Africa.

3 _____ Mount Everest is the highest mountain in _____
Himalayan Mountains to _____ north of India.

4 _____ Jamaica is a beautiful island in _____ West
Indies, which are in _____ Caribbean Sea.

5 _____ Suez Canal lies along _____ western edge of
_____ Sinai Desert in _____ Egypt. It connects _____
Mediterranean and _____ Red Sea.

8 Write *the* or nothing (✗).

*Paul Ross is an international rock star now, but life
was not always so good. He grew up in* <u>the</u> *north of
England and went to* <u>✗</u> *school there. He did not
enjoy his schooldays very much, but there was a very good
music teacher at* [1]_____ *school, and she helped him a
lot. He learned to sing well there, and he started to play*
[2]_____ *guitar when he was 12. At the age of 18, he
went to* [3]_____ *music college, and there he studied other
instruments, including* [4]_____ *drums.*

When he left [5]_____ *college, he could not find*
[6]_____ *work, so he started the rock band Magic
Machine with some friends. Soon they were doing well
and they went south to London. They went on* [7]_____
TV for the first time on [8]_____ *day Paul was 22.*

*When they went to London, they drove there in Paul's
old car, but now they travel everywhere by* [9]_____ *air.*

*Paul and the others work hard, but at the moment,
they are on holiday. Paul wakes up late in* [10]_____
morning, and he eats [11]_____ *breakfast late. He
usually stays at* [12]_____ *home for most of the day, and
he listens to new music on CDs or* [13]_____ *radio. Then
in* [14]_____ *evening, he often goes to* [15]_____ *cinema.*

54 Demonstratives   *one* and *ones*
this, that, these, those   one, ones

FORMS

this, that, these and ***those***

this/that vase
these/those tables

one and ***ones***

the large/small this/that	one
the large/small these/those	ones

this, that, these and those as demonstrative adjectives

Use *this* and *these* for things which are near in place or time. Use *that* and *those* for things which are not near in place or time.

> ... on **that** bookcase ...
> ... over there on **those** tables ...

Use *this* or *that* with a singular or uncountable noun.

> **This wallet** is mine.   **That purse** is Sally's.

Use *these* or *those* with a plural noun.

> **These shoes** are cheap.   **Those boots** are really nice!

Use expressions with *that* to say something is right or wrong.

> **That's** right.   No, **that's** wrong.

this, that, these and those as demonstrative pronouns

When the meaning is clear, we can leave out the noun and *one* or *ones*.

> **This** is boring. Let's change channels. (this programme)
> Look at **these**! They're my size. (these shoes or clothes)

one and ones

We use the pronouns *one* and *ones* instead of a noun. Use *one* or *ones* instead of repeating a noun.

> Which **vase**? → Which **one**?
> Which **plants**? → Which **ones**?

Use *one* or *ones* when you can show what you are talking about.

> ● *Which is your jacket? Is it this **one**?* (pointing)
> ○ *No, it's that **one** over there. Look!* (pointing)
>   *It's the green **one** with red buttons.* (describing)
>   *It's the **one** on the chair.* (saying where it is)

Use *ones* just like *one* – for plural countable nouns.

> ● *What colour shirts would you like?*
> ○ *A white **one**, please, and two red **ones**.*

Do not use *one* or *ones* with uncountable nouns. Use *some* instead.

> I'd like **some** white cloth, please, and **some** red cloth.

تستخدم أسماء الإشارة this وthese مع الأشياء القريبة من حيث المكان أو الزمان.

وتستخدم that و those للأشياء البعيدة من حيث المكان أو الزمان.

تستخدم this أو those مع الأسماء في حالة الجمع.

وتستخدم that مع التعبيرات التي تفيد الصواب أو الخطأ.

عندما يكون المعنى واضحاً فإننا نسقط استخدام الأسماء و الضمائر one أو ones.

تستخدم الضمائر one و ones عوضاً عن الأسماء حتى لا نكرر الاسم.

تستخدم one أو ones عندما تستطيع ان تبيّن ما تتحدث عنه.

وتستخدم ones بنفس الطريقة التي تستخدم فيها one ولكن للأسماء المعدودة في حالة الجمع.

لا تستخدم one أو ones مع الأسماء غير المعدودة، وتستخدم some عوضاً عنها.

Exercises

1 Write *this*, *that*, *these* or *those*.

Example: *I can't see. What are <u>those</u> things over there?*

1 *Could you put the bookcase over there between _____ two windows?*

2 *_____ curry last night was very good.*

3 *Look how _____ diamonds shine when I turn them in the light.*

4 *Look, you have to press _____ button here to start the machine.*

5 ● *Do you remember _____ people from Canada? We met them at _____ party in London last November.*

○ *Do you mean _____ teachers – Bob and Lisa?*

● *Yes. Well, they're coming for dinner _____ evening.*

○ *Great!*

2 Write *this*, *that*, *these* or *those*.

Example: ● *Is <u>this</u> your car here?*

○ *No, mine is blue, not red. <u>That</u>'s it over there.*

1 ● *Alice, _____ is Tom Barnes, our new salesperson. Tom, _____ is Alice Parker, our Finance Director.*

○ *Nice to meet you.*

● *Good to meet you too.*

2 ● *Could you look at my book, please Miss. Is _____ the right answer?*

○ *Yes, _____'s right. Well done!*

3 ● *Excuse me. Is _____ Hill Farm here?*

○ *No, _____ is Lower Farm. Just keep going up the hill. _____'s it, up there at the top.*

4 ● *Here you are, Susan. _____ is your desk, and _____ are your files. Enjoy your new job!*

○ *Thanks very much. _____ is a nice office.*

5 ● *No, Tom. You've brought me the wrong books. I don't want _____*

○ *Oh, so do you want _____ over there?*

● *Yes, _____ are the ones.*

3 Write *this/that (one)* or *these/those (ones)*.

Example: ● *Look, <u>this</u> must be your bag.*

○ *No, <u>this one</u> isn't my bag. Mine is <u>that one</u> over there.*

1 ● *Look. Are _____ Tom's shoes here?*

○ *No. _____ over there are his. _____ here are Fred's.*

2 ● *After we turn on the computer, we need to put in a disk. Could you pass me _____ blue _____ on your desk, Bob?*

○ *Do you mean _____ here?*

● *Yes, _____, please.*

3 ● *I need some lights for my bike, please.*

○ *Yes, Sir. Have a look at _____ here.*

● *What about _____ over there?*

○ *They're good too, but _____ are better.*

4 Write *one/ones* or *the one/the ones*.

Example: ● *Excuse me. I'm trying to find a house. It's Number 73.*

○ *Do you see the three small <u>ones</u> there? Number 73 is <u>the one</u> on the left.*

1 ● *Go and say hello to Jim Baker.*

○ *Which _____ is he?*

● *He's _____ over there with dark hair.*

2 ● *I'd like some shoes from the shop window, please.*

○ *Of course. Which _____ would you like?*

● *They're _____ red _____ on the left.*

3 ● *Are David Frost and Roger West here?*

○ *Yes, they're by the window. David is _____ on the right, and Roger is _____ on the left.*

4 ● *Could I borrow some plates for my dinner party?*

○ *Of course. They're all in this cupboard. Which _____ would you like – _____ large _____ or _____ small _____ ?*

5 ● *Hello. You're from the band Magic Machine, aren't you? I'm Pete Price. I'm _____ who's interviewing you. Which of you is _____ who writes the songs?*

○ *I'm Paul, _____ who writes wites the music. Ron and Bob are _____ who write the words.*

127

55 some or any

We've got some olives.   We haven't got anything.

some or any

Use *some* in positive sentences with plural nouns and uncountable nouns.
>   *There are **some green olives**.   There's **some tomato juice**.*

Use *any* in negative sentences with plural nouns and uncountable nouns.
>   *There aren't **any black olives**.   There isn't **any orange juice**.*

Use *any* with plural nouns and uncountable nouns in *Yes / No* questions.
The answer can be *Yes* or *No*.
- ● *Have we got **any** green olives?*   (○ *Yes.*)
- ● *Have we got **any** orange juice?*   (○ *No.*)

When we think the answer to our question is *Yes*, we use *some*.
>   *Are you going to buy **some** things in town today?*

We also use *some* to make requests and offers sound positive.
>   *Could I have **some** money, please?*
>   *Would you like **some** money?*

We sometimes use *any* to talk about things that are possible, but uncertain.
>   *If there are **any** calls, please tell me.*
>   *Please send **any** letters to my new address.* (if there are any letters)

something or anything

We can use *some* and *any* to make these new words.

	thing	body/one	where
some	something	somebody	somewhere
any	anything	anyone	anywhere

We choose them as we choose *some* or *any*.
>   *He told her **something**.* (like *some news* – positive)
>   *We didn't see **anybody**.* (like *any people* – negative)
>   *Are you singing **anything** tonight?* (like *any songs* – uncertain)

(See Unit 63 for more information about *something, anybody*, etc.)

We can use *any, anything* and *anybody* to mean 'it doesn't matter what'.
>   *You can buy these at **any** supermarket.*
>   *You can have **anything** you want. You choose.*
>   *It's easy to make. **Anybody** can do it.*

تستخدم some في الجمل المثبتة مع الأسماء في حالة الجمع وكذلك مع الأسماء غير المعدودة.

تستخدم any في الجمل المنفية مع الأسماء في حالة الجمع وكذلك مع الأسماء غير المعدودة.

تستخدم any مع الأسماء في حالة الجمع مع الأسماء غير المعدودة في الجمل الاستفهامية التي يجاب عنها بـ«نعم» أو «لا». ويمكن أن تقتصر الإجابة على «نعم» أو على «لا».

تستخدم some في السؤال عندما نعتقد بان الرد بالايجاب.

وتستخدم some أيضاً لجعل الطلبات والعروض تعطي انطباعاً ايجابياً.

تستخدم any احياناً للحديث عن اشياء ممكنة ولكن غير اكيدة.

تستخدم some و any لاشتقاق كلمات اخرى جديدة... كما هو مبين في الأمثلة.

وتستخدم الكلمات المستحدثة بنفس طريقة استخدام some أو any.

ويمكن أن يعني استخدام any و anything و anybody لتعني أن الأمرين سيّان.

Exercises

1 Write *some* or *any*.

Dear Aunt Lucy,

Well, here we are on holiday. We're having a good time, and there are <u>some</u> great things about this place, but there are [1]_____ bad things too. The sea is great, but the hotel swimming pool isn't. There isn't [2]_____ water in the pool! There are [3]_____ interesting places to visit near here, but there aren't [4]_____ cars to hire. It's true, there are [5]_____ buses, but those are all in the middle of the day. There aren't [6]_____ in the morning or the evening.

Must stop. See you soon.

Love, Sam

PS We'll bring you [7]_____ local olives. They're really good!

2 Write *some* or *any*.

Example: ● *Come and sit down. Now, have <u>some</u> coffee and biscuits.*

○ *I'm sorry, but I don't drink coffee. Have you got <u>some/any</u> tea?*

1 ● *I'm looking for _____ cups, but I can't find _____*
   ○ *Perhaps there are _____ in the dishwasher.*

2 ● *Rod, could you lend me _____ money?*
   ○ *I'm sorry, Bob, but I haven't got _____ . I wanted to ask you for _____ money!*

3 ● *I need _____ help with this work. Have you got _____ free time today?*
   ○ *OK. I can give you _____ time tonight.*

4 ● *Ben, would you like to spend _____ time with your grandparents this summer?*
   ○ *Well, they're very nice, but I haven't got _____ friends where they live.*

3 Write *some, any, somebody, anybody, something* or *anything*.

Example: ● *I'm getting <u>some</u> things at the market. Can I get you <u>anything/something</u>?*

○ *No, I don't need <u>anything</u> thanks.*

1 ● *Is there _____ good on TV tonight?*
   ○ *No, there isn't _____ really. There's just _____ about wildlife in India.*

2 ● *Listen! I think I heard a noise. Can you hear _____*
   ○ *Do you mean that noise outside? I think _____ is coming to the front door.*

3 ● *Hello! Is _____ at home?*
   ○ *Oh, hello, Richard. Come in. You're just in time for _____ tea.*

4 ● *Could _____ please open the door for me? My hands are full.*
   ○ *Certainly. And would you like _____ help with carrying those things too?*

5 ● *You look hungry. I'll get you _____ to eat.*
   ○ *Thanks. I haven't had _____ to eat since yesterday.*

6 ● *Are there _____ people still living in the house?*
   ○ *No, we looked round, but there wasn't _____ there.*

4 Complete the answers. Use *any* (plus a noun from the question), *anything*, *anybody* or *anywhere*.

Examples: ● *Which car can we hire?*
   ○ *We can hire <u>any car</u> we like.*
   ● *I mustn't spend too much.*
   ○ *Don't worry. You can buy <u>anything</u> you want.*

1 ● *I like this car, but I don't like the colour.*
   ○ *You can have _____ you want, Sir.*

2 ● *I'm from Channel 5 TV, and I'd like to interview some members of the team.*
   ○ *You're welcome to interview _____ you want.*

3 ● *Are you sure you don't want to keep any of these things?*
   ○ *Yes, you can take _____ you want.*

4 ● *Are many people coming to the meeting?*
   ○ *I don't know, but we'll welcome _____ who comes.*

5 ● *Where shall we go on holiday this year, Tom?*
   ○ *You can go _____ you want to go, Penny.*

56 There, It and They

There's a hotel in the village.   It's in the square.

Excuse me ...

FORMS

There is and There are

Driver: *Is there a place to stay near here?*
Man: *Yes, there's a small hotel in the next village.*

It and They

Man: *It's in the village square.*

It for time, weather and distance

Driver: *Good – because it's getting late and it's getting cold. Is it far?*
Man: *No. It's only five kilometres.*

It as a dummy subject

Driver: *All right. It'll be best to stop there for tonight.*

There is and There are

We can use *There is* and *There are* when we talk about something for the first time.
- **Is there** a bakery in the town?   ○ Yes, **there's** one near the bank.

Use *There are* to talk about quantity with, eg *any, some, a lot (of), several, a few, many*.
- **Are there any** other shops?   ○ Not **many**, but **there are a few**.

Use *There* with different forms of *be* – *will be, was/were, has/have been*.
> **Will there be** time to buy some things?
> **There was** no time to do any shopping in the last village.

It and They

We often use *It* and *They* after *There* to introduce something. *It* and *They* refer back to that thing. We often use *It* like this for people (and other living things).
> **There was** a hotel in the last village, but **it wasn't** very nice.
> **There were** some shops too, but **they were** closing.

It for time, weather and distance

Use *It* in expressions about time, weather and distance.
> **It's** getting late. **It's** time to go.
- What time is **it**?   ○ **It's** 5.00.
> **It's** cold. **It's** going to rain.   **It** was a hot day. **It** was very sunny.
- Is **it** far to the village?   ○ **It's** two miles.
- How far is **it** to London?   ○ **It's** a long way.

It as a dummy subject

Use *It ... to* and *It ... that* in expressions like these.
> **It's** a good/bad idea **to** stop.   **It** was good/lovely **to** see her.
> **It's** sad/a pity **that** you can't stay.   **It's** true **that** he's leaving.

Use *It ... verb + ing* in these expressions.
> **It's** (not) worth **buying** that old car.
> **It's** no use **talking**. He never listens.

يمكن استخدام there is و there are عند الحديث عن شيءٍ ما للمرة الأولى.

تستخدم there are للحديث عن الكم وذلك مع أي من الكلمات المذكورة.

تستخدم there مع تصاريف فعل be المختلفة كما هو مبين.

نستخدم they و it غالباً بعد استخدام there لتقديم شيء لأن it وthey يدلان عليه. وغالباً ما تستخدم it في هذا المقام للدلالة على الأشخاص والأشياء الحية الأخرى.

تستخدم it في التعابير التي تتعلق بالزمن والطقس والمسافة.

استخدم it... to و it...that في التعبيرات التي توضحها الأمثلة.

تستخدم it مع فعل مضاف له ing في التعبيرات المبينة.

130

Exercises

1 Write questions and answers. Use *there* + the correct form of *be*.

Examples: *(sugar?) (Yes/over there)*
- *Is there any sugar?*
- *Yes, there's some over there.*

(onions?) (No/buy some)
- *Are there any onions?*
- *No, there aren't. I'll buy some.*

1 *(potatoes?) (Yes/in the bag)*
- _____
- _____

2 *(coffee?) (No/buy some)*
- _____
- _____

3 *(large pan?) (No/buy one)*
- _____
- _____

4 *(carrots?) (No/buy some)*
- _____
- _____

5 *(butter?) (Yes/in the fridge)*
- _____
- _____

6 *(teapot?) (Yes/on the shelf)*
- _____
- _____

2 Write *There was*, *There were*, *There wasn't* or *There weren't*.

Example: *There weren't many people at the party.*

1 _____ much food in the house.

2 _____ no time to talk.

3 _____ many shops open after 9.00.

4 _____ a lot of strange noises outside in the forest.

5 _____ no bank in the village.

6 _____ only a few days left before the exams.

7 _____ very little time to do anything.

3 Write *There* + the correct form of *be* and pronouns.

Examples: *There was a dog in our garden yesterday. It came from next door.*

There isn't any butter. We finished it yesterday.

1 _____ some flowers for Ann. _____ 're from Tom.

2 _____ much sugar last night. Mum used most of _____ to make a cake.

3 _____ many people at the concert last night, but I think _____ enjoyed it.

4 _____ somebody on the phone for you. His name is Peter. Do you know _____

5 _____ any matches. Have you used _____ all?

6 _____ much water, so we'll have to use _____ very carefully.

4 Complete the statements. Choose from these expressions.

It's	a good/bad idea to ...
It was	good/lovely/sad to ...
	sad that ...
	a pity that ...
	not worth ...
	no use ...

Example: *It was a bad idea to go camping in the middle of winter.*

1 _____ see all the family together again today.

2 _____ walking ten kilometres yesterday just to see that boring view.

3 _____ shouting at the children. It doesn't do any good.

4 _____ we lost the match after we had done so much training.

5 _____ he died so young. He was only 32.

57 Quantity
a lot of, many, much, a few, a little

With countable nouns use *a lot of, many* and *a few*. Use *a lot of* and *many* for a large number of things. The noun has an *s*, eg *a lot of cassettes* and *many videos*

With uncountable nouns use *a lot of, much* and *a little*. Use *a lot of* and *much* for a large amount of something. The noun has no *s*, eg *a lot of pop music* and *much time*.

Use *a lot of* with both countable and uncountable nouns. We use it in positive sentences more than in questions and negative sentences.

> *She's got **a lot of cassettes**.*   *She's got **a lot of pop music**.*

We can use the informal *lots of* instead of *a lot of*.

> *He's got **lots of cassettes**.*   *He's got **lots of pop music**.*

We can use short forms in answers to questions.

> ● *Are there many songs on the CD?*   ○ *Yes, there are **a lot/lots**.*

We usually use *many* and *much* in questions and negative sentences (but sometimes in formal positive sentences too). We can use *much* and *many* by themselves in answers to questions.

> ● *Are there **many** songs on the cassette?*
> ○ *No, **there aren't many**.* OR *Yes, **lots**.*
> ● *Is there **much** music on the cassette?*
> ○ *No, **not much**.* OR *Yes, **a lot**.*

We usually use *a few* and *a little* in positive statements, and also in requests and offers.

> *There were **a few** people in the room.*
> *There was **a little** food on the table.*
> *Could I borrow **a few** stamps?*   *Would you like **a little** money?*

a few is for a small number of something, but positive. *few* is also for a small number of something, but negative. The noun is plural.

> *I'm going to see **a few friends** this evening.* (positive)
> ***Few people** live to 100.* (negative)

a little and *little* are similar and are for a small amount of something. The noun has no *s*.

> *We've got **a little time**, so let's have tea.* (positive)
> *Hurry! There's very **little time**.* (negative)

تستخدم a lot of و many و few a مع الأسماء المعدودة. وتستخدم a lot of و many عند الحديث عن عدد كبير من الاشياء. وتلحق الاسم علامة الجمع s.

تستخدم a lot of و much و little a مع الأسماء غير المعدودة. وتستخدم much و a lot of مع الكميات الكبيرة، ولا تضاف علامة الجمع s إلى الاسم.

تستخدم a lot of مع الأسماء المعدودة وغير المعدودة وتستخدم في الجمل المثبتة أكثرمما تستخدم في الجمل الاستفهامية والجمل المنفية.

ويمكن استخدام صيغة lots of غير الرسمية عوضاً عن a lot of.

ويمكن استخدام الصيغ المختصرة عند الإجابة على الأسئلة.

تستخدم many وmuch عادةً في الجمل الاستفهامية وفي الجمل المنفية (وأحياناً في الجمل الرسمية المثبتة أيضاً). ويمكن استخدام much و many بمفردهما عند الإجابة عن الأسئلة.

تستخدم a few و a little عادةً في الجمل الخبرية المثبتة وكذلك في الطلبات والعروض.

تستخدم a few لأعداد قليلة من الأشياء ولكن ايجاباً. أما few فتعبر عن عدد صغير من الأشياء ولكن سلباً. ويكون الاسم في حالة الجمع.

وينطبق الشيء نفسه على a little و little ويستخدمان لكميات صغيرة، ولا تضاف علامة الجمع s إلى الاسم.

Exercises

1 Complete the statements and questions. Use *a lot (of)*, *lots (of)*, *many* or *much*.

Example: ● Have we got <u>much</u> tea?

○ No, we haven't, but we've got <u>a lot of/ lots of</u> coffee.

1 Let's hurry. There's _____ work to do, and there isn't _____ time.

2 Harry talks to _____ people in his work, but he hasn't got _____ close friends.

3 I haven't got _____ money. How _____ have you got?

4 Some people spend _____ time at the office, but they don't really do _____ work.

5 ● Are there _____ people in the shops today?

○ No, not _____ , even though _____ the shops are having sales.

6 ● How _____ time do you spend travelling every week?

○ _____ Probably about 20 hours.

7 ● How _____ times have you been to France?

○ Not _____ Three times altogether.

8 ● How _____ do you weigh?

○ Too _____ Nearly 85 kilos.

2 Complete the statements and questions. Use *a few*, *few*, *a little* or *little*.

Examples: You'd better go to the corner shop. We've only got <u>a few</u> eggs and <u>a little</u> milk. We'd better hurry. There's very <u>little</u> time.

1 We'd better go to the supermarket. There's only _____ orange juice, and there are only _____ tomatoes.

2 My motor-bike is very cheap to run. It uses very _____ petrol, and very _____ ever goes wrong with it.

3 Smoking is going out of fashion. _____ still smoke at work, but _____ of them think it's a good thing to do.

4 The soup isn't ready yet. I think it needs _____ cream and _____ more chopped vegetables.

5 We can only afford _____ small presents this year. We've got very _____ money.

6 Could you lend me _____ money? I only need _____ pounds.

7 The generals of the First World War were men with _____ ideas and _____ imagination.

8 ● I put on _____ weight while I was on holiday.

○ How much?

● Only _____ kilos.

3 Complete the conversation. Choose from these forms.

a few, few, a little, little, a lot (of), lots (of), many, much

● How's business, Fred?

○ It's quite good. We're getting <u>a lot of</u> orders this year. Not like last year. Last year we had very ¹_____ work, and ²_____ of our staff lost their jobs. How's your company doing?

● It's still not very good, I'm sorry to say. We've only got ³_____ new orders at the moment, and not ⁴_____ of those are big ones.

○ I'm sorry to hear that.

● There's another big problem too. Some customers owe us ⁵_____ money from jobs that we did months ago.

○ That's terrible. How ⁶_____ money do they owe you?

● About £50,000. That's ⁷_____ for a small company like mine.

○ Can you do anything to make them pay?

● No, I can't really do very ⁸_____ If a company really decides not to pay me on time, there's very ⁹_____ that I can do about it.

○ Perhaps you should get them to pay you ¹⁰_____ each month.

● That's a good idea. I might try it.

58 Partitives

All of, Most of, None of, Both of, Neither of, etc   every, each

Our weekend at Brill Adventure Centre

FORMS

All of, Both of, etc

All of us enjoyed the trip.
We had two instructors. Both of them helped us a lot.

every and each

The weather was good every day except Thursday.

All of, Both of, etc

All of means 100% of a group. *None of* means 0% of a group.
> ***All/None of*** *us enjoyed rock climbing.*

Most of means nearly all. *A few of* means a small number. *Some of* is between *Most* and *A few*. (Other phrases: *A lot of, Half of, One or two of*.)
> ***Most/Some/A few of*** *us wanted to do more archery.*

Both of means 100% of a pair. *Neither of* means 0% of a pair.
> ***Both/Neither of*** *the instructors taught us sandsurfing.*

With *Both* and *All* + noun, you can leave out *of*. With *Both* + noun, you can also leave out *the*.
> ***Both*** *(of) (the) instructors helped* ***all*** *(of) the students.*

But you must use *of* before object pronouns and after *Most, Some, A few* and *Neither*.
> *Both of them, All of us, Most of you, One of them*
> *Most of the students, Neither of the instructors*

One of is different from *either of* and *any of*.
> *You can use* ***either of*** *the cars. (It doesn't matter which of the pair you use.)*
> *You can book* ***any of*** *the 200 rooms in the hotel. (It doesn't matter which of the rooms you book.)*

Compare *None of* and *Neither of* above with *not ... any of* and *not ... either of*.

	Subject	**Object**
Group:	*None of*	*not ... any of*
Pair:	*Neither of*	*not ... either of*

> ***None of*** *us enjoyed it. They didn't help* ***any of*** *the students.*
> ***Neither of*** *them taught us. We didn't like* ***either of*** *them.*

Compare talking about a group and talking in general.
> ***Most of*** *the students enjoyed it. (most of the groups of students)*
> ***Most*** *students work hard. (most of the group of students)*

Use *All, Some* and *No* to talk in general.
> ***All*** *cats like milk.*   ***Some*** *trees grow fruit.*   ***No*** *man can fly.*

every and each

We use *every* and *each* to talk about all members of a group. Use a singular noun and verb.
> ***Every*** *day was fun. (all group members together)*
> ***Each*** *day was different. (all group members one by one)*

يفيد استخدام all of جميع المعنيين، ولا يفيد استخدام none of أحداً منهم.

ويفيد استخدام most of الغالبية العظمى في حين تعني a few of عدداً قليلاً. وتستخدم some of لتعبر عن حالة وسط بين most و a few، لاحظ العبارات الاخرى المستخدمة.

ويعني استخدام both of كلا الاثنين في حين تفيد neither of الانتفاء عن الاثنين.

يمكن الاستغناء عن of عندما تأتي مع both و all + اسم. وكذلك يمكن الاستغناء عن الاداة the عند استخدام both + اسم.

يجب استخدام of قبل الضمير في موقع المفعول به، وكذلك بعد most و some و a few و neither. وتختلف of عن either of او any of.

قارن بين الاستخدام السابق لـ none of و neither of، اعلاه، وكيفية استخدام not... any of و not... either of.

قارن كيفية الحديث عن مجموعةٍ ما وكيفية الحديث بشكل يتصف بالعمومية.

تستخدم all و some و no للحديث عن العموميات.

تستخدم every و each للحديث عن جميع افراد مجموعة. استخدم فعلاً واسماً في صيغة المفرد.

Exercises

1 Complete the statements about the students. Use these words.

all, almost all, a few, most, one, some

A teacher checked her class register for the last 15 lessons.

NAME	PRESENT	ABSENT
John	14	1
Lisa	1	14
Lucy	4	11
David	15	0
Robin	8	7
Greg	12	3
Sally	6	9

Examples: *John came to <u>almost all of the lessons.</u>*
Lisa only came to <u>one of them.</u>

1 *Lucy only came to _____*

2 *David came to _____*

3 *Robin came to _____*

4 *Greg came to _____*

5 *Sally only came to _____*

2 Complete the second statement in each pair. Use these words.

all of, both of, most of, half of, a few of, us, you, them

Example: *Rob and I don't always get to work on time.*
<u>Both of us</u> were late again today.

1 *You and your brother look ill. _____ need to see the doctor.*

2 *The teacher put the class in two groups. _____ prepared questions, and the other half prepared their answers.*

3 *Well, everybody, you did very badly in the test. _____ got less than 50%. That's really not good enough!*

4 *The senior and the junior basketball teams are doing very well. _____ reached the national championships.*

5 *About 60 supporters went to the championships. The team coach took _____ in his car, but _____ went by bus. We had a great time.*

3 Complete the negative statements. Use these words.

any of, either of, neither of, none of

Examples: *The couple next door are strange. I don't like <u>either of</u> them much.*
<u>None of</u> the children wanted to go home at the end of the party.

1 *I asked Wayne and Brian, but _____ them could lend me any money.*

2 *I offered all the old people a trip to London, but _____ them wanted to go.*

3 *We looked at several restaurants, but we didn't like _____ them.*

4 *Peter tried two different hotel jobs, but he wasn't very good at _____ them.*

5 *_____ Joe's clothes fitted him any more because he was growing so fast.*

6 *_____ the teams scored, and the match ended at 0 – 0.*

7 *I test drove a number of new cars, but I didn't buy _____ them.*

8 *I took two exams, but because I hadn't done enough work, I didn't pass _____ them.*

9 *I've read both of these books and I didn't like _____ them. They were very boring.*

10 *I asked the class if _____ them would help me move the tables, but _____ them did. So I did it myself.*

4 Complete the paragraph. Use these words.

all, both, each, every

Jamie and his friends, Bob and Pete, go to judo classes <u>every</u> week. He and [1]_____ his friends love judo, and they never miss their class [2]_____ Friday evening. There are about 20 people in the class, and [3]_____ of them train very hard. To start with, they [4]_____ do exercises together. Then the teacher works with [5]_____ member of the class, one by one. [6]_____ student trains at his or her own standard. [7]_____ three months, they take a test. If they pass, they go up to the next grade.

59 Pronouns: subject and object
You can give it to me.

BSL INTERNATIONAL

We must get this package to the Manchester office fast.

Give it to me. I'm going there tomorrow.

FORMS			
	1st person	**2nd person**	**3rd person**
Singular			
Subject	*I*	*you*	*he she it*
Object	*me*	*you*	*him her it*
Plural			
Subject	*we*	*you*	*they*
Object	*us*	*you*	*them*

Personal pronouns refer to people and things. We use pronouns instead of nouns, eg for people's names, when the meaning is clear.

First person pronouns refer to the speaker, or to the speaker and one or more other people.
> *We must get ...* (the two speakers)
> *Give it to me.* (the speaker)

Second person pronouns refer to the person or people listening.
> *You can give ...* (the listener)

Third person pronouns refer to either a person or people or a thing or things. These are outside the 1st and 2nd persons' conversation.
> *Give it to them.* (the package and some other people)

A personal pronoun can be the subject or the object of a sentence.

Subject	**Object**
I'm going home now.	*Peter doesn't know me.*
Is she working tomorrow?	*Sally called her three times.*
They don't like loud music.	*We answered them.*

An object pronoun can be either a direct object or an indirect object. (See Unit 62 for more information about direct and indirect objects.)
> *Joe sent it.* (direct object)
> *Joe sent it to her.* (indirect object)

You can use pronouns in short answers to questions. The other way of doing this – with object pronouns – is informal.
- *Who broke this dish?* ○ *I did./I didn't.* OR *Me./Not me.*
- *Who'll wash the car for me?* ○ *We will./We won't.*
  OR *Us./Not us.*

There are ways of talking about people in general. The pronoun *you* is informal.
> *You never know what's going to happen.*

The pronoun *one* is very formal.
> *One cannot judge people by the way they look.*

The pronoun *they* refers to other people in general, or to people who are in charge.
> *They say some people hardly ever sleep.*
> *They don't let foreigners visit without a visa.*

تشير الضمائر الشخصية الى الاشخاص والاشياء. وتستخدم الضمائر عوضاً عن الاسماء عندما تكون المعاني قد اتضحت.

ويشير الضمير المفرد الاول الى المتحدث كشخص فرد، في حين يشير الضمير we الى متحدثين اثنين او اكثر.

ويشير الضمير الثاني you الى المخاطب كفرد أو إلى مخاطبين اثنين أو أكثر.

وتشير ضمائر الغائب (3rd person) الى فرد او الى افراد، او الى شيء واحد، أو اشياء، خارج حدود المحادثة بين المتحدث او المتحدثين.

يمكن ان يأتي الضمير الشخصي في موقع الفاعل، أو المبتدأ في الجملة، أو في موقع المفعول به.

عندما يأتي الضمير في موقع المفعول به، يمكن ان يكون مفعولاً به مباشراً او غير مباشر. (انظر unit 62 للمزيد من المعلومات عن المفعول به المباشر وغير المباشر)

يمكن استخدام الضمائر في الاجابات القصيرة عن الاسئلة. لاحظ كيف تستخدم الضمائر في صيغة المفعول به بطريقة غير رسمية.

يستخدم الضمير you للحديث عن الناس بشكل عام. ويعتبر استخدام الضمير you هنا استخداماً غير رسمي.

يعتبر استخدام الضمير one في هذا المقام صيغة رسمية جداً.

ويشير الضمير they الى الآخرين بشكل عام او الى اشخاص بعينهم من المسؤولين.

Exercises

1 Read the conversation. Then write the meanings of the underlined pronouns.

Paul: *What are ¹you doing tomorrow?*

Bill: *²I'm going to a football practice in the morning.*

Paul: *³I'd like to go to that too. I love football. What time does ⁴it start?*

Bill: *At 10.00. Why don't ⁵you come with ⁶me? Then after that, we can meet Neil in town. ⁷He wants to see the new Batman film.*

Paul: *Oh, yes. People say ⁸it's good.*

Bill: *Yes, ⁹they say it's the best Batman film yet. So I think ¹⁰we should all go and see it together. What do you think?*

1 you = _Bill_   6 me = _____

2 I = _____   7 He = _____

3 I = _____   8 it = _____

4 it = _____   9 they = _____

5 you = _____   10 we = _____

2 Write the correct subject pronouns and short forms of *be*.

Example: ● *What are <u>you</u> doing, Sally?*
            ○ *<u>I'm</u> making a cake.*

1 ● *Where are Tom and Bill going?*
   ○ _____ *going to the cinema.*

2 ● *Susan looks great in that dress.*
   ○ *Yes,* _____ *a beautiful girl.*

3 ● *What are* _____ *and the boys doing?*
   ○ _____ *going to the swimming pool.*

4 ● *What's that dog doing in our kitchen?*
   ○ _____ *taking our lunch!*

5 ● *Do you know Peter Wells?*
   ○ *Yes,* _____ *the man with the big house at the end of our street.*

6 ● *How are* _____ *travelling round France, Fred?*
   ○ _____ *travelling by bike.*

7 ● _____ *looking very happy today, Sally.*
   ○ *Yes,* _____ *my birthday and* _____ *18 today.* _____ *having a party tonight. Please come.*

3 Write the correct object pronouns.

Example: ● *Where did you put my hat?*
            ○ *I put <u>it</u> on the table.*

1 ● *Do you know where Ann is?*
   ○ *Yes. I can see* _____ *over there.*

2 ● *I'll be at home this evening.*
   ○ *All right. I'll call* _____ *at 7.00.*

3 ● *I need to see Mr Brice, please.*
   ○ *Certainly. You can see* _____ *at 3.00.*

4 ● *Do you like these shoes?*
   ○ *Yes. I'm going to buy* _____

5 ● *Why does Peter always call* _____ *in the evening, Tony?*
   ○ *Because he always wants* _____ *to help* _____ *with his homework.*

6 ● *Were there any calls for* _____ *while we were out?*
   ○ *There weren't any calls for Bill, but there was a call for* _____ *. Mrs Tucker phoned and she wants* _____ *to call* _____ *back.*

4 Write the correct subject and object pronouns and short froms of *be*.

It's Tom's first day at the office.

Jim: *Tom, come and meet Ann Scott. <u>She's</u> our Finance Director. Ann, this is Tom Blake.* ¹_____ *our new sales assistant.*

Ann: *It's nice to meet ²_____ , Tom.*

Tom: *³_____ good to meet ⁴_____ too, Mrs Scott.*

Ann: *Oh, please call ⁵_____ Ann. ⁶_____ all use our first names here.*

Later the same day

Jim: *Tom, could ⁷_____ help ⁸_____ please?*

Tom: *Yes, of course. What can ⁹_____ do?*

Jim: *Take this report to Finance and give ¹⁰_____ to Ann. And give ¹¹_____ these papers too.* ¹²_____ *very important.* ¹³_____ *needs* ¹⁴_____ *for a meeting.* ¹⁵_____ *starting in a few minutes from now.*

Tom: *Right.* ¹⁶_____ *'ll go immediately.*

60 Pronouns: possessive

Is this your jacket?   It's mine.   It's Tim's.

Possessive determiners and possessive pronouns

my, your, their, etc, come before a noun. They are determiners. They are also posssessive – they show who or what owns something.

> *Is this **your** jacket?*
> *Where are **my** shoes? I can't see them.*

We can use *mine, yours, theirs*, etc, instead of a possessive determiner + noun. They are pronouns.

> *This jacket isn't **mine**. Is it **yours**?*
> *That car isn't **ours**. It's **theirs**.*

Note that *his* and *its* are determiners and also pronouns. (But *its* as a pronoun is rare.)

> ● *Perhaps this is **his** bag.*
> ○ *No, it isn't **his**. It's mine.*

its is different from *it's*. *its* is a possessive determiner. *it's* is short for *it is* or *it has*.

> *Here's the camera, and this is **its** case.* (possessive)
> *Look. Now **it's** raining.* (**it's** = it is)
> *There's the bus! At last **it's** arrived.* (**it's** = it has)

Possessive with *'s*

Use noun + *'s* like a possessive determiner.

> *This is **her** coat.* → *This is Sally**'s** coat.*

Use noun + *'s* like a possessive pronoun.

> *This hat is **hers**.* → *This hat is Sally**'s**.*

After a plural noun with *s*, write noun + *s'*.

> *These are the **girls'** coats.*
> *These coats are the **girls'**, not the **boys'**.*

تأتي الضمائر my وyour وtheir... الخ قبل الاسم، وتعمل هنا كمحددات، كما انها تفيد الملكية اذ تبين لنا من يملك ماذا.

ويمكن استخدام صيغ الملكية mine... الخ عوضاً عن محددات الملكية مضافاً لها الاسم... وتعتبر هنا ضمائر.

تعمل his وits عمل المحددات وعمل الضمائر ايضاً. ولكن استخدام its كضمير امر نادر.

تختلف its التي تفيد تحديد الملكية عن it's التي تأتي اختصاراً it is او it has.

عندما يضاف للاسم 's' فانها تكون محددة للملكية.

تعمل صيغة استخدام الاسم مع 's' عمل ضمير الملكية.

توضع 's' بعد الاسم في حالة الجمع s +.

Exercises

1 Write possessive adjectives.

Example: *Hello. My name is Bob.*

1 *Could you write _____ address here, please?*

2 *The boy fell down and hurt _____ arm.*

3 *Let's take _____ holidays at the same time and go away together.*

4 *Could you call at Mr and Mrs Hill's house and give back _____ books?*

5 *Is Sally Barrett here? This is _____ bag.*

6 *That's _____ pen! Give it back to me!*

7 *The cat wants _____ dinner. Look, it's waiting outside.*

2 Write the answers.

Example: ● *Are these shoes Sally's? (No/bigger)*
　　　　　 ○ *No, they aren't hers. Hers are bigger.*

1 ● *Is that coat John's? (No/older)*
　 ○ _____

2 ● *Are those magazines Julie's? (No/newer)*
　 ○ _____
　　 _____

3 ● *Is that car Tom's and Lucy's? (No/smaller)*
　 ○ _____
　　 _____

4 ● *Is that coat mine? (No/nicer)*
　 ○ _____

5 ● *Are these reports ours? (No/longer)*
　 ○ _____
　　 _____

6 ● *Is this umbrella yours?*
　 ○ *Yes, it is _____! Thank you very much!*

3 Write the answers.

Example: ● *Is this bag his or hers? (hers)*
　　　　　 ○ *It's hers. Look, it's got her name inside.*

1 ● *Are these boots yours or mine? (yours)*
　 ○ _____
　　 _____

2 ● *Is this briefcase his or hers? (his)*
　 ○ _____
　　 _____

3 ● *Are these shoes ours or theirs? (theirs)*
　 ○ _____
　　 _____

4 ● *Is that jacket hers or yours? (mine)*
　 ○ _____
　　 _____

5 ● *Are those T-shirts hers or mine? (hers)*
　 ○ _____
　　 _____

6 ● *Is this book yours or his? (ours)*
　 ○ _____
　　 _____

4 Write *its* or *it's*.

Examples: *The dog ate its food in less that a minute.*
　　　　　　 It's 1.00 and this is the News.

1 *The sky has gone dark and _____ started to rain.*

2 *Here's the cassette, but I've lost _____ case.*

3 *Let's stay indoors. _____ too cold to go out.*

4 *I know _____ hard for you, but you must finish the work.*

5 *This is our cat. _____ name is Fluffy.*

6 *Don't try to move your leg. I think _____ broken.*

5 Complete the words with *'s* or *s'*.

Examples: *Look at Tony 's pictures. They're lovely.*
　　　　　　 The two boy s' bikes are in the garage.

1 *My parent___ phone number is 345-321. You can call them any time.*

2 *My brother Peter___ phone number is 345-789.*

3 *Please, can you tell me Sally West___ room number?*

4 *A policeman___ job is often difficult.*

5 *The government has refused to raise hospital worker___ pay again this year.*

6 *Why did you laugh at Tony___ suggestions? I don't understand why you can't accept other people___ ideas.*

61 Pronouns: reflexive
You'll hurt yourself.

Be careful, or you'll fall and hurt yourself.

Use a reflexive pronoun when the subject (S) of a verb (V) is also the direct object (DO) of the action. Compare the following.

S	V	DO		S	V	DO
You'll	*hurt*	*him.*		*You'll*	*hurt*	**yourself**.
He's	*cut*	*her.*		*He's*	*cut*	**himself**.

Use a reflexive pronoun when the subject of an action is also the indirect object (IO) of an action. Compare the following.

S	V	IO		S	V	IO
She	*talked*	*to me.*		*She*	*talked*	*to* **herself**.
He	*works*	*for us.*		*He*	*works*	*for* **himself**.

Use a reflexive pronoun as an indirect object with a direct object. (See Unit 62 for more information about direct and indirect objects.) Compare the following.

S	V	IO	DO	S	V	IO	DO
She	*bought*	*me*	*a book.*	*She*	*bought*	**herself**	*a book.*
We	*taught*	*them*	*Arabic.*	*We*	*taught*	**ourselves**	*Arabic.*

Note the singular → plural change in *self* → *selves*.
> *I enjoyed* **myself** *at the party.*
> *We enjoyed* **ourselves** *at the party.*

Also use a reflexive pronoun to emphasize the subject of an action. This type of reflexive comes after the object of the verb.
- ● *Let me buy the ticket for you.*
- ○ *No, thanks. I'll buy* **it myself**. (I want to do it – not you.)
  Jamie's five now, so he can put on **his clothes himself/by himself**. (He doesn't need his parents' help.)

Also use *by* + a reflexive pronoun to emphasize that the subject of an action does the action alone.
> *John climbed the mountain* **by himself**.
> *The teacher made Ann sit* **by herself**, *away from the other girls.*

يستخدم الضمير المنعكس عندما يكون الفاعل هو المفعول به المباشر في الوقت نفسه، ويتضح ذلك من خلال مقارنة الجمل التالية.

يستخدم الضمير المنعكس عندما يكون فاعل الفعل هو نفسه المفعول به غير المباشر للعمل. ويتضح الامر من خلال مقارنة الجمل التالية:

يستخدم الضمير الانعكاسي كمفعول به غير مباشر مع مفعول به مباشر. (انظر unit 62 للمزيد من المعلومات حول المفعول به المباشر وغير المباشر) وقارن ما يلي:

تجدر ملاحظة التغييرات التي تطرأ على الضمير الانعكاسي self في حالة المفرد والذي يصبح selves في حالة الجمع.
ويستخدم الضمير المنعكس للتأكيد على الفاعل.
ويأتي هذا النوع من الضمائر الانعكاسية بعد المفعول به مباشرة.

وتستخدم by + ضمير منعكس لتأكيد ان الفاعل هو الذي يقوم بالفعل منفرداً.

Exercises

1 Write the correct reflexive pronouns.

Example: *Stop shouting. Control* <u>*yourself.*</u>

1 *Tell the children to dry* _____ *or they'll catch cold.*

2 *The light turns* _____ *off automatically.*

3 *Her real name is Monica, but she calls* _____ *Mo.*

4 *I was tired, so I gave* _____ *a day off work.*

5 *Dan injured* _____ *badly at work.*

6 *We need to protect* _____ *from the sun. We'd better wear hats.*

7 *Don't play with knives or you'll cut* _____

8 *Children, while I'm out I want you to behave* _____

2 Write the correct verbs and reflexive pronouns. Use these verbs.

bought, burn, kill, look after, looked at, made, push, save, wash

Example: *Be careful with the pan. It's hot. Don't* <u>*burn yourself.*</u>

1 *The boat crashed into the rocks, but Fred managed to* _____

2 *Drive more slowly in future, or you'll* _____ *one day.*

3 *Tina tried on the hat, and then she* _____ *in the mirror.*

4 *I was tired when I got home, so I* _____ *a cup of tea.*

5 *Everybody in the team went to the sports shop and they* _____ *the same kind of baseball cap.*

6 *We're not doing enough training. We've got to* _____ *even harder if we want to win the championship.*

7 *Our cat is a very clean animal. It likes to sit in the sun and* _____

8 *I shall miss you both while you're away. Be careful and* _____

3 Write the correct types of pronoun.

Examples: *Then I saw Bob. He was quite near, so I called* <u>*him.*</u>
Sue bought some books, and she taught <u>*herself*</u> *to cook.*

1 *I looked at Sam. He looked back at* _____

2 *Look at* _____ *in the mirror! You're all in a terrible mess.*

3 *Sue doesn't think about other people. She only thinks about* _____

4 *Your house is very near ours. You must come and visit* _____ *soon.*

5 *Let's put on the cassette recorder, and then we can record* _____

6 *They never help us, so I don't want to help* _____

7 *My son is going to university soon. I shall miss* _____ *very much.*

4 Write the answers. Use reflexive pronouns for emphasis.

Example: ● *Did Alan's assistant send the letters?*
○ <u>*No, he sent them himself.*</u>

1 ● *Did your dad pay for your car?*
○ _____

2 ● *Does Sue's secretary prepare the reports?*
○ _____

3 ● *Is Steve's brother bringing the equipment?*
○ _____

4 ● *Will I have to tidy the children's room?*
○ _____
_____

5 ● *Are the boys going to clean our car?*
○ _____
_____

6 ● *I'm hungry! Are you going to make dinner now?*
○ _____
_____

62 Direct and indirect objects
She sent them a card.

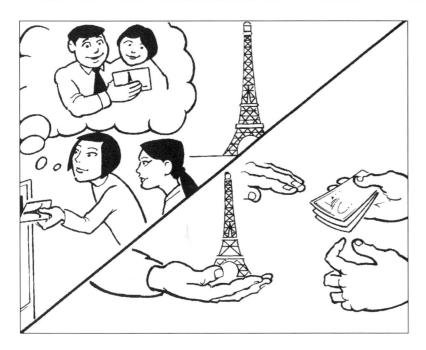

FORMS			
S	**V**	**(DO)**	
Susan	*laughed.*		
Susan	*studies*	*(French).*	
Susan	*sent*	*a card.*	
Form 1 Indirect objects			
S	**V**	**DO**	**IO**
Susan	*sent*	*a card*	*to her parents.*
Form 2 Indirect objects			
S	**V**	**IO**	**DO**
Susan	*sent*	*her parents*	*a card.*
Form 3 Indirect objects			
S	**V**	**IO**	
Susan	*laughed*	*at us.*	

Some verbs (V) do not take a direct object (DO).
> *Susan **laughed**.   We **talked**.*

Some verbs can be with or without a direct object.
> *Susan **studies**.   Susan **studies French**.*

Most verbs must take a direct object.
> *Susan **sent a card**.   She **bought a souvenir**.*

Some verbs take a direct object and an indirect object (IO) too. After these verbs we introduce the indirect object with *to: bring, give, lend, pass, pay, sell, show, take, teach, tell, throw.*

S	**V**	**DO**	**IO**
He	***paid***	***the money***	***to her***.
Bob	***gave***	***his old car***	***to his brother***.

After these verbs we introduce the indirect object with *for: bring, buy, cook, do, get, make, order, take.*

S	**V**	**DO**	**IO**
I've	***brought***	*some books*	***for you***. *Here you are.*
I'm	***doing***	*a letter*	***for the boss***.

We can use *bring* and *take* with both *to* + indirect object and *for* + indirect object.

S	**V**	**DO**	**IO**
I	***took***	*the books*	***to the teacher***.
I	***brought***	*some flowers*	***for Mary***.

We often use Form 1 (see FORMS above) for emphasis.
> *Don't pass **the ball to him**! Pass **it to me**.*

But we usually use Form 2.
> *He paid **her money**.   I've bought **you a book**.*

In Form 3 there is no direct object, only an indirect object.
> *Sue laughed **at us**.   We smiled **at each other**.*

بعض الافعال لا تتعدى إلى مفعول به مباشر.

وبعض الافعال يمكن ان تتعدى إلى مفعول به مباشر، أو لا تتعدى.

معظم الافعال يجب ان تتعدى إلى مفعول به مباشر.

وبعض الافعال تتعدى إلى مفعول به مباشر وآخر غير مباشر، ايضاً. وهنا نقدم على المفعول به غير المباشر اداة الجر to. وفيما يلي قائمة بهذه الافعال.

بعد هذه الافعال التالية تدخل المفعول به غير المباشر مع for.

يمكن ان نستخدم الفعلين bring وtake مع to + مفعول به غير مباشر، وكذلك مع for + مفعول به غير مباشر.

غالباً ما تستخدم الصيغة الاولى to + لتفيد التأكيد (لاحظ forms اعلاه)

ولكن تستخدم الصيغة الثانية (form 2) عادة.

لا تحتوي الصيغة الثالثة (form 3) على مفعول به مباشر ولكنها تحوي مفعولاً به غير مباشر فقط.

Exercises

1 Write statements with the indirect objects in the correct position.

Examples: *I'm writing a letter. (to my sister)*
<u>*I'm writing a letter to my sister.*</u>
I'm writing a card. (my brother)
<u>*I'm writing my brother a card.*</u>

1 *Ann gave a present. (her parents)*
_____

2 *Nick sent a book. (to his niece)*
_____

3 *Did you really buy it? (for me)*
_____

4 *Could you lend some money? (Harry)*
_____

5 *Susie's grandmother made a lovely dress. (her)*
_____
_____

6 *I'll take some magazines next time I visit her in hospital. (Celia)*
_____
_____

7 *Could you pass the report when he arrives? (to the boss)*
_____
_____

8 *I offered a place to stay as he had nowhere else to go. (Rob)*
_____
_____

2 Write replies. Use Form 1 indirect objects for emphasis.

Example: ● *Could you give Bob this magazine? (Kim)*
○ <u>*No, don't give it to Bob. Give it to Kim.*</u>

1 ● *I'm going to sell my pictures to Sally. (me)*
○ _____
_____

2 ● *I'd better take the car to the garage in town. (one near my house)*
○ _____
_____

3 ● *I think I'll buy a computer game for Sally. (her brother)*
○ _____
_____

4 ● *I'm going to show this information about Mr Blake to him. (the police)*
○ _____
_____

5 ● *I think I'll cook the steak for the children. (the adults)*
○ _____
_____

6 ● *Do I have to pay the money to Tom's teacher? (the school secretary)*
○ _____
_____

7 ● *I'll buy a present for you while I'm in Paris. (the children)*
○ _____
_____

3 Complete the memo with *to* or *for*.

Memo

From: JJ
To: KL   *Date: 3rd March*

Ken,
Could you do a few things <u>for</u> me while I'm away in Rome? Could you finish the report on my desk [1]_____ *me? I've been writing it specially* [2]_____ *the Head of Sales, so could you please give it* [3]_____ *him personally by midday on Thursday? Please explain the special items* [4]_____ *him. I've made some notes* [5]_____ *you, so you'll know what to write.*
    We've ordered some new computer equipment [6]_____ *the Sales Department. Could you ask the men from Compu-Tech to take the equipment* [7]_____ *Room 508? Please give the cheque on my desk* [8]_____ *the men when they come.*
    Thanks. I'll get some really good Italian olive oil [9]_____ *you while I'm in Rome.*

See you next week.
                    Jack

---

63 *something, anybody, everyone, etc*

There's something for everyone.

FORMS				
	thing	*body*	*one*	*where*
some	something (a thing)	somebody (a person)	someone (a person)	somewhere (in a place)
any	anything (a thing)	anybody (a person)	anyone (a person)	anywhere (in a place)
every	everything (all the things)	everybody (all the people)	everyone (all the people)	everywhere (in all the places)
no	nothing (no things)	nobody (no person)	no one (no person)	nowhere (in no place)

We can put *some*, *any*, *every* and *no* together with *thing*, *body*, *one* and *where* to form new words.

> *My book is **somewhere** in this room.*
> *Has **anyone** seen my book?*
> ***Everybody**! Please help me find it!*
> *I looked, but I found **nothing**.*

The words *something* and *anything*, etc, are like *some* and *any*.
Positive statements: *He told her **something**.*
Negative statements: *We didn't see **anybody**.*
Yes / No questions: *Did you go **anywhere**?*
Positive questions: *Did you find **something**?*
Offers: *Can I help **anyone**?*
Requests: *May I see **someone** in the office?*
Things that are possible, but not certain: *If **anybody** calls, tell me.*
(See Unit 43 for more information.)

All the words in this group are singular, including the words with *every*.

> *Is **everyone** here now?*   ***Everything** takes a long time.*

The words with *no* are negatives, so use the 3rd person singular positive forms of verbs.

> ***Nobody** is happy with the plan.*   ***No one** wants to go out.*

We can use an adjective, eg *strange*, *funny* and *boring*, after words with *some*, *any* and *no*, (but not usually after words with *every*).

> ***Somebody** came to the door.*   *Is there **anything** funny on TV?*

We can use *else* after all these words.

> *We haven't got **anything else** to eat.*
> *There's **nowhere else** to go.*

We can use the possessive *'s* form with the words that end with *body* or *one*.

> *Is this **anybody's** jacket?*   *The accident was **no one's** fault.*
> ***Somebody's** car is in our parking space!*

يمكن تكوين كلمات جديدة عند اضافة الكلمات some وany وevery وno للكلمات thing وbody وone وwhere.

وتعامل الكلمات something وanything... الخ نفس معاملة some وany.. ويتضح ذلك من خلال الامثلة. (انظر unit 43 للمزيد من المعلومات).

تعتبر جميع الكلمات في هذه المجموعة في حالة المفرد بما في ذلك الكلمات التي تأتي مع every.
تكون الكلمات التي تأتي مع no في صيغة النفي، الأمر الذي يتطلب وضع الفعل المضارع مع الضمير المفرد الغائب في صيغة الاثبات.
يمكن استخدام صفة بعد الكلمات التي تضاف لـ some وany وno، ولكن ذلك ليس شائعاً بعد الكلمات التي تضاف لـ every.
يمكن استخدام كلمة else بعد كل هذه الكلمات.

يمكن استخدام صيغة الملكية 's مع الكلمات التي تنتهي بـ body او one.

Exercises

1 Write *some, any, something, anybody, somewhere*, etc.

Examples: I met <u>some</u> old friends yesterday.

Yesterday I met <u>somebody</u> who knows you.

1 I've got _____ free time tomorrow.

2 I can't think of _____ to do.

3 Have you got _____ money?

4 Tony must be _____ in the park.

5 Does _____ here know how to work this machine?

6 Could I take _____ paper, please?

7 If _____ asks for me, just say I'm busy.

8 Would you like _____ coffee?

9 She can't find her glasses _____

10 I've got _____ for you to do this afternoon.

2 Complete the statements with the correct words beginning with *some-, any-, every-,* and *no-*.

Examples: I don't know <u>anybody</u> as clever as Tom. (any-)

1 If _____ is here now, the meeting can begin. (every-)

2 _____ we went in Africa, we found the people very friendly. (every-)

3 Excuse me. I've got _____ important to say. (some-)

4 _____ in the world can run as fast as Steve. (no-)

5 If there's _____ still in the building, tell them to come out quickly. (any-)

6 Is there _____ quiet near here for us to talk? (any-)

7 Is there _____ I can do to help you? (any-)

3 Write *something, anybody, everyone, nowhere*, etc.

- Has <u>anybody</u> seen my new Bruce Springsteen cassette? I've been looking for it [1]_____ – all over the house.
- ○ I don't think it's [2]_____ in this room.
- Well, it must be [3]_____ round here. It can't have disappeared. [4]_____ must have seen it.
- ○ Did you lend it to [5]_____ Or did you take it [6]_____ with you – into town, for example?
- No, I've been absolutely [7]_____ since yesterday morning. I've just been at home. And [8]_____'s borrowed it either.
- ○ Wait. Look! There's [9]_____ under that chair. Is that it?
- Where? I can't see [10]_____ Oh, I see it now. You're right. That's it! Thanks very much!

4 Complete the statements. Use the words in brackets.

Examples: There's <u>something good</u> on TV tonight. (a good thing)

We're all here now. There's <u>nobody else</u> to come. (not another person)

1 There's _____ on TV tonight. (no interesting thing)

2 I haven't told you the whole story. I've got _____ to tell. (another thing)

3 This beach is too crowded. Isn't there _____ we can go? (another place)

4 I've looked for the money _____ _____ (all possible places)

5 Is _____ coming to dinner this evening? (a nice person)

6 There's _____ to look for the money. (no other place)

64 Relative clauses 1
He's the person who caused the accident.

FORMS		
He's the person	who that	caused the accident.
That's the car	which that	he was driving.

A clause is a group of words with a subject and a verb. It can be a complete, simple sentence, or it can be a part of a larger sentence. A relative clause is only a part of a sentence. It adds meaning to the main clause of a sentence.

who, *which* and *that* introduce relative clauses. They refer back to a noun and stand instead of the noun.

> He's **the person who** ...
> That's **the car which** ...

They introduce a new idea about the noun.
> ... **who caused the accident**.
> ... **which he was driving**.

Below, idea 2 shows which bus and which friends the speaker means. Idea 1 is the main clause. Idea 2 supports it and completes the meaning of the sentence. It is a defining relative clause.

1 *The bus is going to London.*
2 *~~The bus~~ (which) has just left.*
→ *The bus **which has just left** is going to London.*

1 *I often see some old friends.*
2 *~~Some old friends~~ (who) live in Oxford.* → *I often see some old friends **who live in Oxford**.*

Use *who* or *that* for people.
> **The man who/that** bought the coat is standing over there.

Use *which* or *that* for things and animals.
> Those are **the cars which/that** crashed.

Use defining relative clauses in general statements.
> People **who do dangerous jobs** are usually paid well.
> A nice car is something **which most people want**.

Use defining relative clauses to define and identify.
> Gold is a heavy metal **which is very valuable**.
> Bell was the man **who invented the telephone**.

We usually use *who* or *which* in more formal writing, eg in business letters and reports.
> Dear Sir,
> Thank you for the catalogue and price list **which** I recently requested. The person **who** spoke to me on the phone also promised to send some samples, but these ...

تعني كلمة "clause" عبارة تتكون من مجموعة من الكلمات تحوي فاعلاً وفعلاً، ويمكن ان تكون جملة كاملة، بسيطة، او جزءاً من جملة اكبر. اما العبارة الموصولية فتكون فقط جزءاً من جملة تضيف معنى للجزء الرئيسي في الجملة.

تقدم العبارات الموصولية بالكلمات who وwhich وthat، وهي تشير الى اسم سبق ذكره، وتأتي عوضاً عنه. وتضيف هذه الكلمات فكرة جديدة عن الاسم.

توضح الفكرة 2 أدناه، اي حافلة وأي اصدقاء يعنيهم المتحدث. وتشكل الفكرة 1 الجزء الرئيسي في الجملة، تدعمها الفكرة 2 وتُكمّل معنى الجملة. وبالتالي فهي العبارة الموصولية المعرّفة.

تستخدم who او that للأشخاص.

وتستخدم which وthat للأشياء والحيوانات.

تستخدم العبارات الموصولية المعرّفة في الجمل الخبرية العامة.

وتستخدم العبارات الموصولية المعرّفة للتعريف والتحديد.

تستخدم who او which عادة في الاسلوب الكتابي الرسمي مثل الرسائل التجارية ورسال الاعمال والتقارير.

Exercises

1 Write *who, which* or *that*.

Arthur Penn is an old farm worker <u>who/that</u> lives in our village. He lives in a small house [1]_____ his family have had for 100 years. Recently, he was outside, moving a pile of stones and bricks [2]_____ used to be an old garden shed. Suddenly his spade hit something [3]_____ wasn't stone or brick. It sounded like metal. He dug a little more, and he found it was a very old box. He called to a friend [4]_____ was passing the garden gate. They worked together until they were able to pull the heavy box out. 'Perhaps it's something valuable [5]_____ somebody wanted to hide years ago,' Arthur said. 'Let's open it and see,' his friend said. 'Come on. You're the one [6]_____ should do that.' Arthur broke open the box, but there was no gold or silver – just a set of old-fashioned garden tools! 'They're the tools [7]_____ my grandfather used,' Arthur said. 'He was the one [8]_____ built the shed 100 years ago.'

2 Join each pair of statements to make one statement with a relative clause.

Example: A girl won the prize. She wrote the best essay.
<u>The girl who/that wrote the best essay won the prize.</u>

1 A pilot escaped without injury. He crashed his plane in the lake.

_____

_____

_____

2 A student has got a place in the national team. He broke the 10,000-metre record.

_____

_____

_____

3 A bus broke down. It takes people to the airport.

_____

_____

4 A file is on the top shelf. It has all the information.

_____

_____

_____

5 A policeman has recevied an award. He rescued 15 people from a fire.

_____

_____

_____

6 A woman wanted to speak to you. She phoned last night.

_____

_____

_____

3 Write relative clauses with *who, which* or *that*. Use these endings.

It teaches Japanese.
She painted that picture.
They built the first aeroplane.
It will pay a better salary.
She was lost for five days.
They are warm and friendly.
He scored all the goals.
He discovered America.
He can repair my old car.

Example: Were the Wright brothers the ones <u>who/that built the first aeroplane?</u>

1 What was the name of the player _____

_____

2 I want to get a new job _____

_____

3 Where can we find a mechanic _____

_____

4 Ann wants to find a book _____

_____

5 I like people _____

_____

6 Do you know the artist _____

_____

7 Mountain rescuers have found the climber _____

_____

8 Columbus was the man _____

_____

65 Relative clauses 2

The man they want is wearing a coat.

The man we want is coming now.

Reduced relative clauses with objects

who, *which* and *that* can be the subject of a clause, or they can be the object. If they are the object, we can leave them out.

> **The man who wants us** *is coming now.* (subject – no change)
> **The man who we want** *is coming now.* (object – change possible) → **The man we want** *is coming now.*
> *Did you see* **the dress which she bought**? (object – change possible) → *Did you see* **the dress she bought**?

ing and *ed* participles with relative clauses

The verb in a relative clause can be in a continuous tense. If it is, we can leave out *who*, *which* or *that* and then just use the *ing* (present) participle.

> *His case is the one* **which is coming now**. → *His case is the one* **coming now**.
> *I was angry with the people* **who were shouting last night**. → *I was angry with the people* **shouting last night**.

The *ed* (past) participle can be part of a passive tense. If it is, we can leave out *who*, *which* or *that* and then use the *ed* participle.

> *His case is the one* **that is marked** *with a cross.* → *His case is the one* **marked** *with a cross.*
> *He's the man* **who was followed** *by the police.* → *He's the man* **followed** *by the police.*

With a continuous passive tense use *being + ed* participle.

> *He's the man* **who is being watched** *by the police.* → *He's the man* **being watched** *by the police.*
> *Those were the cases* **which were being checked** *by Customs.* → *Those were the cases* **being checked** *by Customs.*

يمكن ان تكون الكلمات who و which و that في موقع الفاعل من العبارة الموصولية، كما يمكن ان تكون في موقع المفعول به. وعندما تأتي في موقع المفعول به يمكن ان نغفل ذكرها.

يمكن ان يكون الفعل في العبارة الموصولية في أحد الازمنة المستمرة... عندها يكون بالإمكان إغفال ذكر الكلمات who وwhich وthat، والاكتفاء بذكر الفعل مضافاً له ing فقط.

يمكن ان يكون الفعل المنتهي بـ ed جزءاً من الفعل في حالة المبني للمجهول، عندها يمكن إغفال ذكر who وwhich وthat، والاكتفاء بذكر ed التصريف الثالث.

تُستخدم مع الازمنة المستمرة في حالة المبني للمجهول، being + ed التصريف الثالث.

Exercises

1 Join each pair of statements to make one statement. Use *who, which* or *that* as the subject of the relative clause.

> **Example:** *The person wasn't there. She had sold the watch.*
> <u>*The person who/that had sold the watch wasn't there.*</u>

1 *The book has disappeared. It has all the answers.*
_____
_____

2 *We climbed over the fence. It separates the fields.*
_____
_____

3 *The old man can't see well. He crashed his car.*
_____
_____

4 *I'm going to give the boy some money. He found my camera.*
_____
_____

2 Join each pair of statements to make one statement. Use *who, which* or *that* as the object of the relative clause.

> **Example:** *The house stood by the river. We bought it.*
> <u>*The house which/that we bought stood by the river.*</u>

1 *The girls seemed sad. We met them at the wedding.*
_____
_____

2 *I want to go to the museum. You told me about it.*
_____
_____

3 *The taxi finally arrived. I'd ordered it.*
_____
_____

4 *The flowers are dying. She gave us them.*
_____
_____

3 Write *who, which, that* or nothing (✗)

> **Example:** *The house* <u>**✗**</u> *we bought stood by the river.*
> *The person* <u>*who/that*</u> *had sold the watch wasn't there.*

1 *The bus _____ we caught got to town early.*

2 *The man _____ will meet you is my brother.*

3 *Here's the money _____ I owe you.*

4 *Rob is the player _____ won the game.*

5 *This goes in the file _____ I put on the shelf.*

4 Write the active participle form of these verbs.

> *enter, finish, go, show, stand, wear*
>
> **Example:** *The police stopped a car* <u>*going*</u> *at 220 kph.*

1 *We listened to the guide _____ us round the palace.*

2 *Did you see anybody _____ the house?*

3 *I took photos of people _____ the race.*

4 *Can you pass me the vase _____ on the cupboard?*

5 *I didn't like that man _____ a red jacket.*

5 Write the passive participle form of these verbs.

> *build, find, make, mend, paint, prepare, use, write*
>
> **Examples:** *This is the gun* <u>*found*</u> *in the car.*
> *The houses* <u>*being built*</u> *in London Street will soon be ready.*

1 *This was the plane _____ by the President on his trip to Australia.*

2 *I'm now going to show you a pot _____ by hand. Watch carefully.*

3 *As we watched, there were two ships _____ to go to sea.*

4 *This is a story _____ for young people.*

5 *That's the bridge _____ after the storm. It'll be closed for another week.*

6 *I prefer shoes _____ of real leather.*

66 Relative clauses 3

There was a time when you could live well.

FISHERMEN FACE HARD TIMES

The fishing industry is going from bad to worse. There are now fishermen whose debts are rising and pushing them out of business.

Tom Billings, aged 58, says, 'There was a time when you could live well from the sea. But not any more. All the best areas where we used to fish are dead now.'

The main reason why this has happened is the fishing industry itself. With too many boats and efficient modern methods, the fishermen have fished the sea to death.

Relative clauses with *whose*

whose is a relative pronoun like *who*, but it is also possessive like *his, her, its, their*, etc.

1 *There are many fishermen with debts.*
2 ~~*Their*~~ *(whose) debts are rising.* → *There are many **fishermen whose debts are rising**.*

We usually use *whose* with people. We sometimes also use it with things and animals too.

> *Mary Owen was **the girl whose** story won first prize.*
> *Japan is **a country whose** economy is very successful.*
> *The boys found **a bird whose** wing was broken.*

Relative clauses with *whose* are formal. We often use them in more formal writing. We do not use them much in conversation.

> *Dear Sir,*
> *I wish to complain about a member of your sales staff **whose behaviour towards my wife was very unpleasant**.*

Relative clauses with *when*, *where* and *why*

We can use several sorts of relative clauses about a 'time' noun.

> *There was **a time when** you could live well.*
> *There was **a time that** you could live well.*
> *There was **a time** you could live well.*

'Time' nouns include words like *summer, year, week, day,* and *moment*.

> *Do you remember that **summer when** we went to France?*
> *I shall never forget the **day when** my sister was born.*

We can also use *where* to refer to a 'place' noun such as *house, street, town* and *city*.

> *I remember the **house where** I grew up.*
> *That's the **street where** John lives.*

We can use *why* to refer to the noun *reason* in the same way.

> *He's lazy! That's the **reason why** he failed.*

تعتبر whose أحد ضمائر الوصل، مَثَلُها مَثَلُ who ولكنها تفيد الملكية ايضاً، مثل his و her...الخ.

تستخدم whose عادة مع الاشخاص، واحياناً تستخدم مع الاشياء والحيوانات ايضاً.

تعتبر العبارات الموصولية بـ whose ذات طابع رسمي وتستخدم غالباً في الكتابة الرسمية، ولا تستخدم في المحادثة كثيراً.

يمكن استخدام العديد من العبارت الموصولية في جمل تنعت كلمة time عندما ترد كاسم.

وهذه العبارات التي تتعلق بالزمن تضم كلمات مثل year, summer...الخ.

ويمكن ايضاً استخدام where للاشارة الى اسم مكان وتحديده.

كذلك يمكن استخدام why التي تشير الى السببية وبالطريقة نفسها.

Exercises

1 Complete the questions with *whose, who, which* or *that*. Answer the questions.

Examples: ● What was the name of the man _who_ first
reached America from Europe in 1492?
○ _Christopher Columbus._
● What is the name of the country _whose_
capital is Kuala Lumpur?
○ _Malaysia._

1 ● What is the English name for the three ancient
man-made structures _____ stand near Cairo?
○ _____

2 ● What was the man _____ first flew in space called?
○ _____

3 ● Name the woman scientist _____ most important
work was the discovery of radium.
○ _____

4 ● What was the name of the Italian _____ travelled
to China and home again 700 years ago?
○ _____

5 ● What is the country _____ flag is a red circle on
a white square?
○ _____

6 ● Name the US state _____ is famous for cowboys
and _____ symbol is a yellow rose?
○ _____

2 Answer the questions. Use *whose* as the subject of the relative clause.

Your friend is looking at a wedding party guest list and
trying to remember people.

Example: ● Who was Yvonne Laroche? (Her husband
had a large beard.)
○ _She was the one whose husband_
had a large beard.

1 ● Which one was George Barret? (His wife had a
wonderful diamond necklace.)
○ _____
_____

2 ● Do you remember the Schmidts? (Their children fell
in the pool.)
○ _____
_____

3 ● Who was Lucy Rosser? (Her hat flew off in the wind.)
○ _____
_____

4 ● Do you remember the Lewis family? (Their car refused
to start after the party.)
○ _____
_____

5 ● And which ones were Mario and Maria di Stefano?
(Their daughters wore lovely blue dresses.)
○ _____
_____
_____

3 Write statements about the underlined parts of the conversation. Use *when, where* or *why* as the subject of the relative clause.

Example: ● Do you remember that _time_ on the river?
○ Oh, yes. Our boat nearly sank!
They talked about the _time when_
their boat nearly sank.

1 ● Our boat nearly turned over because you turned it in
front of that big river cruiser.
○ Yes, that was the _reason_.
They talked about the _____
_____

2 ● And then we stayed at that _old hotel_.
○ Yes. We dried out our clothes there.
They talked about the _____
_____
_____

3 ● And what about the _night_ of the storm?
○ Yes. The rain almost washed our tent away.
They talked about the _____
_____
_____

He's the driver who won.   Alan Brant, who won in France, is ...

NEW WORLD NUMBER ONE

Alan Brant, who yesterday won in France, is now Number One in the world. The race, which was watched by 100 million people world-wide, took place in temperatures of up to 40°C.

FORMS

Defining relative clauses

Anna: *Who's that in the picture?*
Jean: *Alan Brant. He's the driver who won the big race yesterday.*
Anna: *What race was that?*
Jean: *The race which they showed on TV yesterday.*

Adding clauses

Alan Brant, who won in France yesterday, is now Number One in the world. The race, which was watched by 30 million people world-wide, took place ...

Compare defining relative clauses with another type – adding clauses.

CROSSCHECK

Defining relative clauses	Adding clauses

Defining relative clauses

These clauses explain which driver and which race. The sentences are not complete without these clauses.

> *He's the driver **who/that won the big race**.*
> *The race **which/that they showed on TV**.*

These clauses do not have commas. They are a main part of the sentence.

We can use *that* instead of *who* or *which*. We can often use reduced forms. (See Unit 65.)

> *We mended the window **which/that was broken**.*
> *They'll only give jobs to pilots **who/that are very experienced**.*
> *Visitors should come on a day **when the castle is open**.*

which can refer to a noun phrase or a whole sentence.

> *I mended **the doll**, **which** was broken.*
> *They worked on the car all night, **which** helped Alan win.*

Most relative clauses are defining relative clauses. (See Units 64, 65 and 66.) We use them in speaking and in writing.

Adding clauses

These clauses add extra information to the basic sentences. The basic sentences are complete without these clauses.

> *Alan Brant, **who yesterday won in France**, is now ...*
> *The race, **which was watched by 30 million**, took place ...*

We separate this type of clause from the basic sentence with commas (,), dashes (–) or brackets ( ).

We cannot use *that* instead of *who* or *which*. But we can use *whose*, *when* and *where*.

> *We mended the kitchen window, **which was broken**.*
> *The pilots – **who are very experienced** – will be given jobs.*
> *Visitors should come on Sunday (**when the castle is open**).*

We use non-defining relative clauses mainly in writing. Newspaper reports use them a lot because they give a lot of information quickly.

تحدد العبارات الموصولية التعريفية ماهية السائق والسباق ولا تكتمل الجمل بدونها. ولا تستخدم في هذه الجمل الفواصل حيث تكون العبارات الموصولية هنا جزءاً أساسياً فيها. هذه العبارات تضيف معلومات الى الجمل الاساسية التي تعتبر كاملة في حد ذاتها من دون هذه العبارات. ويتم فصل هذا النوع من العبارات الموصولية عن الجملة الاساسية بفواصل او قواطع او اقواس.

يمكن في العبارات الموصولية التعريفية استخدام that بدلاً من who او which، كما يمكن استخدام الصيغ المختصرة في أغلب الاحيان. (انظر 65 unit). اما في العبارات الموصولية الاضافية فلا يمكن استخدام that بدلاً من who او which، ولكن يمكن استخدام whose وwhich وwhere.

يمكن في العبارات الموصولية التعريفية استخدام which، للاشارة الى شبه جملة اسمية، او الى جملة كاملة.

تعتبر معظم العبارات الموصولية تعريفية وتستخدم في الحديث وكذلك في الكتابة (انظر 64,65,66 units) وتستخدم العبارات الموصولية غير التعريفية في الكتابة اساساً، كما تستخدم كثيراً في كتابة التقارير الصحفية لانها توفّر معلومات وافية بشكل سريع.

Exercises

1 Are the clauses in *italics* defining or adding? Write commas if necessary.

Example: *Beethoven, whose music is loved by millions, was born in 1770 and died in 1827.* adding

1 Dover Castle *which is a very impressive building* was built by the Normans. _____

2 The girl *who found the wallet* handed it in to the police. _____

3 The programme *that we watched last night* was awful. _____

4 The writer Pete Holmes *whose most famous book is 'Glory'* has died today. He was 75. _____

2 Join each pair of statements to make one statement with an adding clause with *who* or *which*.

Examples: *Harry Lane is a rich man now. He was at college with me.*

 Harry Lane, who was at college with me, is a rich man now.

1 *Old Professor Jones is going to stop work soon. He's nearly 70.*

_____

_____

2 *To the north of India are the Himalayas. They include the highest mountains in the world.*

_____

_____

_____

3 *I bought myself some good, new clothes. I needed them for my new job.*

_____

_____

_____

4 *Barry Stone has built his own house. He works as a computer programmer.*

_____

_____

_____

3 Match the statements 1–7 and a–g. Join each pair changing a–g into adding clauses with *which*.

1 *The baby cried all night.*
2 *The old ship stayed in port.*
3 *I was out when Peter called.*
4 *The company has won the contract.*
5 *They've started doing road repairs.*
6 *They sun has come out at last.*
7 *The school is building a new gymnasium.*

a *That saved it from the storm.*
b *It's causing bad traffic delays.*
c *That was why I didn't hear the news.*
d *It meant I was tired all next day.*
e *That means we can go to the beach.*
f *It's going to help their basketball teams a lot.*
g *That's good news.*

 1– _d_ 2– ___ 3– ___ 4– ___ 5– ___ 6– ___ 7– ___

1 *The baby cried all night, which meant I was tired all next day.*

2 _____

_____

_____

3 _____

_____

_____

4 _____

_____

5 _____

_____

6 _____

_____

_____

7 _____

_____

_____

68 Adjectives 1

It's large.   It's a large suitcase.

Adjectives describe nouns and pronouns. They give us more information about things. Their form is the same with singular and plural nouns. They do not add *s*.

> *red, green, blue   dark, light, bright   large, small   beautiful, ugly*
> *Japanese, English   my, your, her   this, that, these, those* + noun

Word order 1

Most adjectives can go in two places. They can go before a noun and the pronouns *one* and *ones*.

> *I've got a **blue bag**.   That **one** is **my bag**.*

They can also go after a noun. Link verbs include *be, become, get* (become), *stay, feel, smell, sound, taste, look, seem* and *appear*.

> *The **bag** is **blue**.   I'm getting **tired**.   He seems **nice** – but is he?*

Word order 2

When you use two or more adjectives, put them in the right order. Put a 'feeling' adjective, eg *beautiful* and *terrible*, before an 'information' adjective, eg *red* and *dark*.

> *Ann bought a **beautiful red** dress.   It was a **terrible dark** night.*

Adjectives can give different types of information. We sometimes put different 'information' adjectives together. They go in the following order. We often put commas between several adjectives together.

1 Feeling	+	2 Size	3 Age	4 Shape	5 Colour	6 Origin	7 Material	+ Noun
ugly beautiful		big little	old new	square round	red blue	French German	metal wooden	

> *I bought a **beautiful**, **old**, **round**, **French** clock.*
> *He saw an **ugly**, **little**, **blue**, **wooden** box.*

Adjective + to + infinitive

'Feeling' adjectives can take *to* + infinitive. The adjective usually follows *It*. Some common 'feeling' adjectives are *dangerous, delighted, difficult, easy, funny, important, pleased, safe, sorry* and *stupid*.

> *It's **dangerous to play** in the road.   I'm **pleased to meet** you.*

تصف النعوت الاسماء والضمائر، فهي تعطي مزيداً من المعلومات عن الاشياء، وهي لا تتغير تبعاً لإفراد او جمع الاسماء التي تصفها، ولا يضاف لهاs الجمع.

تأتي معظم النعوت من حيث موقعها في احد مكانين: قبل الاسم وقبل الضمائر one وones.

وتأتي ايضاً بعد الاسم... وهذه قائمة بأفعال الوصل.

عند استخدام النعوت، فإن النعوت المستخدمة توضع حسب ترتيب خاص بحيث تأتي النعوت التي تتعلق بالمشاعر (مثل beautiful) قبل تلك التي تزود بالمعلومات (red).

تزودنا نعوت بأنواع مختلفة من المعلومات. ونضع احياناً نعوتاً مختلفة «مزودة بالمعلومات» معاً، في جملة واحدة، وتكون بالترتيب التالي، ادناه. وغالباً ما توضع فواصل بين النعوت التي يجتمع استخدامها في الجملة.

يمكن ان تأتي النعوت المشاعر مع to + المصدر. ويوضع النعت عادة، بعد it. وهذه قائمة بالشائع من نعوت هذا النوع.

154

Exercises

1 Complete the statements. Use these link verbs and adjectives.

Link verbs

feel, get, look, seem, smell, sound

Adjectives

angry, delicious, happy, right, terrible, tired

Example: *I'll have to check the sales figures again. They don't <u>look right</u>.*

1 ● *Dinner's ready.*
  ○ *Mmm! It _____*

2 *I didn't get enough sleep last night. I still*
  _____

3 *Don't try to take a dog's food away, or it'll*
  _____

4 ● *The children are all laughing.*
  ○ *Yes, they _____ really _____*

5 *Oh, no! Annie's doing her music practice again. It*
  _____

2 Write the words in the correct order.

Example: *(beautiful/a/flower/red)*
  <u>*a beautiful red flower*</u>

1 *(book/old/a/boring)*
  _____

2 *(blue/an/diamond/unusual)*
  _____

3 *(film/exciting/new/an)*
  _____

4 *(yellow/light/a/strange)*
  _____

5 *(an/clock/German/interesting)*
  _____

6 *(little/a/lovely/baby)*
  _____

7 *(green/a/valley/pleasant)*
  _____

8 *(a/man/tall/young)*
  _____

9 *(round/box/a/plastic)*
  _____

3 Report the answers. Use commas between the adjectives.

Example: ● *What was the snake like?*
  ○ *It was big! It was green! It was horrible!*
    <u>*It was a horrible, big, green snake.*</u>

1 ● *What was the man like?*
  ○ *He was little. He was old. He was funny.*
  _____

2 ● *What was the box like?*
  ○ *It was ugly. It was brown. It was metal.*
  _____

3 ● *What were the jackets like?*
  ○ *They were silk. They were new. They were Italian. They were beautiful.*
  _____
  _____

4 ● *What were the vases like?*
  ○ *They were tall. They were wonderful. They were Chinese. They were round.*
  _____
  _____

4 Complete the statements. Use these endings.

to go home.   to drive when you're tired.
to have you with us.
to meet you.   to play with matches.
to remember to post them.   to understand.

Example: *Goodbye for now. It was nice <u>to meet you.</u>*

1 *Put them down. It's dangerous _____*
  _____

2 *I've really enjoyed this holiday. I'll be sorry*
  _____

3 *Please don't forget these letters. It's very important*
  _____

4 *Of course you can come too. We'll be delighted*
  _____

5 *They were speaking very fast, so it was difficult*
  _____

6 *You should have a sleep before you go. It isn't safe*
  _____

155

69 Adjectives 2

The programme is interesting.   Alan is interested.

FORMS

Adjectives with *ing* endings

The programme is interesting.
(interesting, boring, exciting, surprising, worrying)

Adjectives with *ed* endings

Alan is interested.
(interested, bored, excited, surprised, worried)

There are some pairs of important adjectives with the endings *ing* and *ed*.

هناك ازواج من بعض النعوت المهمة تنتهي بـ ing وكذلك بـ ed.

CROSSCHECK

Adjectives with *ing* endings	Adjectives with *ed* endings
These describe something, eg a TV programme, a film, a book or a person.	These describe your feelings about something, eg a TV programme, a film, a book or a person.
Compare these examples.	Compare these examples.
*Ann thinks computer games are **boring**.*	*Ann gets **bored** when her brother plays computer games.*
*The football match was **exciting**.*	*Everybody at the match was **excited**.*
*Rod works at an **amazing** speed.*	*We are **amazed** at the speed Rod works.*
*A bad school report is very **depressing**.*	*Mum will be very **depressed** when she reads my school report.*

تصف النعوت التي تنتهي بـ ing شيئاً ما كبرنامج تليفزيوني او فيلم او كتاب او شخص.

وتصف النعوت التي تنتهي بـ ed مشاعر الشخص تجاه شيء ما مثل برنامج او فيلم او كتاب او شخص.

ويتضح الامر من خلال مقارنة الامثلة من النوعين من النعوت.

Be careful about the difference between these sentences. You will be embarrassed if you say the wrong one!

   *I'm **boring**!   I'm **bored**!*

(*I'm **boring**!* means that other people are not interested in me.)

يجب الانتباه الى الفارق بين هذه الجمل لانك ستصاب بالحرج اذا استخدمت العبارة الخاطئة.

This is a list of common pairs of adjectives with *ing* and *ed* endings.

وهذه قائمة بازواج النعوت الاكثر شيوعاً والتي تنتهي بـ ing و ed.

amazing/amazed	*horrifying/horrified*
amusing/amused	*infuriating/infuriated*
annoying/annoyed	*interesting/interested*
astonishing/astonished	*irritating/irritated*
boring/bored	*puzzling/puzzled*
confusing/confused	*relaxing/relaxed*
depressing/depressed	*satisfying/satisfied*
disappointing/disappointed	*shocking/shocked*
disgusting/disgusted	*surprising/surprised*
embarrassing/embarrassed	*terrifying/terrified*
exciting/excited	*thrilling/thrilled*
exhausting/exhausted	*tiring/tired*
fascinating/fascinated	*worrying/worried*
frightening/frightened	

Exercises

1 Write the correct adjectives.

Example: *Thunderstar 2 is the most __exciting__ film of the year. (exciting/excited)*

1 *Everybody was _____ when we reached the huge waterfall. (exciting/excited)*

2 *The map of the city was out of date, and I was soon _____ (confusing/confused)*

3 *One of the _____ things about Steve is his stupid laugh. (annoying/annoyed)*

4 *I was _____ by the engines in the Science Museum. (fascinating/fascinated)*

5 *We were all _____ after walking round town all day. (exhausting/exhausted)*

6 *The police have found the facts of this crime very _____ (puzzling/puzzled)*

7 *It's _____ that Tina is late. She's usually on time. (surprising/surprised)*

8 *The story of the Earth's development is _____ (amazing/amazed)*

2 Write the correct adjectives.

Example: *(bore)*
● *This programme is __boring.__*
○ *Yes, I'm __bored__ with it too. Let's turn it off.*

1 *(astonish)*
● *I was _____ that Tim passed the exam.*
○ *Yes, he found it _____ too!*

2 *(shock)*
● *The way Sam talks to people is _____.*
○ *I know. I was _____ when I heard him being so rude.*

3 *(embarrass)*
● *It was really _____ to ask for my money.*
○ *Why? You shouldn't be _____ to ask for the money they owed you.*

4 *(depress)*
● *I've failed my driving test again. I'm very _____ about it.*
○ *I remember the feeling. It certainly is _____*

5 *(interest)*
● *Here is an _____ job advert in the paper. Look.*
○ *Are you _____ in applying for it?*

6 *(disappoint)*
● *The team were very _____ that they only came fifth in the competition.*
○ *The trouble is, the way they played was so _____*

7 *(irritate)*
● *Don't you get _____ when you see the same TV commercial all the time?*
○ *Yes, there are some really _____ ones on TV at the moment.*

8 *(tire)*
● *I've been working all day, but I don't feel _____ at all.*
○ *Well, you're lucky. I find this job very _____*

3 Complete the statements. Use these words with the correct endings.

amuse, disgust, frighten, horrify, infuriate, relax, satisfy, terrify, worry

Example: *I don't like being high up. It's really __frightening.__*

1 *That boy always wants more to eat! He's never _____*

2 *The assistant manager lost his job because everybody was _____ by his lies.*

3 *Susan keeps refusing to eat and is losing weight. It's very _____*

4 *When we got back to town, we saw the _____ damage done by the storm.*

5 *The President is feeling _____ after a good holiday.*

6 *The film isn't very funny, but it's quite _____*

7 *Oh, no! The train is going to be late again. It's really _____*

8 *We thought the plane was going to crash. We were all _____*

70 Adjectives and adverbs

He's a slow worker.   He always works slowly.

FORMS

Adjective or adverb

Noun + adjective   Verb + adverb

Adjective → regular adverb

slow   → slowly

Irregular forms

1   good / well
2   hard, fast, etc
3   hard / hardly, etc
4   friendly, lively, likely, etc

CROSSCHECK

Adjectives

Adjectives say more about nouns.

That boy is	**slow**.
	quick.
	bad.

النعوت تقول المزيد عن الاسماء. اما الظرف فيقول المزيد عن الفعل .

This sentence uses a link verb, *is*. Other link verbs include *become, get* (become), *stay, feel, smell, sound, taste, look, seem* and *appear*.

That boy	**is**	**slow**.
	looks	
	seems	

Adverbs

Adverbs say more about verbs.

He works	**slowly**.
	quickly.
	badly.

يستخدم في هذه الجملة الفعل be كاحد افعال الوصل المبينة.

This sentence uses an action verb, *works*. Other action verbs include *run, talk, drive* and *write*. Adverbs go with action verbs, not link verbs.

That boy	**works**	**slowly**.
	moves	
	runs	

وتحوي هذه الجملة (الثانية) فعلاً حركياً. ويأتي الظرف مع الافعال الحركية وليس مع افعال الوصل.

Some verbs are both link and action verbs, but with different meanings.

Ann **looked** happy.

Peter **looked** quickly in the cupboards.

I **felt** awful, so I went to bed.

The chef **felt** the vegetables carefully and bought the best ones.

The milk **tasted** bad.

I **tasted** the food nervously. It was OK.

بعض الافعال هي افعال وصل وافعال حركية ولكن بمعانٍ مختلفة.

Adjective → regular adverb

We form most adverbs from adjective + *ly*, eg *slow + ly → slowly*.
   beautifully, carefully (note ... l + ly), *coldly, freely, quickly, quietly, sadly, safely, warmly*

تتشكل معظم الظروف (adverbs) من النعوت وذلك بإضافة ly لها.

We form other adverbs according to special spelling rules. (See Appendix 2.)

   angry → angrily, easy → easily, lucky → luckily
   comfortable → comfortably, gentle → gently, possible → possibly
   true → truly, whole → wholly

وتتشكل ظروف (adverbs) اخرى وفق قواعد هجائية خاصة (انظر الملحق 2).

Irregular forms

good → well

Note this irregular form – *good → well*. *well* is also an adjective.

> *The car goes **well**.*
> ● *Is she **well**?* ○ *No, she's ill.*

يجب ملاحظة أن *good* ← *well* تشكلان صيغة غير قياسية ولا تسيران حسب القاعدة.

hard, fast, etc

These are both adjectives and adverbs: *deep, direct, early, far, fast, free, hard, high, late, long, low, near, right, short, straight, wrong.*

> *It's a **deep** swimming pool.* *He dived **deep** into the water.*
> *It's a **fast** car.* *He climbed the tree **fast**.*
> *We must catch the **late** bus.* *He didn't want to arrive **late**.*

تأتي القائمة التالية من الكلمات كصفات وكذلك كظروف.

hard/hardly, etc

A few words have two adverb forms – one form is like the adjective and one form ends in *ly*. They have different meanings. Compare the sentences in CROSSCHECK below.

> *direct/directly, free/freely, hard/hardly, high/highly, late/lately, near/nearly, short/shortly*

تأتي بعض الكلمات كظروف في صيغتين إحداهما كالصفة وتنتهي الأخرى بـ *ly*. وتعطي كلتا الصيغتين معنىً مختلفاً... لاحظ ذلك من خلال مقارنة الأمثلة.

CROSSCHECK

Adjective/adverb form

> *I went **direct** from the station to the wedding.* (straight)
> *Airline staff can fly **free**.* (without paying)
> *We worked **hard** all night.* (with a lot of energy)
> *John works **high** above the city, on the 183rd floor.* (above)
> *I have to work **late** this evening.* (a long time after normal)
> ● *Is the hotel far?* ○ *No, it's quite **near** now.* (close)
> *My brother was very ill, so we cut **short** our holiday and went home.* (reduced)

ly form

> *I'll phone you **directly** I hear anything.* (immediately after)
> *The animals can move round **freely**.* (without control)
> *We had **hardly** any sleep that night.* (almost no)
> *This snake is **highly** poisonous. Don't touch it!* (very)
> *What's Sue doing these days? I haven't seen her **lately**.* (recently)
> *We've **nearly** run out of bread. I'll buy some more.* (almost)
> *The bus will be here **shortly**.* (soon)

ly adjectives

These adjectives end in *ly*: *deadly, friendly, likely, lively, lonely, lovely, silly, ugly.*

> *They're a very **friendly** family.* *That poor girl is **lonely**.*

تنتهي القائمة التالية من الصفات بـ *ly*.

We cannot use them as adverbs. We have to say something like *in a* + adjective + *way*.

> *He spoke **in a lively, friendly sort of way**.*
> *He always speaks **in that silly way of his**.*

لا يمكن استخدام الصفات التي تنتهي بـ *ly* كظروف بل كما يلي (*in a* + صفة + *way*).

Exercises

1 Write an adjective after a link verb or an adverb after an action verb.

Examples: *The old man looked* <u>sad.</u> *(sad)*
The old man spoke <u>sadly</u> *to us. (sad)*

1 *We finished the work _____ so we could go home early. (quick)*

2 *Ann looks very _____ in that dress. (nice)*

3 *This soup tastes _____ What's in it? (wonderful)*

4 *Have a good trip home. It's a little foggy so drive _____ (safe)*

5 *Spring is coming and the weather is getting _____ (warm)*

6 *Mrs Pearce greeted the new neighbours _____ and she invited them for coffee _____ (warm) (immediate)*

7 *Old Tom seems very _____ , but he's really very _____ (hard) (kind)*

8 *The back of the ship rose _____ high into the air, and then the whole ship slid _____ into the cold, black sea. (slow) (quiet)*

2 Write the correct adjectives or adverbs.

Example: *(slow/slowly)*
● *Arthur is a* <u>slow</u> *worker.*
○ *Yes, he's very* <u>slow.</u> *He does everything very* <u>slowly.</u>

1 *(proper/properly)*
● *Is this the _____ tool for the job?*
○ *No, I'm afraid this one won't do the job _____*

2 *(quiet/quietly)*
● *Lucy is a very _____ person, isn't she?*
○ *Yes, she talks so _____ that it's sometimes difficult to hear her.*

3 *(smooth/smoothly)*
● *I drove the new Mitsui Tiara the other day. It was a very _____ drive.*
○ *I agree. And it handles extremely _____ in wet road conditions too.*

4 *(pleasant/pleasantly)*
● *The weather is very _____ at this time of year.*
○ *And the garden looks really _____ now, with all the flowers coming out.*

5 *(intelligent/intelligently)*
● *Sally dealt with the problem very _____ , I thought.*
○ *Yes, she's a very _____ woman.*

6 *(bad/badly)*
● *Look, the builders have built this wall really _____*
○ *You're right. They've done a very _____ job. They'll have to do it again.*

7 *(effective/effectively)*
● *Which of these cleaning chemicals is more _____ , do you think?*
○ *Well, Clean-ezy works more _____ with really heavy dirt, but Clean-up seems just as _____ as Clean-ezy for most jobs.*

3 Write the correct adverbs.

Examples: *Ann sang that song* <u>beautifully.</u> *(beautiful)*

1 *Ellen didn't panic after the accident. She acted very _____ (sensible)*

2 *We were able to cut through the dead wood _____ (easy)*

3 *The pilot is looking for somewhere to land _____ (safe)*

4 *The astronauts completed all their tasks _____ (successful)*

5 *I had forgotten to take any cash. _____ , I had my cheque book with me. (lucky)*

6 *We don't usually think _____ , but this time I agree _____ with you. (similar) (whole)*

7 *_____ , everything went wrong with my plan and now I'm _____ and _____ sorry for the problems I've caused you all. (unfortunate) (real) (true)*

4 Complete the statements. Use these irregular adverbs.

direct, early, far, hard, high, late, low, short, straight well, wrong

Example: *The horse jumped* <u>high</u>. *It got over every fence.*

1 *We got home very _____ that night.*

2 *They'll have to leave _____ in the morning, or they'll miss the train.*

3 *The bus goes _____ from Oxford to London without stopping.*

4 *They worked _____ all night to get the car working again.*

5 *The plan seemed to be working, but then everything went _____ at the last minute.*

6 *I tried to throw a rope up to the girl, but it fell _____*

7 *The Clark family don't live _____ from here – just five minutes on foot.*

8 *The children sang _____ in the concert.*

9 *You don't need to ask the hotel telephone operator. You can call any outside number _____*

10 *The helicopter flew _____ over the trees and then landed near them.*

5 Write the correct forms of the adverbs.

Example: *(late/lately)*

    a) *Have you seen Peter* <u>lately?</u>

    b) *He'll be in trouble if he goes back to college* <u>late.</u>

1 *(hard/hardly)*

    a) *The people in this part of Africa have got _____ any food left to eat.*

    b) *The UN are fighting _____ to get help to the people soon.*

2 *(high/highly)*

    a) *Our pilots are all _____ aware of the need for safety in the air.*

    b) *They watch the plane's control systems at all times as they fly _____ above the ground.*

3 *(near/nearly)*

    a) *The ball landed on the ground _____ the house.*

    b) *It very _____ hit the kitchen window.*

4 *(free/freely)*

    a) *After the borders were opened, people like us were able to move much more _____ round Europe.*

    b) *As we were students, we couldn't afford to pay much for our travel, but we often travelled _____ by hitchhiking.*

5 *(short/shortly)*

    a) *Unfortunately, we have fallen _____ of our sales target for this year.*

    b) *However, the economy is getting better, and we expect better sales _____*

6 *(direct/directly)*

    a) *Please call me _____ you get any more news.*

    b) *You can call me _____ on this number.*

6 Write the correct adverbs or adjectives. Choose from these changing the form where necessary.

early, easy, hard, late, quick, serious, tired

Ann: *Hi, Tom. I haven't seen you for ages. What have you been doing* <u>lately?</u>

Tom: *Good to see you, Ann. I've been working really [1]_____ to pass my exams.*

Ann: *Oh, I'm sure you'll pass them [2]_____ No problem. You should relax more. Why not finish work [3]_____ this evening and come out with us for an hour or two? You don't need to stay out very [4]_____*

Tom: *No, sorry, I don't think I should. I'm feeling really [5]_____ and I'd like to finish as [6]_____ as possible and then just go to bed.*

Ann: *Well, all right, but I think you should take life a bit less [7]_____*

71 Adverb positions
He drove slowly.   He slowly drove.

FORMS

Adverbs in front, middle and end positions

It's a quiet road, and Brian *usually* drives *quite fast there. Luckily* he was *only* driving *slowly that day. Suddenly* he saw the tree. He hit it, but he wasn't hurt.

Questions

Have you ever been to Rome?
Who was working quickly?

Front position

We often use an adverb in front position to show a feeling or for special emphasis. The adverb adds its meaning to the whole sentence.

> *Luckily* he was only driving slowly. (speaker's feeling)
> *Slowly* the car began to move. (special emphasis)
> *Finally* we all decided to go. (special emphasis)

يستخدم الظرف غالباً في بداية الجملة، وذلك بقصد تبيان مشاعر المتحدث او بقصد وضع تشديد خاص ويضفي الظرف معناه على الجملة برمتها.

Middle position

Main verb only – put the adverb before the main verb.

> He *usually* drives a long way.
> We *quickly* finished dinner.

عندما تحوي الجملة فعلاً أساسياً واحداً يأتي الظرف قبل الفعل مباشرة.

Auxiliary verb only – put the adverb after a positive auxiliary verb.

> He *is certainly* the best player.

We often put the adverb before a negative auxiliary verb.

> You *certainly weren't* very good today.

Auxiliary + main verb – put the adverb between the auxiliary and the main verb.

> He was *only* driving a short distance.
> Ron has *always* lived in London.

عندما تحتوي الجملة على فعل مساعد واحد فقط يأتي الظرف بعد الفعل في حالة صيغة الاثبات.
وغالباً ما يأتي الظرف قبل الفعل في حالة النفي.
عندما تحوي الجملة فعلاً مساعداً بالإضافة الى فعل اساسي يأتي الظرف بينهما.

End position

We often put the adverb after the verb, at the end of a sentence. An adverb of time goes after any other adverb or an adverbial phrase.

> He was driving *slowly today*.
> I'll be working *over there tomorrow*.
> We're living *in London now*.

غالباً ما يأتي الظرف بعد الفعل في نهاية الجملة، ويأتي الظرف الذي يعبر عن الزمن بعد اي ظرف آخر في الجملة وبعد عبارة ظرفية.

Questions

We do not usually put the adverb in front position in questions. The adverb usually goes in middle or end position.

> Has Ron *always* lived in London?
> Where has Ron *always* lived?
> Was he driving *slowly*?
> Who was driving *slowly*?

لا يأتي الظرف عادة، في الموقع المتقدم في الجملة الاستفهامية، ولكنه يأتي في منتصف الجملة او في آخرها.

Exercises

1 Write these adverbs in front position.

Speaker's feeling
amazingly, frighteningly, hopefully, luckily, sadly

Special emphasis
angrily, finally, quietly, stupidly

Example: <u>*Amazingly,*</u> *John learned French in a month.* (Speaker's feeling)

1 _____ *we'll be able to finish work in time to go to the cinema.* (Speaker's feeling)

2 _____ *I forgot to take my passport with me to the airport.* (Special emphasis)

3 _____ *the boss banged his desk and shouted, 'Get out!'* (Special emphasis)

4 _____ *pieces from the ceiling started to fall around us.* (Speaker's feeling)

5 _____ *the bus arrived – 45 minutes late!* (Special emphasis)

6 _____ *Bob moved past the sleeping dogs and escaped.* (Special emphasis)

7 _____ *the great painter died before finishing the picture.* (Speaker's feeling)

8 _____ *the burning plane managed to land without crashing.* (Speaker's feeling)

2 Write the adverbs in middle position.

Example: *(is flying) (probably)*
John <u>*is probably flying*</u> *home now.*

1 *(get) (always)*
I _____ to work at 8.30.

2 *(only) (was trying)*
Everybody was angry with Sam, but he _____ to help them.

3 *(sometimes) (can see)*
You _____ France from England.

4 *(will be) (only)*
Peter _____ here for two days.

5 *(don't work) (usually)*
We _____ on Saturdays.

6 *(clearly) (has been failing)*
Alan _____ to do this job properly.

7 *(have you been) (ever)*
_____ to Japan before?

8 *(must talk) (never)*
You _____ like that again.

3 Write the adverbs in end position.

Example: *(all day) (very hard)*
I've been working <u>*very hard all day.*</u>

1 *(very soon) (there)*
Don't worry. We'll be _____

2 *(in America) (for five years)*
Brian lived _____

3 *(yesterday) (very heavily)*
It snowed _____

4 *(since last September) (much harder)*
Lisa has been studying _____
_____

5 *(as soon as possible) (over here)*
Please get _____
_____

6 *(wrong) (all the time)*
Poor old Paul. He gets things _____
_____

4 Write these adverbs in the letter.

over here, usually, last week, sadly, last year, definitely, this time, soon

Dear Chris,
It was good to hear from you [1]_____ *. We were pleased to hear you'll be travelling* [2]_____ *.*
[3]_____ *, we were away when you visited Miami* [4]_____ *. So you* [5]_____ *must stay with us* [6]_____ *We're* [7]_____ *at home in the evening, so call us* [8]_____ *.*

FORMS

A breakdown truck *soon* got there from a local garage. *Fortunately* the garage was able to repair Brian's car *quite quickly*. *Now* he *always* drives *extremely carefully*.

Adverb type	Explains	Examples
Manner	how	*fast, slowly, wrongly*
Place	where	*there, here, outside*
Time	when	*today, now, then*
Frequency	how often	*usually, always*
Degree	how much	*very, only, quite*
Sentence	the speaker's feeling	*luckily, certainly*

Adverbs of manner (*fast, quickly*, etc)

These usually go in end position and sometimes middle position. Irregular adverbs, eg *fast*, *well*, etc, go in end position. Use front position for emphasis.

> Peter **quickly** stopped.
> Peter stopped **quickly**.
> **Quickly** Peter stopped.

Adverbs of place (*there, outside*, etc)

These usually go in end position. They do not go in middle position. Use front position for emphasis. An adverb of place usually goes after an adverb of manner.

> The children are playing **outside**.
> I know I'll find her **somewhere**.
> **Somewhere** I know I'll find her.

Adverbs of time (*today, tomorrow*, etc)

These usually go in front position or end position. In end position, a time adverb goes after any other adverb.

> **Tomorrow** we're all going to the beach.
> We're all going to the beach **tomorrow**.

Adverbs of frequency (*usually, always*, etc)

These usually go in middle position. Adverbs of frequency include *always, almost always, usually, generally, normally, often, frequently, sometimes, occasionally, hardly ever, rarely* and *never*. (See the diagrams on the facing page for more information.)

> I **always** go to bed at 10.30.
> Pete **usually** plays football on Sundays.
> It's sad, but I **hardly ever** see my brother because he lives in Australia.
> They **never** ate sweets when they were children.

يأتي ظرف الحال عادة في نهاية الجملة واحياناً يأتي في وسطها. وظروف الحال اللاقياسية مثل fast وwell تأتي في نهاية الجملة. وعندما يأتي ظرف الحال في بداية الجملة فانه يفيد التوكيد.

يأتي ظرف المكان في نهاية الجملة ولا يأتي في منتصفها، وعندما يأتي في بداية الجملة فإنه يفيد التوكيد... ويأتي ظرف المكان عادة، بعد ظرف الحال.

يأتي ظرف الزمان في بداية الجملة او في نهايتها. ويأتي ظرف الزمان في نهاية الجملة بعد اي ظرف آخر.

تأتي ظروف التكرار في وسط الجملة. وتشمل ظروف التكرار ما يلي:

always	sometimes, occasionally
almost always	hardly ever, rarely
usually, generally, normally	never
often, frequently	

We often use *ever* in questions about frequency.

- *Have you **ever** visited London?*   ○ *Yes, I've often been there.*

غالباً ما تستخدم كلمة ever عند السؤال عن التكرار .

You can show frequency with adverbial phrases like these. They usually go in end position.

ويمكن تبيان التكرار باستخدام عبارات ظرفية تأتي عادة، في نهاية الجملة.

once	a	day
twice		week
three times		month
several times		year

*Most people eat **three times a day**.*
*I take the medicine **once a day**.*

Adverbs of degree (*very*, *quite*, etc)

Use these adverbs to make an adjective or another adverb weaker or stronger.

تستخدم الظروف التي تبين درجة القوة لجعل صفة من الصفات، او ظرف آخر، اضعف او اقوى.

Weak: *slightly, a little, a bit* (informal)
   *I felt **slightly** ill, but I didn't stop.*

Stronger: *quite, fairly, rather, pretty* (informal)
   *It isn't snowing, but it's **quite** cold. Bring some warm clothes!*

Strongest: *very, extremely*
   *Eddy is **extremely** good at tennis. In fact, he's Number 10 in the world.*

Be careful. *very* and *too* are different. *too* means more than a certain amount. (See Unit 75.)
   *I was **very** tired, but I went on walking.*
   *I was **too** tired to walk. I had to stop.*

تجدر ملاحظة اختلاف very و too. too تعني اكثر من كمية او حدّ معين. (انظر unit 75).

Sentence adverbs (*luckily*, *probably*, etc)

Sentence adverbs often go in front position. They give their meaning to the whole sentence. They show the speaker's feeling about the information in the sentence. Sentence adverbs include *luckily, sadly, surprisingly, disappointingly, obviously, certainly, probably* and *perhaps*.
   *Then we ran out of petrol. **Luckily** there was a petrol station 300 metres along the road.*
   ***Sadly** Alan is ill and can't be with us.*
   *The train will **probably** be late, and then we **obviously** won't get to the meeting.*

الظروف التي تعطي معناها للجملة بكاملها غالباً ما تأتي في مقدمة الجملة.

فهي تبين مشاعر المتحدث تجاه ما تحويه الجملة من معلومات. وهي تشمل ما يلي:

Exercises

1 Find and write the adverbs.

Example: *My brother arrived yesterday.* <u>*yesterday*</u>

1 *The boys are working upstairs.* _____

2 *The train is definitely late.* _____

3 *Time passed slowly as we waited.* _____

4 *I'm tired, so I'm going to bed now.* _____

5 *This book is very hard to understand.* _____

6 *John always does what he promises.* _____

7 *Luckily the tree fell just behind our car.* _____

2 Name the types of adverb and adverbial phrase in *italics*. Choose from these.

degree, frequency, manner, place, sentence, time

I remember one Japanese national holiday ¹*well*. Some friends and I decided to go to the mountains 100 kilometres from Tokyo in two cars. The problem was that everybody else in Tokyo seemed to be going ²*there* too. The road was ³*very* busy and we moved ⁴*extremely* ⁵*slowly*. We travelled ⁶*all night* and we ⁷*finally* got to the house ⁸*at 6.00*. We were ⁹*terribly* tired, and we went to sleep ¹⁰*immediately*.

We enjoyed the next three days ¹¹*a lot*. We walked through the woods to the village ¹²*once a day* to buy food. And ¹³*every day* we cooked our meals ¹⁴*outside* on a barbecue. Time went ¹⁵*quickly*, and the last day came. We ¹⁶*certainly* didn't want to return to Tokyo but, ¹⁷*sadly*, we had to go.

'Let's leave ¹⁸*late*,' somebody said. 'That way the roads will be quieter.' ¹⁹*Unfortunately* everybody else had the same idea. The journey home was just as slow as the trip from Tokyo. We seemed to get ²⁰*nowhere* in the long, long line of cars. At 2.00 the people in the first car ²¹*suddenly* left the main road to try a smaller road. We followed in the second car. Five more cars followed us, so we thought, 'This must be a good road. The Japanese are using it too.'

²²*Strangely,* the road became narrower. At 2.45 it came to an end. We were back in the mountains again. The cars stopped, and everybody ²³*slowly* got out. The Japanese were embarrassed. 'We didn't know you were foreigners,' one of them said. 'You ²⁴*definitely* seemed to know the way, so we followed you.' Everybody laughed ²⁵*politely*, but we all felt ²⁶*really* tired.

We reached Tokyo ²⁷*early in the morning*, and ²⁸*then* we all had to go to work.

²⁹*After that* I ³⁰*always* stayed at home during national holidays!

1 *well* – <u>*manner*</u>

2 *there* – _____

3 *very* – _____

4 *extremely* – _____

5 *slowly* – _____

6 *all night* – _____

7 *finally* – _____

8 *at 6.00* – _____

9 *terribly* – _____

10 *immediately* – _____

11 *a lot* – _____

12 *once a day* – _____

13 *every day* – _____

14 *outside* – _____

15 *quickly* – _____

16 *certainly* – _____

17 *sadly* – _____

18 *late* – _____

19 *Unfortunately* – _____

20 *nowhere* – _____

21 *suddenly* – _____

22 *Strangely* – _____

23 *slowly* – _____

24 *definitely* – _____

25 *politely* – _____

26 *really* – _____

27 *early in the morning* – _____

28 *then* – _____

29 *After that* – _____

30 *always* – _____

3 Write the adverbs and phrases of manner, place and time in end position.

Example: (soon) (somewhere)
I'm tired of driving. Let's stop <u>somewhere soon.</u>

1 (before midday) (there)
Hurry up! We have to get _____

_____

2 (beautifully) (yesterday)
The team played _____

3 (for a year) (everywhere)
The police looked for the two men _____

_____

4 (angrily) (last night) (at the meeting)
A lot of people spoke _____

_____

5 (at college) (these days) (well)
Harry is doing _____

_____

4 Write the adverbs and phrases of frequency in the most usual position – middle or end.

Examples: Jack goes into town. (sometimes)
<u>Jack sometimes goes into town.</u>
A ship visits the island. (twice a month)
<u>A ship visits the island twice a month.</u>

1 I do the washing on Monday. (usually)

_____

_____

2 Do you visit your old school? (ever)

_____

_____

3 Flights to New York leave. (once an hour)

_____

_____

4 You have to take the medicine. (twice a day)

_____

_____

5 Emphasize the speaker's feeling. Change the adjective in the second sentence into an adverb in front position. Leave out unnecessary words.

Example: I fell. It was lucky that I managed to catch a tree branch.
I fell. <u>Luckily, I managed to catch a tree branch.</u>

1 I called Ann at 7.00. It was sad that she'd already gone.
I called Ann at 7.00. ____ _____

_____

2 Bill is getting better. We're hopeful that he'll be well soon.
Bill is getting better. _____

_____

3 My wife and I are scientists. We were surprised that our children were good at Art.
My wife and I are scientists. _____

_____

4 The prize goes to Clint Starr. It's unfortunate that he isn't here to receive it.
The prize goes to Clint Starr. _____

_____

6 Write the words in the best order.

Example: (will be) (probably)
Ann <u>will probably be</u> late home.

1 (has finished) (definitely)
The football game _____

_____ now.

2 ('ll visit) (never)
I _____ that place again!

3 (are delivered) (always)
New books _____ on
Monday morning.

4 (hasn't understood) (clearly)
She _____
anything I've said.

5 ('ll see) (hardly ever)
If you move, I _____ you
again.

FORMS

Comparison with adjective + *er/est*

The Highlight is cheaper than the Gazelle. It's the cheapest of the three.

Comparison with *more/most*, *less/least* + adjective

The Rebel is more expensive than the Gazelle. It's the most expensive car.

Comparison with two-syllable adjectives

He wants the Rebel, but she is happier with the Gazelle.

Comparison with adverbs

The Rebel accelerates more quickly than the others. It accelerates the most quickly.

We use a comparative form of an adjective (adjective + *er* or *more* + adjective) to compare two things. We use a superlative form of an adjective (adjective + *est* or *most* + adjective) when one of a group is beyond the others, eg *the cheapest* and *the most expensive*. Compare the following comparative and superlative forms.

Comparative adjectives:	*cheaper (than)*	*more*	*expensive (than)*
		less	
Superlative adjectives:	*(the) cheapest*	*(the) most*	*expensive*
		(the) least	

We usually use *than* after a comparative form. It connects the two things that we are comparing. We usually use *the* before a superlative form. It refers to the thing which we are describing.

Comparison with adjectives + *er/est*

We use *er/est* with nearly all one-syllable adjectives. Note the spelling changes. (See Appendix 2 for more information on spelling rules.)

Adjective	**+ *er***	**+ *est***	**Adjective**	**+ *r***	**+ *st***
small	*smaller*	*smallest*	*nice*	*nicer*	*nicest*
slow	*slower*	*slowest*	*large*	*larger*	*largest*

Adjective + doubled consonant		**+ *er***	**+ *est***
big	*+g*	*bigger*	*biggest*
hot	*+t*	*hotter*	*hottest*

*His house is **smaller** than hers.*
*Mexico City is the **largest** city in the world.*
*Today is the **hottest** day of the year.*

Comparison with *more/most* or *less/least* + adjective

We use *more/most* or *less/least* for all adjectives with three syllables or more. We also use these forms for all adjectives ending in *ing* or *ed*, eg *pleasing/pleased, tiring/tired, worrying/worried* and *embarrassing/embarrassed*.

*Cars are **more reliable** now than they were 20 years ago.*
*She's the **most beautiful** girl in the world!*
*I'm **less tired** than I was yesterday.*   *It's the **least tiring** job.*

تستخدم صيغة التفضيل (صفة+ er او more + صفة) للمقارنة بين شيئين. وتستخدم صيغة التفضيل العليا لصفةٍ ما (صفة + est او most + صفة) عندما يفوق فرد ما غيره في المجموعة.

ويتضح الفرق بين الصيغتين من خلال مقارنة الامثلة المبينة.

تستخدم than عادة بعد صيغة التفضيل فهي التي تربط بين الشيئين اللذين تجري مقارنتهما. وتستخدم the عادة قبل صيغة التفضيل العليا فهي تشير الى الشيء موضع الوصف.

تستخدم er / est مع جميع الصفات التي تتكون من مقطع واحد تقريباً. وتجدر ملاحظة التغييرات التي تطرأ على الهجاء.

تستخدم more / most او less / least مع جميع الصفات التي تتكون من ثلاثة مقاطع او اكثر. وتستخدم ايضاً مع جميع الصفات التي تنتهي بـ ing او ed.

We can also use these forms for all adjectives with two syllables.

> *Jack is the **most lazy** boy I know.*
> *John's work is **less careful** than it should be.*

We can also use *more/most* and *less/least* like *fewer/fewest* to talk about quantity.

ويمكن استخدام صيغ *more* و *most* و *less* و *least* مع جميع الصفات التي تتكون من مقطعين.

كما يمكن استخدامها مع الصفات التي تتعلق بالكميات. وبنفس الطريقة يمكن استخدام *fewer* و *fewest*.

Comparison with two-syllable adjectives

You can use *more/most* and *less/least* for all adjectives with two syllables. But we often use *er/est* with two-syllable adjectives.

> *The road is **more narrow/narrower** here.*
> *He's the **most lazy/laziest** boy in the class.*

يمكن استخدام *most/more* و *least/less* مع جميع الصفات التي تتكون من مقطعين، ولكن غالباً ما يتم استخدام صيغة *est/er* مع الصفات التي تتكون من مقطعين أيضاً.

We often use *er/est* with these very common two-syllable adjectives: *clever, cruel, gentle, narrow, pleasant, polite, quiet, simple, stupid, tired.*

> *Ann is **politer** than her sister.*
> *Tom is the **cleverest** boy in the class.*

غالباً ما تستخدم *est/er* مع الصفات الشائعة التالية والتي تتكون من مقطعين.

We also often use *er/est* with two-syllable adjectives ending in a consonant + *y*, eg *dirty, easy, funny, happy, lazy, lovely, pretty, silly, sunny* and *tidy*. They change like this: *dirty + ier/iest → dirtier/dirtiest.*

> *Jack is the **laziest** boy I know.*
> *Question 2 is **easier** than question 1.*

غالباً ما تستخدم *est/er* مع الصفات التي تتكون من مقطعين والتي تنتهي بحرف ثابت + *y*، ويتغير حرف *y* إلى *iest/ier*.

Comparison of adverbs

We use a comparative form of an adverb (adverb + *er* or *more* + adverb) to compare two actions. We use a superlative form of an adverb (adverb + *est* or *most* + adverb) when one of a group does something beyond the others, eg *... accelerates the most quickly.*

تستخدم صيغة المقارنة للظرف (*er* أو *more* + ظرف) للمقارنة بين حدثين. وتستخدم صيغة التفضيل العليا (ظرف + *est* أو *most* + ظرف) عندما يقوم شخص بعمل يفوق قدرة الآخرين.

Many adverbs have the form adjective + *ly*, eg *quickly, slowly* and *nicely.* (See Unit 70 for more information on adjectives, adverbs and adverb formation.) Just like longer adjectives, these *ly* adverbs take the forms *more/most* and *less/least.*

> *Rob works **more quickly** than Steve.*
> *Jane sings the **most beautifully** in the class.*

تتكون كثير من الظروف بزيادة *ly* على الصفات، وبالتالي فإنها تعامل بصيغة *most/more* و *least/less*.

Some adverbs look like short adjectives which take *er/est*, eg *deep, early, fast, hard, high, late, long* and *near.* Just like these short adjectives, these adverbs usually take the forms *er/est.*

> *The Rebel goes **faster** than the Gazelle.*
> *I arrived the **earliest** at the meeting.*

هناك بعض الظروف التي تبدو وكأنها صفات قصيرة وتستخدم معها صيغة *est/er*.

Note the irregular forms.

Adjective	Adverb	Comparative	Superlative
good	well	better	best
bad	badly	worse	worst
far	far	farther/further	farthest/furthest

كذلك يجب ملاحظة الحالات اللاقياسية المبينة.

> *This year's results are **better** than last year's.*
> *My headache is getting **worse**.*
> *We can't go any **farther** tonight.*

Exercises

1 Write the *er* and *est* forms.

Adjective	*er* form	*est* form
1 short	*shorter*	*shortest*
2 pretty	*prettier*	*prettiest*
3 long	_____	_____
4 ugly	_____	_____
5 large	_____	_____
6 big	_____	_____
7 small	_____	_____
8 nice	_____	_____
9 cool	_____	_____
10 easy	_____	_____
11 simple	_____	_____
12 fine	_____	_____
13 thin	_____	_____
14 hot	_____	_____

2 Write the correct *er* forms of the underlined adjectives.

Example: Bill has a <u>large</u> car. It's even *larger* than my brother's.

1 Yesterday's test was <u>easy</u> – much _____ than last month's.

2 Question 2 was <u>simple</u>. It was certainly _____ than question 1.

3 My cousin is <u>nice</u> – a lot _____ than my brother.

4 It's been <u>hot</u> today, and it'll be even _____ tomorrow.

5 The job took a <u>long</u> time. It took _____ than I thought.

3 Write the *est* forms. Use these adjectives.

early, fit, funny, late, narrow, quick

Example: There's a train at 5.30 am. That's the *earliest* one.

1 This is the _____ model. It's just come out.

2 Which is the _____ way to Paris, please?

3 We're coming to the _____ part of the river now. Here it's only five metres wide.

4 Rod is the _____ member of the team. He's been training very hard.

5 He was the _____ man I've ever heard. I couldn't stop laughing.

4 Complete the radio adverts with regular *er* and *est* forms. Use these adjectives.

easy, fast, fine, fit, low, white

Example: SPEED CLEAN was always the *fastest* home cleaner. Now it's *faster* than ever before. It does the job in seconds.

1 You'll be _____ in just three days with the HOME EXERCISER. And after a month you'll be the _____ you've ever been in your life.

2 There's no _____ watch in the world than the perfect TIME PERFECTA. Remember, we've been makers of the _____ watches in the world for 30 years.

3 You'll find the _____ prices in town at GOOD WAY SUPERMARKETS. And that's a promise. If you can find _____ prices anywhere else, we'll give you your money back.

4 GLEAM CREAM cleans your teeth _____ than white. For the _____ , cleanest teeth of all, choose GLEAM CREAM.

5 Do you hate all those video controls? Well, now TELE-SELECT is here. It's the _____ thing in the world to use. Just talk to it. Tell it the time, the channel and the film to record, and TELE-SELECT does the rest. What could be _____ than that?

5 Complete the conversations. Use *more/most, less/least* or *fewer/fewest*.

Example: ● I've just moved to a bigger apartment in the same building.
○ Do you have to pay *more* rent?
● Yes, it's the biggest in the building, so it costs the *most.*

1 ● Bob seems to get richer, but meaner every day. I can't stand him these days.
○ Yes, he's got _____ money than ever before, but he's got _____ friends!

2 ● *I'm still hungry. Is there any* _____
   ○ *But you've already had the* _____ *out of everybody. Don't be so greedy!*

3 ● *This motor-bike is certainly quite cheap. It costs* _____ *than all the other models we've looked at.*
   ○ *I've read that it also costs the* _____ *to run out of all the bikes this size. And I've also heard that it has the* _____ *mechanical problems.*
   ● *But if there's a mechanical problem, spare parts are very expensive. In fact, they cost the* _____ *out of all the models in the 750cc class.*

6 Write the comparative and superlative forms of the adjectives.

Example: *No language is easy to learn, but Italian is* <u>*less difficult*</u> *than I thought. In fact it's the* <u>*least difficult*</u> *language I've ever studied. (difficult)*

1 *Joe is doing well at art college. He isn't the* _____ *student in his year, but he's* _____ *than 90% of the other students. (talented)*

2 *Why do you always have to buy the* _____ *thing in the shop? Couldn't you choose something* _____ *(expensive)*

3 *I think rock climbing is even* _____ *than deep sea diving. In fact, I think it's one of the* _____ *outdoor activities you can do. (dangerous)*

4 *Uncut diamonds are* _____ *than diamonds that are cut. A diamond that was recently sold for $975,000 is the* _____ *one in the world at the moment. (valuable)*

5 *I don't like Robin Black's new book as much as his last one. It's* _____ *In fact, I think it's the* _____ *book he's ever written. (interesting)*

7 Complete the statements with a verb and comparative adverb.

Examples: *Ann is a quicker worker than Sue.*
Ann <u>*works more quickly*</u> *than Sue.*

1 *Grandad is a slower driver than his me.*
   Grandad _____ *than me.*

2 *Stephen Prince is a more exciting writer than Sid Shelley.*
   Stephen Prince _____ *than Sid Shelley.*

3 *Don is a lighter sleeper than his brother.*
   Don _____ *than his brother.*

4 *Ron is always an earlier arrival at work than Bob.*
   Ron always _____ *at work than Bob.*

5 *Joe is a less intelligent football player than Steve.*
   Joe _____ *than Steve.*

8 Write statements with superlative adverbs.

We tested three washing machines – the Crystal, the Wash-Tech and the Snowline. Here are the results.

Examples: *(Snowline/wash/+ good/Crystal/wash/ - effective)*
<u>*The Snowline washed the best, and the Crystal washed the least effectively.*</u>

1 *(Crystal/perform/+ reliable/Wash-Tech/perform/ - reliable)*

_____
_____
_____
_____

2 *(Wash-Tech/run/- economical/Crystal/run/+ cheap)*

_____
_____
_____
_____

3 *(Crystal/finish/+ fast/Snowline/finish/- quick)*

_____
_____
_____

Comparison 2: sentence patterns

Hill finished faster than Rossi.   *He's the fastest man in the world.*

Fantastic! Nigel Hill is first on Number 32! And Carlo Rossi is second. So Hill is the new champion – the fastest man in the world on two wheels!

Sentence patterns with comparatives

Hill finished faster than Rossi.

Sentence patterns with superlatives

Hill is the fastest man in the world.

Sentence patterns with (not) as ... as

Rossi is good, but he is not as good as Hill.

Comparison and object pronouns

I drove faster than he did. → than him.

Sentence patterns with comparatives

A comparative sentence compares two things. When we mention both things, we link them with *than*.

> Hill is **faster than** Rossi.   A CD lasts **longer than** a cassette.

When we compare with an adjective, we do not always mention both things.

> ● *Which is your jacket?*   ○ *The **bigger** one.*

Sentence patterns with superlatives

We usually use *the* before superlative adjectives.

> *Paul is **the tallest** person here.*

We do not often use *the* before superlative adverbs. Compare the following.

> ● *Which is **the best** song?*   ○ *I like Sad Heart **best**.*

We can use *in* or *of* after a superlative. Use *in* to talk about places and groups. Use *of* to talk about other things, including numbers.

> *I'm the **tallest boy in the class**.*
> *July is the **warmest month of the year**.*

Sentence patterns with (not) as ... as

Use *as ... as* to say that two things or actions are equal.

> *Paul is **as tall as** his father now.*   *I drive **as well as** Tom.*

Use *not as ... as* (or *not so ... as*) to say that two things or actions are not equal.

> *English **isn't as difficult as** Maths.* (Maths is harder than English.)
> *He **can't work as quickly as** I can.* (I can work faster than he can.)

Comparison and object pronouns

After a comparative with *than* or *as ... as*, we often talk about another person. If we use a name we can do it in these two ways.

> *I drove faster **than Carlo did**.*   *I drove faster **than Carlo**.*

If we use a pronoun, the subject pronoun + auxiliary verb change to an object pronoun.

> *I drove faster **than he did**. → I drove faster **than him**.*
> *He can't run as quickly **as I can**. → He can't run as quickly **as me**.*

تقارن جمل التفضيل بين شيئين او بين شخصين. وعند ذكر الاثنين نربطهما بكلمة than.

وعند المقارنة مع صفة، لا نذكر كلا الشيئين دائماً.

تستخدم the عادة قبل صفة التفضيل العليا.
لا تستخدم the غالباً، قبل ظروف التفضيل العليا. قارن ما يلي:

ويمكن استخدام in او of بعد صفة التفضيل العليا.
وتستخدم in عند الحديث عن المكان والمجموعات في حين تستخدم of للحديث عن الاشياء الاخرى بما فيها الاعداد.

تستخدم صيغة as...as للقول بان شيئين او حدثين متساويان.

وتستخدم not as... as او (not so... as)، للقول بان شيئين او حدثين غير متساويين.

غالباً ما نتحدث بعد صفة التفضيل مع than او as... as عن شخص آخر. وعند ذكر الاسم يمكن استخدام اي من الصيغتين المبينتين.
اذا استخدمنا الضمير، فان صيغة ضمير الفاعل + الفعل المساعد تتغير الى صيغة ضمير المفعول به.

Exercises

1 Write statements with comparative adjectives.

Example: *Tom is 17. Sam is 19. (old)*
Sam is older than Tom.

1 *Sue is 10. Ann is 12. (young)*
_____

2 *The Honda costs £10,000. The Toyota costs £12,000. (expensive)*
_____
_____

3 *Robin can do 100 metres in 10 seconds. Jack runs 100 metres in 10.5 seconds. (fast)*
_____

4 *Five climbers have died on Mount George. Eleven climbers have been killed on Mount Egmont. (dangerous)*
_____
_____

5 *The journey by sea is an hour. The journey by tunnel is only half an hour. (short)*
_____
_____

2 Write statements with superlative adjectives and *be* in the correct form.

Example: *(the new Boeing/be/big/plane in the world)*
The new Boeing is the biggest plane in the world.

1 *(yesterday/be/hot/day of the year)*
_____
_____

2 *(the XL400/be/popular/car in Europe this year)*
_____
_____

3 *(Tom and Sam/be/good/players in last year's team)*
_____
_____

4 *(some people say Casa Blanca/be/fine/film ever)*
_____
_____

3 Correct the statements. Use *isn't nearly as ... as ...*

Example: ● *Kuwait is larger than Saudi Arabia.*
○ *That's not right. Kuwait isn't nearly as large as Saudi Arabia.*

1 ● *A Jumbo 747 is faster than a Concord.*
○ *That's wrong. _____*
_____

2 ● *Britain is warmer than Egypt.*
○ *I'm afraid that's not quite right. _____*

3 ● *Silver is more expensive than gold.*
○ *I'm sorry, but that's wrong. _____*

4 ● *Rome is older than Athens.*
○ *No, it's the opposite. _____*

5 ● *English food is better than French food.*
○ *I'm afraid I don't agree. _____*

4 Write the correct pronouns.

Examples: *He's cleverer than <u>they</u> are. (they/them)*
He's cleverer than <u>them</u>. (they/them)

Tom: *Sue, why did you give the mailroom manager's job to Tim. Ann is twice as clever as [1]_____ is. (he/him)*

Sue: *Yes, but he knows the work better than [2]_____ (she/her) Remember, he's been with the company much longer than [3]_____ has. (she/her)*

Tom: *Well, what about Alan and Emma? Tim hasn't been here any longer than [4]_____ have. (they/them) And he certainly doesn't know the work any better than [5]_____ (they/them)*

Sue: *Yes, but they're both cleverer than [6]_____, and I'm going to give them better jobs. (he/him)*

Tom: *Well, I still don't agree about Tim.*

Sue: *Believe me, you don't know him as well as [7]_____ do. (I/me) If you did, I'm sure you'd make the same decision as [8]_____ (I/me)*

173

75 *too* and *enough*

He's too young.   He isn't old enough.

too and *enough*

We use *too* and *enough* when we talk about the right amount of something, eg *money, clothes size, exam marks* and *age*.

too and *enough* go with adjectives and adverbs. *too* goes before an adjective/adverb. *enough* goes after an adjective/adverb.

Adjectives
*Len is **too young** to get the job.*
*Len isn't **old enough** to get the job.*

Adverbs
*Slow down! We're going **too fast**.*
*Hurry! We aren't going **fast enough**.*

too + adjective/adverb

too means more than the right amount. *not too* means the right amount. Note that we often leave out the last part in brackets.

> *Ron is 50, so he's **too old** (to get the job).*
> *Bob is 25, so he is**n't too old** (to get the job).*
> *The plane won't take off. It's going **too slowly** (to take off).*

too is not the same as *very*. Compare the following. (See also Unit 76.)

> *Harry was **very old**, but he kept on working.*
> *Harry was **too old** to work. He had to stop.*

Adjective/adverb + *enough*

enough means the right amount – not more, not less. *not enough* means less than the right amount. Note that we often leave out the last part in brackets.

> *Bob is 25, so he's **old enough** (to get the job).*
> *Len is only 20, so he is**n't old enough** (to get the job).*

Further patterns

enough can go with a noun – before, not after. *too* needs *much* or *many* to go with a noun. (We sometimes also say *too little/too few*.)

> *Is there **enough orange juice**?   We haven't got **enough sandwiches**.*
> *There's **too much orange juice**.   Have we got **too few sandwiches**?*

After *too* and *enough* we can use *to* + infinitive + noun or *for* + noun.

> *He's **too young to get the job**.   He isn't **old enough for the job**.*

We can also use them together.

> *This shirt is **good enough to wear** at home, but it's **too old-fashioned for the party** tonight.*

تستخدم too وenough عند الحديث عن الكمية الصحيحة من شيء ما مثل المال وقياس الملابس.. الخ.

تستخدم too وenough مع الصفات ومع الظروف. تأتي too قبل الصفة او الظرف في حين تأتي enough بعد الصفة او الظرف.

تعطي too معنى الزيادة على الكمية الصحيحة، وتفيد not too بأن الكمية صحيحة. ولاحظ باننا غالباً ما نحذف الجزء الاخير من الجملة كما هو مبيّن.

too ليست مثل very. قارن ما يلي. (وانظر ايضاً unit 76)

تفيد enough ان الكمية صحيحة بلا زيادة ولا نقصان. وتعني not enough ان الكمية اقل مما ينبغي. وتجدر الملاحظة ان الجزء الأخير من الجملة غالباً ما يُحذف.

يمكن ان تأتي enough قبل الاسم ولكنها لا تأتي بعده. وتحتاج too إلى استخدام much او many، واحياناً نقول too little أو too few.

يمكن استخدام to + مصدر + اسم بعد too وenough، وكذلك يمكن استخدام for + اسم.

Exercises

1 Write *too* + these adjectives or adverbs.

Adjectives	Adverbs
late, strong, young	quickly, quietly, slowly

Example: *Can't you work faster? You're working*
<u>*too slowly.*</u>

1 *I'm only 15, so I can't drive yet. I'm* _____
2 *Time goes* _____ *when you're having fun.*
3 *I couldn't hold the thief. He was* _____
4 *I ran, but I missed the train. I was* _____
5 *Tell Ann to speak up. She's talking* _____

2 Write these adjectives or adverbs + *enough*.

Adjectives	Adverbs
big, good, soon	carefully, hard, quickly

Example: *Can't you work faster? You aren't working*
<u>*quickly enough.*</u>

1 *I can't climb through the window. It isn't*
_____

2 *I can tell you the answer tomorrow. Is that*
_____

3 *The engine broke down. The engineers hadn't checked it*
_____

4 *Nick is going to lose the race. He hasn't trained*
_____

5 *I'm going to buy the smaller sound system. It isn't the best, but it's* _____

3 Complete the dialogues. Use *too* + *little/few*, *enough* or *not/n't ... enough*.

Mr Simpson and his assistant are checking stock in his small stationery shop.

1 *(✓ A5 paper/✗ A4 paper/✗ brown envelopes)*
Mr S: *We've got* <u>*enough A5 paper,*</u> *but we have* <u>*n't*</u>
got <u>*enough A4 paper.*</u>
Asst: *And we've got* <u>*too few brown envelopes.*</u>

2 *(✗ large paper clips/✗ medium clips/✓ small clips)*
Mr S: *We have* ___ *got* _____
_____ *and we have got*
_____
Asst: *But we've got* _____

3 *(✗ brown sticky tape/✗ clear tape/✓ elastic bands)*
Mr S: *We've got* _____
_____ *and we have* ___ *got*
_____
Asst: *But we've got* _____
_____

4 *(✗ glue/✗ stapling machines/✗ staples)*
Mr S: *We've got* _____ *and we've*
got _____
_____
Asst: *And we have* ___ *got* _____

4 Write statements.

Example: *The boys don't like the weather. It's too hot.*
<u>*The weather is too hot for the boys.*</u>

1 *I really want a holiday. I haven't got enough money.*
_____
_____

2 *Your mother won't like this coffee. It's too strong.*
_____
_____

3 *The family are all very happy with the new house. It's big enough.*
_____
_____

5 Write statements.

Example: *I don't want to go out. It's too hot.*
<u>*It's too hot to go out.*</u>

1 *We don't want to go out. It isn't warm enough.*
_____

2 *They tried to catch the bird. It was too fast.*
_____

3 *We wanted to catch the bus. We were too late.*
_____

4 *The plane missed the mountain. It was flying just high enough.*
_____
_____

76   *a bit, very*   *much, a lot*   *so, such*

I felt a bit ill.   *I felt much better.*   *I felt so tired.*

a bit, very, etc + **adjective/adverb**

He felt a bit tired, but he did not stop.

much, a lot, etc + **comparative adjective/adverb**

He was able to come down much more quickly. He felt a lot better.

so + **adjective/adverb**, *such* (+ **adjective**) + **noun**

Back at home, he was so tired that he went straight to sleep. It had been such a hard journey that he rested all next day.

a bit, very, etc + adjective/adverb

Use these words to give an adjective or an adverb a weaker or stronger feeling. *a bit, pretty* and *really* are informal. Use them in friendly conversation.

Weakest	Weak	Stronger	Strongest
not (+ verb) + *very*	*slightly, a little, a bit*	*quite, rather, fairly, pretty*	*very, extremely, really*

*He did**n't** feel **very well**. In fact, he felt **quite ill**.*
*Eddy is **extremely good** at tennis. He's Number 10 in the world.*

very and *too* are different. Compare the following. (See also Unit 75.)
*He was **very** tired, but he went on climbing.*
*He was **too** tired to walk. He had to stop.*

much, a lot, etc + comparative adjective/adverb

Use these words to give a comparative adjective or adverb a weaker or stronger feeling.

Weak	Strong	Strongest
slightly, a little, a bit	*much, a lot*	*far*

*Could you please talk **a little more quietly**?*
*I felt **a lot better** after a good night's sleep.*
*Susan can speak Japanese **far better** than she can write it.*

so + **adjective/adverb**

Use *so* to make an adjective or adverb very strong.
*The film was **so boring**!*
*What took you **so long** to get here?*
*I didn't see. It happened **so quickly**!*

We can add a *that* phrase to show the result of the *so* part of the sentence.
*The story was **so exciting that** I couldn't stop reading.*
*I was **so cold that** I wore two sweaters.*

such (+ **adjective**) + **noun**

Use *such* (+ adjective) + noun in the same way.
*He always talks **such rubbish**!*
*What took you **such a long time**?*
*This is such **a beautiful house**.*

We can do exactly the same with a sentence containing *such*.
*It was **such an exciting story that** I couldn't stop reading.*
*It was **such a cold day that** I wore two sweaters.*

تستخدم هذه الكلمات لإضافة احساس اقوى او اضعف، على صفة او ظرف. وتستخدم الكلمات a bit و pretty و really في المواقف غير الرسمية وفي الاحاديث الودية.

ويتضح الفرق بين استخدام very و too من خلال مقارنة الامثلة المبينة. (انظر ايضاً، unit 75)

وتستخدم هذه الكلمات المبينة لتضيف، على صفة المقارنة، وعلى ظروف المقارنة، مشاعر اضعف او اقوى.

تستخدم so لتضيف على الصفة او على الظرف درجة عالية من القوة.
وتستخدم such (+ صفة) + اسم بنفس الطريقة.

يمكن اضافة العبارة التي تستخدم فيها that بغرض تبيين الأثر الناتج عن استخدام so في الجملة. ونستطيع فعل الشيء نفسه مع الجملة التي تحتوي على such.

Exercises

1 Complete the statements. Use these words.

a bit, not very, quite, very

Example: *The traffic was travelling at 5 kph. The journey was <u>very</u> slow.*

1 *Sally is doing much better at Maths now, but she's still _____ slow.*

2 *I like football, but I'm _____ good at it.*

3 *I'm _____ hungry. I need food now!*

4 *The new XR200 is _____ a good car, but it isn't my favourite.*

5 *Don't climb on that old fence. It's _____ strong.*

2 Complete the statements. Use these words.

a little, far, much

Example: *Tony is still very ill, but he's getting <u>a little</u> better every day.*

1 *These shoes look the same, but these are £50 more than those. They're _____ more expensive.*

2 *I failed my driving test badly the first time, but I did _____ better the second time, and I passed.*

3 *Sue is _____ older than Tim. She's 10 and he's 9.*

4 *Our new house is _____ bigger than our old one. It's got four bedrooms instead of two.*

5 *Tony drives _____ more carefully than he did a few years ago, but he still frightens me!*

3 Complete the conversation with *so* or *such*.

● *You're <u>so</u> quiet! Is anything wrong?*

○ *It's my exams. They're [1]_____ soon, and I've got [2]_____ a lot of work. I've got to stay up all night.*

● *Don't be [3]_____ an idiot! You're obviously [4]_____ tired that you can't work properly. It would be [5]_____ a waste of time if you stayed up all night! What's more, you'd be [6]_____ exhausted tomorrow that you'd waste the whole day!*

○ *But I'm [7]_____ worried! If I don't pass, it'll be [8]_____ a disaster!*

● *You'll pass. The trouble with you is that you're [9]_____ a worrier, and you've really [10]_____ little to worry about!*

4 Match statements 1–8 and a–h. Then join them using *so* or *such ... (that)*.

1 *The weather was bad.*
2 *The students are making a noise.*
3 *The birds are friendly.*
4 *The children made a mess.*
5 *Everybody is busy.*
6 *I haven't driven for a long time.*
7 *After the trip we were all tired.*
8 *They took a long time to get ready.*

a *All the neighbours are complaining.*
b *They nearly missed their plane.*
c *We went straight to sleep.*
d *They even take food from your hand.*
e *We gave up our holiday and went home.*
f *Nobody is answering the phone.*
g *I feel quite nervous about going on the road.*
h *It took an hour to clean the room.*

1 – <u>e</u>   2 – __   3 – __   4 – __   5 – __   6 – __
7 – __   8 – __

1 <u>*The weather was so bad (that) we gave up our holiday and went home.*</u>

2 _____

_____

3 _____

_____

4 _____

_____

5 _____

_____

6 _____

_____

7 _____

_____

8 _____

_____

Prepositions 1: place and movement

on, onto, into, out of, across, by, down, from, in, through, under, etc

The prepositions in this unit express their place or movement. The preposition refers to the noun which always follows it. (See Unit 78 for differences between the prepositions of place *in*, *on* and *at*.)

>The hotel is **down** the hill. (place)
>The Wood family are walking **down** the hill. (movement)

تتعلق أدوات الجر في هذه الوحدة بالمكان والحركة. وهي ترتبط بشكل دائم بالاسم الذي يليها.

on, on top of

>There's a suitcase **on** the chair.
>There's another suitcase **on top of** the cupboard.

on, onto, off

>Nick Wood is putting a pile of clothes **onto/on** the bed.
>His cap is falling **off** the pile.

in, into, out of

>There are some clothes **in** the suitcase.
>He's putting them **into/in** the case.
>Nick is taking some more clothes **out of** the cupboard.

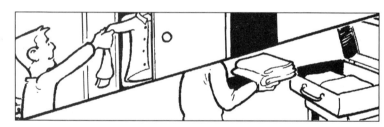

down, up

>Nick is taking his case **down** the stairs.
>His sister is going **up** the stairs.

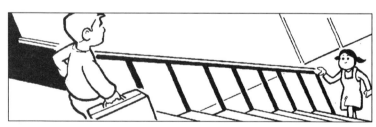

inside, outside

>There are two sports bags **inside** the front door.
>There are some beach things **outside** the front door.

behind, in front of, around, round

>The car was in the garage **behind** the house.
>Now it's **in front of** the house.
>Mr Wood has brought it **around/round** the house.

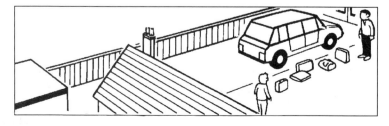

next to, by, beside

The car is **next to/by/beside** the garden fence.
There are some pieces of luggage **next to/by/ beside** the car.
Mr Wood is standing **next to/by/beside** the car.

across, along

Mrs Wood is going **across** the road.
A friend is coming **along** the road.

near, from, to

The Wood family live in Sandford **near** Oxford.
Today they're driving **from** Sandford **to** Heathrow Airport.

away from, towards, past

They're driving **away from** Sandford.
They're going **towards** the motorway.
They're driving **past** the motorway sign.

over, under, through

They've just driven **over** a bridge. (**across** a bridge is also possible.)
There's a river **under** the bridge.
They're going to drive **through** a tunnel.

above, below

The Wood family catch their plane. Soon it's **above** the clouds.
Nick watches the clouds **below** the plane.

between, among, opposite

The Woods finally reach their hotel. It's **between** the hills and the sea.
It stands **among** a lot of trees.
It's **opposite** a small island.

Exercises

1 Look at the picture. Then complete the statements with these prepositions.

above, behind, between, in, in front of, near, next to, on, opposite, under

Example: *There is a light* <u>*near*</u> *the window.*

1 *There is a desk _____ the window too.*

2 *There is a light _____ the desk.*

3 *There is a chair _____ the desk.*

4 *There is a lamp _____ the desk.*

5 *There is a paper bin _____ the desk.*

6 *There is an empty box _____ the paper bin.*

7 *There is a phone _____ the desk.*

8 *There is a filing cabinet _____ the desk.*

9 *There is a large wall map _____ the window.*

10 *The desk is _____ the window and the wall map.*

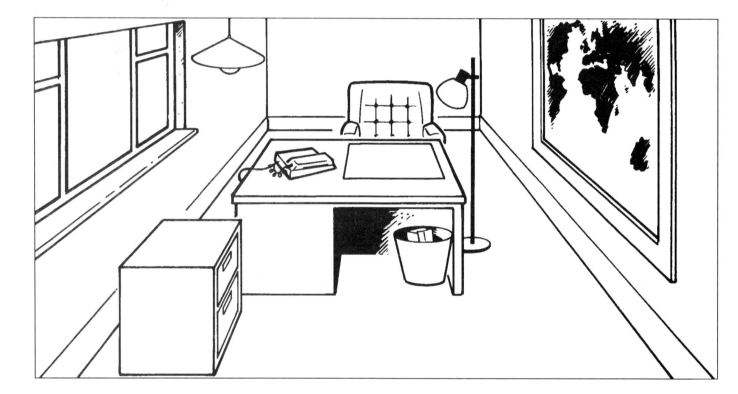

2 Write the correct prepositions.

Example: *There were a lot of people* <u>*outside*</u> *the cinema before the doors opened. (inside/outside)*

1 *There's someone ___ the door. Could you answer it, please? (in/at)*

2 *Is Lucy ___ home today? (in/at)*

3 *Listen! I think I can hear somebody ___ the garden. (in/at)*

4 *I'm sorry. Mr Davis isn't ___ his office just now. He's seeing the Director. (in/at)*

5 *There's a newspaper shop on the other side of the road, _____ our house. (opposite/in front of)*

6 *Please don't stand _____ the children. They can't see what's happening. (opposite/in front of)*

7 *Look! Can't you see your glasses now? They're right _____ you. (opposite/in front of)*

8 *Swindon is a large town that stands on the road _____ London and Bristol. (between/among)*

9 *_____ all the white sheep in the field there were a few black ones. (between/among)*

10 *The woods are lovely there, and we camped _____ the trees by the stream. (between/among)*

3 Look at the picture. Then complete the statements with prepositions.

   Example: (across, along, into, past, through)
   The cat walked <u>along</u> the road for a while.

1 It went _____ the bus stop.

2 Then it suddenly ran _____ the road.

3 It came _____ our garden.

4 It came in _____ the gate.

   (along, over, round, towards, up)

5 It walked a little way _____ the garden path.

6 Then it ran _____ the tree.

7 Next it went _____ our summer house.

8 It jumped _____ the flower bed on the way.

9 It climbed _____ one side of the summer house.

   (away from, down, inside, out of, under)

10 And it climbed _____ the other side.

11 It crawled _____ the summer house.

12 Then it went _____ the summer house for a moment.

13 But then it jumped _____ the window.

14 Finally, it ran _____ the summer house and left the garden.

78 Prepositions 2: place
at, in, on

at

Use *at* to talk about an exact place.

> He lives **at Number 25, Park Road**.
> Where's Mary? She isn't **at her desk**.
> I'll meet you **at the cinema entrance**.

Use *at* to talk about an event.

> Were you **at the football match**?
> Over 100 people were **at the meeting**.

تستخدم *at* عند الحديث عن مكان محدد.

وتستخدم *at* عند الحديث عن حدث ما.

in

Use *in* when there is something around, eg a person in a country or a pen in a pocket.

> He lives **in Sandford, in England**.
> ● Is she **in the TV room**?   ○ No, she's **in the garden**.
> Did you put the pen **in your pocket**?

تستخدم *in* عند الحديث عن شيء في الجوار، مثل شخص في بلد ما أو قلم في الجيب.

Compare the use of *in* and *at*.

> The meeting was **in Room 93**. (the place)
> Over 100 people were **at the meeting**. (the event in the place)

ويصبح الفرق أكثر وضوحاً عند مقارنة استخدام *in* و *at* فيما يلي.

on

Use *on* for any surface.

> Nick was standing **on the chair**.   Her name is **on the door**.
> There's a mark **on the ceiling**.   The answer is **on page 75**.

تستخدم *on* عند الحديث عن شيء موجود على أي سطح.

Use *on* for a line that runs between two places.

> Sandford is **on the River Thames, between Oxford and Abingdon**.
> The Wood family were **on the road to the airport**.
> There were guards **on the frontier between India and Pakistan**.

وتستخدم *on* عند الحديث عن شيء أو عن خط يصل بين مكانين.

Note these common expressions of place.

وتوضح الأمثلة المبينة الاستخدامات الشائعة لأدوات الجر التي تتصل بالمكان.

at	*in*	*on*
at school/work/home/college	*in hospital/town*	*on holiday/business*
at the library/bus station/ cross roads	*in the country/ shopping centre*	*on the beach/lake/ island*
at the (third) turning	*in the middle of the road*	*on the right/left*
at the top/bottom of the hill	*in the middle/centre of the city/town/village*	*on the edge/outskirts of town/the city*
at a party/meeting/lesson	*in a group/queue/line*	*on the front/back of an envelope/a book*
at the front/back of a queue/hall/bus	*in the front/back of a car*	*on TV/cassette/disk*
at the end of a corridor/ queue		

Exercises

1 Match statement halves 1–10 and a–j. Then write the complete statements.

1 Tom lives at
2 There's a notice on
3 Ann is buying some things in
4 Dad is having a sleep in
5 My aunt lives in
6 Come and meet all the trainees in
7 I want you to introduce me to everyone at
8 There are two men working up on
9 Sally put the vase of flowers on
10 Both London and Oxford are on

a the shopping centre.
b Room 564.
c a small town outside London.
d the small bedroom.
e the roof.
f the party.
g Number 25, North Street.
h the River Thames.
i the wall outside my office.
j the table.

1 – _g_ 2 – ___ 3 – ___ 4 – ___ 5 – ___ 6 – ___
7 – ___ 8 – ___ 9 – ___ 10 – ___

1 _Tom lives at Number 25, North Street._
2 _____
_____
3 _____
_____
4 _____
_____
5 _____
_____
6 _____
_____
7 _____
_____
8 _____
_____

9 _____
_____
10 _____
_____

2 Complete the statements. Use these phrases.

at that desk, at the entrance, at the meeting, in a village, in the garden, in the middle of, on that wall, on the way, on the bottle, on the edge of

Example: Sally lives _on the edge of_ London. She can see the country from her house.

1 I live _____ London. It takes an hour to get out of the city.
2 We can stop for some petrol _____ to the shops.
3 A lot of people spoke _____
4 Let's put this picture _____
5 What does the label _____ say?
6 My brother usually works _____
7 You can buy your ticket _____
8 Mary is picking some flowers _____
9 My sister lives _____ near Oxford.

3 Complete the dialogues. Use in, on or at.

● Excuse me. Where can I find a photocopier?
○ There's one _in_ Room 303. Go upstairs and turn right ¹___ the top of the stairs. It's ²___ the right ³___ the end of the corridor.

● Look. There's a note ⁴___ the front door.
○ Oh, yes. It's written ⁵___ the back of an envelope. It's from Jenny. She says she's ⁶___ a meeting ⁷___ college. She'll be back for dinner.

● Is Sue ⁸___ home this afternoon?
○ No, sorry. She's ⁹___ the library.
● Is that the one ¹⁰___ Bath Street ¹¹___ town?
○ No, she always uses the one ¹²___ the shopping centre ¹³___ the edge of town.

79 Prepositions 3: time

at, in, on   past, to

> We'll arrive at 12.40 local time.

FORMS

at, in and on

The Wood family had their holiday in July.
They left on Saturday.
They left on 7th July.
They left at 7.20.

past and to

They left at twenty past seven.
They arrived at twenty to one.

at

Use *at* for time.

> *Lunch will be at 1.00.*
> *Mum called us at dinner time.*

Use *at* for a known point in the past or the future.

> *They married young. At that time, they were poor.*
> *We will arrive at 10.00. At that point, you will open the main door.*

Use *at* for special days, short holidays and festivals.

> *We always have a party at New Year.*

in

Use *in* for centuries, years, months and seasons.

> *The car was invented in the 19th century.*
> *We bought our house in 1989.*
> *School started again in September.*
> *We always go skiing in (the) winter.*

Also use *in* for periods of time.

> *We don't do much work in the holidays.*
> *Are you going away in the summer break?*

Compare these examples with *at* + short period of time.

> *We always have a party at New Year.*
> *What are you doing at the weekend?*

Use *in* for parts of the day (but not usually with the word *night*).

> *I ate in the morning/afternoon/evening.*
> *We arrived late at night.*

Use *in* for a measured time.

> *Tony finished the job in three weeks.*
> *Your pizzas will be ready in ten minutes.*

تستخدم at عند الحديث عن الزمن.

وتستخدم at عند الحديث عن نقطة زمنية محددة في الماضي او في المستقبل.

وتستخدم at عند الحديث عن أيام خاصة او عن العطلات القصيرة او عن الاعياد.

وتستخدم in مع القرون والسنوات والشهور والفصول.

وتستخدم in مع الفترات الزمنية.

وتتضح الصورة عند مقارنة الامثلة المبينة، حيث تستخدم at + فترة زمنية قصيرة.

وتستخدم in مع اجزاء اليوم ولكنها لا تستخدم عادة، مع كلمة الليل.

وتستخدم in مع الوقت الذي يجري تحديده وقياسه.

on

Use *on* for days and dates.

> *They arrived **on Saturday**.*
> *We left **on 7th July**.*

تستخدم *on* مع الأيام ومع التواريخ.

Use *on* for special days.

> *I visited my parents **on New Year's Day**.*
> *I didn't have a party **on my birthday**!*
> *Did things go well **on your wedding day**?*

وتستخدم *on* مع الأيام الخاصة والمعروفة.

Use *on* for parts of a particular day. Compare the following.

> *Did they go **on Saturday morning**?*
> *Did they go **in the morning**?*

وتستخدم *on* عند تحديد جزء من يوم معين. ويتضح الفرق من خلال مقارنة المثالين:

Do not use *in* or *on* with *this, last, next, yesterday, tomorrow, each* and *every*.

> *I came to work late **this morning**.*
> *Did you go away **last weekend**?*
> *Tom cleans his car **every weekend**.*

لا تستخدم *in* أو *on* مع أي من الكلمات المبينة.

Note these common expressions of time with *at, in* and *on*.

> *He's usually happy, but **at times** he feels sad.* (sometimes)
> *He's rich now, but **at one time** he was very poor.* (for a time in the past)
> *The soldiers climbed the ropes three **at a time**.* (three together)
> *We met **in time** to talk before the film.* (with enough time)
> *The plane took off **on time**.* (at the right time – not too early, not too late)
> *You must always get to work **on time**.* (You must not be late for work.)

لاحظ التعبيرات الشائعة المبينة التي تعبر عن الزمن باستخدام *at* و *in* و *on*.

past and to

We can tell these times in different ways.

> *12.15 → twelve fifteen* OR *quarter past twelve*
> *12.30 → twelve thirty* OR *half past twelve*
> *12.45 → twelve forty-five* OR *quarter to one*
> *12.50 → twelve fifty* OR *ten to one*

يمكن التعبير عن الوقت بطرق مختلفة توضحها الأمثلة المبينة.

We can also tell these times in different ways. If you use the second way, you must say *minutes*.

> *1.03 → one oh three* OR *three minutes past one*
> *1.39 → one thirty-nine* OR *twenty-one minutes to two*

ويمكن التعبير عن الأوقات المذكورة بعدة طرق. وفي حالة استخدام الطريقة الثانية، يجب ذكر كلمة *minutes* في الجملة.

Exercises

1 Complete the conversation. Use *at*, *in* and *on*.

Tony and his mother are talking on the phone.

Mum: *So can you come home* on *Saturday, Tony?*

Tony: *I'm sorry, Mum, but I can't come* [1]___ *the weekend this week or next week.*

Mum: *Well, are we going to see you* [2]___ *the holidays? Can you get away from London* [3]___ *the last week of December?*

Tony: *Well, I can get away* [4]___ *the 30th.*

Mum: *The 30th. That'll be a Thursday, won't it?*

Tony: *That's right. And I can stay for three days.*

Mum: *Good! So you'll be with us* [5]___ *New Year. It's good to be at home with your family* [6]___ *that time of the year.*

Tony: *Right. And we'll have a good time* [7]___ *New Year's Eve – just like the old days.*

Mum: *Wonderful! So what time can we expect you* [8]___ *Thursday? Will you be arriving late* [9]___ *night?*

Tony: *I'll probably leave London* [10]___ *lunchtime, so that means I'll get to you* [11]___ *about 6.00.*

Mum: *So you'll be with us* [12]___ *the evening. Dad and the children will be pleased.*

2 Complete the statements. Use *at*, *in* and *on*.

Example: *I'll be away* on *Thursday.*

1 *The meeting will start* ___ *10.00.*

2 *I took a short holiday* ___ *January.*

3 *Columbus sailed across the Atlantic* ___ *1492.*

4 *We flew to Malta late* ___ *Saturday.*

5 *Are you doing anything special* ___ *your birthday?*

6 *The telephone was invented* ___ *the nineteenth century.*

7 *I'll be in New York* ___ *this time next week.*

8 *We always go to France* ___ *the summer.*

9 *I won't be away for long. I'll be home* ___ *three days.*

10 *The President is arriving* ___ *midday.*

11 *Ann usually watches TV* ___ *the evening.*

12 *What are you doing* ___ *Wednesday evening?*

13 *We'll be at a party* ___ *New Year's Eve.*

14 *We'll be away for a week* ___ *New Year.*

15 *Hurry! We have to leave* ___ *an hour's time.*

16 *The climbers reached the top* ___ *the fifth day.*

17 *Tom left home* ___ *the age of 15.*

18 *We finished the job* ___ *less than a week.*

19 *I haven't got any money* ___ *the moment.*

3 Complete the conversation. Use *at*, *in* or *on* or nothing (✗).

● *Hello, Fred. I was trying to call you* ✗ *last weekend.*

○ *Did you call* on *Saturday?*

● *Yes, that's right. I phoned* [1]___ *Saturday morning and again* [2]___ *lunchtime.*

○ *I'm sorry, but I was out. I always go sailing* [3]___ *Saturdays.*

● *So I suppose that means you're going sailing again* [4]___ *Saturday* [5]___ *this weekend too.*

○ *I'm afraid so. What's the problem?*

● *Well, I'd like your help with a new computer that I bought* [6]___ *last week.*

○ *Sure. No problem. I can help you* [7]___ *Sunday night.*

● *Ah, but I'll be away all day until late. You see, I visit my parents* [8]___ *each Sunday.*

○ *I see. Well, what about* [9]___ *the evening? I'm free after I finish work* [10]___ *5.30. In fact, I don't usually do much* [11]___ *the week these days, and I'm free* [12]___ *nearly every evening.*

● *Well, I have to go out* [13]___ *tonight, but could we get together* [14]___ *tomorrow evening?*

○ *Fine. I'm free* [15]___ *the evening tomorrow too. I'll come round to your place* [16]___ *7.00.*

● *Thanks. That'll be really great!*

4 Complete the statements. Use these phrases.

at times, at a time, at one time, in time, on time

Example: *Don't be late. Make sure you're there* on time.

1 *The runners left in groups every two minutes. They left six* _____

2 *I enjoy life most of the time, but* _____ *I'd like to go back to the old days.*

3 We arrived just _____ The shop was just going to close.

4 There are factories everywhere here now, but _____ there were just green fields.

5 The trains always leave _____ They're never late.

5 Write the times in words. Use *past* and *to*.

Examples: 12.15 – *a quarter past one*

10.41 – *nineteen minutes to eleven*

1 3.10 – _____

2 7.50 – _____

3 9.30 – _____

4 2.45 – _____

5 5.15 – _____

6 1.13 – _____

7 11.31– _____

8 12.59 – _____

6 Rewrite the diary notes as full statements. Use the present continuous.

You work for a busy company director. Remind him of his activities in the next two weeks.

Example: *On Monday the 26th you're travelling to New York at 8.30 in the morning.*

1 _____
_____
_____

2 _____
_____
_____
_____

3 _____
_____
_____
_____

4 _____
_____
_____
_____

5 _____
_____

6 _____
_____
_____

7 _____
_____

8 _____
_____
_____

Diary

May

Mon, 26th May
8.30 a.m. – travel to NY

Wed, 28th May
3.45 p.m. – return to London

Fri, 30th May
all day – meet Japanese visitors from the Subarashi Corporation

Sat, 31st May
evening – speak at the goodbye party for the Managing Director

June

Mon, 2nd June
p.m. – attend the sales conference

Tues, 3rd June
a.m. – talk at the sales conference

Thurs, 5th June
7.15 a.m. – fly to Rome

Fri, 6th June
11.45 a.m. – leave Rome for Madrid

Sat, 7th June
midday – travel back to London

80 Prepositions 4: time

for, since   ago, before   during, while   until/till, by

> *I've lived here for 50 years. And I'll stay here till I die.*

FORMS

for and **since**

He has lived there for 50 years.
He has lived here since 1945.

ago and **before**

He moved there 50 years ago.
He had lived with his parents before that.

during and **while**

A lot has changed during those 50 years.
A lot has changed while he has been there.

until/till and **by**

He will be there until/till he dies.
By the year 2,000 he will be 75 years old.

CROSSCHECK

for

We use *for* to say how long in any tense, in the past, present or future.
> *It rained **for three hours**.*

We use *for* with the present perfect to say how long up the the present. *for* refers to the time between the start and now. (See also Unit 10.)

ago

We use *ago* to say when something happened in the past. Count back from the present.
> *Where's my book? It was here **a minute ago**!*

during

Use *during* + noun, eg *the day*, or + noun phrase, eg *the early afternoon*.
> *I'll call again **during the week**.*

until/till

until/till refers to a period continuing to a point in time.
> *I'll be busy **until 5.00**. (I have no free time between now and 5.00. Therefore I can't call before 5.00, but I will be able to call at 5.00.)*

since

We use *since* to say how long mainly in the present perfect.
> *He's lived here **since 1945**.*

We use *since* with the present perfect to say how long up to the present. *since* refers to the start. (See also Unit 10.)

before

We use *before* to say when something happened in the past. Count back from another event in the past.
> *I finished at 4.30, but the others had finished **two hours before**.*

while

Use *while* + verb, eg *I was training*, or + clause, eg *I was away on holiday*.
> *I'll visit you **while I'm in town**.*

by

by refers to a point in time.
> *Please reply **by 5.00**. (Please call at or before 5.00. 5.00 is the latest possible time. Before 5.00 is better.)*

تستخدم كلمة for للتعبير عن الفترة الزمنية في الماضي او في الحاضر او في المستقبل.

وتستخدم كلمة since للتعبير عن «منذ متى» وغالباً في زمن المضارع التام.

تستخدم for مع المضارع التام للتعبير عن مدة الفترة الزمنية حتى الوقت الحاضر. وهي تشير الى الزمن بين البداية والآن.

كما تستخدم since مع المضارع التام للتعبير عن مدة الفترة الزمنية حتى الوقت الحاضر ولكنها تشير الى البداية. (انظر ايضاً unit 10).

تستخدم ago للدلالة على وقت حدوث شيء ما في الماضي، والعدّ الرجعي يبدأ من الوقت الحاضر.

وتستخدم before للتعبير عن وقت حدوث الفعل في الماضي، والعدّ الرجعي يبدأ من حدث آخر في الماضي.

تستخدم كلمة during + اسم او عبارة اسمية.

وتستخدم كلمة while + فعل او جزء كامل من جملة، كما في المثال.

تعبر until و till عن فترة زمنية تستمر حتى نقطة زمنية محددة.

وتشير by الى نقطة زمنية محددة.

Exercises

1 Complete the story with *for* or *since*.

Oxford Lasers has not been in business *for* very long. In fact, the company has only existed *since* 1977. The five directors had done a lot of work on lasers at Oxford University [1]_____ several years before that. They continued to work at the University [2]_____ some time after 1977 too, so their new company developed very slowly. In fact, [3]_____ a while it seemed likely to close down. But [4]_____ the introduction of new products in 1982, Oxford Lasers has grown fast. There were financial problems in the early 1990s [5]_____ a year or two, but the company has remained a top laser producer [6]_____ the mid-1980s. [7]_____ a number of years it has been developing sales world-wide. It has also owned a company in the USA [8]_____ 1985.

2 Complete the dialogues with *ago* or *before*.

Examples: ● Tim bought a BMW two days *ago.*
○ He had an old Fiat *before,* didn't he?

● You went to Ibiza two years [1]_____ , didn't you?
○ That's right. We'd never been there [2]_____

● How long [3]_____ did you try to call her?
○ An hour [4]_____ But she'd left ten minutes [5]_____

● Lucy went away to college three years [6]_____ , didn't she?
○ Yes, and it was a hard time because she hadn't been away from home very much [7]_____

3 Complete the statements with *during* or *while*.

Examples: Jim Brown called *while* you were out.
There will be a fire practice *during* the morning.

1 What's Tom going to do _____ he's in America?
2 _____ the meeting, we'll discuss the sales report.
3 _____ you're cleaning the car, could you clean the ashtrays too?
4 Are you going to visit Australia _____ your trip round the world?

5 Somebody got into the house _____ the night.
6 They'd never seen anything like that _____ their whole lives!
7 I worked out my travel plans _____ I was waiting for the train.

4 Complete the dialogues with *by* or *until/till*.

Examples: ● Do you think you'll be able to finish the picture *by* tomorrow morning?
○ Yes, but I'll have to work *until* midnight to do it.

● Ann was already married [1]_____ the age of 19.
○ She lived at home [2]_____ then, didn't she?

● I'm sorry, Sir. Your car won't be ready [3]_____ early tomorrow afternoon.
○ So, if I come at 4.30, will it be ready [4]_____ then?
● Oh, yes. No problem, Sir.

○ [5]_____ this time tomorrow, I'll be in Tokyo.
● How long are you going to stay there?
○ [6]_____ this time next week.

● I'm sure Tony has left the office [7]_____ now.
○ I don't think so. He said he'd have to work [8]_____ late this evening.

5 Complete the story.

Arthur had worked in the same, large office *for* 30 years. 'I've worked here [1]_____ I was 19,' he often thought. 'And [2]_____ all those years I haven't done anything very exciting.'

One day, [3]_____ he was at a very boring meeting, he suddenly decided to change his life completely. He thought, 'I'll go on working [4]_____ another six months – [5]_____ my 50th birthday – and then I'll stop. I'll sell the house, buy a boat and go sailing.'

[6]_____ the middle of the following year he had done all these things. As he sailed among the Scottish islands on his first long trip, he thought, 'Why didn't I do this [7]_____ ? I should have left that office ten years [8]_____ !'

Preposition + noun

Some expressions have the form preposition + noun. These are some of the most common.

تستخدم بعض التعبيرات اللغوية أداة جر + اسم وهذه أكثرها شيوعاً.

> *It's a picture **by Rembrandt**.*
> *I paid **by cheque/credit card**. (but in cash)*
> *They cut through the rock **by hand**.*

> *There's someone on the phone. It's **for you**.*
> *We're having fish **for dinner**.*
> *Let's go out **for a walk/swim/run/meal**.*
> *They've gone **for a short holiday**. (but go on holiday)*

> *I heard it **on the radio**. (but at the cinema/theatre)*
> *He hurt her **on purpose**. (but by accident/mistake/chance)*
> *The house is **on fire**.*
> *Sally is **on a diet**. She wants to lose six kilograms.*

> *The bus leaves at 12.00, so be there **on time**.*
> *We're going to stop for tea **on the way** there.*
> *Bill is going to Africa **on business/holiday/safari**.*
> *They're going **on a trip/bus tour**.*

> *We're going **by car/bike/plane/train/ship/road/air/rail/sea**, etc. (but on foot/in his car/on his bike/the bus/the plane/the train/the ship)*

Noun + preposition

Some expressions have the form noun + preposition. These are some of the most common.

وتستخدم بعض التعبيرات اسماً + أداة جر، وهذه أكثرها شيوعاً.

> *Tom's teacher sent the theatre a **request for** 60 tickets. (also application for/need for/reason for)*
> *He was very pleased as the theatre reduced the **price of** the tickets by 20%. (also cost of/hope of/way of)*
> *Unfortunately, there was a **problem with** the bus company. (also trouble with/matter with)*
> *There was a **rise in** the price of the bus. (also fall/increase/decrease in)*

Exercises

1 Complete the dialogues with *at*, *by*, *for*, *in* and *on*.

Example: ● *Did you go by bus?*
○ *No, we went* <u>in</u> *Steve's car.*

1 ● *Let's go to the beach _____ foot.*
○ *No, let's go _____ bike. It's quicker.*

2 ● *I saw you! You hit Sam _____ purpose!*
○ *No, I didn't. I did it _____ accident!*

3 ● *Someone is _____ the phone. It's _____ Bob.*
○ *He isn't here. He's gone out _____ a run.*

4 ● *I'm going to have some toast _____ breakfast.*
○ *No, you aren't. It's _____ fire! Can't you smell it?*

5 ● *Are you here _____ holiday?*
○ *No, I'm _____ a short business trip.*

6 ● *Can I pay _____ credit card?*
○ *I'm sorry, Sir. We can only accept payment _____ cash or _____ cheque.*

7 ● *Is there anything good _____ TV tonight?*
○ *No, and there's nothing interesting _____ the radio either.*

8 ● *What's the new play _____ the theatre this week?*
○ *It's called 'Paris in the Spring'. It's _____ that new writer, Mark Ross.*

2 Complete the statements with these words. Put a preposition before each one.

a diet, air, an artist, a school trip, a tour, a walk, dinner, his bike, my car, plane, the cinema

Example: *I'm hungry. Let's stop at that restaurant* <u>for dinner.</u>

1 *My cousins from Australia are visiting Britain. They're _____ of the country.*

2 *Their car is full. You'd better go _____*

3 *Tony's class is going _____ to Italy.*

4 *Tony and his friends are travelling to Italy _____*

5 *Can you see Rob? He's over there. He's _____*

6 *It's a nice day. Let's go _____ along the river.*

7 *They're showing a new film _____ in George Street.*

8 *If you want to get this package to America fast, send it _____*

9 *We aren't eating very much at the moment. We're _____*

10 *It's a wonderful picture. It's _____ who lived about 600 years ago.*

3 Complete the statements with these words. Put a preposition after each one.

applications, call, difficulties, fall, hope, increase, interested, matter, need, problem, way

Example: *We've had a lot of* <u>applications for</u> *the job of Chief Engineer.*

1 *What's the _____ you? You always seem angry about something.*

2 *Could you please keep quiet? There's no _____ all this noise.*

3 *We'd better stop here for tonight. There's no _____ reaching the village before dark.*

4 *Prices have gone up a little this year. There's been a small _____ the cost of living.*

5 *Scientists have found a new _____ producing electricity cheaply.*

6 *There's a _____ your plan. I'm afraid it won't work.*

7 *The rescue team has had a _____ help. They're on their way to the accident now.*

8 *There has been a _____ the size of families. They're smaller nowadays.*

9 *I'm very _____ photography.*

10 *Peter had _____ his homework.*

82 Adjective + preposition
He's good at Maths.

Some adjectives often take one or more prepositions.
These are some of the most common.

تأتي مع بعض الصفات في الغالب أداة جر واحدة أو
أكثر، وهذه أكثرها شيوعاً.

*Sam is a junior accountant. He's **excited about** his first business trip next month.*
*He's **worried/anxious about** his accountancy exams next week.*
*He got **angry/annoyed about** a noisy party next door last night.*
*His neighbour was **sorry about** the noise.*

*He got **angry/annoyed with** his neighbour last night.*
*He sometimes gets **bored/fed up with** his work.*

*He's **afraid/nervous of** failing his exams next week.*
*His family will be **proud of** him if he passes.*
*He's **tired of** studying late every night.*

*He's not **used/accustomed to** so much hard work.*
*Luckily, he's very **interested in** what he's doing.*

*Sam was **amazed/surprised/shocked at/by** the number of books he had to read for the exams.*

*His boss is **pleased/happy with/about** Sam's work now.*
*He was **disappointed with/about** Sam's work at first.*
*Sam is very **careful/careless with/about** his work.*

*Sam is **responsible for** the weekly sales figures.*
*The figures are nearly **ready for** printing.*
*He's **late/early for** a meeting.*
*Sam's family feel **sorry for** him when he works late.*
*His mother thinks the work is **bad for** his eyes.*
*His father knows the work is **good for** his future.*

*He's **good/brilliant at** figures and Maths.*
*He's **bad/terrible/hopeless at** languages.*

*He sometimes thinks life is very **similar to** school again.*
*He sometimes thinks life is no **different from/to** school.*

192

Exercises

1 Complete the statements with *about, at, for, of* and *with*.

Example: *I feel very sorry _for_ Ann. The poor girl has been ill for so long.*

1 *Are you ready _____ a big surprise?*

2 *Tim is quite good _____ sport.*

3 *I'm very angry _____ Sam. He never answers my letters.*

4 *We really thought our team would win, so we were disappointed _____ the bad result.*

5 *I wish they'd be more careful _____ their work.*

6 *You must stop working day and night. It's very bad _____ you.*

7 *I'm fed up _____ eating at home all the time. Let's go out.*

8 *Tony and Lisa were so annoyed _____ the people next door that they called the police.*

2 Complete the statements with these words. Put a preposition after each one.

different, early, good, late, proud, responsible, shocked, terrible, worried

Example: ● *I was _shocked at_ the bad sales figures.*
○ *Me too. I'd expected much better sales.*

1 ● *I can't understand this Maths problem.*
○ *But it's easy! You must be really _____ Maths*

2 ● *People in Manchester are very _____ their football team.*
○ *Yes, especially as they've won the championship again.*

3 ● *The men have done the job again, but it still looks bad.*
○ *I agree. It's no _____ last time.*

4 ● *It isn't _____ small children to stay up late at night.*
○ *That's right. It means they're very tired the next day.*

5 ● *Calm down! Why are you running around like that?*
○ *Because I'm _____ a very important meeting.*

6 ● *Have you heard? Joe's a senior manager now.*
○ *Yes, I hear he's _____ the whole factory now.*

7 ● *I hope you got to the interview on time.*
○ *Yes, I did. In fact, I was twenty minutes _____ it.*

8 ● *Have Robin and Steve reached Australia in their little boat yet?*
○ *No. They're two weeks late, and we're very _____ them.*

3 Write a statement using the underlined words and the words in brackets.

Example: *Ann reads a lot about sailing. (interested)*
She's _interested in sailing._

1 *Bob is going to give away his old computer games. (tired)*
He's _____
_____

2 *Working at night was strange at first, but it's all right now. (used)*
I'm _____

3 *Mrs Elfin shouted at her children. (angry)*
She was _____

4 *Peter isn't sure if his first business trip will go well. (anxious)*
He's _____
_____

5 *The airline staff felt bad because of the long delay at the airport. (sorry)*
They were _____
_____

6 *Bill decided to turn the radio programme off. (bored)*
He was _____
_____

7 *Old Mrs Price doesn't like going out alone. (nervous)*
She's _____
_____

8 *It was a fantastic surprise to see the huge number of people at the concert. (amazed)*
We were _____
_____

83 Prepositional verbs
She applied for several jobs. *He stole $600 from her.*

Verb + preposition

Some verbs often take one or more prepositions.
These are some of the most common.

غالباً ما تأتي مع بعضِ الأفعال أداة جر واحدة أو أكثر
وهذه أكثرها شيوعاً.

> *Claire **looked for** a job before she left college.*
> *She **asked for** details of lots of jobs.*
> *She **applied for** several jobs.*
> *She **applied to** several companies.*
> *She **waited** hopefully **for** the replies, but they were all negative.*
>
> *She **heard about** a good job in New York.*
> *She **talked about** it with her friend.*
> *She **asked about** the company at the US Embassy.*
> *She **thought about** the job a lot.*

> *In the end, she **wrote to** the company in New York.*
> *They **replied to** her letter immediately.*
> *They **talked to** her on the phone.*

look + different prepositions has different meanings.

> ***Look at** this photo. It's beautiful.*
> *I'm **looking for** my glasses. Can you see them?*
> *Could you **look after** the baby for a few minutes?*

think and *dream* + different prepositions have different meanings.

> *Claire **thought about** the job carefully.*
> *When I **dream about** the crash, I always wake up.*

> *I've just **thought of** a great idea!*
> *Harry **dreams of** becoming rich one day.*

Verb + object + preposition

Some verbs often take an object and then a preposition.
These are some of the most common.

وتأخذ بعض الأفعال غالباً مفعولاً به متبوعاً بأداة جر،
وهذه أكثرها شيوعاً.

> *The company **invited her to** an interview.*
> *They **provided her with** air tickets.*
> *When she got to New York, she **asked somebody for** directions to the company.*

> *At the interview, she **asked them about** the job.*
> *They **told her about** the pay and conditions.*
> *She accepted the job, and they **congratulated her on** her decision.*

> *She also **had a bad experience in** New York. A thief **robbed her of** her money. He **stole $600 from** her. Fortunately, she had **insured herself against** theft. She **blamed herself for** the theft because she had left her purse on a restaurant table. She **described the purse to** the police, but they never found it.*

Exercises

1 Complete the statements with *about*, *for*, and *to*.

Example: *A boy came to the door and asked ＿for＿ a glass of water.*

1 *Danny dreams ＿＿＿＿＿＿ being famous one day.*

2 *I'll wait ＿＿＿＿＿＿ you outside the cinema.*

3 *Ann is on the phone. Could you talk ＿＿＿＿＿＿ her, please?*

4 *They're very bad. They take ages to reply ＿＿＿＿＿＿ letters.*

5 *The family talked ＿＿＿＿＿＿ their plans every night.*

2 Complete the dialogues with the correct forms of the verbs and prepositions.

Example: ● *There's Mark Blake. He's famous!*
　　　　　 ○ *Mark Blake? I've never ＿heard of＿ him!*
　　　　　 (hear)

1 ● *Hello, I'm Terry Grant.*
　 ○ *Hello. I've often ＿＿＿＿＿＿＿＿ you. It's nice to meet you at last. (hear)*

2 ● *I hear you're looking for a new job.*
　 ○ *That's right. I've ＿＿＿＿＿＿＿＿ several companies. (apply)*

3 ● *What sort of job are you ＿＿＿＿＿＿＿＿ (apply)*
　 ○ *I'm trying to get a job in sales.*

4 ● *Have you found an answer to the problem yet?*
　 ○ *No. I've been ＿＿＿＿＿＿＿＿＿＿ it for ages, but I haven't got any ideas. (think)*

5 ● *Can you see what to do about the problem?*
　 ○ *Well, yes, I've suddenly ＿＿＿＿＿＿＿＿ a new idea! (think)*

6 ● *Who waters the plants when you're away?*
　 ○ *My neighbours ＿＿＿＿＿＿＿＿ them. (look)*

7 ● *What sort of bike would you like?*
　 ○ *One like this! Come and ＿＿＿＿＿＿ it. (look)*

8 ● *Oh, no! I've lost my wallet.*
　 ○ *Don't worry. I'll help you ＿＿＿＿＿＿ it. (look)*

3 Complete the statements with these verbs. Add prepositions.

ask, congratulate, insure, provide, tell

Example: *Companies need to ＿insure＿ themselves ＿against＿ injuries to their staff.*

1 *The old man ＿＿＿＿＿＿＿ us ＿＿＿＿＿ some money, so we gave him £1.*

2 *Mrs Brett, we'd all like to ＿＿＿＿＿＿＿ you ＿＿＿＿＿ reaching the fantastic age of 100.*

3 *We ＿＿＿＿＿＿＿ all visitors to the company ＿＿＿＿＿ identity cards.*

4 *There's a reporter here. He wants to ＿＿＿＿＿＿＿ you some questions ＿＿＿＿＿ your plans for a new factory.*

5 *The reporter said, 'Could you please ＿＿＿＿＿＿＿ me ＿＿＿＿＿ your ideas for a new factory in town?'*

4 Complete the statements. Write the words in order and put the verbs in the correct forms. Add prepositions.

Example: *Yesterday a thief ＿stole my wallet from my pocket.＿ (my/my/steal/pocket/wallet)*

1 *Tim couldn't understand, so he ＿＿＿＿＿＿＿＿＿＿＿＿＿＿＿＿＿＿＿＿＿＿＿ (the/help/ask/teacher)*

2 *We phoned the doctor, and we ＿＿＿＿＿＿＿＿＿＿＿＿＿＿＿＿＿＿＿＿＿＿＿ (him/the/tell/accident)*

3 *It wasn't Tony's fault, but they still ＿＿＿＿＿＿＿＿＿＿＿＿＿＿＿＿＿＿＿＿ (him/the/crash/blame)*

4 *The police are coming soon, so you can ＿＿＿＿＿＿＿＿＿＿＿＿＿＿＿＿＿＿＿＿ (them/man/describe/the)*

5 *It's my birthday next week, and I'm ＿＿＿＿＿＿＿＿＿＿＿＿＿＿＿＿＿＿＿＿ (my/my/invite/all/party/friends)*

84 Phrasal verbs

come in, sit down, give out, pick up, turn over, etc

You can turn over your papers and begin.

A phrasal verb is a verb + adverb. Some phrasal verbs do not have an object, but most do.

Subject	Verb + adverb	Subject	Verb + adverb	Object
The boys	**came in**.	*The teacher*	**gave out**	*the exam papers.*
They	**sat down**.	*The boys*	**picked up**	*their pens.*

An object can usually go before or after the adverb in a phrasal verb. Compare the following.

> *The boys **put down their pens**.*   *The boys **put their pens down**.*

But when the object is a pronoun, it must go before the adverb.

> *The boys put **them** down.* (their pens)
> *He put **them** away in his bag.* (the exam papers)

In a phrasal verb, the adverb completes the meaning of the verb. Some phrasal verbs are easy to understand and learn. They mean exactly what you expect, eg *pick up/put down*, *give out/take in* and *sit down/stand up*.

Others are not so easy to understand. Their meaning is not clear from the verb and the adverb together. Compare the following. The first example is clear, but the second is not.

> *They **turned over** the papers.*
> *Another boy **turned up**.* (arrived)

We use phrasal verbs a lot, so you have to learn them as you meet them. Write down the meanings when they are not clear. Here are some more examples.

> *The car **broke down**.* (stopped working)
> *He was too tired to do any more and he **gave up**.* (stopped trying to do something)
> *The man **made off** with my bike.* (ran away)
> *The weather is **picking up**.* (getting better)

الافعال الظرفية هي التي تتكون من فعل + ظرف، وبعضها لا يتعدى إلى مفعول به، ولكن معظمها يتعدى إلى مفعول به.

يمكن ان يأتي المفعول به قبل الظرف او بعده في الفعل الظرفي. ويتضح الامر من خلال مقارنة المثالين.

ولكن عندما يكون المفعول به ضميراً، يجب وضعه قبل الظرف.

يكمل الظرف في الفعل الظرفي معنى الفعل. وبعض الافعال الظرفية يسهل فهمها وتعلمها. وهي تعني تماماً ما تتوقعه.

ومنها ما يصعب فهمه، فمعانيها ليست واضحة من الفعل والظرف معاً. قارن المثالين، فالاول واضح والثاني غير واضح.

كثيراً ما تستخدم الافعال الظرفية، الامر الذي يوجب تعلمها كل على حدة. ويساعد في تعلمها كتابة المعاني عندما تكون غير واضحة.

Exercises

1 Complete the statements with these phrasal verbs.

come in, give out, pick up, put away, sit down, turn over, turn up

Example: *I can't find my book now, but I know it'll* <u>turn up</u> *later.*

1 *Could you _____ all the rubbish on the floor, please? It looks very untidy.*

2 *I'm going to _____ sets of working clothes to all the new trainees.*

3 *Please _____ on the chairs over there.*

4 *We always have to _____ our papers when we finish work and leave our desks clean.*

5 *_____ the paper and start the exam, please.*

6 *Don't wait outside the door. Please _____*

2 Complete the statements with these phrasal verbs without objects.

Moving
come in, come back, go away, go out, move on, turn round
Resting
get up, lie down, wake up

Example: *Please* <u>come in.</u> *The door is open.*

1 *I'm tired. I'm going to _____ and rest.*

2 *If you _____ and live somewhere else, we may we may not see you again.*

3 *Let's _____ and get some fresh air for an hour.*

4 *This place is horrible. Let's _____ and stay in the next town.*

5 *You can go home now, but please _____ to the office by 2.00.*

6 *I don't _____ immediately in the morning. I lie in bed and plan my day.*

7 *That coat looks good on you, but does it look all right from the back? _____ slowly and let me see.*

8 *Pat was so tired that she couldn't _____ She didn't open her eyes for ten minutes.*

3 Complete the statements with these phrasal verbs without objects.

pay in/take out (eg money at the bank)
put on/take off (eg clothes)
put up/bring down (eg shop prices)
switch on/switch off (eg lights)
turn up/turn down (eg radio volume)

Example: *It's getting dark. I'll* <u>switch on</u> *the lights.*

1 *Could you _____ £50 for me? I need some money for the weekend*

2 *Look. They've _____ the price of these computers. They're only $950 now.*

3 *Could you _____ the TV, please? It's too loud.*

4 *Tom _____ his dirty boots before he went into the house.*

5 *It was raining, so I _____ a coat when I went out.*

6 *Oh, no! The Government is_____ the price of petrol again!*

4 Complete the statements. Change the noun objects into pronoun objects.

Example: *Bob told me to give out the clothes, so I* <u>gave them out.</u>

1 *Ann wanted Tom to pick up the rubbish, so she _____*

2 *Dad asked us to switch off the TV, so we _____*

3 *My boss told me to put away my papers, so I _____*

4 *Sue asked the men to put down the cases, so they _____*

5 *Steve wanted his brother to turn up the stereo, so he _____*

6 *Mum told Tina to turn over the chicken legs, so she _____*

7 *The boss asked us to pay in the money at the bank, so we _____*

Word classes
Verb, adverb, noun, adjective, etc

FUN RIDE TURNS TO DANGER

An enjoyable day out at Britain's biggest fun park, Alton Towers, turned to danger yesterday. It happened when high winds hit the Skyride cable-cars and stopped them in mid-air.

Specially trained firemen safely brought 59 people down from several cable-cars 30 metres above the ground. They successfully used their climbing techniques and equipment to climb along the cables and enter the cars.

Although some passengers needed first aid when they reached the ground, nobody had to go to hospital.

FORMS

There are eight different word classes in English. They are:

Verb:	*hit, stop, use, climb*
Adverb:	*yesterday, successfully, down, safely*
Noun:	*day, Alton Towers, danger*
Adjective:	*enjoyable, high, special*
Pronoun:	*they, them, nobody*
Determiner:	*a/an, the, their, some*
Preposition:	*at, from, above, along*
Linking word:	*and, although, when*

We often use one word in different ways. It may be just a different word class with a similar meaning.

> *Did they **climb**?* (verb)
> *It's a long **climb**.* (noun)
> *Some needed **first aid**.* (part of a noun)
> *We climbed along **first**.* (adverb)

Or a word may have different meanings.

> ***High** winds hit the cable-cars.* (adjective = strong)
> *The tower is 30 metres **high**.* (adjective = off the ground)
> *The price of tickets is too **high**.* (adjective = expensive)

غالباً ما نستخدم كلمة واحدة بطرق مختلفة. فقد تكون فعلاً في الجملة، واسماً من جملة اخرى، ويكون المعنى متشابهاً.

ويمكن ان تحمل الكلمة الواحدة معاني مختلفة.

CROSSCHECK

There are different kinds of determiners and pronouns.

Determiners	**Pronouns**
Articles: *a/an, the*	Personal: *I, he, she* (subject) *me, him, her* (object)
Quantifiers: *some, a lot of, no* (+ noun)	Quantifiers: *some, a lot, nobody* (+ verb)
Demonstratives: *this, those* (+ noun)	Demonstratives: *this, those* (+ verb)
Possessives: *my, your* (+ noun)	Possessives: *mine, yours* (+ verb)
Use a determiner before a noun.	Use a pronoun instead of a determiner + noun.

> **The** car was in the street.
> They brought down **all** the people.
> I took **that** photo.
>
> Is it **my** newspaper or **your** newspaper?

> **It** was in the street.
> **Nobody** had to go to hospital.
> **That** is one of the cable-car passengers.
>
> Is it **mine** or **yours**?

هناك انواع مختلفة من المحددات والضمائر.

يستخدم المحدد قبل الاسم.

ويستخدم الضمير بديلاً من المحدد + الاسم.

Exercises

1 Label the words in *italics* with these word classes.

Adjective, Adverb, Determiner, Linking word, Noun, Preposition, Pronoun, Verb

Noun   An ordinary English *family*

¹*We* are an ordinary ²*English* family – a mother, ³*father* and ⁴*two* children – ⁵*and* we ⁶*live* very ⁷*ordinarily* in a small town ⁸*near* London.

1 _____   5 _____

2 _____   6 _____

3 _____   7 _____

4 _____   8 _____

2 Complete the paragraph. Use the correct forms of these nouns.

bathroom, bedroom, dining-room, dish, flower, food, garden, house, kitchen, living-room, shop, television, time, vegetable, visitor

An ordinary English home

Upstairs in our __house__ *there are three* ¹_____ *and a* ²_____ *Downstairs there is a* ³_____ , *where we sometimes watch* ⁴_____ *Then there is a* ⁵_____ , *but we only eat there when we have* ⁶_____ *When there are only four of us, we usually eat in the* ⁷_____ *It's easier to serve* ⁸_____ *there and clear away the dirty* ⁹_____ *Outside, there is a large* ¹⁰_____ *We spend a lot of* ¹¹_____ *out there, so we keep it looking nice with lots of* ¹²_____ *We also grow our own* ¹³_____ *They taste better than the ones from the* ¹⁴_____ !

3 Complete the paragraph. Use the correct forms of these verbs in the present simple.

be, cook, drive, drop, get, have, have to, leave, make, take, work

Ordinary weekday mornings

In the morning, I always __make__ *tea for everybody. Then Rosie* ¹_____ *breakfast while Peter and Lisa*

²_____ *ready for school. We all* ³_____ *the house at 8.00. Rosie* ⁴_____ *always the driver. First she* ⁵_____ *me at the station because I* ⁶_____ *in London and I* ⁷_____ *catch the 8.20 train. Next she* ⁸_____ *the children to school. Then she* ⁹_____ *back into town, where she* ¹⁰_____ *a job at a bank.*

4 Complete the conversation with adjectives or adverbs.

Another ordinary morning

Peter: *I* __really__ *don't want to go to school* __today.__ *I'm* __ill__ ! (ill, really, today)

Lisa: *You're* ¹_____ *saying that because you've got a* ²_____ *exam and you know you're going to do* ³_____ ! (badly, big, only)

Mum: *I think Lisa is* ⁴_____ *You look* ⁵_____ , *Peter. So finish your breakfast as* ⁶_____ *as you can, and let's go. It's* ⁷_____ *8.00. (fast, fine, nearly, right)*

Dad: *Yes, come on, everybody. Let's go* ⁸_____ *or I'll be* ⁹_____ *for the train, and I* ¹⁰_____ *mustn't miss it this morning. (certainly, late, quickly)*

5 Complete the story with pronouns, determiners or prepositions.

Finally ... a very unusual day

Last weekend __we__ *took Peter and Lisa* __to__ *Alton Towers.* ¹_____ *was* ²_____ *nice day, but rather windy. (a, it, to, we)*

When ³_____ *arrived,* ⁴_____ *decided to take* ⁵_____ *cable-car. Soon after* ⁶_____ *started,* ⁷_____ *wind got worse. Then* ⁸_____ ⁹_____ *cable-car system stopped and* ¹⁰_____ *cars stopped moving. (a, it, the, the, the, we, we, whole)*

¹¹_____ *was over* ¹²_____ *deep valley.* ¹³_____ *people* ¹⁴_____ *our car waited calmly, but* ¹⁵_____ *child kept crying. (a, in, most, one, ours)*

¹⁶_____ *hour later,* ¹⁷_____ *group* ¹⁸_____ *rescuers climbed* ¹⁹_____ ²⁰_____ *cable to help* ²¹_____ . ²²_____ *helped* ²³_____ *climb down* ²⁴_____ ²⁵_____ *ground. (a, along, an, of, the, the, they, to, us, us)*

86 Sentences: types and structure
Statement, question, etc   Subject, verb, object, etc

You're driving very fast, Tom!

FORMS

Sentence types
There are four types of sentence in English. They are:

Statement: *You're driving very fast.*

Question: *How fast are you driving?*

Order: *Don't drive so fast.*

Exclamation: *Help!*

Sentence structure
There are several possible parts of a sentence. They include:

Subject	**Verb**	**Object**	**Adverbial**
The car	*is following*	*us*	*very fast.*

Sentence types

A statement gives information. A question requests information or action. An order requires action. An exclamation expresses an emotion. (See Units 23/24 for more on question forms. See Unit 1 for more on orders.)

In writing, a sentence starts with a capital letter, eg *You, How, Slow, Help.* It ends with a full stop (.), a question mark (?) or an exclamation mark (!).

Sentence structure

Most sentences contain different parts. These parts can include a subject, verb, object, complement and adverbial. A subject is the focus of the sentence. A verb shows an action or a state, eg *brings* and *is*. An object is the thing or person affected by the verb. A complement gives more information about the subject. An adverbial gives more information about the verb. Look at the following statements. The simplest statement contains only two parts. The longer statements contain four. (But a statement or other type of sentence can contain many more parts than this.)

1	**Subject**	**Verb**		2	**Subject**	**Verb**	**Complement**
	Tom	*is driving.*			*Tom*	*is*	*the driver.*

3	**Subject**	**Verb**	**Object**	4	**Subject**	**Verb**	**Adverbial**
	Tom	*is driving*	*his new car.*		*Tom*	*is driving*	*dangerously.*

5	**Subject**	**Verb**	**Object**	**Adverbial**
	Tom	*is driving*	*his new car*	*dangerously.*

All of these statements have a subject and a verb. They are the most important parts. In statements the subject goes before the verb. (See Unit 23 for word order in questions.) If there is an object or a complement, this goes after the verb.

In statements 4 and 5 the adverb comes at the end of the sentence, but it can also come in other places. (See Unit 71.)

> *Unfortunately, he's probably going to stop us **at the side of the road now.***

تزودنا الجملة الخبرية بمعلومة، في حين تستفسر الجملة الاستفهامية عن معلومة او عمل. ويتطلب الامر القيام بعمل ما في حين يعبر التعجب عن مشاعر معينة. (انظر units 23/24 لمزيد من المعلومات عن صيغة الاستفهام. وانظر unit 1 للمزيد عن صيغة الامر).

عند الكتابة، تبدأ الجملة بحرف كبير وتنتهي بنقطة او بعلامة استفهام او بعلامة تعجب.

تحوي معظم الجمل اجزاء مختلفة يمكن ان تضم فاعلاً وفعلاً ومفعولاً به وكذلك تكملة واضافة ظرفية. ويشكل الفاعل نقطة التركيز في الجملة، في حين يبين الفعل عملاً ما او حالة. اما المفعول به فهو الشيء او الشخص الذي يتأثر بالفعل، وتعمل التكملة على اضافة معلومات عن الفاعل. اما الإضافة الظرفية فتعطي المزيد من المعلومات عن الفعل. انظر الى الامثلة التالية من الجمل الخبرية. ان ابسطها تحتوي على جزءين، اما الجملة الاطول فتحوي اربعة اجزاء (ولكن الجملة الخبرية، او نوعاً اخر من الجمل يمكن ان تحوي اجزاءً اكثر من ذلك كثيراً).

لكل هذه الجمل الخبرية فاعل وفعل يشكلان اهم جزءي الجملة. ويأتي الفاعل في الجملة الخبرية قبل الفعل (انظر unit 23 لترتيب الكلمات في الجمل الاستفهامية). واذا كان هناك مفعول به او تكملة، فيأتيان بعد الفعل.

يأتي الظرف في الجمل ٤، ٥ في نهاية الجملة، ولكنه يمكن ان يأتي في مواقع اخرى ايضاً. (انظر unit 71).

Exercises

1 Label the sentences with the following.

Exclamation, Order, Question, Statement

Example: *Are you all right?* _Question_

1 *How much money have you got?* _____

2 *Take these letters to the post office.*
_____

3 *Fantastic!* _____

4 *John's birthday is next week.* _____

5 *We all understand what we've got to do, don't we?*
_____

6 *I don't like this sort of music.* _____

7 *Absolutely amazing!* _____

8 *Don't spend any more time on this job.*
_____

2 Label the sentence parts with the following.

Adverb (A), Adverb phrase (AP), Complement (C),
Object (O), Subject (S), Verb (V)

Example:

Is Lucy singing well?

1 *Lucy   has become   a great singer.*

2 *Don't drop   those glasses.*

3 *The boys   quickly   mended   the bike.*

4 *Quickly   write down   these addresses.*

5 *Has   anybody   seen   my glasses?*

6 *Are   the pictures   safe?*

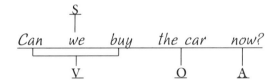

7 *When do   the boys   see   their parents?*

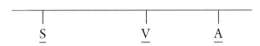

8 *Luckily,   we   reached   the airport   in time.*

3 Re-order the words to form different types of sentences.

Example: Question *(the/now/we/can/buy/car)*

Can   we   buy   the car   now?

1 Statement *(fast/the/climbed/plane)*

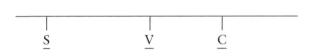

2 Statement *(seems/brother/tired/very/your)*

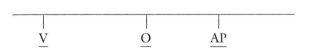

3 Order *(there/the/put/over/don't/boxes)*

4 Statement *(as/as/is/Robert/soon/coming/possible*

5 Question *(see/you/the/did/yesterday/news)*

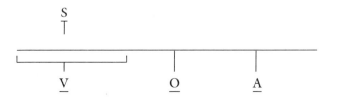

201

87 Connecting clauses

and, but, or, so, because, if, when, even though, who, to, for

FORMS

Two main clauses

Ann has got a case, and Jan has got a bag.
They can take a bus, or they can take a taxi. They have to choose.
The taxi is faster, but it is more expensive.
They are late, so they will take a taxi.

Main clause + sub-clause

They need the taxi because they are late.
If they arrive late, they will miss their plane.

Two main clauses

A main clause has a verb and can be a complete sentence.

> ***Ann went by bus.***   ***Jan went by taxi.***

The words *and*, *but*, *or* and *so* connect two main clauses. *and* adds one thing to another. *but* sets one thing against another. *or* expresses one possibility instead of another. *so* introduces a result.

Main clause		Main clause
Ann went by bus,	**and**	*Jan went by taxi.*
The taxi was faster,	**but**	*it was more expensive.*
You can take a bus,	**or**	*you can take a taxi.*
There are no buses,	**so**	*we'll have to take a taxi.*

In writing, we usually put a comma (,) between two main clauses, especially long clauses. Compare *and* and *or* in these negative sentences.

> *They **didn't take** a taxi, **and** they **didn't take** a bus.*
> *They **didn't take** a taxi **or** a bus.*

Main clause + sub-clause

We often put a sub-clause with a main clause. A sub-clause has a verb like a main clause. But it is not a complete idea. It adds to a main clause.

Main clause	Sub-clause
They need a taxi	***because they're late.***

We can use a sub-clause by itself in a short answer to a question.

> ● *Why are they late?*   ○ ***Because Jan's watch was wrong.***

Here are some other types of sub-clauses. Most sub-clauses can go before the main clause (but not relative clauses). When we put the sub-clause first, we usually put a comma (,) between the two clauses.

> ***If you ask Alex***, *he'll go to the party.* (conditional)
> *Someone came to the door **when I was working in the garden**.* (similar to *while* and *as*)
> ***Even though Tom's leg hurt***, *he managed to run.* (similar to *although* and *though*)
> *Bill jumped into the river **to save the child**.* (similar to *in order to* and *so as to*)
> *She's the girl **who won the prize**.* (similar to *that* and *which*)

Note that *because* introduces a reason and *so* introduces a result.

> ***Because they're late***, *they need a taxi.*
> *They're late, **so they need a taxi**.*

يضم الجزء الرئيسي (main clause) في الجملة فعلاً، ويمكن ان يكون جملة كاملة.

تعمل الكلمات and وbut وor وso على ربط جزءين متكاملين في جملة واحدة. وتعمل and على اضافة جزء لآخر في حين تضع but جزءاً ضد الآخر. اما or فتعبر عن وجود احتمال بديل عن آخر. واما so فتقدم النتيجة.

توضع فاصلة(،) عادة بين الجزءين الرئيسين المكونين للجملة خصوصاً عندما تتكون الجملة من جزءين طويلين. ويوضح المثال الفرق بين استخدام and وor في جملتين منفيتين.

يُوضع عادة جزء رئيسي مع جزء فرعي يحوي فعلاً، مثله في ذلك مثل الجزء الرئيسي، ولكنه لا يعطي فكرة متكاملة بل يضيف معنى للجزء الرئيسي.
ويمكن استخدام الجزء الفرعي بمفرده، في الاجابة المختصرة عن سؤالٍ ما.

وهذه مجموعة من انواع اخرى من الاجزاء الفرعية (sub-clauses). وتأتي غالباً قبل الجزء الرئيسي (ولكن ليس في حالة relative clauses) التي تعتمد على الجزء الرئيسي بشكل كلي. وعندما نضع الجزء الفرعي في بداية الجملة نستخدم الفاصلة(،) عادة بين الجزءين.

تجدر ملاحظة ان because تقدم السبب في حين تقدم so النتيجة التي تترتب على الفعل.

Exercises

1 Connect the clauses with *and, but, or* or *so*.

Example: *You can buy <u>or</u> rent the apartment.*

1 *I'm tired _____ I'm hungry too.*

2 *The train was late, _____ we couldn't get to the meeting on time.*

3 *The Prince was rich, _____ he wasn't happy.*

4 *You can take the money now, _____ you can take it later.*

2 Connect clauses 1–4 and a–d with *and, but, or* or *so*.

Example: *We usually eat at 8.00,*
           <u>*but we're eating at 7.30 tonight.*</u>

a *he can go at 4.00.*

b *he seems very tired at the moment.*

c *he's got to come by taxi instead.*

d *he owns a house in Scotland.*

1 *Ben has an apartment in London, _____*
_____

2 *Tom's car is at the garage for repairs, _____*
_____

3 *Sam can see the film at 1.45, _____*
_____

4 *John is usually very energetic, _____*
_____

3 Rewrite the *so* statements using *because/as*.

Example: *It was dark, so we couldn't see much.*
          <u>*We couldn't see much because/as it*</u>
          <u>*was dark.*</u>

1 *I was very tired, so I went to bed.*
_____

2 *My car is old, so I'm getting a new one.*
_____
_____

3 *I have to go out now, so I'll call you later.*
_____
_____

4 Rewrite the *but* statements using *even though/although*.

Example: *The engine is new, but it's already going wrong.*
          <u>*The engine is already going wrong*</u>
          <u>*even though/though it's new.*</u>

1 *Sally is young, but she does her job well.*
_____
_____

2 *The film is old, but it's still very popular.*
_____
_____

3 *Their new house was expensive, but it looks terrible.*
_____
_____

5 Connect the clauses with *because, if, when, even though* or *who* in the correct position.

Examples: _____ *Mary would lend you £100 <u>if</u> you asked her.*
          <u>*When*</u> *I got home, _____ everybody was eating.*

1 _____ *I'd known about Ann's illness* _____ *I wouldn't have bothered her.*

2 _____ *Mr Hardy is the man* _____ *bought my company.*

3 _____ *I phoned home* _____ *I got to the office.*

4 _____ *Harry worked all day* _____ *he still couldn't finish the job.*

5 _____ *Annie ran home* _____ *she was afraid of the dark.*

6 _____ *Tony gets this note,* _____ *I'll already be in Canada.*

7 _____ *Dr Ross still works very hard* _____ *he's nearly 70.*

8 _____ *Tony has looked after our old car so well,* _____ *I think we should give it to him as a present.*

Dear Sir,

Thank you for your order of 13th March for 4,000 K52 Matsuo CD players.

We note your specific colour requirement for black. *In addition*, we note your required delivery date of 30th March. *However*, we are sorry to say we cannot meet that schedule. Demand has been heavy for this popular product. *As a result*, we are now out of stock and are waiting for new supplies from Japan. *Despite this*, we can promise delivery by 10th April. *Alternatively*, we can offer you immediate delivery of the K53 model.

Sentence connectors instead of *and, but, or* and *so*

We use *and, but, or* and *so* to link parts of sentences. (See also Unit 87.)
> *The day was warm **and** sunny.*
> *Harry found some bread, **but** no butter.*

We also often want to connect the ideas in two separate sentences. In spoken English, we often use *and, but, or* and *so*.
> *He's very good at football. **And** he's a great runner too.*

In formal and written English, we usually avoid *and, but, or* and *so* at the start of a sentence. Instead, we can use connectors like these. (Note that we put a comma (,) after these sentence connectors.)
> ***In addition/Furthermore**, we note your required ...* (instead of *and*)
> ***However**, we cannot meet that schedule.* (instead of *but*)
> ***Alternatively/Instead**, we can offer you the ...* (instead of *or*)
> ***As a result/consequence**, we are now out of stock.* (instead of *so*)

Sentence connectors with pronouns

Subject pronouns often refer to things outside their own sentence.
> *The children are tired. **They**'d better go to bed.*

We often use demonstrative pronouns in the same way.
> ● *Let's have a rest.*   ○ ***That**'s a good idea.*

Many sentence connectors include demonstrative pronouns or nouns. Some sentence connectors can be with or without demonstrative pronouns or nouns.
> ***In addition to** this/your colour requirement, we note your ...*
> ***As a result of** this/the heavy demand, we are now out of stock.*
> ***Instead of** that/the K52, they will take the K53.*

Some sentence connectors must include a pronoun or noun.
> ***Because of this**, we are now of out stock.*
> ***Due to the heavy demand**, we are now out of stock.*
> ***Despite this**, we can promise delivery by ...*
> ***In spite of that**, we can promise delivery by ...*
> ***Except for the K52**, we have stock of all models.*
> ***Apart from that**, we have stock of all models.*

تستخدم كلمات الربط and و but و or و so لربط اجزاء الجمل. (انظر unit 87).

غالباً ما نريد ان نربط فكرتين في جملتين منفصلتين. وفي الانجليزية المحكية غالباً ما نستخدم and و but و or و so.

ولكن في الامور الرسمية وعند الكتابة، نستبعد عادة استخدام كلمات الربط هذه، ونستعيض عنها باستخدام كلمات ربط اخرى كالكلمات الموضحة في الامثلة، وعندها يصير استخدام الفواصل بعد كلمات الربط.

غالباً ما يشير ضمير الفاعل الى اشياء او الى اشخاص خارج نطاق الجملة ذاتها.

وغالباً ما تستخدم ضمائر الإشارة بالطريقة نفسها.

وتضم كلمات الربط بين الجمل ضمائر إشارة او اسماء. كما ان بعض كلمات الربط يمكن ان تأتي مع ضمائر اشارة او بدون ضمائر اشارة او اسماء.

تتطلب بعض كلمات الربط بين الجمل استخدام ضمائر او اسماء.

Exercises

1 Change the informal spoken statements to formal statements from a business report. Use full verb forms and change *and*, *but*, *or* or *so* to the following.

Alternatively, As a result, However, In addition

Example: *We're unable to meet the schedule, so we won't get the contract.*
<u>*We are*</u> *unable to meet the schedule.*
<u>*As a result, we will not get*</u> *the contract.*

1 *It's possible to up-date our present model, or it's possibly the right time for a completely new model.*
_____ *possible to up-date our present model.*
_____ *possibly the right time for a completely new model.*

2 *We've reached this year's production target already, and we've managed to cut waste by 8%.*
_____ *this year's production target already.* _____
_____ *to cut waste by 8%.*

3 *We're cutting most costs successfully, but we're failing to hold down the cost of wages.*
_____ *most costs successfully.*
_____ *to hold down the cost of wages.*

4 *We haven't tried selling to America up till now, so we don't yet know if it'll be a good market for us.*
_____ *selling to America up till now.* _____
_____ *if _____ a good market for us.*

2 Write nothing (✗) or one of these words to complete the connectors.

for, from, of, to

1 *Apart* <u>*from*</u> *this*
2 *As a result _____ this*
3 *Despite _____ this*
4 *Due _____ this*
5 *Except _____ this*
6 *In addition _____ this*
7 *In spite _____ this*
8 *Instead _____ this*

3 Choose the right connecting statements from a–g to complete the teacher's reports 1–6.

Example: *Susan has not worked hard this year. Despite this,* <u>*she has done enough to pass the year.*</u>

a *she has behaved badly in class all year.*
b *she could go on to do extra Science.*
c *she has achieved a Grade A.*
d *she has found it difficult to improve.*
e *she has done enough to pass the year.*
f *she has often failed to complete her homework.*
g *she must learn to do some hard work.*

1 *Sally is very intelligent and has worked extremely well. As a result,* _____
_____
_____

2 *Lisa has worked very well in class. However,* _____
_____
_____
_____

3 *Tessa has failed to produce any good work. In addition,* _____
_____
_____

4 *Lucy is clever, but she seems to spend her time thinking about pop music. Instead,* _____
_____
_____

5 *Kate has tried hard this year. In spite of this,* _____
_____

6 *Denise is very talented at both Maths and Science. She may decide to take Higher Maths. Alternatively,* _____
_____
_____

Appendix 1 Irregular verbs

These common irregular verbs have the following forms.

A Verbs with no change

Infinitive	Past tense	Past participle
cost	cost	cost
cut	cut	cut
hit	hit	hit
hurt	hurt	hurt
let	let	let
put	put	put
set	set	set
shut	shut	shut
spread	spread	spread

B Verbs with one change

Infinitive	Past tense	Past participle
beat	beat	beaten
bring	brought	brought
build	built	built
burn	burnt/burned	burnt/burned
buy	bought	bought
catch	caught	caught
deal	dealt	dealt
dream	dreamt/dreamed	dreamt/dreamed
feel	felt	felt
fight	fought	fought
find	found	found
get	got	got
have* (see below)	had	had
hear	heard	heard
hold	held	held
keep	kept	kept
lay	laid	laid
lead	led	led
learn	learnt/learned	learnt/learned
leave	left	left
lend	lent	lent
lose	lost	lost
make	made	made
mean	meant	meant
meet	met	met
pay	paid	paid

*Note that the 3rd person singular of *have* in the present simple is *he/she/it has.*

read (sounds like *need*)	*read* (sounds like *red*)	*read* (sounds like *red*)
say	*said*	*said*
sell	*sold*	*sold*
send	*sent*	*sent*
sit	*sat*	*sat*
shoot	*shot*	*shot*
sleep	*slept*	*slept*
slide	*slid*	*slid*
smell	*smelt/smelled*	*smelt/smelled*
spell	*spelt/spelled*	*spelt/spelled*
spend	*spent*	*spent*
stand	*stood*	*stood*
swing	*swung*	*swung*
teach	*taught*	*taught*
tell	*told*	*told*
think	*thought*	*thought*
understand	*understood*	*understood*
win	*won*	*won*

C Verbs with two changes

Infinitive	Past tense	Past participle
be * (see below)	*was/were*	*been*
become	*became*	*become*
begin	*began*	*begun*
bite	*bit*	*bitten*
blow	*blew*	*blown*
break	*broke*	*broken*
choose	*chose*	*chosen*
come	*came*	*come*
do * (see below)	*did*	*done*
draw	*drew*	*drawn*
drink	*drank*	*drunk*
drive	*drove*	*driven*
eat	*ate*	*eaten*
fall	*fell*	*fallen*
fly	*flew*	*flown*
forget	*forgot*	*forgotten*
give	*gave*	*given*
go	*went*	*gone*
grow	*grew*	*grown*
hide	*hid*	*hidden*

*Note that *be* in the present simple is *I am*, *he/she/it is* and *you/we/they are*.
*Note that the 3rd person singular of *do* in the present simple is *he/she/it does*.

know	*knew*	*known*
lie	*lay*	*lain*
ride	*rode*	*ridden*
ring	*rang*	*rung*
rise	*rose*	*risen*
run	*ran*	*run*
see	*saw*	*seen*
shake	*shook*	*shaken*
show	*showed*	*shown*
sing	*sang*	*sung*
sink	*sank*	*sunk*
speak	*spoke*	*spoken*
steal	*stole*	*stolen*
swim	*swam*	*swum*
take	*took*	*taken*
throw	*threw*	*thrown*
wake	*woke*	*woken*
wear	*wore*	*worn*
write	*wrote*	*written*

Appendix 2 Some spelling rules

These spelling rules deal with spelling changes with grammatical word endings.

A Some spelling terms

To study this Appendix you need to know the terms **vowel** and **consonant**.

Vowel letters are *a, e, i, o* and *u*.

Vowel sounds are sounds written with two or more vowel letters, eg
ai, au, ea, ee, ei, ie, oa, oo, ou, etc.

Consonants are the other letters of the alphabet and their sounds, eg *b, c, d, f, g*, etc.

A **short vowel** is, eg *e* in *get* and *o* in *got*.

A **long vowel** is, eg *ee* in *keep*, *ea* in *heat*, *oo* in *soon* and *ou* in *route*.

You also need to know the term **syllable**. This is a unit of sound within a word.
stand (1 syllable)   *un•der* (2 syllables)   *un•der•stand* (3 syllables)
mis•un•der•stand (4 syllables)   *mis•un•der•stand•ing* (5 syllables)

B Word endings

English adds the following grammatical word endings to words.

Noun + s + s	Verb + ing	Verb + ed	Verb + er	Adjective + est	Adjective + ly	Adjective
cars	looks	looking	looked	quicker	quickest	quickly
planes	works	working	worked	slower	slowest	slowly
(Plural)	(3rd person present simple)	(Present participle)	(Past simple, past participle)	(Comparative)	(Superlative)	(Adverb)

Sometimes there is a spelling change when we add an ending to a word. There are clear rules for these changes – see sections below.

C Noun and verb endings with *es*

Add *es* when the word ends in *s, ss, sh, ch* and *x*.

bus	boss	dish	match	box
buses	bosses	dishes	matches	boxes

Many verbs and nouns end in an *e* which we do not say. But if the silent *e* comes after *c, s, x* or
z, just add *s*. We then sound the *e + s* together.

race	practise	axe	organize
races	practises	axes	organizes

After other consonants, we do not sound the silent *e* – see Section D below.

bikes	scenes	tapes	votes	consumes

We add *es* after some nouns ending in *o*, but not others. Compare the following.

cargoes	heroes	potatoes	tomatoes	volcanoes
discos	studios	photos	radios	stereos

Note also the verbs *go → goes* and *do → does*.

Some nouns which end in *f* or *fe* change their endings to *ves*.

knife	life	loaf	shelf	wife
knives	lives	loaves	shelves	wives

D Words that end in silent *e*

After final, silent *e* just add *s*.

bikes	*scenes*	*tapes*	*votes*	(Plural nouns)
consumes	*hopes*	*rules*	*types*	(3rd person present simple)

But see Section C for pronunciation of words like these.

races *practises* *axes* *organizes*

Leave out *e* and add *ing* to form the present participle.

dance	*handle*	*hope*	*smile*	*write*
dancing	*handling*	*hoping*	*smiling*	*writing*

After *e* just add *d* for regular past tense and past participle forms.

consumed *hoped* *ruled* *typed*

Just add *r* and *st* for comparative and superlative forms.

brave	*large*	*rude*	*wide*
braver	*larger*	*ruder*	*wider*
bravest	*largest*	*rudest*	*widest*

Just add *ly* to most adjectives for adverb forms.

bravely *largely* *rudely* *widely*

But if an adjective ends in *le*, leave out *e* and just add *y*.

able	*capable*	*horrible*	*probable*
ably	*capably*	*horribly*	*probably*

Note these special *ly* cases.

day	*due*	*true*	*whole*
daily	*duly*	*truly*	*wholly*

E Words that double the final consonant

Words that end in one short vowel + one consonant often double that consonant before *ing*, *ed*, *er* and *est*.

plan	*chop*	*permit*	(Verb)
planning	*chopping*	*permitting*	(Present participle)
planned	*chopped*	*permitted*	(Past simple, past participle)

fat	*wet*	*thin*	(Adjective)
fatter	*wetter*	*thinner*	(Comparative)
fattest	*wettest*	*thinnest*	(Superlative)

Most words like *occur*, with two syllables or more, double the last consonant when the last syllable is stressed. Compare the following.

occur	*frighten*	*permit*	*benefit*
occurring	*frightening*	*permitted*	*benefited*

But words which end in one vowel + *l* are different in British English (though not American English). They all double the *l*.

quarrel	*quarrelling*	(Present participle)
travel	*travelled*	(Past simple, past participle)
beautiful	*beautifully*	(Adverb)

210

F Words that end in *y*

Before *s*, *y* changes to *ie* and becomes *ies*.

body	*copy*	*family*	*sky*	(Noun)
bodies	*copies*	*families*	*skies*	(Plural)

apply	*empty*	*study*	*try*	(Verb)
applies	*empties*	*studies*	*tries*	(3rd person present simple)

Before *ed*, *y* changes to *ie* and becomes *ied*.

applied   *emptied*   *studied*   *tried*   (Past simple, past participle)

Before *er* and *est*, *y* changes to *i* and becomes *ier* or *iest*.

happy	*lucky*	*pretty*	*silly*	(Adjective)
happier	*luckier*	*prettier*	*sillier*	(Comparative)
happiest	*luckiest*	*prettiest*	*silliest*	(Superlative)

But a *y* ending does not change before *ing*.

applying   *emptying*   *studying*   *trying*   (Present participle)

Most words with a vowel + *y* ending (*ay*, *ey*, *oy*) do not change at all.

play	*grey*	*boy*
plays	*greyer*	*boys*
playing	*greyest*	
played		

But note these special cases.

day	*lay*	*pay*	*say*
daily	*laid*	*paid*	*said*

G Words that end in *ie*

A few verbs end in *ie*. With these, *ie* changes to *y* and becomes *ying*.

die	*lie*	*tie*
dying	*lying*	*tying*

Appendix 3 Punctuation

A Types

Study the punctuation in the following.

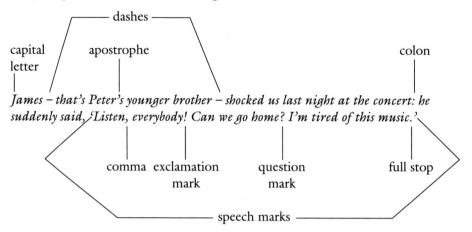

B Apostrophe (...')

Use this:

● in short forms of verbs: **It's** *cold.* (**It's** = *It is*)   I **don't** *want to go out.* (**don't** = *do not*)
Be careful with the different meanings of *'s* and *'d*: **He's** *working.* (**He's** = *He is*)
He's *finished.* (**He's** = *He has*)   **We'd** *finished by 5.00.* (**We'd** = *We had*)
We'd *like to go home now.* (**We'd** = *We would*)

● in short forms of other words, mainly years: *I met Joe in June* **'89**.

● to show possession after nouns: *I'm* **Peter's** *younger brother.*

A possessive apostrophe goes after a plural noun with *s*: *We can use my* **parents'** *car.*

Possessive adjectives and pronouns do not take apostrophes: *This is my coat, and this is hers.*

Be careful with *its* (possessive adjective) and *it's* (*it is/it has*): *Look at the fish.* **It's** *opening and closing* **its** *mouth.*

C Capital letter (*I, P, J, L,* etc)

Use this:

● for the 1st person singular: *I*

● for the name of a person, place, geographical name, country, nationality: *James,*
The Palace Hotel, London, the River Nile, Canada, Canadian

● for abbreviations: *the* **UN** *(the United Nations), the* **USA** *(the United States of America)*

D Colon (:)

Use this:

● to introduce a list of things: *Remember to bring the following: thick jacket, walking boots, leeping bag.*

● to lead from a general heading into a particular example: *Summer camp: equipment*

● to show a connection between two ideas: *I've got the answer: 2,301.*   *You should take a coat: it's going to rain.*

E Comma (,)

Use this:

- between separate clauses in one sentence: *We were shocked, but Peter just smiled.*
- to separate other parts of a sentence, eg connectors and sentence adverbs: *We were tired.* **However,** *we had to keep running.* **Surprisingly,** *it got easier as we continued.*
- between words in lists: *I bought some bread, butter, cheese and tomatoes.   It was a lovely, warm, sunny day for a picnic.*
- to introduce direct speech in a story: *Bob arrived and said, 'Hello.'*

F Dash (–)

Use this:

- to show an extra idea added to a sentence: *I met Carol* **– she's the one in a blue dress –** *when we were both students. She's going to France next month* **– or at least that's what she told me**.

G Exclamation mark (!)

Use this:

- to show strong feeling in written form: *'I'm so happy!'   'That was really stupid!'   'Listen! I've got an idea!'   'Help!'*

This takes the place of a full stop – see below.

H Full stop (.)

Use this:

- to show the end of a statement: *The men are not due to go home this week. They will return next week.*
- in abbreviations (optional): *I work for the B.B.C.   It's 10 a.m.   Have you seen Mrs. Jones?*

I Question mark (?)

Use this:

- to end a sentence in question form: *Can they do the job?   They can do it, can't they?*
  This takes the place of a full stop – see above.

J Speech marks (' ... ')

These are also called quotation marks or inverted commas.

Use these:

- to mark direct speech in a story: *Ann turned to Bob and said, 'Hi.'*
  You can also use speech marks in double form: *Ann turned to Bob and said, "Hi."*
- to mark something for special attention: *The letters 'Dr' stand for 'Doctor'.*

Appendix 4 Numbers

A Whole numbers

Write	Say
101	*a hundred and one*
199	*a hundred and ninety-nine*
235	*two hundred and thirty-five*
1,001	*a thousand and one*
1,135	*one thousand, one hundred and thirty-five*
1,000,001	*a million and one*
1,135,199	*one million, one hundred and thirty-five thousand, one hundred and ninety-nine*

Compare the following.

a hundred BUT *exactly one hundred*

about a hundred BUT *exactly one hundred and twelve*

B Telephone numbers

Write	Say
521 301377	*five two one ... three oh one ... three seven seven* OR *five two one ... three zero one ... three double seven*
999 775666	*nine nine nine ... seven seven five ... six six six* OR *treble nine ... double seven five ... treble six*

C Decimals

Write	Say
31.3166	*thirty-one point three one six six*
33.3333	*thirty-three point three recurring*

D Fractions

Write		Say			
½	*1½*	*a half*	OR	*one half*	*one and a half*
⅓	*2⅔*	*a third*	OR	*one third*	*two and two-thirds*
¼	*5¾*	*a quarter*	OR	*one quarter*	*five and three quarters*
⅕	*7⅘*	*a fifth*	OR	*one fifth*	*seven and four-fifths*
⅙	*9⅚*	*a sixth*	OR	*one sixth*	*nine and five-sixths*
¹⁄₁₀	*10 ⁷⁄₁₀*	*a tenth*	OR	*one tenth*	*ten and seven-tenths*

E Mathematical terms

Write	Say
7 + 2 = 9	*seven plus/add/and two equals/is nine*
9 − 3 = 6	*nine minus/take away three equals/is six*
6 × 3 = 18	*six times/multiplied by three equals/is eighteen*
18 ÷ 2 = 9	*eighteen divided by two equals/is nine*

F Ordinal numbers

Write (eg in dates)	Write or say	Write (eg in dates)	Write or say
1st	first	20th	twentieth
2nd	second	21st	twenty-first
3rd	third	22nd	twenty-second
4th	fourth	23rd	twenty-third
5th	fifth	24th	twenty-fourth
6th	sixth	...	
7th	seventh	30th	thirtieth
8th	eighth	40th	fortieth
9th	ninth	50th	fiftieth
10th	tenth	60th	sixtieth
11th	eleventh	70th	seventieth
12th	twelfth	80th	eightieth
13th	thirteenth	90th	ninetieth
14th	fourteenth	100th	hundredth
15th	fifteenth	101st	hundred and first
...			...
19th	nineteenth		

Appendix 5 Days, dates and times

A Days and months – abbreviations

Note that the short forms of days and months may have a full stop, eg *Mon.* and *Oct.*

Days		Months			
Full	Short	Full	Short	Full	Short
Monday	*Mon*	*January*	*Jan*	*July*	*Jul*
Tuesday	*Tue/Tues*	*February*	*Feb*	*August*	*Aug*
Wednesday	*Wed*	*March*	*Mar*	*September*	*Sep*
Thursday	*Thu/Thur/Thurs*	*April*	*Apr*	*October*	*Oct*
Friday	*Fri*	*May*	*–*	*November*	*Nov*
Saturday	*Sat*	*June*	*Jun*	*December*	*Dec*
Sunday	*Sun*				

B Dates – word order

Write	**Say**
1st January	*the first of January*
January 1st	*January the first*

C Dates – abbreviations

Write	**Say**
Monday, 21st January	*Monday, the twenty-first of January*
Mon, 21st Jan	
Mon, 21 Jan	

D Dates in numbers

Write	**Say**
30/6	*the thirtieth of June*
31/12/94	*the thirty-first of December, 1994*

E Times

Write	**Say**
10.00	*ten o'clock*
10 a.m.	*ten a.m./ten o'clock* (in the morning)
3.00 p.m.	*three p.m./three o'clock* (in the afternoon)
10.00 p.m.	*ten p.m./ten o'clock* (at night)
12 a.m./12 p.m.	*midday/midnight*
1.15/1.30/1.45	*a quarter past one/half past one/a quarter to two* OR *one fifteen/one thirty/one forty-five*
2.10/2.20/2.40	*ten past two/twenty past two/twenty to three* OR *two ten/two twenty/two forty*
3.13/3.59	*thirteen minutes past three/one minute to four* OR *three thirteen/three fifty-nine*

Index

(The numbers in the index refer to the units, not the pages.)

a and *an*   49, 52–53

a bit
    a bit + adjective or adverb   *a bit tired*   76
    a bit + comparative   *a bit better*   76

about
    adjective + preposition   *angry about*   42

above   77

accommodation   51

across   77

adding clauses   67

adjectives   42, 68–70, 73–74, 85
    adjective + preposition + noun   *tired of work*   42, 82
    adjective + preposition + *ing* form   *tired of working*   42
    word order   68
    adjective + *to* + infinitive   *Pleased to meet you.*   68
    boring and *bored*   69
    adjectives and adverbs   *slow* and *slowly*   70
    adjectives ending in *ly*   70
    comparative forms   *cheaper, more expensive*   73
    superlative forms   *cheapest, most expensive*   73
    irregular forms   *better, best*   73
    comparison: sentence patterns
        faster than   74
        the tallest boy in the class   74
        isn't as tall as   74
    comparison and object pronouns   *faster than him*   74
    spelling rules with comparison   Appendix 2

adverbials   86

adverbs   70–74, 85, 86
    adverbs and adjectives   *slowly* and *slow*   70
    irregular forms   70
    word classes   85
    adverb positions   *He drove slowly., He slowly drove.*   70
    adverb types
        manner   *quickly*   72
        place   *there*   72
        time   *today*   72
        frequency   *usually*   72
        degree   *very*   72
        sentence   *luckily*   72
    comparative forms   *more quickly*   73
    superlative forms   *most beautifully*   73
    irregular forms   *better, best*   73
    comparison: sentence patterns   73
        lasts longer than   74
        likes best   74
        works as quickly as   74
    comparison and object pronouns   *faster than him*   74
    word classes   85

advice   51
    spelling rules with comparison   Appendix 2

advise doing and *advise me to do*   40

a few
    a few and *a little*   57

a few and *few*   57

after
    in connecting clauses   *Susan cried after he had gone.*   13
    in prepositional verbs   *look after*   83

against
    in prepositional verbs   *insure against*   83

ago
    with past simple   6
    ago and *before*   80

a little
    a little and *a few*   57
    a little and *little*   57
    a little + adjective/adverb   *a little tired*   76
    a little + comparative   *a little better*   76

all
    all (of) the students   58
    all cats   58
    all morning/day/week   12

allow smoking and *allow people to smoke*   40

along   77

a lot
    a lot/a lot of   57
    a lot and *much* or *many, a little* and *a few*   57
    a lot + comparative   *a lot better*   76

already   9

alternatively   88

am, is and *are*   3

among   77

an and *a*   49, 52–53

and   87–88

any
    any and *some*   55
    anything, somebody, etc   55, 63
    any of   58
    not ... any of and *none of*   58

apart from   88

apostrophe   *'s, s'* punctuation   Appendix 3

appear   5

around   77

articles   49, 52–53
    a, an and *some*   49, 52
    a, an and *the*   52
    a and *an* with rates   *100 kph*   52
    no article with plurals   49
    the   52
    the with positions   *on the right*   52
    the with superlatives   *the cheapest, the best*   52
    the with groups   *the rich, the French, the Himalayas*   53
    the with regions and other names   *the Far East*   53
    school and *the school*   53
    the with time expressions   *in the morning*   53
    by plane and *on the 5.00 plane*   53
    general statements   *A plane is a beautiful thing.*   53

general and specific   *students* and *the new students*   53

as
  linking word   8
  as soon as   13
  as long as   43
  (*not*) *as ... as*   74
  as a result and *as a result of*   88
  as a consequence   88

at
  with indirect objects   *Sue laughed at us.*   62
  at, in and *on* for place   77, 78
  at, in and *on* for time   79

auxiliary verbs review   *be, do, have*   21

away from   77

baggage   51

be
  be with present forms   *am, is, are*   3
  be with past forms   *was, were*   7
  be in continuous tenses   *I am/was doing*   16
  auxiliary verb forms   *be, do, have*   21
  main verb form   21
  be in passive verb forms   *it is done, it is being done*   37–38

be able to   29, 36

because
  in connecting clauses   *Because they're late, they need a taxi.*   87
  because and *so*   87

been to and *gone to*   10

before
  in connecting clauses   *It had begun before you arrived.*   13
  before + time   17
  before and *ago*   80

behind   77

being
  as a main verb   *He's being stupid.*   21
  in continuous passive tenses   *It's being done.*   38

believe   5

belong   5

below   77

beside   77

better and *best*
  good, well, better, best   73
  had better   31, 36

between   77

be used to + noun/*ing* form   *I'm used to hard work., I'm used to working hard.*   82

bit
  a bit + adjective/adverb   *a bit tired*   76
  a bit + comparative   *a bit better*   76

both (*of*)   58

but   87–88

by
  by + time   *by 10.30*   17, 80
  by and *until/till*   80
  by + place   *by the supermarket*   77
  by + noun   *by car*   81
  adjective + *by*   *surprised by*   82

can   29–30, 34–36
  can't have   29, 34–35
  can't be   34

capital letter   *A, B, C,* etc   punctuation   Appendix 3

colon   :   punctuation   Appendix 3

comma   ,   punctuation   Appendix 3

comparative forms   *cheaper, most quickly*   73–74

comparison: adjective and adverb forms   *cheaper, most quickly*   73

comparison: sentence patterns
  is faster than   74
  is the tallest boy in the class   74
  isn't as tall as   74

complement   *Tom is the driver.*   86

conditional forms   43–45

connectors   *in addition, however,* etc   88

consonants   *b, c, d, f, g, h,* etc   49, Appendix 2

continuous tenses
  I am doing   4
  I was doing   8
  I have been doing   12
  I will be doing   16

could   29–30, 34–36, 44–45
  could have   29, 34–35
  couldn't have   29, 36
  could in conditional forms   44–45

countable and uncountable nouns   *olives, olive oil*   51

'd, they would and *they had*   22

dash   –   punctuation   Appendix 3

dates   Appendix 5

days   Appendix 5

demonstratives   *this, that, these, those*   54

despite   88

determiners
  word classes   85
  determiners and pronouns   85

detest   5

did   6

direct and indirect objects   62

do
  do and *does*   2, 5
  auxiliary verb forms   *do, be, have*   21
  main verb form   21

down

movement   77
    with phrasal verbs   77
dream about and *dream of*   83
due to   88
during   80
    during and *while*   80

each and *every*   58
ed participles
    with present perfect   9–11
    with past perfect   13
    with future perfect   17
    with passive sentences   37–38
    with relative clauses   65
either
    either of   58
    not ... either of and *neither of*   58
enough and *too*   75
even though   87
ever   10, 72
every and *each*   58
except for   88
exclamation mark ! punctuation   Appendix 3
exclamations   86
extremely   76

fairly, pretty, quite and *rather*   78
farther and *farthest*   73
few and *a few*   57
for   10
    for and *since*   10
    for + indirect object   62
    time   80
    with nouns   81
    with adjectives   82
    in prepositional verbs   83
forget   5
    forget to do and *never forget doing*   40
from   77
    with adjectives   *different from*   82
full forms and short forms   *he is* and *he's*   22
full stop . punctuation   Appendix 3
furniture   51
furthermore   88
future   5, 14–18
    present tenses for the future   5
    going to   14
    will   15
    will and *going to*   18
future continuous   *I will be doing*   16
    I will be doing and *I will*   18
future perfect   *I will have done*   17

future perfect with *before, by* and *not ... until/till*   17
    I will have done and *I will be doing*   18

genitive *'s*   *Tom's book*   60
geographical names   *the Himalayas, Mount Everest*   53
get/have something done   38
going to
    I am going to do and *I am doing*   14
    I am going to do and *I will do*   18
gone to and *been to*   10
go on to do and *go on doing*   40
got, have got and *have*   19

had
    with past perfect   *I had done*   13
    had better   31, 36
    had to   35, 36
hair   51
hard and *hardly*   70
hate   5
have
    with present perfect   *I have done*   9–12
    present perfect and past simple   *I have done* and *I did*   11
    with present perfect continuous   *I have been doing*   12
    present perfect continuous and present perfect   *I have been doing* and *I have done*   12
    have and *have got*   19
    have a rest   19
    auxiliary verb forms   *have, be* and *do*   21
    main verb form   21
    can't have, could have and *couldn't have*   29
    should have and *ought to have*   31
    have/get something done   38
    have to and *have got to*   32, 36
he   59
health   51
hear   5
help   41
her
    object pronoun   *I called her.*   59
    possessive adjective   *This is her number.*   60
hers   60
herself   61
him   59
himself   61
his
    possessive adjective   *This is his car.*   60
    possessive pronoun   *This car is his.*   60
how, how much, how many, how old, etc   24

if   43–45, 87
    conditional forms   *If it rains, we'll ...*   43–45

if only 44, 45
    in connecting clauses 87
imperatives *Do/Do not ...* 1
in
    in, *on* and *at* for place 77, 78
    in, *on* and *at* for time 79
    in phrasal verbs 84
in addition and *in addition to* 88
indirect forms *I wonder what time it is.* 27
infinitives *hold, talk, play,* etc 1, Appendix 1
information 51
in front of 77
ing participles
    with present continuous *I am doing* 4
    with past continuous *I was doing* 8
    with present perfect continuous *I have been doing* 12
    with future continuous *I will be doing* 16
    with relative clauses 65
in order to, so as to and *to* 87
inside 77
in spite of 88
instead and *instead of* 88
into 77
irregular adverbs *well, fast, hard* 70
irregular comparative and superlative forms *better, worst,* etc 73
irregular noun forms *clothes, sheep, men,* etc 50
irregular verb forms *break, broke, broken,* etc Appendix 1
    in past simple 6
    infinitive, past form and past participle 9
it
    it and *there* *There was a hotel. It wasn't ...* 56
    it for time, weather and distance *It's 5.00.* 56
    it as dummy subject *It's a good idea to ...* 56
    subject pronoun *It saw me.* 59
    object pronoun *I saw it.* 59
its
    possessive pronoun *This is its.* 60
    possessive adjective *This is its food.* 60
it's and *its* 22, 60
itself 61

just 9

know 5
knowledge 51

like 5
    like doing and *like to do* 40
linking words *and, although, when,* etc 85, 87–88
    word classes 85
    connecting clauses 87
    connecting sentences 88
little
    a little and *a few* 57
    little and *a little* 57
    a little + adjective/adverb *a little tired* 76
    a little + comparative *a little better* 76
look 5
look after, look at and *look for* 83
lot
    a lot/a lot of 57
    a lot and *much* or *many, a little* and *a few* 57
    a lot + comparative *a lot better* 76
love 5
luggage 51

main clause 87
main verb forms 20
many
    how many 24
    many, much and *a lot of* 57
may 30, 34–36
    may be 34
    may have 34–35
me 59
mean 5
mean to do and *mean doing* 40
might 34, 36, 44–45
    might be 34
    might have 34
    might in conditional forms 44
    might have in conditional forms 45
mine 60
modal auxiliary verbs *can, must,* etc 29–36
    can, could and *be able to* 29
    can't have, could have and *couldn't have* 29
    can, could, would and *may* 30
    should, ought to and *had better* 31
    should have and *ought to have* 31
    must and *have to* 32
    mustn't, can't and *not have to* 32
    needn't and *mustn't* 33
    needn't have and *didn't need to* 33
    may, might and *could* 34
    may be, might be, must be and *can't be* 34
    may have, must have and *can't have* 34
    could, had to and *needed to* 35
    may have, must have, can't have and *could have* 35
    review of modal auxiliary verbs 36
most
    most of the students and *most students* 58
    in superlative forms *most quickly* 73–74
much
    how much 24
    much, many and *a lot of* 57

much + comparative *much better* 76

music 51

must 32, 34–36
   must be 34, 36
   must have 34–36

mustn't, can't and *not have to* 32

mustn't and *needn't* 33

my 60

myself 61

near 77

need 5

needed to 35

needn't 33, 35–36
   needn't and *mustn't* 33, 36
   needn't have and *didn't need to* 33, 35

need to 35

need to do and *need doing* 40

negative questions 21, 23–24

neither/nor and *so* 21, 28

neither and *neither of* 58

never 10, 72

news 51

next to 77

no
   There is no ... 56
   No man can fly. 58

none and *none of* 58

not and *so* *I'm afraid not.* and *I think so.* 28

nouns 49–51, 85
   singular and plural 49
   irregular forms 50
   countable and uncountable 51
   noun + preposition *the price of* 80
   word classes 85

numbers 52, Appendix 4

object pronouns
   me, him, us, etc 59
   after comparison *faster than him* 74

objects
   direct and indirect objects 62
   objects in sentence structure 86

of
   in partitives *all of us* 58
   noun + preposition *the price of* 81
   adjective + preposition *nervous of* 82
   verb + preposition *dream of* 83

off
   preposition 77
   in phrasal verbs *make off* 84

on

on, in and *at* for place 77, 78
on, in and *at* for time 79
on with nouns *on holiday* 81
on with verb + object + preposition *congratulate her on* 83

once connecting clauses 13

one
   one and *ones* 54
   one of 58

onto 77

on top of 77

opposite 77

or 87, 88

orders 86

ought to 31, 36

ought to have 31, 36

our 60

ours 60

ourselves 61

out of 77

outside 77

over
   movement 77
   in phrasal verbs *turn over* 84

own 5

passive verb forms 37–38
   forms with simple tenses *It is mended.* 37
   by + agent *It was mended by the mechanic.* 37
   forms with continuous tenses *It is being mended.* 38
   forms with modal verbs *It can be mended.* 38
   have/get something done 38
   irregular past participles Appendix 1

past
   movement 77
   telling the time with *past* and *to* 79

past continuous *I was doing* 8
   past continuous and past simple *I was working* and *I worked* 8
   with linking words *when, as* and *while* 8
   spelling rules Appendix 2

past participle 9–13, Appendix 1

past perfect *I had done* 13
   past perfect and past simple *I had worked* and *I worked* 13
   with linking words *when, after, before, once, until* and *as soon as* 13
   irregular past participles *break, broken,* etc Appendix 1

past simple *I did* 6–8, 11
   past simple of main verbs *I worked* 6
   used to 6
   past simple of *be* *I was, they were* 7
   past simple and past continuous *I worked* and *I was working* 8

with linking word *when*   8

past simple and present perfect   *I worked* and *I have worked*   11

past simple and past perfect   *I worked* and *I had worked*   13

irregular past forms   *break, broke*, etc   Appendix 1

phrasal verbs   *come in, sit down*   84

noun and pronoun objects   *put down their pens* and *put them down*   84

plural and singular nouns   49–50

regular plurals   *book, books*, etc   49

plurals without articles   *They're maps.*   49

irregular plurals   *man, men*, etc   50

spelling rules   Appendix 2

possessive forms

possessive pronouns   *mine, yours*, etc   60

possessive determiners/adjectives   *my, your*, etc   60

noun + *'s   Sally's cat*   60

punctuation   *'s* and *s'*   Appendix 3

prefer   5

prefer doing and *prefer to do*   40

prepositional verbs   *apply for*   80

prepositions   77–83, 85

place   *on, in, behind*   77–78

movement   *onto, into, out of*   77

time   *at, in on*,   79

time   *for, since, ago, before, during, while, until/till, by*   80

preposition + noun   *for the children*   81

noun + preposition   *price of*   81

adjective + preposition   *worried about*   82

present continuous   *I am doing*   4–5

present continuous and present simple   *I am doing I do*   5

future meanings   4–5

spelling rules   Appendix 2

present participle   4, 8, 12, 16

spelling rules   Appendix 2

present perfect   *I have done*   9–12

with *yet, just, still (not)* and *already*   9

with *for* and *since*   9

with *ever* and *never*   10

gone to and *been to*   10

present perfect and past simple   *I have worked* and *I worked*   11

present perfect and present perfect continuous   *I have worked* and *I have been working*   12

irregular past participles   *broke, broken*, etc   Appendix 1

present perfect continuous   *I have been doing*   12

present perfect continuous and present perfect   *I have been working* and *I have worked*   12

spelling rules   Appendix 2

present simple   *I do*   2, 5

present simple of main verbs   *I work, she works*   2

present simple of *be   I am, he is, you are*   3

verbs taking simple not continuous tenses   2, 5

present simple and present continuous   *I do* and *I am*

doing   5

future meanings   2, 5

spelling rules   Appendix 2

pretty, quite, rather and *fairly*   76

pronouns   54–60, 85

demonstrative pronouns   *this, that, these* and *those*   54

demonstrative pronouns and demonstrative adjectives   54

one and *ones*   54

there, it and *they*   56

subject pronouns   *I, you, he, she, it, we* and *they*   59

object pronouns   *me, you, him, her, it, us* and *them*   59

possessive pronouns   *mine, yours, his, hers, its, ours* and *theirs*   60

possessive pronouns and possessive determiners/adjectives   *my, your, his, her, our* and *their*   60

reflexive pronouns   *myself, yourself, himself, herself, itself, ourselves, yourselves* and *themselves*   61

something, anybody, everywhere, etc   55, 63

relative pronouns *who, which* and *that*   64–65, 67

relative pronoun *whose*   66

provided that   43

punctuation   Appendix 3

quantity   *a lot of, many, much, a few* and *a little*   57

question forms   23–25

Yes/No questions   *Are you from Japan?*   23

Wh questions   *Where are you going?*   24

negative questions   *Why aren't you going?*   24

tag questions   *You're 18, aren't you?*   21, 25

question mark *?* punctuation   Appendix 3

questions   23–25, 86

question words   *what, where, who*, etc   24

quite, rather, fairly and *pretty*   76

rather, fairly, pretty and *quite*   76

realize   5

reflexive pronouns   *myself, yourself, herself*, etc   61

regret to do and *regret doing*   40

relative clauses   *He's the person who …*   64–67

defining relative clauses   *He's the person who …*   64

relative pronouns   *who, which* and *that*   64

relative pronoun *whose*   66

reduced relative clauses   *The man they want is wearing …*   65

relative clauses with *ing* and *ed* participles   *The people shouting last night …*   65

relative clauses with *when, where* and *why*   66

adding clauses   *Alan Brant, who won in France, is …*   67

remember   5

remember to do and *remember doing*   40

reported speech   46–48

statements   *He said he would go.*   46

questions   *He asked if he could go.*   47

orders, requests and invitations   *He told me to go.*   48

promises and offers *He promised to go.* 48
    suggestions and apologies *He suggested going.* 48
reporting verbs *invite, promise*, etc 48
round 77

's possessive *This is Tom's.* 60
see 5
seem 5
sentence connectors *In addition, However,* etc 88
sentence structure subject, verb, etc 86
sentence types statement, question, etc 86
short answers
    Yes, I do. 21, 26
    with *so* and *neither/nor So do I.* 21, 28
short forms and full forms *he's* and *he is* 22
should 31, 36
should have 31, 35–36
since and *for* 10, 80
singular and plural 49–50
smell 5
so
    so and *neither/nor* 21, 28
    so and *not I think so.* and *I'm afraid not.* 28
    so and *such so long* and *such a long time* 76
    connecting clauses 87, 88
    so and *because* 87
    so as to, in order to and *to* 87
some
    some, a and *an* 49
    some and *any* 55
    somebody and *anything*, etc 55, 63
    some of 58
    Some trees grow fruit. 58
sound 5
speech marks ' ' punctuation Appendix 3
statements 86
still (not) 9
stop to do and *stop doing* 40
sub-clauses 87
subject 86
subject pronouns *I, he, we*, etc 59
subject questions with *who* and *what* 24
such and *so such a long time* and *so long* 76
suggest 48
superlative forms *cheapest, most quickly* 73–74
syllable Appendix 2

tag questions 21, 25
taste 5
than 73–74
that

demonstrative adjectives and pronouns 54
    that, who and *which* in relative clauses *There's the car
        that ...* 64–67, 87
their 60
theirs 60
them 59
themselves 61
there is and *there are* 56
they 59
    they and *there There were some shops. They were ...* 56
think about and *think of* 42, 83
this, that, these and *those* 54
through 77
till/until 13, 17, 80
    till/until and *by* 80
times Appendix 5

to
    with indirect objects *Pass it to me.* 62
    movement 77
    time 79
    adjective + preposition *used to* 82
    prepositional verb *talk to* 83
    to, in order to and *so as to* 87
too
    too and *enough* 75
    too and *very* 76
towards 77
travel 51
trouble 51
try to do and *try doing* 40

under 77
understand 5
unless 43
until/till 13, 17, 80
    until/till and *by* 80
up
    movement 77
    in phrasal verbs *pick up* 84
us 59
used to + infinitive *I used to go training.* 6
be used to + noun/*ing* form *I'm used to hard work.* 82

verb forms, auxiliary *be, do, have* 21
verb forms, main *break, breaks, broke, broken, breaking* 20
verb + object + preposition + noun/*ing* form *I thanked her
    for coming.* 42, 83
verb + preposition + noun/*ing* form *I'm thinking about the
    race.* 42, 83
verb tenses, active 1–18

verb tenses, passive   37–38

verb + object + *to* + infinitive   *I want you to go.*   41

verb + *to* + infinitive or verb + *ing* form   *want to go* and *like doing*   39–40

very and *too*   76

vowels   *a, e, i, o, u*   49, Appendix 2

was and *were*   7, 8

we   59

were
   in past tenses   7, 8
   in conditional sentences   *If I were you, I'd …*   44

when
   linking word   8, 13, 43
   when with past simple and past continuous   8
   Wh question word   24
   when, where and *why* in relative clauses   *There was a time when …*   66

where
   Wh question word   24
   where, when and *why* in relative clauses   *I remember the house where …*   66

which, who and *that* in relative clauses   *There's the car which …*   64, 67, 87

while
   linking word   8
   while and *during*   80

who
   who and *what* subject questions   *What's happening?*   24
   who, which and *that* in relative clauses   *He's the man who …*   64, 67, 87
   Wh question words   *what, where, who,* etc   21

whose
   Wh question word   24
   in relative clauses   *He's the man whose car …*   66

why
   Wh question word   24
   why, where and *when* in relative clauses   *That's the reason why …*   66

will   15–18, 36
   You'll pass your exams.   15
   Will you post this?   15
   will and *shall*   15
   I will be doing   16
   I will have done   17
   I will do and *I am going to do*   18
   I will do and *I will be doing*   18

wish   44

with
   noun + preposition   *problem with*   81
   adjective + preposition   *angry with*   82
   verb + object + preposition   *provide her with*   83

word classes   verb, noun, etc   85

work   51

worse and *worst*   73

Yes/No questions   *Are you from Japan?*   23

yet   9

you   59

your   60

yourself and *yourselves*   61

Answer key

Unit 1

Exercise 1
1 *Be*
2 *don't be*
3 *Be*
4 *Don't be*
5 *Be*
6 *Don't be*
7 *Be*
8 *Don't be*

Exercise 2
1 *Don't play*
2 *Take*
3 *Turn off*
4 *Don't talk*
5 *Don't forget*
6 *press*
7 *Don't drive*
8 *Write*

Exercise 3
1 *put in*
2 *place/put*
3 *press/push*
4 *choose*
5 *place/put*
6 *press/push*
7 *take*
8 *enjoy*

Exercise 4
1 *go*
2 *Turn*
3 *Turn*
4 *Take*
5 *Pass*
6 *Follow   turn*
7 *Cross   turn*
8 *Go   take*

Unit 2

Exercise 1
1 *live*
2 *like*
3 *cries*
4 *start*
5 *goes*
6 *fetches*
7 *has*

Exercise 2
1 *want   love*
2 *use   doesn't work*
3 *doesn't get   eats*
4 *don't like   don't enjoy*
5 *doesn't swim   goes*

6 *don't drink   keeps*
7 *doesn't drive   walks*

Exercise 3
1 *Does Tom drive?*
2 *Do you know Ann Smith?*
3 *Does the TV work?*
4 *Do you go out much?*
5 *Does Marie speak French?*
6 *Do Fred and Mary live near here?*

Exercise 4
1 *How does Tom go to work?*
2 *When does Sally visit her parents?*
3 *Where do they go on holiday every year?*
4 *What time do you/I get home in the evening?*
5 *Why do you/we always make mistakes?*
6 *How long do the children watch TV after school?*
7 *What does the cat have for lunch?*

Unit 3

Exercise 1
1 *are*
2 *Is*
3 *is*
4 *Am*
5 *Are*
6 *is*
7 *Are*
8 *am   is   are*

Exercise 2
1 *I'm*
2 *he's*
3 *they're*
4 *you're*
5 *I'm not*
6 *he isn't/he's not*
7 *they aren't/they're not*
8 *you aren't/you're not*

Exercise 3
1 *I'm not 80 kilos. I'm 85 kilos.*
2 *isn't in Berlin. He's in Paris.*

3 *aren't 1 metre 75. You're 1 metre 80.*
4 *aren't at home. They're at school.*

Exercise 4
1 *Yes, she is.*
2 *No, you aren't. You're very late.*
3 *No, it isn't. It's 30th April.*
4 *Yes, there are.*
5 *No, I'm not. I'm only 28.*

Exercise 5
1 *How old is he? He's 25.*
2 *What's his job? He's a designer.*
3 *Where is his office? It's on the second floor.*
4 *How many people are there? There are six.*
5 *Which is his desk? It's the one by the window.*

Unit 4

Exercise 1
1 *I'm going.*
2 *You aren't going./ You're not going.*
3 *He isn't going./He's not going.*
4 *They're going.*
5 *It isn't going./It's not going.*

Exercise 2
1 *'m not feeling*
2 *'re going*
3 *aren't working.*
4 *is ringing   isn't answering*
5 *'m looking for   isn't working   's visiting*
6 *'s having*
7 *aren't watching   're listening*

Exercise 3
1 *are the children doing?   They're playing*
2 *Are you enjoying   am.*

3 *is Bill training He's trying*
4 *Is Sally going   isn't.*
5 *are we flying? We're doing*
6 *Are the boys washing aren't   They're cutting*
7 *'s the cat eating? It's eating*

Exercise 4
1 *'s getting*
2 *are choosing*
3 *Are you writing*
4 *'m planning*
5 *'re leaving*
6 *are you cutting*
7 *is making*

Exercise 5
1 *'m working*
2 *'re building*
3 *are*
4 *studying*
5 *'m not*
6 *'m training*
7 *is*
8 *going*
9 *'s starting*

Unit 5

Exercise 1
1 *Are you going*
2 *Are you doing*
3 *is staying*
4 *'m taking*
5 *aren't doing*
6 *aren't going*
7 *are you planning*
8 *'re having*

Exercise 2
1 *don't need*
2 *look*
3 *do you say*
4 *don't like*
5 *Does the bus stop*
6 *doesn't do*
7 *does he leave*
8 *goes*
9 *walk*
10 *don't mind.*
11 *Do you know*

Exercise 3
1 *'re*
2 *don't*

3 *is*
4 *Are*
5 *does*
6 *do*
7 *isn't*
8 *doesn't*
9 *Do*
10 *aren't*

Exercise 4

1 *'m making*
2 *'m staying*
3 *do*
4 *get up*
5 *start*
6 *eat*
7 *owns*
8 *'m living*
9 *takes*
10 *train*
11 *'s finishing*
12 *'m writing*

Unit 6

Exercise 1

1 *asked*
2 *was/were*
3 *broke*
4 *called*
5 *did*
6 *drove*
7 *ate*
8 *found*
9 *went*
10 *had*
11 *invited*
12 *jumped*
13 *kept*
14 *left*
15 *met*
16 *needed*
17 *opened*
18 *ran*
19 *saw*
20 *woke up*

be, break, do, drive, eat, find, go, have, keep, leave, meet, run, see and *wake up* are irregular verbs.
be, do and *have* can be main verbs and auxiliary verbs.

Exercise 2

1 *saw*
2 *jumped*

3 *ran*
4 *ate/had*
5 *had*
6 *left*
7 *drove*

Exercise 3

1 *found my old suit didn't find my new one.*
2 *cleaned her red shoes didn't clean her black ones.*
3 *called their mother didn't call their sister.*

Exercise 4

1 *Did Tim and Fred visit Paris too?*
No, they didn't.
2 *Did Ann run well too?*
Yes, she did.
3 *Did they have a French test too?*
No, they didn't.
4 *Did Peter practise the piano too?*
Yes, he did.

Exercise 5

1 *When did she go there?*
2 *How did she go?*
3 *Why did she go?*
4 *What time did she get there?*
5 *Who did she meet?*
6 *Where did they meet?*

Unit 7

Exercise 1

1 *was   were*
2 *were   was   were*
3 *were   was   was*
4 *were   was   was*

Exercise 2

1 *was*
2 *Was*
3 *was.*
4 *were*
5 *were*
6 *was*
7 *wasn't*
8 *weren't*
9 *were*

Exercise 3

1 *How old was the house?*
About 100 years old.

2 *How many bedrooms were there?*
Four.
3 *How big was the living-room?*
12 x 5 metres.
4 *Where was the kitchen?*
At the back of the house.
5 *What was outside?*
A garden with a stream.
6 *What was the only problem?*
The price.
7 *How much was the house?*
£200,000.

Exercise 4

1 *are   are*
2 *was   isn't*
3 *were   're*
4 *weren't   was*
5 *was   is   is*

Unit 8

Exercise 1

1 *was calling*
2 *were swimming*
3 *was watching*
4 *were having*
5 *was getting*
6 *were riding*

Exercise 2

1 *were   swimming*
were swimming
Were they swimming
weren't.   were swimming
2 *Was   listening*
wasn't.   was watching
was he watching?
was watching
3 *were   riding their bikes?   were riding*
4 *was   calling?*
was calling

Exercise 3

1 *were you doing*
2 *was he running*
3 *was driving   broke down.*
4 *opened   was shining*

5 *were working   rang*
6 *hit   was trying*
7 *was trying   crashed*

Exercise 4

1 *was*
2 *were singing.*
3 *was walking*
4 *noticed*
5 *was playing*
6 *called*
7 *looked*
8 *shouted*
9 *invited*
10 *were playing*
11 *stopped*
12 *were eating*
13 *decided*
14 *happened.*
15 *was getting*
16 *started*
17 *fell*
18 *were watching*
19 *laughed*
20 *felt*

Unit 9

Exercise 1

1 *asked*
2 *been*
3 *chosen*
4 *done*
5 *eaten*
6 *found*
7 *given*
8 *had*
9 *invited*
10 *joined*
11 *kept*
12 *left*
13 *made*
14 *needed*
15 *opened*
16 *put*
17 *run*
18 *started*
19 *taken*
20 *woken up*

be, choose, do, eat, find, give, have, keep, leave, make, put, run, take and *wake up* are irregular verbs.
be, do and *have* can be main verbs and auxiliary verbs.

Exercise 2

1 *found*
2 *bought*
3 *started*
4 *joined*
5 *made*
6 *met*
7 *been*
8 *invited*

Exercise 3

1 *'ve broken*
2 *have caught*
3 *has painted*
4 *have arrived*
5 *has won*
6 *has got*

Exercise 4

1 *has joined the school drama group, hasn't joined the tennis club.*
2 *has made a cake, hasn't made any sandwiches.*
3 *have brought their books, haven't brought their pens.*
4 *have chosen the carpets for their new house, haven't chosen any furniture.*
5 *'ve washed the car, haven't washed the children's bikes.*
6 *'ve invited Alan to the party, haven't invited Joe.*

Exercise 5

1 *Have the boys done their French homework too? No, they haven't.*
2 *Has Mark been busy all day too? Yes, he has.*
3 *Have you learnt to fly too? Yes, I have.*
4 *Has Sally brought her books too? No, she hasn't.*

Exercise 6

1 *How long has Emma lived in London?*
2 *Why have you come so late?*
3 *What have you done with my skirt?*
4 *Where has Andy put the bike?*
5 *How many kilometres have you driven today?*

Exercise 7

1 *Yes, she's just gone to Rome.*
2 *No, I haven't met them yet.*
3 *Yes, he's just bought some chocolate.*
4 *No, we haven't finished work yet.*
5 *No, they haven't come home yet.*
6 *Yes, I've just bought some.*
7 *Yes, I've just put them in your briefcase.*

Exercise 8

1 *But you still haven't called him.*
2 *We've already bought the tickets.*
3 *But you still haven't packed your bag.*
4 *She's already got £50.*
5 *It's already doing 300 kph.*
6 *But I still haven't had a reply.*

Unit 10

Exercise 1

1 *This land has belonged to Mr Hill since 1950.*
2 *Sally has had the same car for five years.*
3 *We've lived in this house since I was 25.*

Exercise 2

1 *have they had Since*
2 *has he worked For*
3 *have they wanted Since*
4 *has he lived For*

Exercise 3

1 *He hasn't seen Susan for three weeks.*
2 *They haven't met since Claire's wedding.*
3 *We haven't had fish for dinner for months.*

Exercise 4

1 *Have you ever studied English before? Yes, I've studied English once.*
2 *How many times has he seen Superman? He's seen it seven times.*
3 *Have they ever tried Indian food? Yes, they've tried it a few times.*
4 *How often has it rained today? It's rained twice today.*

Exercise 5

1 *Have   been   has gone*
2 *'s gone*
3 *has   been*

Unit 11

Exercise 1

1 *did you do?*
2 *went*
3 *looked*
4 *Did you find*
5 *weren't*
6 *was*
7 *didn't call*
8 *didn't want*
9 *did you do*
10 *phoned*

Exercise 2

1 *have you put haven't seen*
2 *Have you packed 've left*
3 *Has Dad given hasn't.*
4 *'ve brought   has gone*

Exercise 3

1 *asked   asked*
2 *was/were   been*
3 *cut   cut*
4 *did   done*
5 *found   found*
6 *went   gone*
7 *had   had*
8 *invited   invited*
9 *joined   joined*
10 *kept   kept*

be, cut, do, find, go, have and *keep* are irregular verbs. *be, do* and *have* can be main verbs and auxiliary verbs.

Exercise 4

1 *has*
2 *didn't*
3 *hasn't*
4 *Did*
5 *haven't*
6 *Has*
7 *did*
8 *have*

Exercise 5

1 *haven't written*
2 *has been*
3 *have begun*
4 *'ve had*
5 *told*
6 *'s let*
7 *got*
8 *'ve found*
9 *signed*
10 *gave*

Unit 12

Exercise 1

1 *'ve been working*
2 *'ve been playing*
3 *has been using*
4 *'ve been doing*
5 *'s been studying*

Exercise 2

1 *hasn't been spending 's been saving*
2 *haven't been going 've been going*
3 *hasn't been doing 's been listening*

Exercise 3

1 *have you been doing*
2 *has he been getting on*
3 *Has he been learning*
4 *Have you been eating*
5 *have they been working*

Exercise 4

1 has Pam been doing
  She's been looking for
  a new job.
  has she been doing
  Since last month./For
  a month.
2 have Nick and Andy
  been doing
  They've been training
  for the London
  Marathon.
  have they been doing
  For three months.

Unit 13

Exercise 1

1 had gone.
2 had taken
3 had eaten
4 'd changed
5 'd seen
6 had bought
7 'd left
8 'd started

Exercise 2

1 'd already arranged
2 'd never seen
3 had just started
4 'd recently heard
  about
5 still hadn't repaired
6 had already spent
7 had only had

Exercise 3

1 arrived   had gone.
2 had got away
  closed
3 'd crossed   were
  able
4 left   'd done
5 turned back
  'd run out of

Exercise 4

1 We drove out of town
  when we'd loaded the
  jeep.
2 We stopped for a rest
  when we'd driven into
  the hills.
3 We started again
  when we'd had a good
  rest.

4 We stopped for the
  night when we'd been
  on the road for ten
  hours.
5 We started to cook
  dinner when we'd
  unpacked the jeep.
6 We went to sleep when
  we'd finished dinner.

Unit 14

Exercise 1

1 'm going to wash it
  after lunch.
2 's going to clean them
  now.
3 're going to mend
  them this evening.
4 's going to have it in
  a minute.

Exercise 2

1 's going to rain.
  're going to get
2 's not going to get
  's going to miss
3 're going to run
  out of
  're not going to reach
4 's not going to give up
  's going to finish

Exercise 3

1 Is Sam going to pass
  his exams?
  Yes, he is.
2 Are your parents
  going to take you out?
  No, they aren't.
3 Are you going to
  watch TV this
  evening?
  Yes, I am.
4 Is Sally going to buy a
  newspaper?
  No, she isn't.

Exercise 4

1 Where is she going to
  put them?
2 When are they going
  to move out?
3 How many are you
  going to do?
4 What is he going to
  see?

Unit 15

Exercise 1

1 won't find
2 will cross
3 won't open
4 'll do
5 won't be

Exercise 2

1 'll buy
2 won't be
3 'll wash
4 'll close
5 won't make
6 won't forget

Exercise 3

1 He'll get
2 She'll give
3 I'll carry
4 He'll be
5 I'll cut

Exercise 4

1 Will Ann be ten next
  week?
  Yes, she will.
2 Will the boys like their
  new school?
  No, they won't.
3 Will Mr Hall arrive
  tonight?
  Yes, he will.
4 Will next term start
  on 15th April?
  No, it won't.

Exercise 5

1 'll phone
2 won't be
3 Will everybody want
4 will.
5 will we need
6 'll have to
7 Will we need
8 won't.
9 'll have
10 won't rain.

Unit 16

Exercise 1

1 At 10.00 he'll be
  doing Art.
2 At 10.45 he'll be
  learning French.

3 At 11.20 he'll be
  studying Maths.
4 At 12.20 he'll be
  doing English.
5 At 1.05 he'll be
  having lunch.

Exercise 2

1 'll be meeting the
  Sales Manager.
2 'll be visiting the
  factory.
3 'll be having meetings
  with the sales team.
4 'll be showing visitors
  round London all
  day.
5 'll be spending the day
  in Paris.

Exercise 3

1 When will he be flying
  to Florida?
  Next Monday.
2 How long will he be
  riding across
  America?
  For two months.
3 Where will he be
  arriving in ten weeks?
  In California.
4 Where will he be going
  from there?
  To Alaska.

Unit 17

Exercise 1

1 'll have written a
  book of short stories.
2 'll have produced a
  play in London.
3 'll have published a
  best-seller novel.
4 'll have won an
  important
  international prize.
5 'll have made a lot of
  money.

Exercise 2

1 won't have finished
2 will have sold
3 'll have gone
4 'll have got
5 won't have had

Exercise 3

1 What will they have finished
  They'll have put in the windows, but they won't have fitted the doors.
2 What will they have finished
  They'll have done the wiring, but they won't have laid the floors.
3 What will they have finished
  They'll have plastered the walls, but they won't have painted the house.

Unit 18

Exercise 1

1 're going to crash.
  'll be
2 Are we going to eat
  're going to go
3 'll have
4 Will you answer
  'll probably be
5 'll be   are you going to leave
  'm going to study
6 will the meeting start?
  won't be

Exercise 2

1 're taking
2 reaches
3 're flying
4 takes off
5 arrives
6 are staying

Exercise 3

1 'll be flying   will you be doing?
  'll be working
2 'll pass
  won't do
3 will Sam be
  will have
  'll be talking
4 'll be waiting
  'll have

Exercise 4

1 will have laid

---

2 will be working
3 will be working
4 'll be taking
5 'll have left   'll be training
6 will be arriving
  won't have finished

Unit 19

Exercise 1

1 Have you got
  haven't got   's got
  hasn't got
2 's got
  Has he got
  hasn't.

Exercise 2

1 Do you have
  don't have   has
  doesn't have
2 has
  Does she have
  doesn't.
3 Did you have
  did   didn't have
  had
4 do you have?
  don't have   haven't
  had
  did you have?
5 has
  has he had
  's had   doesn't have

Exercise 3

1 have got
2 hasn't got
3 've got
4 've had
5 've   had.
6 didn't have
7 had
8 've got
9 've got
10 's had

Exercise 4

1 has a look
2 has a chat
3 have time
4 have coffee
5 has a game
6 has a swim
7 have lunch
8 have a rest
9 has a run
10 has a chance

Unit 20

Exercise 1

1 know
  drives
2 start?
  begins
3 like
  watches
4 have
  has

Exercise 2

1 finishes
2 'm listening
3 hope
4 is he making
5 does she go
6 Are you enjoying

Exercise 3

1 cost   cost   cost
2 cut   cut   cut
3 hit   hit   hit
4 let   let   let
5 read   read   read
6 learn   learnt   learnt
7 make   made   made
8 pay   paid   paid
9 get   got   got
10 ride   rode   ridden
11 take   took   taken
12 wear   wore   worn
13 see   saw   seen
14 give   gave   given

Exercise 4

1 cut
  cut
2 make
  made
3 ride
  ride   rode
4 let
  let   hit   got

Exercise 5

1 done?
  made
2 seen
  given
3 read
  learnt
4 hit
  cut

Unit 21

Exercise 1

1 'm
2 is
3 'll be
4 has been
5 were
6 've been
7 Are
8 was

Exercise 2

1 do
  don't
2 Do
  don't
3 did
  didn't
4 does
  don't
5 Did
  didn't
6 Does
  doesn't

Exercise 3

1 Have
  haven't   haven't
2 hasn't
3 Have
  've   haven't
4 hadn't
5 'll have
6 has
  's
7 won't have
8 'd

Exercise 4

1 Hasn't Paul come home yet?
2 Why didn't they call the police?
3 Aren't you enjoying the film?
4 Why don't you agree with me?
5 Isn't Rosie going to the wedding?
6 Which questions haven't they answered yet?
7 Don't you have to go home now?
8 Which parts don't we have to learn?

Exercise 5

1 *have you?*
2 *doesn't he?*
3 *weren't they?*
4 *do you?*
5 *didn't he?*
6 *haven't they?*
7 *does he?*
8 *wasn't she?*
9 *are you?*
10 *did he?*

Exercise 6

1 *Neither/Nor do we.*
2 *So does Alan.*
3 *Neither/Nor have I.*
4 *Neither/Nor did Lisa.*
5 *So have her brothers.*
6 *Neither/Nor is she.*
7 *Neither/Nor had we.*
8 *So did the van.*
9 *Neither/Nor are you.*
10 *So has Andy.*

Exercise 7

1 *What are you having for lunch?*
We're having chicken.
What did you have for lunch?
We had chicken.
2 *How much work is he doing?*
He's doing doing ten hours.
How much work did he do?
He did ten hours.
How much work has he done?
He's done ten hours.
3 *Why are they being so slow with their work?*
Because they're being careful.
Why were they so slow with their work?
Because they were careful.
Why have they been so slow with their work?
Because they've been careful.

Unit 22

Exercise 1

1 *You're*

2 *He's*
3 *I'm*
4 *What's*
5 *We'll*
6 *he's   he'll*
7 *you'd*
8 *she'd   she'd*
9 *They've*
10 *I'd*

Exercise 2

1 *don't*
2 *isn't*
3 *hasn't*
4 *won't*
5 *Don't   didn't*
6 *'m not*
7 *isn't   doesn't*
8 *hadn't   wouldn't*
9 *haven't*
10 *wasn't*

Exercise 3

1 *don't*
2 *'m*
3 *'s*
4 *'ve*
5 *'d*
6 *'d*
7 *haven't*
8 *'m*
9 *Don't*
10 *'re*
11 *won't*
12 *doesn't*
13 *'ll*
14 *'ll*
15 *'ll*
16 *'s*

Exercise 4

1 *we have*
2 *are not*
3 *do not*
4 *I am*
5 *they are*
6 *will not*
7 *we are*
8 *have not*

Exercise 5

1 *we had*
2 *you would*
3 *it is*
4 *he has*
5 *He is*
6 *I would*

Unit 23

Exercise 1

1 *Does Bob like football too?*
2 *Is Lucy good at cooking too?*
3 *Has Dad had dinner too?*
4 *Did Jim cook some meat too?*
5 *Are you going out tonight too?*

Exercise 2

1 *Does he have to go now too?*
2 *Must she finish the letters too?*
3 *Can he swim fast too?*
4 *Should we train every evening too?*
5 *Will we have to write to all our friends too?*

Exercise 3

1 *Have they been married for long?*
2 *Did they move to Manchester at that time?*
3 *Have they got any children?*
4 *Do the children go to school?*
5 *Is she starting school soon?*

Exercise 4

1 *Why? Isn't it a good one?*
2 *Really? Don't you like flying?*
3 *Why? Hasn't he gone to college yet?*
4 *Really? Aren't they going to bed soon?*
5 *Why? Didn't she buy one yesterday?*

Unit 24

Exercise 1

1 *Where*
2 *Whose*
3 *How long*
4 *How many*

5 *Which*
6 *When*
7 *Why*
8 *What*

Exercise 2

1 *How old are you?*
I'm ...
2 *What's your address?*
It's ...
3 *What does your father do?*
He's a/an ...
4 *How many brothers and sisters have you got?*
I've got ...
5 *Why are you learning English?*
Because ...

Exercise 3

1 *Why hasn't Tom answered my letter?*
2 *What haven't we done?*
3 *Why won't they be able to go on holiday?*
4 *Where didn't we go?*
5 *Why isn't Ann going to go out tonight?*
6 *Why don't you like this television programme?*

Exercise 4

1 *Who called the police?*
2 *What went wrong?*
3 *What did Bob find by the door?*
4 *Who did Tom phone?*
5 *What did the car run over?*
6 *Who saw Peter?*
7 *What did Julie eat?*

Unit 25

Exercise 1

1 *won't you?*
2 *has it?*
3 *aren't they?*
4 *didn't it?*
5 *is she?*
6 *was he?*
7 *can he?*
8 *shouldn't he?*
9 *need we?*
10 *might she?*

11 *won't he?*
12 *have you?*
13 *won't they?*
14 *has it?*
15 *is it?*
16 *wasn't it?*
17 *doesn't he?*
18 *didn't you?*
19 *don't you?*
20 *didn't she?*

Exercise 2

1 *didn't it?*
2 *were they?*
3 *aren't you?*
4 *do you?*
5 *is she?*
6 *haven't you?*
7 *will they?*

Exercise 3

1 *isn't it?*
2 *are there?*
3 *are they?*
4 *have I?*
5 *didn't you?*
6 *won't we?*

Exercise 4

1 *didn't I?*
2 *haven't you?*
3 *weren't they?*
4 *aren't we?*
5 *does it?*
6 *don't we?*
7 *is there?*

Unit 26

Exercise 1

1 *I haven't.*
2 *I do.*
3 *I'm not.*
4 *we should.*
5 *I would.*
6 *there aren't.*
7 *I haven't.*
8 *he is.*
9 *I can't.*
10 *I did.*
11 *I must.*

Exercise 2

1 *I'm not.*
2 *I haven't.*
3 *I wasn't.*
4 *I didn't.*
5 *I was.*

6 *I was.*
7 *I did.*
8 *I was.*
9 *I did.*
10 *I was.*

Exercise 3

1 *Yes, I am./No, I'm not.*
2 *Yes, I do./No, I don't.*
3 *Yes, it is./No, it isn't.*
4 *Yes, I am./No, I'm not.*
5 *Yes, they do./No, they don't.*
6 *Yes, they do./No, they don't.*
7 *Yes, I do./No, I don't.*
8 *Yes, I will./No, I won't.*
9 *Yes, I have./No, I haven't.*
10 *Yes, I would./No, I wouldn't.*

Unit 27

Exercise 1

1 *Do you know what date it is today?*
2 *Could you tell me when Ann is coming home?*
3 *Do you have any idea why Tom has gone?*
4 *Can you say how long you'll be away?*
5 *Can you tell me where they've gone?*

Exercise 2

1 *Do you know if/whether they have had lunch?*
2 *Can you say if/whether you'll be home tonight?*
3 *Do you have any idea if/whether the team are going to win?*
4 *Can you tell us if/whether we're having a test this week?*

Exercise 3

1 *Can you tell me if/whether Tom goes to*

school?
2 *Can you say if/whether the ring cost a lot?*
3 *Do you have any idea if/whether they play tennis?*
4 *Could you tell us when the bus went?*
5 *Do you know how the engine works?*
6 *Can you tell me where they always go?*

Exercise 4

1 *Why do you think he arrives late?*
2 *Do you think they're going to finish today?*
3 *How far do you think they walked?*
4 *Do you think we've made a mistake?*
5 *Where do you think you will live when you go to college?*

Unit 28

Exercise 1

1 *Neither/Nor do I*
2 *So am I*
3 *So am I.*
4 *So did I*
5 *Neither/Nor did I*
6 *So did I*
7 *Neither/Nor could I*
8 *So was I.*
9 *So is mine.*
10 *So does mine.*
11 *So is mine.*

Exercise 2

1 *neither/nor is Ted.*
2 *so is Sally.*
3 *so does Claire.*
4 *so does Ken.*
5 *so can Ted.*
6 *neither/nor can Claire.*

Exercise 3

1 *I expect so.*
2 *I suppose so.*
3 *I don't think so.*
4 *I'm afraid not.*
5 *I guess not.*
6 *I think so.*

Unit 29

Exercise 1

1 *can see*
2 *can go*
3 *can't walk*
4 *can't catch*

Exercise 2

1 *can't   could*
2 *can   couldn't*
3 *couldn't   can't*
4 *could   couldn't*

Exercise 3

1 *could hear*
2 *could remember*
3 *could understand*
4 *could feel*

Exercise 4

1 *could*
2 *could*
3 *were able to*
4 *was able to*
5 *could*

Exercise 5

1 *were able to*
2 *could*
3 *can*
4 *couldn't*
5 *be able to*
6 *can't*
7 *were able to*
8 *couldn't*

Exercise 6

1 *can't have*
2 *could have*
3 *can't have*
4 *could have*

Unit 30

Exercise 1

1 *can*
2 *Could*
3 *Would*
4 *can*
5 *May*
6 *Could*

Exercise 2

1 *Can I borrow your book?*

2 *Can you lend me your pen?*
3 *Could you tell me your address?*
4 *Would you take a seat, please?*
5 *May I put your bag away?*
6 *Would all passengers remain in their seats until the plane stops?*

Exercise 3

1 *Yes, you can go now.*
2 *No, you can't park here.*
3 *Yes, you can pass the bus.*
4 *No, you can't turn round here.*

Exercise 4

1 *would*
2 *Would*
3 *could*
4 *Can*
5 *can*
6 *can't*

Unit 31

Exercise 1

1 *ought*
2 *should*
3 *ought*
4 *should*
5 *should.*

Exercise 2

1 *ought*
2 *oughtn't*
3 *should*
4 *oughtn't*
5 *shouldn't*
6 *should*
7 *should*
8 *ought*

Exercise 3

1 *'d better*
2 *'d better not*
3 *'d better not*
4 *'d better*

Exercise 4

1 *You ought to do more exercise.*

2 *You'd better see a dentist.*
3 *You shouldn't watch TV so much.*
4 *You oughtn't to use the phone so much.*
5 *You'd better not go out yet.*
6 *You should go to the beach.*

Exercise 5

1 *He should have gone to the doctor.*
2 *They shouldn't have played outside.*
3 *We ought to have turned left at the traffic lights.*
4 *She oughtn't to have bought it.*

Unit 32

Exercise 1

1 *has Paul had to pay for it?*
2 *will Emma have to go to London?*
3 *did the Smith family have to go last week?*
4 *does Ann have to change all her plans?*
5 *have Ed and Sue had to live in the flat?*

Exercise 2

1 *must rest for a week Mr Robbins.'*
2 *have to pay immediately.*
3 *must check in one hour before the flight.*
4 *must complete a registration form.*
5 *must be home by 6.00.'*
6 *has to go to the police station.*

Exercise 3

1 *must*
2 *has to*
3 *must*
4 *had to*
5 *must*
6 *have to*
7 *must*

Exercise 4

1 *mustn't*
2 *don't have to*
3 *mustn't*
4 *mustn't*
5 *doesn't have to*
6 *don't have to*

Unit 33

Exercise 1

1 *needn't*
2 *mustn't*
3 *mustn't*
4 *needn't*
5 *mustn't*
6 *needn't*

Exercise 2

1 *I have to work late.*
2 *Where do they have to go?*
3 *Does she need to go so soon?*
4 *Do you have to work tomorrow?*
5 *I don't need to do my homework.*
6 *Why do they need to learn French?*

Exercise 3

1 *Do you need to*
2 *needn't*
3 *need to*
4 *need to*
5 *needn't*
6 *need to*
7 *mustn't*
8 *do we need to*
9 *need to*
10 *mustn't*

Exercise 4

1 *didn't need to*
2 *needn't have*
3 *needn't have*
4 *didn't need to*
5 *didn't need to*
6 *needn't have*

Unit 34

Exercise 1

1 *may/might*
2 *may/might*
3 *may/might not*

4 *may/might*
5 *may/might not*
6 *may/might not*

Exercise 2

1 *He can't be under 60. He may/might be about 64 or 65. He must be 65 because he's just retired from work.*
2 *It must be Julian because that looks like his jacket. It may/might not be him. He's walking towards some other people. It can't be Rod. Rod is taller.*

Exercise 3

1 *can't be doing*
2 *can't be playing*
3 *must be practising*

Exercise 4

1 *can't have dropped*
2 *may/might have left*
3 *must have put*

Unit 35

Exercise 1

1 *could*
2 *had to/needed to*
3 *was able to*
4 *had to/needed to*
5 *didn't need to/have to*
6 *had to/needed to*
7 *couldn't*
8 *had to*
9 *could*
10 *needed*
11 *couldn't*
12 *couldn't/wasn't able to*
13 *was able to*

Exercise 2

1 *can't have*
2 *may/might/could have*
3 *may/might/could have*
4 *may/might/could have*
5 *must have*

Exercise 3

1 wouldn't have
2 should have
3 needn't have
4 could have
5 would have
6 'd have
7 shouldn't have
8 'd have

Unit 36

Exercise 1

1 can't   Can
2 could
3 couldn't.
4 Could
5 were able to
6 Was he able to

Exercise 2

1 Can I borrow your book?
2 Can I help you?
3 Could you get the red file, please?
4 Would you like a cup of tea?
5 Could I have your name, please?
6 Can you lend me some money?
7 Could I have a day off next week, please?
8 May I park my car outside the entrance?

Exercise 3

1 You should go to the dentist.
2 They oughtn't to watch TV.
3 You'd better get some glasses.
4 He ought to find a better job.
5 He'd better not miss the next test.
6 He shouldn't go out yet.

Exercise 4

1 mustn't   must
2 mustn't   'll have to
3 must   must
4 can't/mustn't
   must/have to

Exercise 5

1 don't need to/needn't
2 didn't need/have to
3 don't have to   have to
4 had to   didn't have/need to
5 don't need to/needn't need/have to
6 have to
   had to

Exercise 6

1 will
2 may
3 may not.
4 'll
5 could
6 might
7 won't

Exercise 7

1 must be meeting Stephen Fisher.
2 may be at the City Hotel   may be at the Ritz Grill.
3 can't be in Birmingham.   must be travelling to Liverpool or Manchester.

Exercise 8

1 should/ought to have
2 can't/couldn't have
3 shouldn't/oughtn't to have
4 needn't have
5 'd have

Unit 37

Exercise 1

1 is made
2 is produced
3 are provided
4 are brought
5 is put
6 are delivered

Exercise 2

1 was built
2 were used
3 were flown
4 were found
5 were carried

6 were begun
7 were provided
8 was employed

Exercise 3

1 First the new factory was built.
2 Then the new Superbike 2,000 was designed.
3 The design wasn't shown to anyone.
4 1,000 were bought in the first year.

Exercise 4

1 When was oil first used?
   It was first used thousands of years ago.
2 Was it burned for light?
   Yes, it was.
3 When was far more oil needed?
   It was needed about 100 years ago.
4 Was more oil found at that time?
   Yes, it was.
5 How many barrels of oil are pumped every day now?
   Nearly 50 million barrels of oil are pumped.

Unit 38

Exercise 1

1 We were being called by someone.
2 They are being pulled down next week.
3 The work wasn't being done efficiently.
4 She was being looked after by Sue.
5 It's being serviced at the garage.

Exercise 2

1 Many new houses have been built.
2 It hadn't been driven for 20 years.
3 We've been left behind.

4 We hadn't been told about it.

Exercise 3

1 Up to five books can be borrowed.
2 Books should be returned on time.
3 Protective clothing must be worn at all times.
4 Food mustn't be eaten in the office.

Exercise 4

1 have/get the window mended now.
2 have/get these films printed soon.
3 have/get this wall rebuilt tomorrow.

Exercise 5

1 This castle was built in 1760.
2 Tony was being pulled along the road.
3 The match won't be won by Alan. It'll be won by Jim.
4 Contracts should always be read before they're signed.
5 A memo has been written and it's being read.

Unit 39

Exercise 1

1 to play
2 to give
3 to see
4 to be
5 to win
6 to move
7 to climb
8 to learn

Exercise 2

1 watching
2 losing
3 buying
4 eating
5 saying
6 waiting
7 smoking
8 walking.

Exercise 3

1 to spend
2 arriving.
3 to have
4 to save
5 smoking.
6 going?
7 to see
8 doing
9 going
10 to go
11 walking

Exercise 4

1 not to mind what he said.
2 not making so much noise?
3 not having the money to repay Sam.
4 not to go out with the others.
5 not to talk to Bill any more.

Unit 40

Exercise 1

1 to be
2 to take
3 to form
4 to provide
5 to ask/asking

Exercise 2

1 getting up
2 to go
3 to check
4 swimming
   swimming
5 reading
6 to do
7 to visit
8 playing
9 to know
10 to live

Exercise 3

1 to post
2 to buy
3 asking
4 hearing
5 saying
6 saying
7 to get
8 to do

Exercise 4

1 to get
   using
2 writing   signing
   to do
3 correcting.
   to do

Exercise 5

1 mean to say those terrible things to Emma.
2 to develop a new kind of engine.
3 remember having fights with other children.
4 stop making so much noise late at night.
5 to tell you that your son has done badly in his exams.
6 stop to buy some things for dinner at this supermarket.
7 throwing your work away and starting again.
8 to telephone you this morning, but I didn't.
9 needs painting.

Exercise 6

1 training
2 to find
3 doing
4 to do
5 thinking
6 passing
7 leaving
8 to take
9 to say.
10 to catch up
11 to study

Unit 41

Exercise 1

1 Alan to be quiet.
2 Rob not to drive so fast.
3 me not to take photos.
4 her son to take his medicine after lunch.
5 everybody to try the cake.
6 the man to stop.

Exercise 2

1 Tina not to buy the dress.
2 the climbers to turn back.
3 our boat to roll over.
4 you buy now and pay later.
5 the boys run five kilometres.
6 us go out.

Exercise 3

1 to buy that car.
2 Tom to get the job.
3 Mrs Jones to leave her cases (there).
4 to see the contract.
5 our friends (to) cut down a tree.
6 you to see your present yet.

Exercise 4

1 to swim
2 to have
3 to help
4 to get
5 (to) buy
6 talk

Unit 42

Exercise 1

1 for breaking
2 on paying
3 about moving
4 to going
5 like doing
6 of joining

Exercise 2

1 You can't prevent me from winning.
2 Ben's father punished him for breaking the window.
3 I must warn you about going sailing in this wind.
4 I can't forgive her for hitting my child.
5 You can't blame him for leaving that terrible job.
6 We can't stop the dogs (from) fighting.

Exercise 3

1 capable of hurting
2 excited about going
3 fond of visiting
4 interested in studying
5 pleased about passing
6 fed up with hearing
7 bad at cooking.

Exercise 4

1 thought about going
2 decided against doing
3 discouraged us from choosing
4 enthusiastic to see
5 looking forward to showing
6 tired of working
7 thank her for asking

Unit 43

Exercise 1

1 the oil light comes on.
2 it becomes ice.
3 it soon goes bad.
4 the lights come on.
5 the machinery soon breaks down.

Exercise 2

1 arrives,
2 will tell
3 won't let
4 don't try
5 'll call
6 will lend
7 won't listen
8 don't come

Exercise 3

1 If the police come, they'll ask about Tom.
2 If you enter the race, you'll probably win.
3 If the party goes on till late, we'll go home early.
4 If you call the office at 2.00, Tony will be there.
5 If Ann doesn't call, I'll be worried.
6 If you finish the job today, you won't have to come tomorrow.

Exercise 4

1 won't be able
2 is
3 decide
4 will come.
5 will you join
6 organize
7 go
8 'll have
9 'll come
10 isn't
11 find
12 'll cost
13 don't act
14 will take
15 'll miss

Unit 44

Exercise 1

1 had
2 'd go
3 lost
4 followed
5 'd be
6 wouldn't believe
7 'd stay
8 didn't get

Exercise 2

1 Ann would be pleased if Tom called.
2 If you didn't visit us again, we'd be very sad.
3 I'd get fit quite fast if I worked out at the gym.
4 Barry wouldn't argue so much if he had more friends.
5 The team would win more games if they trained harder.

Exercise 3

1 'd waste
2 'd become
3 'd enjoy
4 might never see

Exercise 4

1 Where would they stay if they visited Turkey? They'd stay in cheap hotels.
2 Who would we see if we complained at the Head Office? You'd talk to the Sales Manager.
3 How would you travel if you visited Scotland? I'd go by car.
4 What would they do if they left school now? They'd get jobs.

Unit 45

Exercise 1

1 'd have loved
2 'd gone
3 hadn't shown
4 had been
5 'd saved   'd have had
6 wouldn't have asked   hadn't been

Exercise 2

1 If Jim had asked us, we'd have lent him our car.
2 If I hadn't written down her phone number, I'd have forgotten.
3 The car wouldn't have crashed if Tom had kept to the speed limit.
4 I'd have forgotten to buy Ann's present if you hadn't reminded me.

Exercise 3

1 If we'd had a map, we'd have found the house.
2 If the bus hadn't arrived late, we'd have missed it.
3 If they hadn't opened the box, they wouldn't have found the books.
4 If the tree had fallen on the car, the driver would have been hurt.
5 If I'd turned back, I wouldn't have got lost.

Exercise 4

1 he might have won the race.
2 they could have caught the thieves.
3 we'd have got home an hour ago.

Unit 46

Exercise 1

1 they're sitting by their fire.
2 it's hot there and he's sitting by their new pool.

Exercise 2

1 He said he was working outside London that month.
2 He told me he'd finished his college course the year before.
3 He said he hadn't been to see his parents for ages.
4 He told me he'd arrived home with his family the day before.
5 He said they were going back to London the next day.
6 He told me they couldn't stay for long as he had to get back to work.
7 He said they might come back the following year. He didn't know.
8 He told me he'd write soon and send me a photo of the family.
9 He said I should stay with them when I had time.

Exercise 3

1 But you said you loved this music.
2 But you told me he wouldn't sell his bike.
3 But you said you would call her.
4 But you told me it was on today.
5 But you said they'd lose the match.
6 But you told me she'd be at home tonight.
7 But you said they wouldn't send you anything.
8 But you told me they couldn't swim at all.

Unit 47

Exercise 1

1 we're going for our holiday this year. if we're going to visit them again.
2 we're doing this winter.   if we're taking a skiing holiday again.

Exercise 2

1 Jim asked me if I'd sold my terrible old car.
2 Jim asked me if I still lived with my parents.
3 Jim asked me if I was going to visit London soon.
4 I asked him if there was room for me to stay with him.
5 I asked him if I could have his phone number.
6 I asked him if he'd met his wife at college.

Exercise 3

1 They asked him where he came from.
2 They asked him how long he'd been in Britain.
3 They asked him why he'd decided to go there.
4 They asked him how long he was going to stay.
5 They asked him where he was living.

Exercise 4

1 A Swedish student asked me if I knew the way to the station.
2 A Turkish student asked me if I could help him/her find a flat.
3 A Lebanese student asked me which was the best travel agency.

Unit 48

Exercise 1

1 The girl asked me to open the door.
2 Carol instructed the new assistant not to use the photocopier.
3 Tom invited us to come for dinner on Saturday.
4 Celia reminded me not to be late for the party.
5 Ann asked everybody not to make so much noise.
6 Mrs Davis told Tony to give his name to the receptionist.
7 Bob warned Emma not to touch the red button.
8 The manager reminded her assistant to post the letters.

Exercise 2

1 They agreed to meet at 7.30.
2 He promised to be there on time.
3 She threatened not to wait if he was late.
4 He offered to get there an hour early.
5 She threatened she'd leave if he wasn't there at 7.30.
6 He promised not to be late.

Exercise 3

1 Maria suggested going parachuting.

2 Barry insisted going at that moment/ immediately.
3 Barry admitted feeling scared.
4 Maria apologized for suggesting parachuting.
5 Barry insisted on jumping.

Unit 49

Exercise 1

1 an
2 an
3 a
4 an
5 a
6 an
7 a
8 an
9 an
10 a
11 a
12 an

Exercise 2

1 a letter
2 an umbrella
3 some paint(s)
4 some glasses
5 an egg
6 a taxi

Exercise 3

1 Do
2 Is
3 are
4 Does
5 is
6 is
7 Are
8 are

Exercise 4

1 some
2 x
3 some
4 x
5 some
6 some

Exercise 5

1 Colleges are places to study.
2 A large plane can carry a heavy load.

3 Nowadays, students need to learn to use computers.
4 A car uses more energy per person than a train or bus.

Exercise 6

1 some
2 x
3 x
4 a
5 an
6 some
7 some
8 some
9 a
10 an

Unit 50

Exercise 1

1 police
2 cattle.
3 contents
4 scissors?
5 clothes
6 glasses
7 shorts.
8 sheep.

Exercise 2

1 is
2 Does
3 are
4 Is
5 are
6 is
7 is
8 is
9 Does
10 are

Exercise 3

1 children
2 person
3 foot
4 teeth.
5 tooth
6 people.
7 women
8 child

Exercise 4

1 knives
2 matches
3 potatoes
4 loaves

5 photos.
6 wives
7 batteries.
8 lives.
9 roofs

Unit 51

Exercise 1

1 apples
2 bananas
3 beans
4 biscuits
5 carrots
6 eggs
7 olives
8 onions
9 oranges
10 peas
11 potatoes
12 tomatoes
13 apple juice
14 bread
15 butter
16 cheese
17 cooking oil
18 milk
19 mineral water
20 rice
21 salt
22 soup
23 sugar
24 tea

Exercise 2

1 meat.
2 vegetables.
3 beans
4 onions.
5 rice
6 bread
7 bread rolls
8 tomatoes
9 olive oil
10 list

Exercise 3

1 some
2 information
3 ideas
4 is
5 furniture
6 some
7 a
8 luggage?
9 hair.
10 any

Exercise 4

1 e a packet of tea.
2 i a carton of milk.
3 d a five-litre bottle of cooking oil.
4 a a roll of kitchen paper.
5 f three loaves of bread.
6 h four cans of Pepsi.
7 c a box of matches.
8 g a two-kilo bag of potatoes.
9 b a piece of cheese.

Unit 52

Exercise 1

1 an
2 a
3 an
4 a
5 an
6 a
7 an   a
8 an   a

Exercise 2

1 ¹a
   ²a
2 ¹a   ²a
   ³the
   ⁴The ⁵the
3 ¹a   ²the
   ³an   ⁴The   ⁵the
   ⁶a   ⁷The   ⁸an
4 ¹a
   ²the
   ³the
5 ¹the
   ²a   ³a   ⁴the
   ⁵the ⁶the

Exercise 3

1 ¹a   ²the   ³a
   ⁴the ⁵the   ⁶a
2 ¹a   ²a   ³the   ⁴a
   ⁵the ⁶a   ⁷an
   ⁸the ⁹the ¹⁰the
   ¹¹the ¹²The ¹³the
   ¹⁴the ¹⁵the
   ¹⁶a/the ¹⁷the
   ¹⁸the ¹⁹The ²⁰an

Exercise 4

1 the beach.
2 The sun

3 the sky
4 The birds
5 the
6 trees
7 the
8 fields
9 the
10 wind.
11 the
12 sea
13 the
14 waves
15 the
16 sand.
17 the world

Exercise 5

1 the
   a
2 the
   a
3 the
   a
4 a
   the
5 a
   the
6 the
   a
7 the
   a
8 the
   a
9 a
   the
10 the
    a

Exercise 6

1 A reporter answered when I phoned the newspaper.
2 Joe fell and knocked a vase over.
3 The police officer stopped me for driving too fast.
4 The ship can travel from Britain to the USA in four days.
5 When I was away, I brought a present for my parents.
6 I picked the phone up and called my sister.
7 Sarah wrote a long letter to her father.

Unit 53

Exercise 1

1 d A camera is for taking pictures.
2 e A pen is for writing.
3 a A fork is for picking up food.
4 b A file is for holding papers.
5 g A diary is for noting dates of meetings, etc.
6 f A fridge is for keeping food cold.
7 c An answering machine is for taking phone messages.

Exercise 2

1 g Bell invented the telephone.
2 d Otis invented the lift/elevator.
3 b Marconi invented the radio.
4 f Biro invented the ballpoint pen.
5 a Edison invented the electric lamp.
6 c Dunlop invented the modern car tyre.
7 e Singer invented the sewing machine.

Exercise 3

1 I don't like black coffee.
2 I like fast cars.
3 I don't mind homework.
4 I don't like loud rock music.
5 I like swimming.
6 I don't mind tennis.

Exercise 4

1 the horse
2 companies
3 the salt
4 The books
5 Money
6 water.
7 Elephants
8 The phone

Exercise 5

1 the poor.
2 the unemployed
3 the old
4 The young
5 The blind

Exercise 6

1 the Australians
2 the British
3 the Chinese
4 the Danes/Danish
5 the Egyptians
6 the French
7 the Indonesians
8 the Japanese
9 the Kuwaitis
10 the Dutch
11 the Portuguese
12 the Spanish
13 the Russians
14 the Turks/Turkish
15 the Americans
16 the Venezuelans

Exercise 7

1 The   the
2 x   x
3 x   the   the
4 x   the   the
5 The   the   x   the
   the

Exercise 8

1 the
2 the
3 x
4 the
5 x
6 x
7 x
8 the
9 x
10 the
11 x
12 x
13 the
14 the
15 the

Unit 54

Exercise 1

1 those
2 That
3 these
4 this

5 *those*   *that*
   those
   this

Exercise 2

1 *this*   *this*
2 *this*
   that
3 *this*
   this   *That*
4 *This*   *these*
   This
5 *these.*
   those
   those

Exercise 3

1 *these ones*
   Those ones   *These*
   ones
2 *that*   *one*
   this one
   that one
3 *these ones*
   those ones
   these ones

Exercise 4

1 *one*
   the one
2 *ones*
   the   *ones*
3 *the one*   *the one*
4 *ones*   *the*   *ones*
   the   *ones*
5 *the one*   *the one*
   the one   *the ones*

Exercise 1

1 *some*
2 *any*
3 *some*
4 *any*
5 *some*
6 *any*
7 *some*

Exercise 2

1 *some*   *any.*
   some
2 *some*
   any   *some*
3 *some*   *any*
   some
4 *some*
   any

Exercise 3

1 *anything*
   anything   *something*
2 *anything?*
   somebody/something
3 *anybody*
   some
4 *somebody*
   any/some
5 *something*
   anything
6 *any*
   anybody

Exercise 4

1 *any colour*
2 *anybody*
3 *anything*
4 *anybody*
5 *anywhere*

Exercise 1

1 *Are there any
   potatoes?
   Yes, there are some in
   the bag.*
2 *Is there any coffee?
   No, there isn't. I'll buy
   some.*
3 *Is there a large pan?
   No, there isn't. I'll buy
   one.*
4 *Are there any carrots?
   No, there aren't. I'll
   buy some.*
5 *Is there any butter?
   Yes, there's some in the
   fridge.*
6 *Is there a teapot?
   Yes, there's one on the
   shelf.*

Exercise 2

1 *There wasn't*
2 *There was*
3 *There weren't*
4 *There were*
5 *There was*
6 *There were*
7 *There was*

Exercise 3

1 *There are*   *They*
2 *There wasn't*   *it*
3 *There weren't*   *they*

4 *There's*   *him?*
5 *There aren't*   *them*
6 *There isn't*   *it*

Exercise 4

1 *It's good/lovely to*
2 *It's not worth*
3 *It's no use*
4 *It was sad that*
5 *It was sad that*

Exercise 1

1 *a lot of/lots of*
   much
2 *a lot of/lots of*
   many
3 *much*   *much*
4 *a lot of/lots of*
   much
5 *many*
   many   *a lot of/lots
   of*
6 *much*
   A lot.
7 *many*
   many.
8 *much*
   much.

Exercise 2

1 *a little*   *a few*
2 *little*   *little*
3 *Few*   *a few*
4 *a little*   *a few*
5 *a few*   *little*
6 *a little*   *a few*
7 *few*   *little*
8 *a little*
   a few

Exercise 3

1 *little*
2 *many*
3 *a few*
4 *many*
5 *a lot of/lots of*
6 *much*
7 *a lot*
8 *much.*
9 *little*
10 *a little*

Exercise 1

1 *a few of them.*
2 *all of them.*
3 *some of them.*
4 *most of them.*
5 *a few of them.*

Exercise 2

1 *Both of you*
2 *Half of them*
3 *All/Most of you*
4 *Both of them*
5 *a few of us*   *most of
   us*

Exercise 3

1 *neither of*
2 *none of*
3 *any of*
4 *either of*
5 *None of*
6 *Neither of*
7 *any of*
8 *either of*
9 *either of*
10 *any of*   *none of*

Exercise 4

1 *both*
2 *every*
3 *all*
4 *all*
5 *each*
6 *Each*
7 *Every*

Exercise 1

1 *Bill*
2 *Bill*
3 *Paul*
4 *the practice*
5 *Paul*
6 *Bill*
7 *Neil*
8 *Batman film*
9 *People*
10 *Paul, Bill, Neil*

Exercise 2

1 *They're*
2 *she's*
3 *you*
   We're

4 *It's*
5 *he's*
6 *you*
  I'm
7 *You're*
  it's   I'm   I'm

Exercise 3

1 *her*
2 *you*
3 *him*
4 *them.*
5 *you*
  me   him
6 *me/us*
  you   you   her

Exercise 4

1 *He's*
2 *you*
3 *It's*
4 *you*
5 *me*
6 *We*
7 *you*
8 *me*
9 *I*
10 *it*
11 *her*
12 *They're*
13 *She*
14 *them*
15 *It's*
16 *I*

Unit 60

Exercise 1

1 *your*
2 *his*
3 *our*
4 *their*
5 *her*
6 *my*
7 *its*

Exercise 2

1 *No, it isn't his. His are older.*
2 *No, they aren't hers. Hers are newer.*
3 *No, it isn't theirs. Theirs is smaller.*
4 *No, it isn't yours. Yours is nicer.*
5 *No, they aren't ours. Ours are longer.*
6 *mine*

Exercise 3

1 *They're yours. Look, they've got your name inside.*
2 *It's his. Look, it's got his name inside.*
3 *They're theirs. Look, they've got their names inside.*
4 *It's mine. Look, it's got my name inside.*
5 *They're hers. Look, they've got her name inside.*
6 *It's ours. Look, it's got our names inside.*

Exercise 4

1 *it's*
2 *its*
3 *It's*
4 *it's*
5 *Its*
6 *it's*

Exercise 5

1 *s'*
2 *'s*
3 *'s*
4 *'s*
5 *s'*
6 *'s   's*

Unit 61

Exercise 1

1 *themselves*
2 *itself*
3 *herself*
4 *myself*
5 *himself*
6 *ourselves*
7 *yourself.*
8 *yourselves.*

Exercise 2

1 *save himself.*
2 *kill yourself*
3 *looked at herself*
4 *made myself*
5 *bought themselves*
6 *push ourselves*
7 *wash itself.*
8 *look after yourselves.*

Exercise 3

1 *me.*

2 *yourselves*
3 *herself.*
4 *us*
5 *ourselves.*
6 *them.*
7 *him*

Exercise 4

1 *No, I paid for it myself.*
2 *No, she prepares them herself.*
3 *No, he's bringing it himself.*
4 *No, they'll have to tidy it themselves.*
5 *No, we're going to clean it ourselves.*
6 *No, you're going to make it yourself.*

Unit 62

Exercise 1

1 *Ann gave her parents a present.*
2 *Nick sent a book to his niece.*
3 *Did you really buy it for me?*
4 *Could you lend Harry some money?*
5 *Susie's grandmother made her a lovely dress.*
6 *I'll take Celia some magazines next time I visit her in hospital.*
7 *Could you pass the report to the boss when he arrives?*
8 *I offered Rob a place to stay as he had nowhere else to go.*

Exercise 2

1 *No, don't sell them to Sally. Sell them to me.*
2 *No, don't take it there. Take it to the one near my house.*
3 *No, don't buy it for Sally. Buy it for her brother.*
4 *No, don't show it to him. Show it to the police.*

5 *No, don't cook it for the children. Cook it for the adults.*
6 *No, don't pay it to the teacher. Pay it to the school secretary.*
7 *No, don't by one/it for me. Buy it/one for the children.*

Exercise 3

1 *for*
2 *for*
3 *to*
4 *to*
5 *for*
6 *for*
7 *to*
8 *to*
9 *for*

Unit 63

Exercise 1

1 *some*
2 *anything*
3 *any*
4 *somewhere*
5 *anybody*
6 *some*
7 *anybody*
8 *some*
9 *anywhere.*
10 *something*

Exercise 2

1 *everybody/one*
2 *Everywhere*
3 *something*
4 *Nobody*
5 *anybody/one*
6 *anywhere*
7 *anything*

Exercise 3

1 *everywhere*
2 *anywhere*
3 *somewhere*
4 *Somebody*
5 *anyone?*
6 *anywhere*
7 *nowhere*
8 *nobody*
9 *something*
10 *anything.*

Exercise 4

1 nothing interesting
2 something else
3 anywhere else
4 everywhere possible
5 anyone nice
6 nowhere else

Unit 64

Exercise 1

1 which/that
2 which/that
3 which/that
4 who/that
5 which/that
6 who/that
7 which/that
8 who/that

Exercise 2

1 The pilot who/that crashed his plane in the lake escaped without injury.
2 The student who/that broke the 10,000-metre record has got a place in the national team.
3 The bus which/that takes people to the airport broke down.
4 The file which/that has all the information is on the top shelf.
5 The policeman who/that rescued 15 people from a fire has received an award.
6 The woman who/that phoned last night wanted to speak to you.

Exercise 3

1 who/that scored all the goals?
2 which/that will pay a better salary.
3 who/that can repair my old car?
4 which/that teaches Japanese.
5 who/that are warm and friendly.

6 who/that painted that picture?
7 who/that was lost for five days.
8 who/that discovered America.

Unit 65

Exercise 1

1 The book which/that has all the answers has disappeared.
2 We climbed over the fence which/that separates the fields.
3 The old man who/that can't see well crashed his car.
4 I'm going to give the boy who/that found my camera some money.

Exercise 2

1 The girls who/that we met at the wedding seemed sad.
2 I want to go to the museum which/that you told me about.
3 The taxi which/that I'd ordered finally arrived.
4 The flowers which/that she gave us are dying.

Exercise 3

1 x
2 who/that
3 x
4 who/that
5 x

Exercise 4

1 showing
2 entering
3 finishing
4 standing
5 wearing

Exercise 5

1 used
2 being painted
3 being prepared

4 written
5 being mended
6 made

Unit 66

Exercise 1

1 which
The pyramids.
2 who
Yuri Gagarin.
3 whose
Marie Curie.
4 who
Marco Polo.
5 whose
Japan.
6 which   whose
Texas.

Exercise 2

1 He was the one whose wife had a wonderful diamond necklace.
2 They were the ones whose children fell in the pool.
3 She was the one whose hat flew off in the wind.
4 They were the ones whose car refused to start after the party.
5 They were the ones whose daughters wore lovely blue dresses.

Exercise 3

1 reason why their boat nearly turned over.
2 old hotel where they dried out their clothes.
3 night when the rain almost washed their tent away.

Unit 67

Exercise 1

1 adding
2 defining
3 defining
4 adding

Exercise 2

1 Old Professor Jones, who's nearly 70, is

going to stop work soon.
2 To the north of India are the Himalayas, which include the highest mountains in the world.
3 I bought myself some good, new clothes, which I needed for my new job.
4 Barry Stone, who works as a computer programmer, has built his own house.

Exercise 3

1 d   The baby cried all night, which meant I was tired all next day.
2 a   The old ship stayed in port, which saved it from the storm.
3 c   I was out when Peter called, which was why I didn't hear the news.
4 g   The company has won the contract, which is good news.
5 b   They've started doing road repairs, which is causing bad traffic delays.
6 e   The sun has come out at last, which means we can go to the beach.
7 f   The school is building a new gymnasium, which is going to help their basketball teams a lot.

Unit 68

Exercise 1

1 smells delicious.
2 feel tired.
3 get angry.
4 seem   happy.
5 sounds terrible.

Exercise 2

1 a boring old book

2 an unusual blue diamond.
3 an exciting new film
4 a strange yellow light
5 an interesting German clock
6 a lovely little baby
7 a pleasant green valley
8 a tall young man
9 a round plastic box

Exercise 3

1 He was a funny, little, old man.
2 It was an ugly, brown, metal box.
3 They were beautiful, new, Italian, silk jackets.
4 They were wonderful, tall, round, Chinese vases.

Exercise 4

1 to play with matches.
2 to go home.
3 to remember to post them.
4 to have you with us.
5 to understand.
6 to drive when you're tired.

Unit 69

Exercise 1

1 excited
2 confused.
3 annoying
4 fascinated
5 exhausted
6 puzzling.
7 surprising
8 amazing.

Exercise 2

1 astonished astonishing
2 shocking. shocked
3 embarrassing embarrassed
4 depressed depressing.
5 interesting interested
6 disappointed disappointing.

7 irritated irritating
8 tired tiring.

Exercise 3

1 satisfied.
2 disgusted
3 worrying.
4 horrifying
5 relaxed
6 amusing.
7 infuriating.
8 terrified.

Unit 70

Exercise 1

1 quickly
2 nice
3 wonderful.
4 safely.
5 warm.
6 warmly immediately.
7 hard   kind
8 slowly   quietly

Exercise 2

1 proper properly.
2 quiet quietly.
3 smooth smoothly.
4 pleasant pleasant
5 intelligently intelligent
6 badly. bad
7 effective effectively   effective

Exercise 3

1 sensibly.
2 easily.
3 safely.
4 successfully.
5 Luckily
6 similarly   wholly
7 Unfortunately really   truly

Exercise 4

1 late
2 early

3 straight
4 hard
5 wrong
6 short.
7 far
8 well
9 direct.
10 low

Exercise 5

1 hardly hard
2 highly high
3 near nearly
4 freely free
5 short shortly.
6 directly direct

Exercise 6

1 hard
2 easily.
3 early
4 late.
5 tired
6 quickly
7 seriously.

Unit 71

Exercise 1

1 Hopefully,
2 Stupidly,
3 Angrily,
4 Frighteningly,
5 Finally,
6 Quietly,
7 Sadly,
8 Luckily,

Exercise 2

1 always get
2 was only trying
3 can sometimes see
4 will only be
5 don't usually work
6 has clearly been failing
7 Have you ever been
8 must never talk

Exercise 3

1 there very soon.

2 in America for five years.
3 very heavily yesterday.
4 much harder since last September.
5 over here as soon as possible.
6 wrong all the time.

Exercise 4

1 last week
2 over here
3 Sadly
4 last year
5 definitely
6 this time
7 usually
8 soon

Unit 72

Exercise 1

1 upstairs
2 definitely
3 slowly
4 now
5 hard
6 always
7 Luckily

Exercise 2

1 manner
2 place
3 degree
4 degree
5 manner
6 time
7 time
8 time
9 degree
10 time
11 degree
12 time
13 time
14 place
15 manner
16 sentence
17 manner
18 time
19 sentence
20 place
21 manner
22 sentence
23 manner
24 sentence
25 manner
26 degree
27 time

28   *time*
29   *time*
30   *frequency*

Exercise 3

1   *there before midday.*
2   *beautifully yesterday.*
3   *everywhere for a year.*
4   *angrily at the meeting last night.*
5   *well at college these days.*

Exercise 4

1   *I usually do the washing on Monday.*
2   *Do you ever visit your old school?*
3   *Flights to New York leave once an hour.*
4   *You have to take the medicine twice a day.*

Exercise 5

1   *Sadly, she'd already gone.*
2   *Hopefully, he'll be well soon.*
3   *Surprisingly, our children are good at Art.*
4   *Unfortunately, he isn't here to receive it.*

Exercise 6

1   *has definitely finished*
2   *'ll never visit*
3   *are always delivered*
4   *hasn't clearly understood*
5   *'ll hardly ever see*

Unit 73

Exercise 1

1   *shorter   shortest*
2   *prettier   prettiest*
3   *longer   longest*
4   *uglier   ugliest*
5   *larger   largest*
6   *bigger   biggest*
7   *smaller   smallest*
8   *nicer   nicest*
9   *cooler   coolest*
10 *easier   easiest*
11 *simpler   simplest*
12 *finer   finest*
13 *thinner   thinnest*
14 *hotter   hottest*

Exercise 2

1   *easier*
2   *simpler*
3   *nicer*
4   *hotter*
5   *longer*

Exercise 3

1   *latest*
2   *quickest*
3   *narrowest*
4   *fittest*
5   *funniest*

Exercise 4

1   *fitter   fittest*
2   *finer   finest*
3   *lowest   lower*
4   *whiter   whitest*
5   *easiest   easier*

Exercise 5

1   *more   fewer*
2   *more?*
    most
3   *less*
    least   fewest
    most

Exercise 6

1   *most talented   more talented*
2   *most expensive   less expensive?*
3   *more dangerous most dangerous*
4   *more valuable   most valuable*
5   *less interesting.*
    least interesting

Exercise 7

1   *drives more slowly*
2   *writes more excitingly*
3   *sleeps more lightly*
4   *arrives earlier*
5   *plays football less intelligently*

Exercise 8

1   *The Crystal performed the most reliably, and the Wash-Tech performed the least reliably.*
2   *The Wash-Tech ran the most economically, and the Crystal ran the most cheaply.*
3   *The Crystal finished the fastest, and the Snowline finished the least quickly.*

Unit 74

Exercise 1

1   *Sue is younger than Ann.*
2   *The Toyota is more expensive than the Honda./The Honda is less expensive than the Toyota.*
3   *Robin runs/can run faster than Jack.*
4   *Mount Egmont is more dangerous than Mount George./ Mount George is less dangerous than Mount Egmont.*
5   *The journey by tunnel is shorter than the journey by sea.*

Exercise 2

1   *Yesterday was the hottest day of the year.*
2   *The XL400 is/has been the most popular car in Europe this year.*
3   *Tom and Sam were the best players in last year's team.*
4   *Some people say Casa Blanca was/is the finest film ever.*

Exercise 3

1   *A Jumbo 747 isn't nearly as fast as Concord.*
2   *Britain isn't nearly as warm as Egypt.*
3   *Silver isn't nearly as expensive as gold.*
4   *Rome isn't nearly as old as Athens.*
5   *French food is much better than English food.*

Exercise 4

1   *he*
2   *her.*
3   *she*
4   *they*
5   *them.*
6   *him*
7   *I*
8   *me.*

Unit 75

Exercise 1

1   *too young.*
2   *too quickly*
3   *too strong.*
4   *too late.*
5   *too quietly.*

Exercise 2

1   *big enough.*
2   *soon enough?*
3   *carefully enough.*
4   *hard enough.*
5   *good enough.*

Exercise 3

1   *enough A5 paper, n't enough A4 paper.*
    too few brown envelopes.
2   *n't enough large paper clips, too few medium clips.*
    enough small clips.
3   *too little brown sticky tape, n't enough clear tape.*
    enough elastic bands.
4   *too little glue, too few stapling machines.*
    n't enough staples.

Exercise 4

1   *I haven't got enough money for a holiday.*
2   *This coffee is too strong for your mother.*
3   *The house is big enough for the family.*

Exercise 5

1   *It isn't warm enough to go out.*
2   *The bird was too fast to catch.*

3 We were too late to catch the bus.

4 The plane was flying just high enough to miss the mountain.

Unit 76

Exercise 1

1 *a bit*
2 *not very*
3 *very*
4 *quite*
5 *not very*

Exercise 2

1 *much/far*
2 *much*
3 *a little*
4 *a little*
5 *far/much*

Exercise 3

1 *so*
2 *such*
3 *such*
4 *so*
5 *such*
6 *so*
7 *so*
8 *such*
9 *such*
10 *so*

Exercise 4

1 *e* The weather was so bad (that) we gave up our holiday and went home.

2 *a* The students are making so much noise (that) all the neighbours are complaining.

3 *d* The birds are so friendly (that) they even take food from your hand.

4 *h* The children made such a mess (that) it took an hour to clean the room.

5 *f* Everybody is so busy (that) nobody is answering the phone.

6 *g* I haven't driven for such a long time (that) I feel quite

nervous about going on the road.

7 *c* After the trip we were all so tired (that) we went straight to sleep.

8 *b* They took such a long time to get ready (that) they nearly missed their plane.

Unit 77

Exercise 1

1 *near*
2 *above*
3 *behind*
4 *next to*
5 *under*
6 *in*
7 *on*
8 *in front of*
9 *opposite*
10 *between*

Exercise 2

1 *at*
2 *at*
3 *in*
4 *in*
5 *opposite*
6 *in front of*
7 *in front of*
8 *between*
9 *Among*
10 *among*

Exercise 3

1 *past*
2 *across*
3 *into*
4 *through*
5 *along*
6 *round*
7 *towards*
8 *over*
9 *up*
10 *down*
11 *under*
12 *inside*
13 *out of*
14 *away from*

Unit 78

Exercise 1

1 *g* Tom lives at

Number 25, North Street.

2 *i* There's a notice on the wall outside my office.

3 *a* Ann is buying some things in the shopping centre.

4 *d* Dad is having a sleep in the small bedroom.

5 *c* My aunt lives in a small town outside London.

6 *b* Come and meet all the trainees in Room 564.

7 *f* I want you to introduce me to everyone at the party.

8 *e* There are two men working up on the roof.

9 *j* Sally put the vase of flowers on the table.

10 *h* Both London and Oxford are on the River Thames.

Exercise 2

1 *in the middle of*
2 *on the way*
3 *at that meeting.*
4 *on that wall.*
5 *on the bottle.*
6 *at that desk.*
7 *at the entrance.*
8 *in the garden.*
9 *in a village*

Exercise 3

1 *at*
2 *on*
3 *at*
4 *on*
5 *on*
6 *at*
7 *at*
8 *at*
9 *at*
10 *in*
11 *in*
12 *in*
13 *on*

Unit 79

Exercise 1

1 *at*

2 *in*
3 *in*
4 *on*
5 *at*
6 *at*
7 *on*
8 *on*
9 *at*
10 *at*
11 *at*
12 *in*

Exercise 2

1 *at*
2 *in*
3 *in*
4 *on*
5 *on*
6 *in*
7 *at*
8 *in*
9 *in*
10 *at*
11 *in*
12 *on*
13 *on*
14 *at*
15 *in*
16 *on*
17 *at*
18 *in*
19 *at*

Exercise 3

1 *on*
2 *at*
3 *on*
4 *on*
5 *x*
6 *x*
7 *on*
8 *x*
9 *in*
10 *at*
11 *in*
12 *x*
13 *x*
14 *x*
15 *in*
16 *at*

Exercise 4

1 *at a time.*
2 *at times*
3 *in time.*
4 *at one time*
5 *on time.*

Exercise 5

1 *ten past three*
2 *ten to seven*
3 *half past nine*
4 *a quarter to three*
5 *a quarter past five*
6 *thirteen minutes past one*
7 *twenty-nine minutes to eleven*
8 *one minute to one*

Exercise 6

1 *On Wednesday the 28th you're returning to London at 3.45 in the afternoon.*
2 *On Friday the 30th you're meeting Japanese visitors from the Subarashi Corporation all day.*
3 *On Saturday the 31st you're speaking at the goodbye party for the Managing Director in the evening.*
4 *On Monday the 2nd you're attending the sales conference in the afternoon/evening.*
5 *On Tuesday the 3rd you're talking at the sales conference in the morning.*
6 *On Thursday the 5th you're flying to Rome at 7.15 in the morning.*
7 *On Friday the 6th you're leaving Rome for Madrid at 11.45 in the morning.*
8 *On Saturday the 7th you're travelling back to London at midday.*

Exercise 1

1 *for*
2 *for*
3 *for*
4 *since*
5 *for*
6 *since*
7 *For*
8 *since*

Exercise 2

1 *ago*
2 *before.*
3 *ago*
4 *ago.*
5 *before.*
6 *ago*
7 *before.*

Exercise 3

1 *while*
2 *During*
3 *While*
4 *during*
5 *during*
6 *during*
7 *while*

Exercise 4

1 *by*
2 *until/till*
3 *until/till*
4 *by*
5 *By*
6 *Until/till*
7 *by*
8 *until/till*

Exercise 5

1 *since*
2 *during*
3 *while*
4 *for*
5 *until/till*
6 *By*
7 *before*
8 *ago*

Exercise 1

1 *on*
  by
2 *on*
  by
3 *on   for*
  for
4 *for*
  on
5 *on*
  on
6 *by*
  in   by
7 *on*
  on
8 *at*
  by

Exercise 2

1 *on a tour*
2 *in my car.*
3 *on a school trip*
4 *by plane.*
5 *on his bike.*
6 *for a walk*
7 *at the cinema*
8 *by air*
9 *on a diet.*
10 *by an artist*

Exercise 3

1 *matter with*
2 *need for*
3 *hope of*
4 *increase in*
5 *way of*
6 *problem with*
7 *call for*
8 *fall in*
9 *interested in*
10 *difficulties with*

Exercise 1

1 *for*
2 *at*
3 *with*
4 *with/about*
5 *with/about*
6 *for*
7 *with*
8 *with*

Exercise 2

1 *terrible at*
2 *proud of*
3 *different from*
4 *good for*
5 *late for*
6 *responsible for*
7 *early for*
8 *worried about*

Exercise 3

1 *tired of his old computer games.*
2 *used to working at night.*
3 *angry with her children.*
4 *anxious about his first business trip.*
5 *sorry about the long delay at the airport.*
6 *bored with the radio programme.*
7 *nervous about going out alone.*
8 *amazed at the huge number of people at the concert.*

Exercise 1

1 *about*
2 *for*
3 *to*
4 *to*
5 *about*

Exercise 2

1 *heard about*
2 *applied to*
3 *applying for?*
4 *thinking about*
5 *thought of*
6 *look after*
7 *look at*
8 *look for*

Exercise 3

1 *asked   for*
2 *congratulate   on*
3 *provide   with*
4 *ask   about*
5 *tell   about*

Exercise 4

1 *asked the teacher for help.*
2 *told him about the accident.*
3 *blamed him for the crash.*
4 *describe the man to them.*
5 *inviting all my friends to my party.*

Exercise 1

1 *pick up*
2 *give out*
3 *sit down*
4 *put away*
5 *Turn over*
6 *come in.*

Exercise 2

1 lie down
2 go away
3 go out
4 move on
5 come back
6 get up
7 Turn round
8 wake up.

Exercise 3

1 take out
2 brought down
3 turn down
4 took off
5 put on
6 putting up

Exercise 4

1 picked it up.
2 switched it off.
3 put them away.
4 put them down.
5 turned it up.
6 turned them over.
7 paid it in.

Unit 85

Exercise 1

1 Pronoun
2 Adjective
3 Noun
4 Adjective
5 Linking word
6 Verb
7 Adverb
8 Preposition

Exercise 2

1 bedrooms
2 bathroom.
3 living-room
4 television.
5 dining-room
6 visitors.
7 kitchen.
8 food
9 dishes.
10 garden.
11 time
12 flowers.
13 vegetables.
14 shop

Exercise 3

1 cooks
2 get

3 leave
4 is
5 drops
6 work
7 have to
8 takes
9 drives
10 has

Exercise 4

1 only
2 big
3 badly
4 right.
5 fine
6 fast
7 nearly
8 quickly
9 late
10 certainly

Exercise 5

1 It
2 a
3 we
4 we
5 a
6 it
7 the
8 the
9 whole
10 the
11 Ours
12 a
13 Most
14 in
15 one
16 An
17 a
18 of
19 along
20 the
21 us
22 They
23 us
24 to
25 the

Unit 86

Exercise 1

1 Question
2 Order
3 Exclamation
4 Statement
5 Question
6 Statement
7 Exclamation
8 Order

Exercise 2

1 S V C
2 V O
3 S A V O
4 A V O
5 S
 V O
6 V S C
7 S
 V O
8 A S V C
 AP

Exercise 3

1 The plane climbed fast.
2 Your brother seems very tired.
3 Don't put the boxes over there.
4 Robert is coming as soon as possible.
5 Did you see the news yesterday?

Unit 87

Exercise 1

1 and
2 so
3 but
4 or

Exercise 2

1 and he owns a house in Scotland.
2 so he's got to come home by taxi instead.
3 or he can go at 4.00.
4 but he seems very tired at the moment.

Exercise 3

1 I went to bed because/ as I was tired.
2 I'm getting a new car because/as mine is old.
3 I'll call you later because/as I have to go now.

Exercise 4

1 Sally does her job well even though/though she's young.
2 The film is still very popular even

though/ though it's old.
3 Their new house looks terrible even though/ though it was expensive.

Exercise 5

1 If
2 who
3 when
4 Even though
5 because
6 When
7 even though
8 Because

Unit 88

Exercise 1

1 It is Alternatively, it is
2 We have reached In addition, we have managed
3 We are cutting However, we are failing
4 We have not tried As a result, we do not know it will be

Exercise 2

1 from
2 of
3 x
4 to
5 for
6 to
7 of
8 of

Exercise 3

1 she has achieved a Grade A.
2 she has often failed to complete her homework.
3 she has behaved badly in class all year.
4 she must learn to do some hard work.
5 she has found it difficult to improve.
6 she could go on to do extra Science.